Composing Software Components

D1180461

Dick Hamlet

Composing Software Components

A Software-testing Perspective

 Springer

Dick Hamlet
Professor Emeritus
Portland State University
Portland, OR
USA

ISBN 978-1-4419-7147-0   e-ISBN 978-1-4419-7148-7
DOI 10.1007/978-1-4419-7148-7
Springer New York Dordrecht Heidelberg London

Library of Congress Control Number: 2010932008

© Springer Science+Business Media, LLC 2010
All rights reserved. This work may not be translated or copied in whole or in part without the written
permission of the publisher (Springer Science+Business Media, LLC, 233 Spring Street, New York, NY
10013, USA), except for brief excerpts in connection with reviews or scholarly analysis. Use in connection with any form of information storage and retrieval, electronic adaptation, computer software, or by
similar or dissimilar methodology now known or hereafter developed is forbidden.
The use in this publication of trade names, trademarks, service marks, and similar terms, even if they are
not identified as such, is not to be taken as an expression of opinion as to whether or not they are subject
to proprietary rights.

Printed on acid-free paper

Springer is part of Springer Science+Business Media (www.springer.com)

For Corinne, with love always

The Griffin

T HE *griffin*[1] is a fabulous animal with the body of a lion, the head of an eagle, and (sometimes) a snake's tail. The griffin is powerful and fierce because of its parts. It will tear to pieces any human being it comes across. Software developers should pay attention to this, because software also may tear people to pieces. Software made from components has the properties of its parts.

WATERCOLOR BY CAROLYN MCWILLIAMS

---

[1] With apologies to T. H. White, *The Book of Beasts*, a translation from a Latin bestiary of the 12th century, Jonathan Cape, 1954.

Acknowledgements

AVE Mason and Denise Woit are responsible for some of the core ideas that made this work possible. We spent some fine time at University College Galway (UCG) putting the initial theory together. Zheng Tu, Milan Andric, Ben Buford, John Christmann, Alex Corrado, Paul Draghicescu, Michael Plump, and Devon Gleeson (in that chronological order) worked on the prototype tools and early experiments. They all taught themselves Perl and Linux, and they worked long and hard (well, most of them did), I hope because it was fun. Their code, however often I look at it carefully to understand or change it, never ceases to astonish me.

The US National Science Foundation and Science Foundation Ireland provided substantial support for the work. UCG (now the National University of Ireland, Galway, NUIG) Math Department provided me space to work for several years, including a year as a Fulbright fellow. When strings needed to be pulled at NUIG, Ted Hurley pulled them.

A series of meetings on computer-based software engineering (CBSE, first as an ICSE Workshop, now an independent conference) provided a forum for early discussions of these ideas. Two informal meetings organized by K.-K. Lau at Manchester were even more productive. James Bach volunteered to read a draft, with an eye to making the work accessible to a practical audience; alas, I mostly failed to use his advice.

My wife, Corinne McWilliams, mostly smiled bravely and was generously supportive when the vagaries of research and software tool development possessed me.

Contents

Chapter 1
Introduction

THIS book is a monograph, a detailed exposition of ideas about software components and component-based software development (CBSD) from the viewpoint of software testing. Its primary audience is the computer-science and software-engineering research community, those who study software and its testing to understand, to teach, and to conduct research. "Monograph" literally means "...an account of a single thing...". But "*an* account" is important to the definition along with the "single thing." The author of a monograph necessarily brings to it strong views. "Monomania" is a related word: "insanity in which the patient is irrational on one subject, an exaggerated interest in some one thing"[1]. Monograph authors undoubtedly desire to add to the world's stock of knowledge, but frequently they have axes to grind at the same time. At the outset, along with an introduction to this book's content, it may be helpful to set forward the ways in which my treatment is biased, at least insofar as I recognize my biases. In this chapter I write in the first person, because for stating bias the usual passive-impersonal style is so awkward as to be an abuse of English[2]. Perhaps that is why technical computer science papers can appear blindly self-serving. Not to worry—the rest of the book is written in passive-impersonal in which I've had 45 years of practice[3].

---

[1] *The Macquarie Dictionary*, Macquarie Library Pty. Ltd., New South Wales, 1981.

[2] For example, "It may be seen that the use of _____ may perhaps be thought to be less than ideal in this context" means "I made the mistake of using _____ ."

[3] I can date the beginning of my learning experience because my MS thesis adviser—a kind and good man—patiently explained to me in 1963 that my draft thesis, written in best breezy college-humor-magazine style, simply Would Not Do.

D. Hamlet, *Composing Software Components*, DOI 10.1007/978-1-4419-7148-7_1,
© Springer Science+Business Media, LLC 2010

1.1 A 'Clear Drop'

I have been actively investigating CBSD since about 1999. In this section I briefly describe the unusual form that investigation has taken[4]. I published papers as the research progressed, in conferences [52, $\prec A \succ$][50, 51, 49, 35, 41, 43, 44, 45, 47] and in journals [46, $\prec A \succ$][48, $\prec A \succ$]. Part of the reason for writing this book is to collect and present these results in a coherent framework. Technical publications are severely space-limited, and cutting a large subject up into 10- or even 30-page chunks doesn't work very well. Since the research began, I've learned a lot about components, CBSD, and supporting tools, so the early results can now be better presented.

There are three parts to my ideal form of CBSD:

Unit test. Component code is tested in isolation by dividing its input domain into subdomains and recording test results for each subdomain.

System synthesis and prediction. Novel algorithms are used to calculate an approximation to how an arbitrary system built from components will behave.

Support tools. The synthesis algorithms are implemented in tools that support component (unit) testing, then can calculate and display system predictions. Collectively, the support tools are called "SYN " (for "synthesis") tools. The SYN tools are available free on the Internet; they run on UNIX, Mac, and Windows platforms. Go to URL http://cs.pdx.edu/~hamlet/bookload.html to download the tools and many examples.

What is omitted in this Introduction is the theoretical basis for my work. In contrast to the usual formal logic, my underlying theory is functional software testing. Testing theory shows what to measure in unit test and how to use that information for system predictions.

The 'clear drop' of this monograph is a simple example of CBSD along these lines. In a sense, the book is nothing more than a series of similar (more complex) examples, each leading to insights and answering fundamental questions about testing and about CBSD. Along the way, the underlying theory is presented to derive the algorithms used in the SYN tools, and the tools themselves are described in several tutorials.

1.1.1 Testing Components and Recording Approximations

To begin, I put on my hat as a developer of components; two will be needed for this example. The first is component Chopper that 'chops' its input, interspersing

---

[4] Bob Blackburn, a colleague who tried hard to teach me how to teach, always said that a college course should begin with a miniature of the whole at its first meeting. This 'clear drop' of the course's essence would tell students what they were in for, both in subject material and presentation, so that they could drop the course immediately instead of after the deadline when they finally found out what it was all about. A monograph needs a 'clear drop,' too.

short zero output intervals with longer intervals on which the input is reproduced as output[5]. Chopper is written in Perl. I arbitrarily pick the interval $D = [0.0, 12.0)$ on which to experiment with Chopper, and a collection of subdomain intervals on D of equal length 0.5. (That makes 24 subdomains in the experiment.) Figure 1.1 shows some of the graphs produced by the SYN tools[6] for Chopper. The dotted

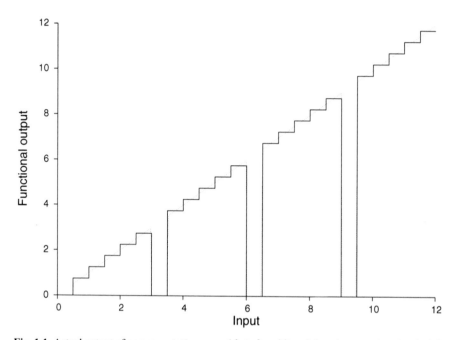

Fig. 1.1 Actual output of component Chopper (*dotted*) and its subdomain approximation (*solid*)

line in the figure is actual measured output of Chopper obtained by running its code on 300 equi-spaced samples from D. This graph aids the developer in checking that the code meets its requirements—the chopping is taking place as described.

The other graph in Fig. 1.1 (solid line) is an approximation to Chopper output obtained by sampling the code three times on each subdomain and averaging the results. Thus where the output is changing, its approximation has stairsteps constant across each subdomain. This approximation graph tells the developer the quality of the unit test . If the subdomains are well located and small enough, the approximation will be be close to the measured output. In Fig. 1.1 the average root-mean-

---

[5] Although the components in this example have no need to be useful (or even sensible) in order to display my idea, a chopping component is useful in converting a slowly changing signal into a similar, but rapidly-alternating one. AC is often better than DC, which is why Tesla's technology replaced Edison's.

[6] The tools also display measured and approximated run time of a component, but this is omitted for clarity. The example is expanded in the stateless tutorial, Chapter 9; it is also used in the study of accuracy in Chapter 17.

square deviation is about 1.8%. On subdomains that are 'chopped' to zero, the error is 0 because output is constant across the subdomain; at worst the error in the stairsteps is about 2.3%. Shrinking the subdomains would reduce these errors, but for this illustration it is good to be able to clearly see the difference between approximation and real output.

Thus `Chopper` seems to be doing what it is required to do, and the tools have recorded an adequate approximation to its behavior. From now on, only this approximation is needed. It might be filed away in a component repository.

My second component provides a signal to chop. The C program `Bell` computes a Gaussian bell function with $\mu = 6.6$ and $\sigma = 2.7$; most of the bell curve falls in the sample interval D. To make `Bell` more interesting, a discontinuous 'bump' is introduced near input 3.3. Again using 24 subdomains, the tools produce Fig. 1.2, showing measured behavior and approximation. The average r-m-s error for the

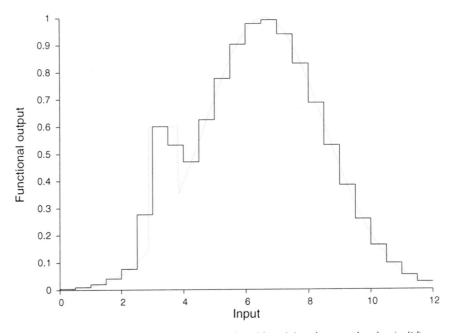

Fig. 1.2 Actual output of component `Bell` (*dotted*) and its subdomain approximation (*solid*)

`Bell` approximation is about 6.1%; it ranges from 0 within the 'bump' to to 38% at a 'bump' edge. Across the bell itself, the error is under 10%. The large errors near the edges of the 'bump' result from a poor choice of subdomains, not aligned on the discontinuities. (For `Chopper` more care was taken with subdomain placement.) The developer, seeing the approximation errors, would choose better subdomains (Fig. 1.2 helps to find where the boundaries should be located), and might choose to shrink the subdomain size where `Bell` is changing most rapidly to reduce the approximation error there. However, to see what happens in synthesis, I choose to place `Bell`'s approximation in the repository as is.

1.1.2 Synthesizing a System

Now I put on a quite different hat and pretend to be a system developer. Perhaps I'm designing a program with (almost) Gaussian output, but I want it to be chopped. Looking in my handy component repository, I find just what I need (surprise!), so I imagine a system that has `Chopper` in series with `Bell`. The conventional way to proceed would be to buy the two components, link their code in series, and experiment with (test) the system. This conventional approach has three serious drawbacks:

- I don't like to buy before I try. The code may be proprietary, so I can't get the sources.
- All of the testing done by the component developers is wasted—I can't trust them, and without the sources I'll have to do some form of blackbox tests.
- Testing a system is time consuming and error prone.

The algorithms and SYN tools described in this monograph solve all three problems.

So instead of proceeding conventionally, I take from the repository not proprietary code or even executables, but *their approximations*. These can be free because presumably they aren't good enough to use in my real system. Each approximation comes with an error analysis that quantifies the developer's unit testing. But the best news is that I don't have to assemble and execute the system. Instead, I can get an approximation to its behavior using support tools. They implement algorithms that *calculate* system output from a description of the connection(s) (here, 'series') and the component approximations. The tools predict that the approximate system output will be that shown in Fig. 1.3. Figure 1.3 appears to be like the approximate parts of Figs. 1.1 and 1.2 for the components, but its meaning is entirely different: The component approximation graphs are measured from code executions, but Fig. 1.3 has nothing to do with code or measurement—its approximation to system behavior is a prediction.

By studying Fig. 1.3, the developer may be able to decide whether or not the components and the system design are meeting requirements. It's pretty clear that they do, except within the 'bump' region near 3.3, where the output should be substantially larger than the prediction. Looking at the component test-quality measurements, the system developer (that's me) decides to blame `Bell`'s testers (me again) for doing a poor job, and goes ahead with the component purchase[7]. Once I have the real components, I assemble the real system and expect it to work. Of course I

---

[7] Since in the illustration I successively play the role of component developer and system designer, there is a certain conflict of interest in the latter deciding to accept the work of the former, and our negotiations over the price of the real components are likely to be a farce. In "The International Christmas Pudding," a 1955 BBC Goon Show broadcast, there is a marvelous interchange between

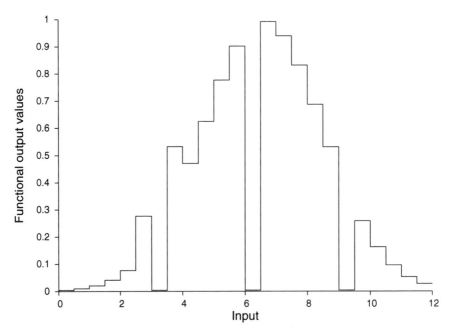

Fig. 1.3 Calculated approximate output of the system `Chopper; Bell`

do a little testing, but only in the region of the 'bump' and perhaps to check a few precise values of the Gaussian. That ends this simple illustration of CBSD.

1.1.3 Discussion of the Example

As befits a 'clear drop,' I chose example a ridiculously simple[8] example. The SYN tools can handle much more elaborate examples, and have many additional features. (See the tutorials in Chapters 9, 10, 11, and the descriptions in Chapter 14 and Appendix A for details.) They work with executable components that originate in any programming language. However, the SYN tools also have stringent limitations, which are the source of their power. Their most serious limitation is that they require components with numerical input domains. Step-function approximations rely on this restriction and the system-prediction algorithms rely on approximation. In real CBSD, such a restriction would be crippling—almost all software is inher-

---

Neddie Seagoon and Major Bloodnok in which hats keep changing in just this way. (The script is on the Internet.)

[8] Some students miss the point. My favorite is the one who does badly but does *not* drop the course in time, and when asked why he wasn't warned off on the first day, replies, "Well, it was dumb and I wasn't interested in that, but it seemed pretty easy, so I figured I'd get a good grade with no work."

ently non-numeric. Perhaps the ideas presented here can be extended to encompass more of reality, as discussed in Chapter 22. But even if the restrictions are inherent in a tractable theory, the restricted case has its virtues. It is usually possible to devise numerical examples to investigate fundamental issues, and insights gained apply to the general case. For example, Chapter 19 studies the roles of unit- vs. system testing, and Chapter 20 looks at the relationship between testing functional and non-functional software properties. Each of the case studies in Chapter 18 answers general question(s) through examples that the tools can handle.

The 'clear-drop' example itself suggests a number of ideas, some related to CBSD and some to exploring features of the SYN tools.

Insights into CBSD. A system developer who selects approximations from a component repository may find that testing done by the component developers is inadequate. In the example, Bell's subdomains should have been adjusted to improve its approximation. A poor Bell approximation in turn leads to larger errors in system prediction, which interfere with the system developer's ability to see if the components and system design are OK. The 'actual' graph of Bell behavior in Fig. 1.2 isn't needed to detect this problem—it's enough to have the approximation and its error analysis[9]. It is a fundamental tenant of CBSD that components are developed and tested in isolation. But nothing precludes negotiations between system designer and component provider once an attempt has been made to employ a component in some unusual way for which it was not well tested. Under the scheme proposed here, those negotiations can take place *before* component purchase, which is evidently better than buying a pig in a poke and trying to get satisfaction afterward.

Tool exploration. Outside the artificial distinctions of wearing a component-developer's hat or a system-designer's hat, a person who wants to understand the software involved in this example of CBSD can use the SYN tools to help. The tools are able to link together actual component code and test a real system for comparison against the tools' predictions. For ideal CBSD that's a no-no, but for exploring and evaluating the tools it's of interest. The average r-m-s error in the prediction is about 6.4% (ranging from 0.3% to 42%); the worst errors, as is to be expected, are at the edges of the 'bump', where the Bell approximation is poor. Chapter 17 explores prediction accuracy in detail, and in particular shows that there is a mostly linear relationship between component test errors and system prediction errors.

The reader might wonder what would happen in the synthesis if Bell's approximation were improved, or about the effect of using more (or fewer) samples in each subdomain of the component tests, or might question why the system was

---

[9] A paranoid component developer might choose not to allow access to graphs of component actual behavior, which could conceivably be reconstructed into code. But the error analysis cannot be suppressed, since it is a marketing tool. Would you be more likely to select a Bell whose tests have a published maximum error, or a competing component whose developer will not release error data, and says only, "Trust me."?

constructed as `Chopper; Bell`, not as `Bell; Chopper`. The tools make it easy to answer such questions.

In addition to measuring and predicting functional behavior as in Figs. 1.1, 1.2 and 1.3, the SYN tools similarly handle non-functional properties like run time. It often happens that run-time approximations are much better than approximations of functional output, because run time varies little across subdomains. In that case, the run-time approximation can be perfect. However, it does not follow that predicated system run times are also perfect, as explored in Chapter 20.

1.2 Roadmap of this Monograph

Part I describes components and CBSD, starting with the analogous ideas in mechanical and electrical engineering in Chapter 2. Chapter 3 traces some of the ideas that lead to components and proposes my simple model based on testing, to be contrasted with commercial practice and logic-based theory in Chapter 4.

Part II is devoted to software-testing background, and includes (Chapter 6) the functional testing theory that underlies my model of component composition.

The heart of the monograph is Part III, where testing theory is applied to derive the algorithms on which my tools are based. Chapter 8 covers composition in the simplest case of stateless, sequential components, with a tutorial on using the SYN tools in Chapter 9. Chapters 10 and 11 extend the composition algorithms to cover components with state and concurrent execution; these chapters each include a tutorial.

The SYN tools themselves are the subject of Part IV. Like most testing tools, these implementations are difficult only because of the bookkeeping required, but in Part IV two novel ideas appear: (1) *Artificial components* make significant, focused experimentation easy. 'Real' components resist alterations to explore something that comes up in an experiment. (2) *An oracle* is available for tool/theory validation. Each example using the tools has a result that can be obtained in two independent ways, making it very unlikely that these agree yet the tools are incorrect.

The case studies in Part V use examples to explore fundamental questions about components and CBSD; each study contains insights that were gained only through tool-supported experiments.

Some insights can be generalized to any sort of software testing, in Part VI. In particular, Chapter 19 provides a new understanding of unit testing and Chapter 20 looks at the issues raised by non-functional software properties and emergent properties. Part VI ends with some speculation about using my ideas outside the restrictions imposed by the support tools.

In the list of references, papers of particular historical interest are annotated. These are marked with "$\prec A \succ$" in the citation.

Appendix A gives details of the SYN tool specifications and designs.

1.2.1 Theory vs. Practice

My formal research training is in recursive-function theory, particularly the theory of undecidability, on top of initial graduate work in experimental solid-state physics. These disciplines strongly imprinted me with the essential role of mathematics in science: precise mathematics is the only satisfying way to describe something, the best way to explain and understand it. True, mathematics is necessarily a *model* of reality, not reality itself, but even when it is a distortion, a model can be so helpful to understanding that it remains in use long past its discard date. How many people still imagine electrons in their orbits around a nucleus, for all they know that quantum mechanics demolished Bohr's model 80 years ago?

Computer science began with a superlative example of a mathematical model: Alan Turing's successful attempt to capture the essence of computation and explore its theoretical limits [94, $\prec A \succ$]. Turing machines (as they are now called), or Turing programs (as they could be called, although Turing thought of the program as a "hard-wired" part of a machine) are literally a stroke of genius. By defining his "computers" mathematically, Turing at once cut through the philosophical haze of what it means to compute and was able to demonstrate the existence of uncomputable problems. Perhaps it is unwise to set before young, enthusiastic, naïve students an example such as Turing's. Few of us are in the genius class, and the world might be better off if we tried a different approach. Be that as it may, I have spent my professional life making mathematical models and looking to them for insight into real problems, mostly in the field of software testing. And in the publishing part of that life, I've sometimes found myself at loggerheads with colleagues who have no use for mathematics in computer science. I've suspected that my antagonists didn't like it because they didn't understand, and that is sometimes true. It takes training and practice to grasp even a straightforward mathematical model. The effort may be rewarded handsomely, but it is never quick and easy. Unfortunately for my ego, I've also disagreed with colleagues whose mathematics is far better than mine. They were just disappointed that I was using Turing's methods without his genius.

Turing's model provides a crystal-clear lesson on the relationship between theory (mathematics) and practice (for example, software engineering):

- A mathematical model should strive for extreme simplicity to maximize ease of understanding and ease of proof.
- A model may differ substantially from reality.
- Insights gained from a model often cross the boundary to reality.

A Turing machine (TM) is nothing at all like a modern PC nor is a Turing program anything like a C program, yet what's possible and impossible is the same[10] for TMs

---

[10] Attempts to formalize 'real' computers (as formal RASP machines [19]) and real languages (e.g., C [91]) because TMs are too far from today's reality have been a dismal failure. These models founder in the complications of reality and yield few insights (except perhaps how messy reality really is). Part of the difficulty is that the extra trappings actually get in the way of replicating Turing's proof. For example, most 'real' computing features of C can't be used to prove the existence of an uncomputable function: Potentially unlimited storage is needed, which precludes

and for PCs running C code. Proofs for TMs are vastly simplified because TMs have only a handful of 'op codes' without complicating exceptions; PCs have closer to 100 CPU operations, each subject to many exceptions involving virtual memory, cache, pipelining, interrupts, etc. TMs aren't 'real,' and a good thing, too. No one would build a TM for daily use, but when it comes to hard questions TMs are better to think about than all-too-real CPU chips and programming languages.

The real-world objects that fit my model of software components are real programs, but strongly constrained to fit the mathematics, which makes them at once 'unrealistic' and easy to understand in depth. In the model I can get results that I could never hope to achieve in a more 'realistic' case. It's my hope that insights gained from the model will be helpful to those who must face reality.

1.2.2 Formal Theory of Software Testing

The substrate underlying my component model is software testing, so it is with a theory of software testing that I begin to develop the model (Chapter 6). I was fortunate that a testing theory was developed and published at the beginning of my career. John Goodenough and Susan Gerhart wrote a seminal article [34, $\prec A \succ$], Bill Howden another [64, $\prec A \succ$]. Their theories were *functional*. A program was modeled as a mapping from input to output; that is, a program's meaning was the *function it computes*[11]. I was even more fortunate in being invited to work with Harlan Mills[12] on his functional theory of program semantics. This theory in turn perfectly supports the Goodenough/Gerhart/Howden testing theory, and extensions of it are also presented in Chapter 6.

Elegant as functional theories of semantics and of testing are, and as much as they dominate testing theory to this day, they are deficient in not encompassing two important ideas: One is program persistent state, the other is concurrent execution. Making state explicit in the composition theory (Chapter 10) yielded a number of insights about how testing should (and should not!) be conducted in the presence of state. Chapter 11 describes adding a basic form of concurrency to composition theory.

---

any use of memory-based constructs like variables, stacks, dynamic arrays, machine arithmetic, etc. In principle, memory in most machines is strictly limited by the size of the address space.

[11] To return to recursive function theory (for the last time, I promise!), that makes a programming language nothing more or less than a Gödel numbering of the partial recursive functions.

[12] Harlan called together six faculty members at the University of Maryland in 1981, and told us that we were going to write a programming textbook that would stand the world on its ear. To a man, we replied, "Sorry, I'd love to help, but I'm already overloaded; I've little to bring to the table; I know nothing about writing a text; it's premature; etc." Half an hour later we had agreed to sign a contract. John Gannon, Vic Basili, and I stayed the course to help Harlan publish his textbook [82, $\prec A \succ$] and teach the innovative freshman programming course it supported. I wish I could say that we stood the world on its ear...

1.2.3 Exploratory Tools

Although I've been a contract programmer, and put in a two-year apprenticeship at the University of Washington at a program help desk[13], I've always been disappointed in programs that merely solve particular problems. A program can aim higher, at helping its users to create and use programs to solve their problems. The self-compiling compiler was my first computing infatuation [37]; I maintained and rewrote commercial operating systems for five years. So in an academic career where I could choose my programming projects, I've concentrated on what are now pretentiously called "software tools." The tools described in Part IV and Appendix A suggest how component developers and designers assembling components into a system can be supported in style. I was able to implement these tools only because of the simplifying restrictions placed on components in my theoretical model.

Implementing tools to support a theory is more fun than any other kind of programming. There are no rigid requirements, but clear guidelines—a tool has to enable its users to try out the theory. Once a tentative implementation of some concept is working, using it suggests a myriad of changes and improvements. When it takes too long to do some calculation, it triggers a search for better algorithms. Each new feature of the tools is easy to test and immediately gratifying when it works. This is 'exploratory programming' at its best.

1.2.4 Insights into Component Composition

It is common wisdom that testing doesn't 'scale,' that is, while it might be possible to do a super job testing a small program, adequately testing large programs is thoroughly problematic. My intuition says that the reason is one of intellectual control: the author of a small program knows all about what it is supposed to do and how it tries to do it, so testing progresses from one trial to another, and if conscientiously done, this 'unit' testing winds up thoroughly investigating the program. At the end the tester cannot say exactly what was done, nor why she is pretty sure that enough was done. Such a seat-of-the-skirts method can't possibly work on a large program. In this situation, it is often possible to divide and conquer by splitting a problem, solving its parts, and recombining the results. Software components would seem to be ideal 'parts,' but while testing them works pretty well, recombining the

---

[13] I can't imagine how anyone accurately views computing without the experience I had consulting with scientists (hard- and social-) to debug their FORTRAN programs and canned-package runs.

Physics post-doc: "But I didn't change anything and it wiped out core!"
Consultant: "Why did you run it again if you hadn't changed anything?"
Post-doc: "Well, I just added 1 to that one subscript..."

Psychology grad student: "What does it mean when I get a negative R^2?"
Consultant: "It means you don't understand the SPSS package, and if you don't learn fast you'll never get your degree."

results doesn't work at all. For components in composition, separately-done tests don't 'match up' at the interface, and if forced to match, intuitively good testing of one component is compromised.

Two insights came together for me to form the solution to composing tests, which is presented in Part III. First, the only plausible method of dividing a program's input domain is by partitioning into subdomains. Subdomain testing has a long history, and there is something intuitively irresistible about it: no matter how badly it works, its proponents continue to tout it. I began studying subdomains as a test-quality measure in 1996 [39]; Chapter 7 summarizes the background. Second, it is essential to view the testing process not as a collection of binary successes/failures, nor as a collection of input values, but *functionally*. That is, the discrete test-input points, paired with their outputs, form a finite graph that is just like the function the program computes, but defined at only a few inputs[14]. The quality of testing is accurately measured by the extent to which the finite test graph matches and captures the real functional behavior. The functional viewpoint applies equally well to so-called 'non-functional'[15] program behavior, e.g., program run time or reliability. Dave Mason and Denise Woit, who were studying composition of component reliabilities in the late 1990s [101], saw the importance of measuring component *mappings* and told me about it.

Putting the two ideas together, an approximation to any program's functional and non-functional behavior can be constructed by interpolating between the test points, joining disparate output at subdomain boundaries [52, $\prec A \succ$]. This approximation may be inaccurate, but it is defined everywhere, and that is just what's needed to compose independent test results. Chapter 8 gives the details of the stateless composition theory, which is extended to cover state in Chapter 10 and concurrency in Chapter 11.

1.2.5 Implications for Testing in General

The novel content of my theory and tool support is its synthesis algorithms and prediction of system properties from measured component properties. Making component measurements with unit tests of the component code is necessary but initially seemed neither novel nor particularly interesting. It was a surprise that many insights into unit testing as a generalization of component testing came from experimenting with the tools. In seeking to get better system predictions, I was led to better unit tests. Good predictions are a metric for good unit test measurements, a metric that is novel but related to coverage metrics (since these are in turn defined using subdomains). The difference is that the usual coverage-testing metrics are weak surrogates

---

[14] In mathematical language, the testing function is a *finite support* for the program function.

[15] The apparent contradiction that 'non-functional' is 'functional' of course arises from using the same word to denote different things. The functional view means a mathematical mapping; 'functional' behavior that is the opposite of 'non-functional' refers to program functionality, that is, intuitive utility.

for quality, but a good prediction intuitively measures real quality in the test that led to it. Furthermore, since the same component can be placed in a variety of systems, the prediction measure varies, providing a way to study the quality of unit testing.

Because the formulation of functional testing theory in the presence of state in Chapter 10 is new, it suggests new ways to test programs with state, and tells some cautionary tales about methods now in use that are plain wrong. Similarly, a new theory of concurrent testing may lead to much-needed insights for software that uses multiple 'independent' versions in an attempt to gain high reliability.

Components as units suggest new ways in which unit testing can be valuable. Current practice simply discards unit test results and begins anew with system test. But if system properties can be predicted from unit-test results, those predictions can stand in for system testing, as described in Chapter 19.

Finally, the theory suggests that non-functional program properties are not really the ugly step-children of functional testing, but themselves deserve close study. Chapter 20 explores both 'compositional' and 'emergent' properties.

Part I
Components and Component-based Development

W HAT is an engineering component? Certainly 'component' is more than just a fancy name for a part, a bit, or an element of a whole artifact designed by an engineer. Engineering components have crucial properties without which they do not deserve the name. The right properties of components also enter into component-based design, the discipline of putting them together to make something larger. With proper parts, a difficult design can be accomplished; without them it may be beyond human ability. It is not too strong a statement to assert that components and component-based design are responsible for many of the miraculous successes of modern engineering.

Part I examines components and design in traditional engineering fields to see what properties of parts and design methods are crucial; then it describes what has been done for software and what might be done.

Chapter 2
Engineering, Components, and Software

A S a verb, "engineer" means to plan, manage, or construct. That's what an engineer does. A craftsperson does the same but in a quite different way. "Craft" carries the meaning of individual creative effort, of 'hand' work, of aesthetic goals as well as utilitarian ones, of less planning and more 'just doing.' The engineer follows rules (learned at an accredited engineering school, of course) while a craftsperson is more likely to have served an apprenticeship, or to make it up as s/he goes along. Both have another discipline to which they may aspire though they may not attain its standard: for the craftsperson it is 'art,' while for the engineer it is 'science.'

Beginning in the late 1960s, 'software engineering' has tried to apply engineering methods to the craft of developing software. There is an ongoing dispute about whether this is always a good idea, and much more dispute about exactly how it might be done. But even 'software cowboys' who despise engineering rules and management[1] can enthusiastically adopt ideas that work. 'Component-based design' is one such idea.

2.1 Standardized Components Make Engineering Possible

When something is to be made from individual parts, there is a clear distinction between craft and engineering methods. A craftsperson makes parts in the same way as the whole object is made: each part is fitted to the others until they work

---

[1] Much of the dispute about software engineering involves engineering methods applied to software *management*. The dispute is almost a replay of a similar controversy that arose at the beginning of the 20th century, when Fredrick W. ("Speedy") Taylor introduced what he called "Scientific Management" (and wrote a book with that title). Scientific management involves finding the best (i.e., cheapest) way to do any task, and then forcing workers who do it to do it that way. Today "time and motion study" or "industrial engineering" are more common terms, but Speedy's critics called it "Taylorism," and said it was just another way to exploit workers. See Donald Roy, "Quota restriction and goldbricking in a machine shop," *American Journal of Sociology*, vol. 67, 1952, no. 2, pp. 427-42.

D. Hamlet, *Composing Software Components,* DOI 10.1007/978-1-4419-7148-7_2,
© Springer Science+Business Media, LLC 2010

together. If the same person makes a second similar object, it won't be exactly the same, and in particular its parts will differ—parts likely won't be interchangeable between the two. That in itself isn't a happy situation: there could be a pile of broken objects, each with one bad part, yet not a single working object could be salvaged from the pile because parts can't be substituted for each other.

The engineering approach is to design parts to specification, and include quality parameters—usually called 'tolerances' for mechanical objects—that define when a part is 'as specified.' Such parts can be used interchangeably, and there is the large advantage that most of the assembly will require far less skill than for a craft object. (Some parts may be harder to make because the necessary tolerances are difficult to achieve.) The final step is *standardization*, where a limited range of parts is made in quantity for use in designing a vast variety of objects, most not even imagined when the parts were designed and fabricated. Mechanical fasteners are a good example: cap screws come in only a few head designs (hex, socket, etc.), only a few diameters ($1/16^{th}$-inch gradations in the English system which now is largely confined to the U.S.), and only a few lengths (quarter- or half-inch increments between roughly one inch and six inches). If you want a weird cap screw to fill some special need, you can have one made with some difficulty. But if instead you can live with one of the standard sizes, there will be one immediately available, it will be cheap, and you can count on it fitting.

Standardized components make engineering work because a design problem can be broken down and many of its pieces then require no design—they are 'off the shelf.' Furthermore, the limited variety of standard parts is actually an advantage because selecting a part helps to determine what goes around it[2]. A 1/4"-diameter cap screw fits a 1/4" nut, it fits through a 1/4" hole (the bolt is really a tad smaller than 1/4" in diameter), the hole can't be too close to the edge of the material, and so on. In today's computer-supported world, it is no small advantage to be designing with standardized parts. So-called computer-aided design (CAD) programs are a big help in design, and when the designer clicks on that 1/4" cap screw the CAD program can draw it and check if the hole is too near the edge...

Standardization plays a subtle role in designing physical systems. To illustrate, think about two pieces of metal that must be fastened together as part of a design. The metal parts come first, since presumably each has a purpose (to cover something, to support something, etc.). Their joint can't be designed until they themselves have been selected or fabricated, because its strength and location depends on their shape, thickness, etc. Suppose the designer decides to use a cap screw, and from a fasteners' catalog it appears that 1/4" diameter is strong enough. Furthermore, the screw needs to be at least 7/8" long to pass through both pieces of metal (and leave room for the nut and a couple of washers). Both of these dimensions are properties derived from the *system* design; nothing was known about them until the two metal

---

[2] Limiting design choices is sometimes thought of as a bad thing, but every designer knows that too much freedom wastes precious creative energy on inconsequential decisions. The hardest part of beginning a design is reducing too many degrees of freedom so that the mental wheels can stop spinning and start designing. The more choices that have been made for a designer, the easier (because the more constrained) the remaining choices are to make.

parts had been designed and the choice made to bolt them together. Looking at the catalog again, the designer finds that there is no 1/4 x 7/8 cap screw (except on 'special order' requiring three weeks lead time), but there is 1/4 x 1, which will do. (The extra 1/8" sticking out on the nut end doesn't interfere with anything. Perhaps it proves necessary to insert the screw from the other side for clearance.) Standardization plays a crucial role in that it allows the cap screw to be 'off the shelf' even though its description was not known when the shelf was stocked.

Craftspeople routinely make use of standardized components, too. A wood turner can buy ballpoint pen units or pepper-grinder mechanisms and then spend his/her creative energy on turning an elegant outer shell. The size of the hole to drill[3] for the mechanism is part of its published description.

In the next two sections, superficial descriptions are given of two component-based hardware designs, with an eye to seeing what makes them successful, and how software might imitate them.

2.2 Mechanical Engineering of a Vacuum System

Physical scientists often use laboratory apparatus that must operate in a vacuum. A qualified lab technician is adept at designing one-of-a-kind vacuum systems with which to conduct experiments. For more than 40 years there has been a vacuum-system components industry manufacturing flanges, pipes, feed-throughs, and other parts that can be bolted together to form a custom vacuum system. These parts are made from carefully selected stainless steels welded equally carefully. Their specifications are published in catalogs (today on the Internet—search terms "vacuum flange"), and the design of each system is a textbook example of component-based design.

The lab tech starts with a set of requirements from a scientist who has an experiment to perform. The requirements are not entirely precise, but they indicate a rough shape for the system, what has to be connected to it internally and externally, and the necessary upper bound on the pressure. It is common for these requirements to be a 'back of the envelope sketch' such as Fig. 2.1. A requirements sketch is the beginning of the 'top-down' part of the system design.

The lab tech starts the 'bottom-up' part of the design by consulting a catalog of vacuum components. Paging through this catalog he/she notes what sizes and qualities of flanges, seals, etc., are available, and matches these with the requirements. Figure 2.2 is an example of the kind of data available for a flange. (Dimensions 'A' and 'B' in the figure, and details of the bolt holes in the flange appear in separate figures[4] not shown here.) It will likely happen that available components will dictate an altered design, which will almost certainly be a wise choice compared to requesting special fabrication of custom parts. The scientist will be consulted about

---

[3] With a standard-size drill bit, of course.

[4] See http://us.trinos.com, where prices are also shown.

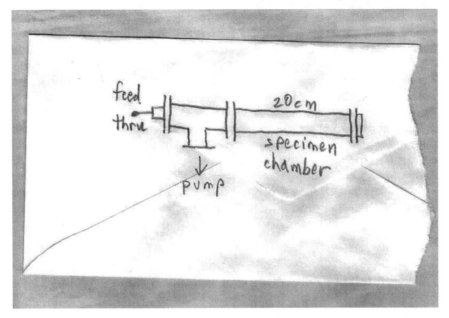

Fig. 2.1 Vacuum system requirements sketch

CF Tee, 316LN ESR
Flange material: 1.4429 316LN ESR
Pressure range: 10^{-13} to 1000 mbar
Temperature range: -196 to 400 °C
Bakeable up to 450 °C
Brinell hardness: 170
Magnetic permeability: < 1.005
Gasket material: Copper, Viton (FPM)
Leak rate: < 10^{-10} mbar l/s

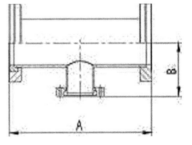

Fig. 2.2 Catalog description of a standard vacuum flange

acceptable changes; this process in turn may result in different component choices. Very quickly the top-down and bottom-up design paths will meet in a likely design.

But before the lab tech writes a purchase order, he will do some crucial calculations. Using the catalog descriptions, it will be possible to calculate important system properties. For example, the total volume is obtained as the sum of volumes of the parts, the vacuum quality will be determined by seal leak rate, the vacuum pump type and speed will depend on seals and volume, etc. These calculations show the technician whether the design will quantitatively meet the requirements, and they may be checked by the scientist. For example, it's a bad design if there is no available pump that can achieve the required vacuum. If that's the case, the volume or the number of seals may have to be reduced. What the tech does *not* do is order the parts and assemble the system to see if it fits together and works as required[5], then if it does not, start making changes. It is fully expected by everyone concerned that when the calculations check out, the required system can be routinely bolted together and it will work.

2.3 Electrical/Computer Engineering of a Laptop

A modern laptop computer is a marvel of component-based hardware design. It is literally possible to buy a CPU, memory, hard drive, CD/DVD drive, keyboard, touchpad mouse, battery, and screen, and plug them together to make most of a working computer[6]. Each component is itself complex, but their interfaces are simple, which is what allows the parts to be selected independently and to work together. In many cases there are several choices for interchangeable components, so a laptop builder can trade speed or quality for price.

Fixing a broken laptop may be as easy as exchanging a broken component for a replacement; in some cases the replacement slides into an existing slot without tools. How hard it is to replace a component mostly depends on packaging. For example, hard drives in a standard shape plug in; screens[7] and keyboards are custom fitted to the case. A traditional way to describe component-based physical systems is an 'exploded view,' a projection drawing showing the whole separated into its parts. Figure 2.3 shows a typical laptop[8]. In Figure 2.3 about half of the 19 components shown can be obtained off the shelf, and these account for perhaps 3/4 of the laptop cost.

There is a peculiarity of the computer market that gives an insight into 'specifications' for laptop components. In practice, virtually all laptops are sold bundled with some version of the Microsoft Windows operating system. There is a measure of 'fit and try' in getting a new version of Windows to work on existing laptops, or in checking that Windows works on a new laptop. Engineers at a laptop manufacturer do the work so that when a customer buys a machine with Windows installed, it works out of the box. This effort would not be required if the published specifications for the hardware were accurate and Windows followed them. One can imagine that data on the magnitude of the adjustment required would be difficult to obtain from either side of the operation. However, there is an independent way to get data. Some laptop purchasers discard Windows and install Linux on their machines. Here there has been no fit and try—Linux, like an ideal 'component' developed in isolation, can use only published hardware specifications[9]. If Linux works 'off

---

[5] To carry this a bit farther, it would be even worse to hand a trial assembly over to the scientist untested.

[6] The case that holds them and some other parts are custom designed.

[7] A website advertising replacement screens lists about 5000 15.4" models. Many of them are probably interchangeable, but no specifications are published on the site.

[8] Taken from the Dell information site http://support.dell.com for the Inspiron 5100.

[9] And damn hard to get them from the laptop makers it is. Why is that?

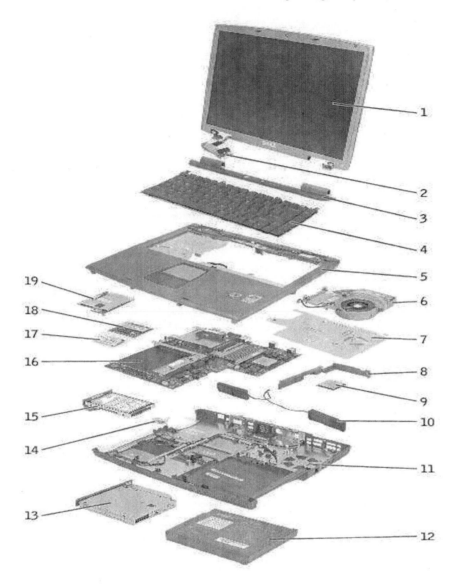

Fig. 2.3 Exploded view of a Dell laptop

the shelf,' it means that the hardware specifications are solid; it may fail because they are inadequate. Judged by the traffic on 'help' forums and Q-A websites, these specifications have improved dramatically in the last ten years. Where it was once necessary to pick from among a few laptop models that worked with Linux, today most models work[10].

2.4 Can It Be Done with Software?

"Software is different." But is it so different that component-based designs cannot work as they do in mechanical and electrical engineering?

From the time when the first program was written for a digital computer, there has been a 'software problem.' This problem is created by expectations that software can be routinely made to do what its creators intend[11] it to do. Many people have pointed out that the 'problem' is caused largely by an interplay between human aspirations and human frailty, compounded by dubious analogies to engineering. It would be as well to speak of an 'automobile problem' because some cars are lemons. But in the case of mechanical failures, humans share the blame with 'Mother Nature,' those forces that bring down the house (literally, in the case of structural engineering). Where Mother Nature is involved, engineering is well understood to be a discipline of trade-offs, in which there are no perfect solutions. A building can be designed to stand against the worst storm or the most severe earthquake in recorded history, but it becomes very expensive to build (and it is likely to be ugly). Besides, there may yet be a worse storm, or a storm coinciding with an earthquake—who knows what Mother Nature will come up with? So the structural engineer balances strength against cost and knows that there is a point beyond which any design will fail. If a building designed to withstand 70-mph wind gusts falls in a freak storm, it's the fault of the weather and the City Fathers who limited what they would pay, not the engineer.

But for software, we humans have only ourselves to blame. Software designs do not face unpredictable weather, the software really does not cost (much) more when it covers all possibilities, and as for ugly—well, code is invisible. What seems to bring down programs is just mistakes that people make. So the 'software problem' is that our creations fail, we trace the causes, try to do better, yet they fail again. It isn't flattering to explain the situation as an intrinsic limitation on human intellectual limitation. It may be true that people simply can't accomplish some tasks that they can perfectly well set themselves, but no one likes to admit it. Instead,

---

[10] PC models have standardized even more quickly; but here's an anecdote: A Dell PC purchased in 2003 with a optional large display worked with Windows, but when Linux was installed the full display resolution could not be selected. When Windows was reinstalled, the high resolution was not restored. After a great deal of Internet searching, the explanation appeared: There was a mistake in the BIOS code that returned an incorrect parameter for the display. The Windows loaded in the machine initially by 'fit and try' fixed this by ignoring the BIOS. But Linux (and the reloaded Windows) used the erroneous BIOS value according to specification. There was probably a single Dell engineer who knew this story, which was later laboriously reconstructed by dedicated (obsessive?) Linux enthusiasts.

[11] Although it may be apocryphal, the story is told that von Neumann's first subroutine failed, and the code was examined only after checking the hardware—how could the program be wrong?

we try to solve the 'software problem,' and what better way than to look to older engineering disciplines[12] for what has worked for them? Over the years, there have been calls for adopting this or that idea that has worked elsewhere, calls that sound good but often amount to nothing more than empty terminology. We need 'software blueprints' (because mechanical engineers use blueprints to get things right), or 'software ICs' (because electrical engineers package designs in integrated circuits), or 'software architects' because in construction engineering there is an important design step that comes before building starts, etc. Seeking common factors in these fads, many of them are ways of saying that for software, the 'problem' is in software requirements/specifications. If only we could say better what it is we mean to do, then perhaps we could get it right.

There are far too many inexcusably vague or shoddy specifications for software. But if the real difficulty is human intellectual limitations, precision in specification may not help much. More precision makes requirements harder to understand, and hence harder to implement correctly. What has been gained if software fails because a precise specification was not understood? Wouldn't it be just as well (and of course a lot less work!) to fail to understand the real-world requirements themselves? It seems that the only real answer lies in limiting the scope of activity: precise requirements for less-ambitious software could be understood, implemented, and the software not fail. In other engineering disciplines limitations are accepted but ascribed to Mother Nature, so it isn't necessary to admit that human rational ability, too, has its limitations[13].

Apart from contested ideas about engineering management and calls for transplanting ideas for their sexy-sounding names, there *are* parts of conventional engineering that software developers might adopt, notably 'components.' There is no doubt that mechanical engineers, for example, benefit immensely from the existence of standardized parts, not least because they interact so well with CAD tools. The issue is not whether similar components would be helpful in software design—of course they would be. But is it possible? *Are* there software units that act as the mechanical components do? Or are 'software components' just another flawed analogy?

The issue of software complexity and human lack of intellectual control cuts both ways for components. On the positive side, breaking up a large system should reduce the difficulty of developing each of its parts. (The issue of putting the parts together will be taken up at the end of this section.) But on the negative size, the description of even a rudimentary software unit is more complex than the descriptions of most mechanical and electrical parts[14].

---

[12] In the 1970s, Harlan Mills and others philosophically said that software's problems were just those of a young discipline. Give us 50 years and we would do better, as the other engineers did in that much time. We have done better, but the time is nearly up...

[13] After all, whose fault is it that people aren't clever enough to construct anything they can imagine? Mother Nature's, that's Who's.

[14] Many people have noticed that as computer CPU chips become more complex, they approach the intricacy of software. Then despite a long tradition of careful engineering design and good

The ability to grasp easily and accurately what a component does is one part of what makes it useful in system design. The other part is that a useful component must live up to its description. It's no good choosing the right part if it turns out its 'rightness' was a lie. When it comes to certifying components—checking to see that they really are as they are described—physical objects have a huge advantage over software. To give a simple example, the strength of a threaded fastener like a cap screw is described by the torque it is safe to use in tightening it. (Too much torque and the head will shear off or the threads strip.) And to measure this parameter takes just one test: the maximum torque is applied, and if the cap screw doesn't shear[15], it passes the test. Mother Nature very seldom (but not never!) allows her things to break at a small stress if they survive a larger. Mechanical engineers also cheat on Mother Nature by including *safety factors* in their component descriptions. If the cap screw is expected to fail at (say) 45 kg-m torque, its description might list the maximum torque as 15 kg-m, a safety factor of 3. Safety factors must cover variations in materials and fabrication and (not so obviously) mistakes in theory—the detailed explanation of how and why cap screws fail could be wrong. If despite the inclusion of a safety factor, some cap screw fails, the safety factor can be increased. However, if the reason for unexpected failure is theoretical, there may be *no* large enough safety factor. A minimum level of understanding is required before trial and error can succeed /citewhat.

Software descriptions are not usually limited to just a few parameters, but suppose for the moment that one is this simple. A reasonable analogy to safe tightening torque for a cap screw might be a bound on response time for a program. But to establish such a bound requires knowing which input excites the longest run time. And to find that input, if it can be found at all, requires extensive trials. Even if a large number of tests execute within the bound, there is no guarantee that for some untried input the run time will not be completely out of line. A program is inherently *discontinuous*; what it does on one input says nothing about another input which might be different only in the least-significant bit. Another way to say this is that there can be no safety factor for programs. This subject will be extensively explored in Chapter 17.

Complexity and certification interact in an important way that makes software unlike most physical objects. Where structural engineers (say) strive to simplify and standardize component parts like I-beams so that they can be reliably described by a handful of parameters and those parameters controlled in the manufacturing process, the essence of software parts is that they are not limited in any functional way. Software can do anything, which is usually thought to be a huge positive advantage over physical artifacts. But when it comes to certification, the advantage becomes a liability: the 'anything' that gets done can differ arbitrarily from what is required, which may be practically impossible to discover by testing. By exert-

---

CAD tools, even electrical engineers have begun to make mistakes similar to those of software developers.

[15] Well, more precisely it should remain elastic, not go into plastic deformation. Deformation on one test could set up quite different behavior on a following one. The analogy to software state is apt (see Chapter 10).

ing rigid control in design and at every manufacturing step, a mechanical part is constrained to behave simply and continuity allows this to be checked; no matter how simple a software part is *supposed* to be, its inherent discontinuity makes it untrustworthy. In general, the response to this intrinsic software property has been to legislate against the human developers who sometimes get it wrong: "You *shall* do it thus (perfectly)." Perhaps it would be better to begin using software's own power against its weakness: to exploit the 'do anything' to check that mistakes have not been made, or to correct them. If there is an aspect of software that has been shamefully neglected, it is self-limitation. For example, it has been known since the 1960s how to surely prevent memory-destruction problems like buffer overruns, yet the vast majority of working (so to speak!) software relies on perfect human effort to prevent them, instead of the foolproof checks that slightly slow program execution.

Much has been made of one unique software advantage: the ability to depend on all copies of a program to be exact duplicates. Manufactured physical objects, even when held to high standards and tested by good sampling methods, are not so trustworthy—Mother Nature can always throw a ringer in the batch. But continuity is worth much more than consistency when one cannot test for conformance—perfect software copies mean no more than that they are all bad. It is a common consumer-protection guarantee to promise a replacement if a product fails; but, if you got a replacement for your copy of Windows that crashes, it will be exactly the same broken Windows[16].

There is nothing practical to be done about software's complex descriptions and hard-to-test behavior, except to strive for simplicity, to be as careful as possible to understand the problem to be solved and the code that tries to solve it, and to use foolproof internal checks to detect or correct mistakes. A good argument can be made for using formal mathematical specifications, which certainly goes along with components of limited functionality—people do not seem able to use formal methods routinely except in restricted cases. The 'component' idea fits well with simplification and careful checking for another reason: it will be worth devoting extensive resources to requirements and certification of a unit that can be employed over and over in many developed systems. If a way can be found to have software check/correct its own actions, it is likely to be expensive; so it will only be worth incorporating in components that can be reused.

Unfortunately, complexity can be the death of standardization, which depends on being able to catalog a reasonable number of items, one that a person can skim through. Perhaps 'standardization' of many software components is outside the range of possibility. Even for mechanical systems there is an important role for the customized component, i.e., one not intended to be used outside of one system. Modern automobiles are full of such things, each designed for just one car, or even just one model of one car[17]. In structural engineering, each large building has a

---

[16] Unless, of course, it is 'new, improved' Windows that is even more complicated and less well tested, i.e., probably worse. And where is the retailer offering any software guarantee?

[17] Pity the car owner with a broken side mirror, who finds that its replacement costs the earth, and to get a used one requires finding a junkyard with exactly the same car. Furthermore, the parts of which the mirror is made are unique—the tiny plastic molding that is actually broken occurs in

unique design that makes crucial use of standardized components like I-beams, yet customized components may be equally important. For example, the joints between structural members can be separately designed and fabricated throughout the building, but it might be cheaper and better to design joints as examples of one custom component [3].

The 'do anything' nature of software certainly encourages custom components.

In summary, although there are important differences between mechanical/electrical components and software units, it should be possible to take the unique strengths and weaknesses of the latter into account and exploit component-based design. However, there remains a single significant issue that distinguishes a 'software component' from a mechanical/electrical one. The older engineering disciplines are able to make quantitative predictions of how their components will behave when combined into system assemblies. In the vacuum-system example, the leak rates of constituent parts can be combined (in ways that depend on the system configuration) to predict the system leakage. In the example of bolting two metal parts together, the forces that will bear on the joint can be calculated and the length is the sum of thicknesses of metal, nut, and washers. The reliability of the whole is determined by the reliability of the parts, and so on. Furthermore, these calculations carry safety factors along. It may happen that safety factors for the parts are not enough for the combination[18], so an aggregate gets an additional safety factor. This ability to make safe system predictions is what makes CAD tools invaluable, and what allows a system designer to work 'at component granularity;' that is, to ignore details of the parts and concentrate on the combinations. Nothing remotely like this has been done for software.

It is not at all certain that properties of software systems can be calculated from properties measured for the parts, because of the problematic nature of descriptions and certifications. The best that one might hope for is that an approximate system prediction could be obtained from imperfect component descriptions, and a quantitative bound placed on the accuracy of the one (system) in terms of the accuracy of the others (components). No matter how loose such a bound might be, it would then be possible to devote sufficient effort to improving the component certifications, with the knowledge that system predictions will get better. The proof that some software-component definition is really similar to the mechanical/electrical case would be the existence of CAD tools to make system-design predictions, including the prediction of safety factors.

This monograph follows exactly that plan. It proposes an approximation to component behavior to be measured by unit testing. It displays CAD tools that use component measurements to make (approximate) system predictions, and it relates the errors that exist in approximations at both levels. The intention is not to propose that the (very restricted) components defined are adequate for practical use nor to tout the CAD tools. Rather, the book is an 'existence proof' for the idea that software

---

no other car. It seems that mechanical engineers are forgetting the truths that software engineers would so like to learn.

[18] If so, the fault necessarily lies with inaccuracy in the theory of composition, since materials have been accounted for in the components.

components *can* be defined so that they act as useful components should. And it is the nature of existence proofs to illuminate the larger subject through a single concrete case. However restricted and 'unreal' the components and tools presented here may be, they are a fully worked out example from which insights and lessons may be drawn, insights that apply to any component scheme worthy of the name.

Chapter 3
Software Components
and Component-based Development

SOFTWARE has since its inception been packaged in self-contained pieces, for the obvious reason that only such pieces can be exchanged and used by others. Indeed, the original IBM user group whose purpose was to exchange code is called SHARE (Society to Help Avoid Redundant Effort according to one source); it was at first concerned with assembly-language subroutines for the 701/704 mainframes. A collection of subroutines is called a 'library,' and includes not only code but documentation. With the advent of FORTRAN, subroutine sources became far easier to read and understand—this goes by the misnomer of 'self-documenting code.'

The first libraries were very focused, particularly on mathematical functions. This made them genuinely useful, indeed, essential. Everyone doing scientific computation needs (for example) Γ-functions, and writing a mathematical library is a non-trivial task that requires great skill and knowledge. So it was natural for people with the required resources to share their work. That they were willing to take some trouble to share is a long-standing testimonial to the human generosity that lies behind today's open-source movement. Two particular mathematical libraries that were (and are) invaluable are statistical routines for data analysis such as SPSS and matrix routines such as LINPACK.

Once libraries for the basics were available, the idea was extended to more arcane subjects. But the more complex and varied the subject, the less valuable its subroutine library is. Providing extensive functionality makes its routines hard to locate in documentation, and when found they don't do quite what is needed. Modern libraries have tried to attack this problem by solving a narrow problem and providing many tailoring 'parameters' common to all their subroutines. A superb current example is the PSTricks package [96] for mixing graphics with TeX document processing.

However important packages and libraries are, the subroutine is just not the right mechanism for sharing arbitrary code. It is ludicrous to imagine one big library containing all the subroutines ever written—searching even the best documentation would almost always take more time than writing code anew. Furthermore, the documentation and search problem is not the only thorny one for sharing code. Equally

D. Hamlet, *Composing Software Components*, DOI 10.1007/978-1-4419-7148-7_3,
© Springer Science+Business Media, LLC 2010

important is the issue of quality: Having at last found the right routine, how can the code be certified? When a programmer writes his own, at least his mistakes are his own, which makes them easier to find and fix (and, oh, so much easier to forgive...).

Software components attempt to handle these issues that subroutine libraries do not address well. Whether components are more than a new name for pieces of code remains to be seen. In this chapter some of the ideas behind components are summarized and explored.

3.1 The Parts: Components

The computing world has changed greatly since SHARE was formed in 1955. By almost any standard, hardware changes are the most striking. But as hardware has improved over many orders of magnitude, software sometimes seems to have gone in the other direction. For the IBM 704 the 'software problem' was that there wasn't much of any, and to avoid every installation writing the same fundamental routines mandated sharing. Today's software problem is that there is too much, it's too complex, and it seems out of human control. 'Components' is one of the ideas that will help software catch up with hardware.

3.1.1 Common Environment for Software

One software aspect that changed all out of recognition but now may be returning to earlier times is commonality of the hardware environment in which software is used. SHARE worked at first because there were essentially no scientific computers except the IBM 704, then because FORTRAN made any scientific machine look much the same[1]. As competition for IBM developed, a plethora of disparate machines appeared, each with a unique operating system. Languages multiplied, sometimes available for just a single machine. 'Porting' significant software between machines was difficult or impossible. Only FORTRAN was close to universal[2]. When IBM decided to publish its PC architecture in 1981, the computing world began to come back together, and today it is almost true to say that there is one machine and three operating systems: the IBM-compatible PC[3]; Microsoft Windows, Apple Mac OS,

---

[1] For numerical computation, the lack of standards for machine arithmetic certainly took more taming than FORTRAN could supply. There were serious differences between IBM, UNIVAC, and CDC machines that could undo the best algorithms, not to mention the floating-point failings of the IBM 360 architecture.

[2] System software could be written in a subset of FORTRAN that would (almost) execute identically on every machine; to gain access to operating-system services that were needed to augment FORTRAN's meager functionality, a small 'kernel' of service routines could be implemented on each different machine [58].

[3] Perhaps Sun Microsystems should count as a second hardware design.

and UNIX[4]. Today an individual computer user often can go to the Internet and download one of three 'binaries' that will run directly under Windows, under Mac OS, or under LINUX. Not all software is like that, but a broad range of languages and applications[5] is, software coming from individuals, open-source centers like SourceForge, and commercial interests. So maybe it's again time to share.

3.1.2 Reuse

Engineering replaces individual craftsmanship when the parts of things can be precisely described and fabricated to closely meet specifications. Then those 'standardized parts' can be mass-produced and will fit interchangeably. In contrast, craft production assembles handmade parts, each adjusted and fitted to the others. Mass-produced articles are seldom as beautiful or even as functional as what a craftsperson makes, but they are much cheaper and can be made by people with less skill.

The software analog of standardized parts is 'reusable code' The expense and difficulty in making software lies not in the replication of many copies, but in the time and care required to fabricate each single complex original. It would not be much advantage for making two bicycle to use standardized pedals[6]—standardization only comes into its own at a dozen, or certainly 100, bicycles to be made. But if a software system can incorporate any substantial chunk of code that is not newly written, there is a large payoff even on the first reuse. For software, it is not 'standardization' that counts, but the mere fact of reuse. Within a particular software development effort, some block of code may be decidedly non-standard: poorly documented, badly coded, with many bizarre features; still, to use it in two distinct system-development projects saves its full cost the second time around. However, it is obvious that standardizing code greatly enhances reuse. Many more people will find and feel comfortable reusing code that is well documented, well coded, with a coherent feature set. The extra dimensions beyond reuse itself are what distinguishes a reusable *component* from reused code.

---

[4] Apple's decision to use Intel PC chips eliminated a second machine. Mac OS is now constructed on top of UNIX, and although it provides a full UNIX interface, most of its users never know. UNIX systems do come with a disparate collection of "environments" that tailor the interface to the user, many of them built on the windowing support of the X11 software. But different environments seldom interfere with exchange of software. Of course, there are still incompatible machines and unique operating systems, but they have a far smaller market share than in 1970.

[5] Those able to use a C compiler have access to more software available in system-independent source form. It is a very unusual machine/system that doesn't have a pretty good C compiler, no small part of today's common environment. Credit is due to the GNU project and their open source gcc compiler.

[6] In 1972 the Lambert bicycle was designed and built using largely non-standard parts, though mass-production techniques were still used. It was not a commercial success. Anyone who has owned a Lambert knows the thrill of replacing a part only to find that the threads don't match—Lambert made their own unique machine screws. (The pedals are one of the few Lambert parts interchangeable with other bicycles.) Lambert owners also know the joy it was to ride those bikes.

Any enhancement of code whose purpose is to encourage and reward its reuse will have a cost above and beyond the minimum for achieving just the required functionality. The argument justifying this cost has its obvious part: there are savings when code is not written again. A less obvious justification is that reuse supports increased quality in software. When a component is reused enough times, its cost is almost immaterial because it is amortized over many systems. With more resources devoted to it, the component code can be better, making each system that reuses it better.

3.1.3 Information Hiding

A big part of what's wrong with software is 'maintenance,' in software jargon meaning changing program code to correct or augment its behavior[7]. Dave Parnas early recognized that code could be designed to make changes far easier, and he proposed [89, $\prec A \succ$] division into modules giving each 'secrets' so that changes would be confined to modules whose secrets were impacted. The name *information hiding* has a dual meaning: storage for data values is encapsulated within a module, but the more important sense is that all characteristics of that data are kept hidden from other modules for their own good[8].

Information hiding is a design technique, but it might be better to call it a design critique—it isn't much help in creating software designs to solve a problem, only in judging whether a design, once found, is 'maintainable.' The idea is language independent: Parnas was thinking of assembly-language software in 1972; even that "best high-level machine language" C can do it naturally [54].

3.1.4 Object-oriented Design

Object-oriented (OO) design techniques are perhaps the most help in creating software to find solutions to problems. To simplify almost to the point of parody, OO design is a process of inventing data types, that is, sets of values and operations on those values. These data types are tailored to a particular problem, to make its discussion easy. The discussion concerns relationships between parts of the problem and actions that simplify or reduce it, which in turn often make a problem solution

---

[7] It is well understood that 'maintenance' is a misnomer that shows just how different software is from other human artifacts and how difficult it is to think and talk about it. So-called 'perfective maintenance,' closely akin to the 'refactoring' step in an agile design process, is more like the usual sense of maintenance that seeks to stave off later failure. The 'wear and tear' that is being compensated for is programmers working on the code!

[8] Code outside the module literally cannot make reference to the hidden information. So although programmers undoubtedly would cheat and look at the module source and its secrets, they *cannot* write outside code that depends on a secret.

apparent. There are few general rules for solving problems, especially using so poor an instrument as a programming language, but being able to talk about a problem in concise, accurate terms may bring a solution within reach of a leap of human intuition.

An object-oriented programming language must provide mechanisms for defining and using the types of an OO design, usually called 'classes.' A class seems a good candidate for a definition of 'component,' because classes are *encapsulated* and one class can *inherit* from another. Encapsulation allows complexity to be hidden inside, so that the interface to the outside user can be narrow but the class capabilities great. Encapsulation can be used to implement information hiding, but that is not its point for reuse. Inheritance addresses the component problem of modifying code that is 'not quite right' for reuse. Changes can be made in a way that preserves some or all of the original class functionality (and quality!).

Unfortunately, across OO languages inheritance is too varied a mechanism to easily standardize. What form and substance are essential to defining 'component'? The subject is fertile ground for 'terminology wars' in which *your* components aren't really components because they differ from true components (that is, *mine*). A related drawback of a definition based on language is the power of the market and a *de facto* standard: the most popular OO language may not have the best features on which to standardize, and unless it has and holds for a long time an overwhelming popularity lead, its competitors will not accept it as definitive. Whatever a 'component' turns out to be, there will be a need for supporting software to make the idea easy to use in development, and it can be the death of a good idea to tie it prematurely to a language or product that is destined to disappear[9].

Finally, the case against using constructions in an OO programming language to define 'component' rests on more general principles. The purpose of programming languages is to provide power and control of machine computation. However well some language happens to intersect with ideas about pieces of code to be standardized and shared, that language will include many, many features that do *not* intersect with the component idea. Indeed, some language features that at first seemed unrelated may turn out to be antithetical. It's unwise to base a definition on ground that's not fully explored. Section 3.2 to follow suggests that the very strength of OO development—the ability to define modified components using inheritance—is a flaw from the testing viewpoint.

3.1.5 Szyperski's Definition

Clemens Szyperski was one of the first to think deeply about what 'component' should mean for software. The subtitle of his 1999 book *Component Software* [93,

---

[9] Harlan Mills's functional semantics was worked out in detail for Pascal at a time when Pascal was the dominant language for teaching programming in U.S. universities. Then along came C++.

$\prec A \succ$] is "Beyond Object-Oriented Programming"[10]. With no attempt to summarize or explain Szyperski's thinking, here's his initial definition:

> A software component is a unit of composition with contractually specified interfaces and explicit context dependencies only. A software component can be deployed independently and is subject to composition by third parties.

Szyperski was not thinking about persistent state when he framed the definition, and state does not much figure in *Component Software*. However, in a footnote he says that if there is to be state in a component, of course it must be local, which might or might not be implied by "...explicit context dependencies only."

It is easy to criticize definitions that strive for generality. They appear vacuous to someone who doesn't already have a good idea of what they mean, while those who already do have ideas, however disparate, tend to think the definition agrees with their narrower view. Szyperski's definition is notable for not explicitly stating that these 'units' have anything to do with computing. The definition could apply to dominoes 'deployed' and 'composed' by laying them out. But extreme abstraction and generality cut through terminology wars, and Szyperski's definition has wider acceptance than any other. The definition adopted for this book is as follows:

In Szyperski's definition	*In this monograph*
software	components are executable
composition	components are to be combined with one another
contractual interfaces	components include descriptions of how they legally can be combined
explicit context	descriptions must include all ways in which components can be influenced by the execution environment
deployed independently	component descriptions may not assume any particular combination of them

In any 'sensible' assembly of such components, their contractual-interface and explicit-context requirements will be observed, although it is not a property of a component that it be sensibly used.

3.2 The Systems: Component-based Software Development (CBSD)

There is no use in software components by themselves; what counts is how they are assembled into software systems. Component-based software development (CBSD)

---

[10] The subtitle probably did not interfere with sales of the book in a world that wasn't yet using 'component' as a buzzword.

is also called component-based software engineering (CBSE), but CBSE implies a precision and process definition that many (most?) development projects lack, yet they may be component-based. Using components to construct software applications is a good idea if more resources spent on the parts reduces resources needed for the aggregate. But the potential gain in quality that results from using better parts is more important than development time and money saved. There is also an important subjective effect of raising the granularity of programming. When the actions that make up the system behavior are large and well controlled because they are component macro-actions rather than micro-actions of programming-language statements, a system designer finds it easier to combine them correctly. The system complexity is reduced by increasing the complexity of its parts; this is a gain because the parts are of a size that people can better manage.

Theoretical investigation of the component idea divides into two camps when system development is considered.

The OO camp, perhaps in response to the practical observation that no third-party component ever seems to do exactly what is needed, believes that reuse in systems is essentially a process of component adaptation. In this view the research questions involve trade-offs between flexibility and stability: one wants a component to allow change, but not so much that its good qualities (of reliability, say) are lost. Much of the research is connected with the technology of writing and modifying components, which in turn comes down to properties of the programming language and component-linking mechanism used.

The opposing, 'immutable' camp, [11] perhaps in response to chaotic OO terminology wars, chooses to consider components as unchanging: their origin, programming language, linking mechanism, etc., are not considered because they must be taken as found. The research questions in the immutable camp center on the implications of this self-imposed limitation: has too much been given away for the sake of simplicity? What properties must inviolate component objects have so that they can be used?

This monograph is clearly in the 'immutable' camp, perhaps at the extreme edge of reducing the inviolate component properties to a minimum.

As the sequel will show, the testing viewpoint adds important dimensions to this issue:

No retesting. For a given fixed component, can a system designer improve the *description* of its behavior, or must the one supplied by the component's author suffice? This additional question is related to the issue of proprietary code: Can component sources be inspected? Can components be retested? The answers here are both 'no'—components are not freely available to a system designer even in binary form. This choice is not intended to support the jealous protecting of code as so-called 'intellectual property.' Surely the tradition of SHARE dictates just the opposite. Rather, inviolate components are dictated by the decision to simplify and go deeply into the fundamentals of CBSD. It certainly muddies the

---

[11] It's not easy to name the alternative to OO. It might be called after Szyperski; would he like that?

water if a 'component' can be a shifting entity hard to distinguish from OO code in general. The strongest open-source advocate might acknowledge that if CBSD is to be profitably studied and used, it would be better *not* to look at (and certainly not to modify) component code.

No bug insertion. The strongest reason for keeping components inviolate is the well known human propensity to destroy what we touch. If a component is complex enough to be worth using, it is probably difficult to understand the detailed workings of its source, and hence all too easy to insert or change code contrary to its intrinsic quality. The more finely tuned and cleverly implemented a component is, the more easily ham-handed 'maintenance' can compromise it. At the heart of CBSD is the idea that implementation and testing effort are effective in the small, so that mistakes in system construction rise above the component level. The best human effort gets components right; then system problems are new and to find them does *not* descend to questioning the parts used.

3.2.1 Product Families

One important form of reuse occupies a unique place in CBSD. In developing *product families* [79], collections of closely related applications, the design of the family and reusable components within it are intermingled. The reuse is important, indeed it underlies the whole idea of a family, but it would be counterproductive to insist that components be designed first and then remain unchanged. It is expected that as system design proceeds, component properties will alter to fit and improve the whole. Of course, the closer the family design comes to completion, the harder it is to alter a component, which must continue to correctly serve in multiple members of the family. Perhaps at some point component designs are best 'frozen,' but this is a practical, not a philosophical issue.

Product families are not studied in this book. There is no reason why, as in any systems, a family could not also make use of the kind of CBSD discussed here, in which some component definitions are fixed at the start. One way in which the ideas fit together is that a fixed component C might be selected initially, then as the family design continues, C might be found to be more trouble than its use is worth, and a new search might look for a better (fixed) C'. This *substitution* of components does not violate the tenets of the simplest CBSD, and is one of the situations to be explored in Chapter 18.

3.2.2 Component Development and Cataloging

If components are to be developed as fixed entities, not to be altered when later deployed in a variety of systems, then the component description released with the component becomes all-important. Following the nomenclature of mechanical and electrical components, this description will appear in a component *catalog* (or *handbook*), and the catalog description is the only information available to system designers. It must therefore have two parts:

Functional and non-functional descriptions. When a systems designer is looking for a component, descriptions of behavior[12] are matched against search keys. It is by no means clear how this is to be done—or even if can be done at all—for software. In other engineering disciplines catalogs are indexed by a small number of general categories such as "fasteners," or "connectors," and within each category there are numerical parameter values and drawings, graphs, or photographs that give details. Searching a catalog for a component means finding the pages for its category, then paging through that section looking at the graphics and parameters. For software components such a scheme is feasible only for a few well defined categories, e.g., "mathematical functions." Those categories are the ones for which subroutine libraries already work fine. The only precise descriptions known for software are the formal ones based on some kind of mathematical logic. These are notoriously difficult to read and seem impossible to usefully index. Non-functional property descriptions play for software something of the same role as mechanical/electrical parameter or tolerance values, but are themselves seldom single numerical values. They would complicate the cataloging problem, but the primary difficulty remains one of indexing 'functionality.'

Certification. There is a place in component catalogs for a wide variation of quality among the entries. But it is essential that the quality be quantitative and explicit in the catalog description. A system designer might be willing to try a low-quality component because it is cheap or the only one available, or to pay more for a component with high quality, but selecting a complete unknown is a recipe for disaster. Again, no one knows much about how quality can be practically described for software. The only clear standard would be something like, "proved correct by Alan Turing in 1937 [95, $\prec A \succ$]." Most known descriptions are subjective and qualitative and would be rejected out of hand for physical objects. It would be unthinkable to describe CPU chip quality as no more than "produced in a level-3 (on a self-assessed subjective scale of 1-5) fabrication facility," yet that is just what some software-process certifications amount to. Software testing seems a good compromise candidate for quality description—it is precise, but not so difficult as proof. Testing needs accurate measures of its adequacy, currently not often available.

In this book component descriptions are finite graphs of functional and non-functional behavior, graphs obtained from testing a component. Details are given in

---

[12] In mechanical and electrical engineering, component descriptions are usually called *specifications*. This word has a different meaning in software development, so it will not be used here in the sense of 'description.' The very fact that terminology is different underlines the disparity between software and physical objects. Handbook descriptions are not comprehensive requirements/specifications in any case, but rather descriptions of actual objects. For the physical objects those descriptions are so good that they might as well be called 'specifications.' Not so for software.

Chapter 8. Certification is also provided by testing, using the accuracy of finite graphs as a test-quality metric. Details are given in Chapter 17.

3.2.3 System Design using Components

When an adequate catalog of components is available, a novice can be instructed to build a system by 'just doing it'. This means that the system requirements must be studied until they become internalized and second nature. The component catalog also has to be studied, to see what is available and what it can do. 'Just doing it' is a description of the intuitive process of top-down decomposition (of system requirements) and bottom-up synthesis (of component descriptions) that sometimes come together in the middle to yield a system design. The difference between a novice and an experienced designer is that this vague process works better for the latter. This does not mean that an old pro can easily describe how it's done. A novice can learn by apprenticeship, that is, watching the process in action, and making attempts that are then criticized to shape his intuition. One way to describe what is being proposed here is to say that by introducing rigorous engineering procedures for software components, it will be possible to produce systems by craft methods.

3.3 The Viewpoint: Testing Simple Components and Systems

This chapter has introduced some ideas in software development that motivate formal 'engineered' components and their use as system building blocks. The particular aspect of this relatively new subject to be studied in this book is the testing of components. It is important to simplify the model in a fundamental study, to eliminate as many extraneous 'real' complications as possible.

3.3.1 Simple Components

Components in this book clearly fall under Szyperski's definition. A component supported by the SYN tools described here is any executable program observing the following rather harsh restrictions. On each execution run of a component:

Input. A single floating-point value must be read from STDIN.

Output. A single floating-point value must be written to STDOUT.

Run time. A single floating-point value must be written to STDERR, representing any non-functional property of the execution.

State. A single floating-point value must be first read from a disk file and later written to replace that same file. (A stateless component is exempt from this requirement.)

Concurrency. If a component uses concurrency, it must start exactly one other component in parallel, passing it an input. The started component's output comes back to the starter, which must rendezvous to wait for it.

The simplicity of requiring a single value in all component interactions with its environment is evident. It enables comprehensible graphs to be drawn describing the testing of behavior. The restriction to numerical inputs is more severe, but it is essential in approximating component behavior and randomly selecting inputs. The real motivation for the restrictions is to enable automatic component testing. A simple, uniform test procedure can be mechanically carried out on any component without any knowledge of it except that it obeys the constraints. The SYN tools implement this procedure.

3.3.2 Simple Systems

'Software architecture' is coming to mean [4] the way in which parts of a system communicate with each other and work together. The simplest architecture is called 'pipe-and-filter' after the UNIX-shell supported '|' (pipe) operator that sends output from one program (filter) into another. The generalization of pipe-and-filter used in this book and by the SYN tools is sequences of components with local state connected by pipes, but additional conditional connections and iterative connections are allowed in which a component can influence the flow of system control[13]. These three structuring operations of sequence, conditional, and iteration have been shown to be adequate to express any computation [10]; they are the operations of 'structured programming' [72] that pushed the goto out of much of programming.

A rudimentary kind of concurrency is also modeled, which corresponds to that started by the UNIX fork system call. But restrictions (given in detail in Chapter 11) are imposed so that neither race conditions nor deadlock can occur.

3.3.3 Critique of the Model

Faced with a model so very restricted, the first response is likely to be: "But those aren't real components or real CBSD! They don't have _____ (and _____ ...)." The rebuttal is that they *are* real components, just not very complicated ones. If a prac-

---

[13] Control extensions have often been imagined for UNIX shells, but they don't have a natural command-line syntax and none ever caught on. Whether or not pipe-and-filter allows the filters to keep persistent state is unclear. In UNIX, the tee command allows file creation, but tee has no UNIX inverse.

tical software developer were forced to use them, the absence of _____ and _____ , etc. would be annoying and frustrating. However, many aspects of CBSD would be no different than in the real situation where components *do* have _____ and _____ etc. So it is possible to hope that this model will yield insights into CBSD, and because of its simplicity, those insights will be comprehensible and revealing. It might be possible for a developer forced to use such simple components and architecture to find workarounds so that more complicated CBSD can be done within the model. For example, the restriction to single input/output/state values might be got around by coding several values into one. The restriction to numerical values could be circumvented by coding other data numerically. Such attempts to evade the model's restrictions are usually counterproductive for understanding. The reason is that by side-stepping the model, its simplicity is lost and the lessons it could teach are obscured. As will be seen in Chapter 18, the most revealing experiments are those in which complications are kept to a minimum.

The model used here is an abstraction of reality, but it is not so abstract as to omit all of reality's stubborn facts. If the right balance has been found, it will be possible to get surprising insights into CBSD. Too much abstraction and the insights won't be real (a little *too* surprising!); too little abstraction and nothing will be learned that could not come from directly observing reality. Chapter 4 to follow describes the state of the practice of CBSD for comparison.

Chapter 4
CBSD in Practice and Theory

W HEN a real-world software engineer talks about system design with components, it may mean following a quite formal process, or it may mean no more than a vague plan to divide the software into parts. Between these extremes, commercial software tools are available to support practical CBSD. Commercial component tools are practical aids to software development; they have no theoretical basis. They are also unlike the SYN tools of this monograph in that the components to which they apply are not restricted as SYN's are. Within their narrow scope, the SYN tools are much more capable. They support a process here called *Immutable*-Component-Based Software Development[1], in which component design, implementation, and testing occur strictly before any system activities and cannot be revisited. Commercial practice and terminology will be briefly explored before continuing with immutable-component investigation.

4.1 Components and Connectors

A diagram something like Fig. 4.1 seems to express everything about a component-based software system. In the figure, within a dashed 'system' boundary, numbered boxes represent components and their connections are shown as 'ball and cup' pairs. The 'ball' indicates that a component *provides* something, and the 'cup' that something is *required*. Pairing them indicates a match (but see below for limitations of the match). For example, in the sample figure, component **1** provides what component **2** requires. Connections extending outside the dashed box show what the system provides/requires. For example, on the upper left side of Fig. 4.1 there is an external 'required' connection. Any component box in such a diagram can be further decomposed into a subsystem of connected boxes; in the other direction, any group of boxes can be lumped into a single component box by erasing its internal detail. In decomposition, connections are invented to link the new parts; in grouping, the

---

[1] I-CBSD. The 'I' could also stand for 'Ideal'.

D. Hamlet, *Composing Software Components,* DOI 10.1007/978-1-4419-7148-7_4, © Springer Science+Business Media, LLC 2010

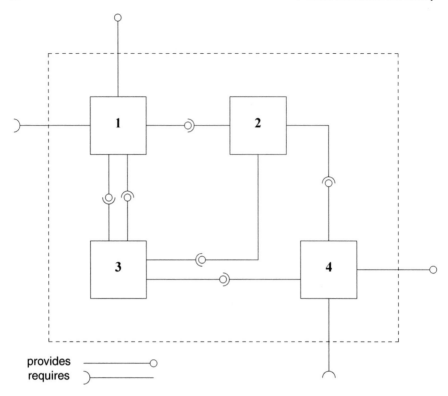

provides ────────○
requires ⊃──────

Fig. 4.1 A system of connected components

lines leading in and out of the identified group become its connections. Designing
with connection diagrams could be described as decomposing a one-box (named say
"SYSTEM") diagram into one with many boxes, each to be implemented as a piece
of code. A number of fancy graphical editors manipulate connection diagrams, and
using an editor is sometimes called 'computer-aided design,' but the 'aid' provided
is small.

These diagrams and tools to edit them are useful, but they apply only to a minor
part of the design process. The diagram is a kind of 'syntax' for the system; it
leaves out the much more important and difficult 'semantics.' Connecting 'ball' to
'cup' in no way implies that 'something' will be properly exchanged. There may
be timing/blocking conditions that do not match, for example. There are almost
certainly expectations on both sides about the form and meaning of the 'something.'
For example, the provider may expect an acknowledgment that the requirer does
not expect to give, or the requirer may need a floating-point number in $[0, 1]$, etc.
Within each component box, the *way* in which things are provided or required is not
described at all. Semantics makes all the difference. For one and the same diagram,
a connection may operate like a subdomain call-return between equals or like a

central program issuing commands. When a human being knows the relationships to be used, it is easy to draw a diagram for it; but very little about the relationships can be surely deduced from a diagram. It's a common human failing to confuse syntax with semantics[2]. In Fig. 4.1, for example, components 1 and 3 have a pair of connections. That's the way it would be drawn if 1 sends 3 a sequence of values which 3 processes to return a composite result. But it could just as well be 3 sending 1 a command and waiting for an acknowledgment, or any number of other meanings.

For the simple components supported by the SYN tools (Section 3.3.1) it is hard to draw a useful connection diagram. The one-in-one-out part is easy, but to show state would require a peculiar internal requires-provides pair of 'connectors.'

Semantic omissions from a connection diagram cannot be supplied in any tidy, general way. In principle semantic content can be described by a detailed description of what takes place inside each box. Descriptions can be given in a precise mathematical form (say as a relational specification); as a vague description in English, e.g., "When the first component receives an outside input, it computes a result and sends it to the second component..."; or even in program-like pseudocode. But detailed descriptions are a mistake at the initial stage in system design, because they put details ahead of large abstractions. Two abstract approaches are useful: 'system architecture' to describe the high-level 'way' of the system, and 'component models' to describe (and partially control) matching at the connectors.

4.2 System Architecture

There is no limit to the number of system patterns behind a connection diagram, but in practice a handful of patterns has proved most useful[3]. The most common, general patterns deserve the name 'architectures.'

The pipe-and-filter architecture of Section 3.3.2 is perhaps the simplest powerful architecture. It is trivial to draw a connection diagram for pipe-and-filter: a system is a single line of components, each 'provides' joined to the following 'requires.' The

---

[2] One of the best confusion mechanisms people use is to employ loaded names for the parts. Calling a component box "sort" doesn't make it so. It is a sobering experience to study syntax labeled in a natural language one doesn't know—what seemed clear becomes instantly incomprehensible. The theory of programming language specification has done a great deal to help straighten out syntax and semantics. But there are still technical experts who believe that a language's context-free grammar tells what its programs do, and others (or the same ones?) who call deterministic type properties 'static semantics.' The rational relationship is that mechanical syntax *carries* non-mechanical semantics, making precise statements about it possible. Nowhere is there a better example of this than the way programming-language grammars provide the terms in which to describe meaning. Given that

   <assignment statement> ::= <variable> = <expression>,

one can say, "The current value attached to <variable> is replaced by..." and thereby describe all possible cases at one go.

[3] A good analogy for physical structures is that although bridges could be built in a vast number of ways, only a few are routinely used, driven by circumstances. For example, a long span without the possibility of supporting piers dictates a suspension bridge.

other operators of conditional, loop, and parallel in Section 3.3.2 are not so easy to represent in helpful connection diagrams—a flowchart does a better job (except for concurrency, which is difficult to capture in any simple diagram). Altogether, the inclusion of state and control flow disqualifies the present model as an 'architecture': it is more a general scheme in which many architectural patterns can be expressed.

4.3 Component Models

Architecture describes system properties, the way in which components cooperate to meet the overall requirements. The other part of system semantics applies to the component connections themselves, describing and constraining the interfaces. Although interface matching is a system property, the descriptions used to check a match are at component level, and can be called a 'component model.'

As a very simple example, UNIX pipe-and-filter connections pass data as character strings, using a bounded buffer and blocking i/o. Output goes into the buffer from a process 'ball,' to be taken out by another process 'cup.' If the processes' i/o rates are not compatible to within the buffer's capacity, one process blocks waiting for the other. In principle arbitrary processes match, but the model is too general to express narrow match requirements such as exchanging a value that must be an integer, and too specific to encompass other synchronizations such as polling. The processes themselves must check the details of a match, and they are expected to properly use blocking i/o. If they fail in these responsibilities, the system may 'hang' or throw bizarre exceptions.

Viewed as a component model, the SYN tools also use only blocking i/o between components, but they enforce exchange of single floating-point numbers over each connection.

Most component models, particularly those implemented as software to aid in systems development (so-called 'middleware'), are unlike UNIX pipe-and-filter and unlike the SYN tools. Commercial middleware provides a choice of interface and its implementation. The middleware helps the components to connect as the component model requires. It is bad form for a component model to allow a connection under its control to misbehave. In contrast, pipe-and-filter and the SYN tools are general connection mechanisms in which the components provide most of the interface, which works only if they happen to behave properly.

4.3.1 Middleware and Container Services

CORBA [12] is a full-blown component model, which can be implemented as middleware. Components call on the middleware software layer to obtain standardized connections, which are guaranteed to function according to the model's definitions. One way to describe middleware is to say that it encloses each component in a 'container' and then connects containers. 'Container services' are the middleware routines that the encapsulated code can use. Interface matching is the most basic container service. Static analysis, or if necessary run-time checking, is used to see that a 'provides' connection does supply what a 'requires' expects. When the interface provided is relatively complicated, its details are sometimes called 'connector semantics.' The most powerful services are declaratory, freeing the component code from implementation altogether. For example, in a connection declared to be 'logged,' the middleware transparently inserts interface code to do the logging, which then appears to happen by magic.

It is a stretch to call UNIX shell features a component model or component middleware, because UNIX's intention is to provide simple, general, and powerful connections over which programmers have full low-level control. Most component models are anything but simple; they sacrifice generality and low-level control to provide high-level services. Similarly, the SYN tools of this monograph are not conventional middleware, because their purpose is to foster experiments and aid understanding, not to help implement applications. But SYN tools use mechanisms very like containers to accomplish their different ends. For example, the interface profiling feature of Section 9.5 to follow is very like a middleware declaration: neither component developers nor system designers write any code for profiles.

4.4 Immutable Components

Component development and system development are usually intertwined in practice, and commercial support tools do not try to separate them. On the contrary, the thesis of this monograph is that the two kinds of development can be kept strictly separate, and the guiding principle for the SYN tools is maximal support while maintaining the separation. For *immutable components* there is a two-fold result of component development:

Actual component code. Whatever process a component developer uses, its outcome is a unit of source code implementing a design, tested or verified in some way, and placed in a repository. The intention is that later the component may be selected and used in some system(s). Restrictions are placed on the information that is released: source code may not be modified in the repository (perhaps it may not be examined even); purchase is required before use of even executable code.

Component description. Restrictions on repository use cannot be overly stringent, otherwise a system designer has no hope of finding and selecting a component. So it is natural to think of a description distinct from code that is fully accessible in the repository. This description could be called a 'catalog entry' or a 'data sheet' in analogy with components in mechanical and electrical engineering. Its precise purpose is to support system design. In CBSD with immutable components it is expected that all system-design activities are accomplished using component descriptions alone. In system design, so-called Computer-Aided

Design (CAD) tools play a crucial role: they compensate for ways in which a catalog entry falls short of the actual code.

It is a consequence of requiring immutable components that systems cannot be actually implemented or tested until actual code is purchased. This might seem like hobbling yourself as a software developer, but it captures a reality in which components have value and quality that their developers protect. It also opens the way to exploring what useful form a less-than-complete component description might take, and what CAD tools might do with it.

The ideal CBSD that assumes immutable components, *Immutable-Component--Based Software Development, I-CBSD*, requires that component development be entirely uninfluenced by system-design considerations. It is not part of the definition that there be component descriptions other than code itself, nor that supporting tools avoid using code. But the SYN tools are an existence case for an approximate description based on subdomain testing and what can be done with it. By investigating this extreme, insights are gained about component/system separation, what tools should (and can!) do, and about the very idea of 'component.'

4.5 Broader Theory of CBSD

Before plunging into a detailed investigation of I-CBSD with approximate component descriptions measured by testing, the subject of chapters to follow, some mention should be made of alternative theories, to place what follows in perspective. This monograph's I-CBSD theory could be described as bottom-up, testing-based; the alternative is top-down, proof-based.

The "D" in CBSD is "Development," not "Design." Design is only a part of development[4], though arguably the most important part. What characterizes I-CBSD is its use of pre-existing, unchanging, *independent* components. They are developed in isolation, they have intrinsic fixed properties, and "SD" is "I-CB" if this decomposition plays a substantial role in the process of creating the software.

4.5.1 General Component-based System Design Theory

Given the infrastructure for CBSD—that is, a repository of independently developed components and a collection of architectures that might be used for a system[5] whose requirements must be satisfied by a design—the design process begins with an intuitive guess about an architecture and rough ideas about the main components to be tried. An experienced designer remembers successful past efforts and selects

---

[4] Unfortunately, software-engineering terminology is still in some disarray, and the two words are sometimes used to mean the same thing. Here, "Development" is the larger, encompassing process.

[5] Confusing the "Software" "S" in CBSD with "System" is no big deal.

the closest fit. This first intuitive leap from requirements to design is an essential feature of routine engineering. Creativity—conceiving of a design that has never been tried[6]—is a last resort: engineers are hired to make working systems and there is nothing safer than repeating a past success.

It may help with the first intuitive choices to assume a particular component model and to sketch diagrams appropriate to that model.

The design process can be viewed as refining a vague collection of components within an architecture into precise component descriptions for acquisition or construction. If a dead end is encountered along the way, it may be necessary to change component(s) or architecture. There are two general ways to conduct design within CBSD:

Top-down. Each component inherits local requirements from those of the proposed system. For example, the fields and query capabilities of a relational database could be induced from system requirements to retrieve certain information. A database component could then be selected by its ability to store those fields and handle needed queries.

Bottom-up. Properties of components to be used can be matched to see if together they do what's needed. For example, if a GUI component does not record user input choices in enough detail to construct queries for a database component, together the two cannot satisfy a system requirement for responding to questions about past history.

After an architecture and trial components have been selected, detailed design is best done bottom-up. For example, top-down partitioning of an available total run time among a set of components can be done in many, many ways, most of which don't correspond to what any available components do; bottom-up adding of particular components' run times to learn if they meet a performance requirement is far less problematic.

Imagining ideal tools to support system design makes a clear distinction between top-down and bottom-up design. The tool input would be similar for the two methods: the system requirements, a description of the architecture, and information about the component division to be tried. But the tool output for top-down design would be component requirements, which must be computed largely from the architecture and system requirements; for bottom-up design the tool output would be system properties whose computation comes largely from information about the components and the architecture. A top-down system designer would next look for more detailed component descriptions to satisfy the computed requirements; a bottom-up designer would check the computed properties to see if they satisfy the given system requirements.

'Imagining' tools to support practical CBSD describes the state of the art today. Nothing like the grand concepts described above has been implemented or even

---

[6] An innovative software architecture is the most risky choice, because it cuts the designer loose from all experience. In contrast, when designing a physical building it is the architect who most often takes the liberty to be creative, and structural engineers follow along as best they can. However, a good case can be made for structural-engineering creativity even for a conventional building [3].

proposed. It would not be unfair to say that existing CBSD tools do little more than help designers draw pretty diagrams and check the syntax of interfaces. The SYN tools described in this monograph do much more; they completely implement bottom-up component synthesis.

4.5.2 Component-based Verification

In a perfect world, a perfect design method would require no verification of its designs. The rules it supplies would be guaranteed to in turn produce software meeting system requirements. However, that isn't how engineering typically works. It is obvious that safety factors must be included to cover materials variation in a physical design; it is less well understood that safety factors must also cover errors in the theory behind design rules. So when a design has been obtained, even though it should be safe, the engineer checks it[7]. Part of the reason for verification is that checking is intrinsically easier than generation[8]. When perfect design rules are too difficult to discover or impractical to use, easier, perhaps incorrect rules fill the vacuum; the result must be checked. It is an important advantage of verification that it deals with final objects, and so covers more potential mistakes. It does no good to design a perfect system if the code file for one of its components is accidentally corrupted; verification looks at the actual file.

In I-CBSD where components are developed in isolation for reuse in an arbitrary system, verification, like design, is expected to benefit from the division.

Verification is usually described using pre- and post-conditions for parts of a system. These logical assertions apply just before execution and just after execution. A proof that code is correct takes the pre-condition as hypothesis and demonstrates the post-condition using properties of the code. For a complete system the pre-condition is usually empty[9] and the post-condition is an assertion that the system's requirements are fulfilled. Verification of a system can be performed top-down or bottom-up. In the former, assertions are traced through the system starting at its input; in the latter, assertions are built up from assertions about the parts. Verification using

---

[7] Indeed, Turing called his informal proof of the correctness of a subroutine "Checking" it [95].

[8] There is strong mathematical backing for this statement: For example, the algorithm for checking the result of division by multiplying quotient by divisor is simpler (for people and for CPUs) than performing the division. In mathematical logic there are important classes of problems whose solution is not algorithmic, but checking a solution is.

[9] A non-empty pre-condition is dangerous in practice. The software developer may know very well that the input must be a positive integer (to take one common pre-condition), but users forget (or never know) so it is much better for the code to check every input and reject the non-integer. There is a place for pre-conditions if software is to be used only by other software which can first check them, but that's a description of how components are used, not of a system. Except in unusual time-constrained circumstances, a case can be made for *always* eliminating pre-conditions—checking and re-checking conditions that are supposed to hold but by mistake don't hold has saved many's the day at small cost.

formal methods makes direct use of assertions and implications to be proved among them; a theory of verification by testing is more convoluted.

4.5.3 Testing vs. Proving

The components of CBSD are independent entities, each with an independent description. The form taken by component descriptions determines how design and verification are done, but there is an important element common to all descriptions: they exist in isolation, independent of any system in which the component might later be used. Imagine some particular executable code component C to be described in isolation. This might be done using formal methods: assertions that describe C's behavior can be proved using a mathematical definition of code semantics[10]. In principle, there are 'best' assertions for a formal description[11], which capture exactly what the code does, in the sense that from them any other valid assertion can be derived, but in practice these may be particularly difficult to find or to prove. If it were not for the requirement to work with C in isolation, the necessary assertions (from properties of a system in which C is placed) might be available and they might be easier to work with.

In practice, instead of proving assertions about C, C is likely to be tested. Again because of the isolation, a tester is working blindly, without knowing what test points may later be important. There is in principle no 'best' test[12]. For the test points that are tried, results are checked against requirements, and nothing need be proved[13]. An execution on (say) input 2.71 can be described by the proof theory as follows: Let the input variable be x. The pre-condition is then $P \equiv (x = 2.71)$. If the requirements post-condition is Q, the test will succeed if the semantics of the program establishes Q given the assumption P. Actually conducting the test execution differs only in that no proof using the program semantics is needed[14]: An output value y results from input 2.71 and y can be substituted in Q to check success. Although having a pre-condition like $x = 2.71$ often makes a proof easy, the proof may be possible with an empty pre-condition, in which case it holds for all inputs; on the other side, executing a test point like 2.71 never establishes anything about other points.

---

[10] It's important not to confuse assertions about what C *does* do according to its formal semantic definition, with what it *should* do according to the wishes (requirements) of some person. Wishes at best supply some trial assertions whose proof can be attempted.

[11] For example, given any post-condition Q, there exists a weakest pre-condition P such that given P the execution of C establishes Q. P is weakest in that any other pre-condition implies it. The empty pre-condition is of course always weakest, but it may not be sufficient to prove Q.

[12] Except of course an exhaustive one trying all points in C's domain. The distinction between proving, which is in principle perfect but in practice less so, and testing, which is in principle and practice imperfect, may not be so great.

[13] In practice the possible difficulty of checking requirements is ignored, but it can happen that a program gets results that a human being can't validate.

[14] With the dubious assumption that all the hardware and software involved is perfect.

Once descriptions of C and other needed components have been obtained in isolation, properties of a system built from them can be deduced. The formal-methods derivation proceeds top-down: starting with a pre-condition for the whole system, that pre-condition establishes a post-condition after the first component (through its independent formal description), this post-condition is the pre-condition for the next component, and so on until the post-condition for the last component becomes the system post-condition. The testing-based synthesis must go bottom-up: starting with a test input for the system, the first-component output comes from its independent testing, that output is the input to the next component, and so on until the last component output becomes the system output.

Michael Ernst has invented a clever way to relate test executions to proofs. His analysis software DAIKON [23] takes as input a program and a testset, executes the program for these test points, then produces as output a collection of post-condition assertions (expressed in values of program variables) that hold *for just those test-point inputs*. That is, each assertion Q calculated by DAIKON from a program and test point values $x_1, x_2, ..., x_n$ can be proved as post-condition for that program from any one of preconditions $x = x_1, x = x_2, ..., x = x_n$. But DAIKON does no proofs; instead it finds its assertions using the input-output pairs of the tests. For example, for the input-output pairs $(0,3), (2,6), (5.5, 8.25)$, DAIKON finds $Q \equiv (y = 1.5x + 3)$. Evidently, DAIKON makes fixed heuristic choices about what assertions to try for the given test data[15]. Insofar as these mirror common relationships that programs do compute, its assertions may be useful for understanding a program. For one thing, they could be used as candidates for which to attempt a general proof.

4.6 Summary of CBSD Issues

Any precise theoretical meaning for CBSD must approach the ideal that component properties have an existence independent of systems in which the components will figure. Component properties may be obtained by formal methods; then their description is pre- and post-condition assertions, and systems can be designed and verified top-down. Or, if components are tested, they have finite (and hence necessarily only approximate) descriptions, which must be combined bottom-up to get system properties. The strict separation of component development from system development hampers component analysis in either case. For formal methods it deprives component proofs of strong pre-conditions that actually hold in some system; in testing it prevents test points from concentrating on situations that will be important in some system. In compensation, once the component work is done, however much more difficult it may have been, the system work is made easier. The value of the tradeoff largely depends on the complexity of the components. If they are small

---

[15] For example, DAIKON tries a linear relationship, which gives the example result. It does not try a quadratic, which would have produced the assertion $y = -0.\overline{16438356}x^2 + 1.\overline{171232876}x + 3$. Both are correct for the given test data (along with many other relationships such as $y > x$), and neither may actually be correct for the program.

and simple, they are easy to code and (relatively) easy to describe (analyze). Then the design and verification tasks for a system are overall easier to accomplish. In the limiting case that a component is used and reused often, its contribution to system cost falls to zero, and CBSD is a clear win over any other development method.

Part II
Software Testing: Practice and Theory

SOFTWARE testing's strong suit is its practicality—software is written to be used (executed), and an execution is a test case, so a tester is just a 'pre-user[16].' It was a breakthrough when Glenford Myers [85] (and others) realized that what testing does best is expose failures: a user wants software to work, to accomplish what's required; but a tester does better to look for what's wrong. Testing principles are derived empirically and sanctioned by what works. Not content with this practical situation, software engineers have called for a testing theory to give the subject more respectability. Beginning in about 1975, computer scientists began to supply the perceived lack. Their theory is derived from Floyd's seminal work in proving programs correct. Originally testing theory applied only to stateless, sequential programs, but it can be extended to cover state and concurrency.

Practical testing has a practical problem, however. The input domain of even the simplest program is huge, so it cannot be sampled with a reasonable density. Furthermore, since program behavior is inherently discontinuous, nothing short of exhaustive testing can establish that a program will not fail if its tests do not fail. Hence almost all testing methods are *subdomain* based: they divide the input domain into 'same-behavior' regions and sample each one at most a few times. In principle subdomains are not a sound idea, because 'sameness' in each subdomain can only be established by testing, which is subject to the same difficulties as for the whole domain. Be that as it may, subdomain methods are in constant use.

---

[16] Instead of 'tested software,' developers might advertise 'pre-used' software, yet another example of software's unique character: 'pre-used' is better than 'brand new' (i.e., 'never been tried').

Chapter 5
Software Testing's Place in Development

SOFTWARE may be unique among engineered artifacts in that its testing has a formal place among the processes of development, a place with methods and measures all its own that are integrated into development itself. Products of the older engineering disciplines get tried, of course, but in a significantly different way. The test of a skyscraper is that it stands against the forces of nature. But structural engineers do not typically bother to check their calculations, say by attaching strain gauges to the beams as they are put in place. And they certainly do not expect nasty surprises as the building rises[1]. One way to look at the special place of testing in software development is as a transitory phenomenon in an immature discipline. As software developers better learn to design, they may not need to test as they do at present. There is a lot to be said in favor of this view, and the use of software components and component-based development is partially directed to mimic what has helped other branches of engineering to get away from the build-test-fail-rebuild cycle of development. But there is also reason to believe that the unique properties of software and software design make a place for extensive testing as part of development, and that place cannot and should not be eliminated. In the latter view, a goal of software engineering should be to test better, not less. There are strong feelings on both sides of this question, which is open today. Those who find testing a distasteful expedient are working to eliminate it (so far with only limited practical success); most of testing's practitioners are doing it because they have no real alternative. This monograph tries to focus on 'better testing.' Testing theoreticians, after all, would be sad to see their subject relegated to an historical footnote.

---

[1] Bill Addis [2] gives a fascinating history of the transition from elastic design theory to plastic-deformation theory in skyscraper design in the mid-20th century. The elastic theory was successfully used for many years even though its assumptions were often violated in the field. The beams were often *not* in elastic deformation, but no one bothered to find out. The buildings stood and are still standing.

D. Hamlet, *Composing Software Components,* DOI 10.1007/978-1-4419-7148-7_5,
© Springer Science+Business Media, LLC 2010

5.1 'Lifecycle' Models of Development

Starting in the late 1960s, software development has been formally studied as a purposeful process divided into distinct 'phases.' The principle of defining phases is often called 'separation of concerns.' Problems are better solved by breaking them down only if each part has unique aspects that make solution easier in the breakdown than in the whole. While an engineer is testing, for example, important issues like the maintainability of the software are not relevant and need not complicate the work of the testing phase[2]. The collection of phases, each with its goals and methods, are fitted together into what is called a 'lifecycle (model).'

5.1.1 Development Phases

Separation of concerns identifies four broad activities that seem necessary to software development. There is a disturbing lack of consensus on the name given to each activity, which can lead to pointless argument and confusion.

Requirements analysis. The software to be developed has a purpose and intended use defined by the customer who wants it done, which are described by 'requirements.' These are usually informal natural-language descriptions, so in consultation with the customer the software developer must examine and sharpen them. Requirements are often described as *what* is to be done. An important (but too often neglected) aspect of requirements are the constraints imposed by an environment or resources. The customer might need to use the software with ever-changing and untrained personnel, or might be able to afford only a short development time at a low cost.

Design. The most important technical step in development is the translation of *what* into *how*, which has two aspects. First, algorithms must be found to accomplish what is needed. It could happen that the requirements cannot be satisfied within the constraints[3] or that to satisfy them is very difficult. Second, design must describe the way in which parts of the software are separated from each other and how the parts interact.

---

[2] Obviously it is possible to go too far with division into rigid phases, so that engineers are going through the motions yet missing the substance. The resulting product will be an 'over-engineered' failure. This possibility only emphasizes that phases are artificial and must be controlled by a larger purpose in each actual instance of development.

[3] It is important to computer-science theory that some apparently sensible requirements are *impossible* to satisfy because no algorithm exists for them; for example, termination of programs is not mechanically predictable. Some resource constraints that might seem feasible are not; sorting n items cannot be done is a time proportional to n, for example. But these triumphs of theory seldom arise in practical development. More often there is a simple conflict. It is impossible to achieve a one-second response time for reading 10,000 characters from a device with a maximum transfer rate of 9,600 characters/sec, for example.

Implementation. The 'how' of design is abstract and must be brought down to explicit steps carried out on computer hardware. Programming languages are the vehicle, and implementation means programming. Each design description of a software part constitutes a programming assignment.

Testing. Each part of a software system that is separately programmed can be separately tested. The parts are finally linked together and the system itself can be tried.

Apart from interchangeable names (e.g., 'programming' for 'implementation') it is the use of 'specification' that introduces the most confusion. For some, 'specification' and 'requirements' are much the same; for others, 'specification' overlaps 'requirements' and 'design'; for yet others, 'specification' is a product of development that results from requirements analysis. It seems best to avoid the use of 'specification' in intuitive discussion[4].

5.1.2 Waterfall Models

There are obvious connections and interplay between software development phases. To list just two, (1) feasibility of design might usefully enter into requirements analysis; (2) decomposition into parts might be done in the implementation phase instead of in design. The *waterfall model* rigorously excludes phase interaction and strictly orders the phases. The name comes from an analogy to a river with a series of dams; each reservoir must fill before the water spills over and begins to fill the next. So each phase must be completed, then its result passed to the next phase. Although it is seldom emphasized, the waterfall model also excludes the customer from development as soon as possible, that is, at the end of the requirements-analysis phase.

When the software project is not small, i.e., it requires at least a few people and a few months, the waterfall phases seem natural enough—programming requires a prior design, testing requires a program, etc. Its strong point is the detailed information derived in each phase, which when passed to the next phase makes the work there routine. The difference between several programmers working directly from raw requirements and working on separate parts of a careful design can be the difference between unending chaos and steady accomplishment[5]. This strength is also a weakness: the strict sequences of phases means that everything depends on the customer's requirements remaining unchanged until the software is accepted. If the

---

[4] In the theory presented in Chapter 6, a technical use of the word is so well established that it cannot be avoided.

[5] As one example of the kind of uncontrolled development that the waterfall model was invented to eliminate, in the 1960s the Universal Timesharing System (UTS) was under development for XDS Sigma 7 hardware, and XDS was running advertisements about its imminent release (the ads had photos of reels of magnetic tape as if they contained the UTS code). But in fact UTS was never released, because its modular design had to be abandoned. Changes in one module impacted others and spiraled out of control, so that the project ceased to make progress toward its goal. What UTS lacked was a careful design.

requirements should change, it invalidates all the carefully constructed work in each subsequent phase. Unfortunately, customer requirements evolve with their changing needs, not least between the time when requirements analysis is complete and a delivered system is tried. The most dreaded critique of a newly delivered software system is: "This isn't what I wanted."

Testing's role in waterfall development is to check the correspondence between the requirements that are the result of the first phase and the programs that result from the third phase. If the design calls for implementation of separate parts, it may be that these can be tested in isolation before the whole is assembled for test.

5.1.3 Agile Models

Variations of the waterfall model seemed at first the only possible decomposition of the development task, but a brilliant insight showed there is another: development might be divided into parts by dividing the requirements themselves. Instead of developing one complex system to solve a problem this decomposition develops several simpler systems for parts of it, each an incremental addition to the capabilities of earlier ones, culminating in a complex system (or perhaps a collection of systems) able to solve the original problem. This idea was originally a waterfall variation, sometimes called a 'spiral' development model [9], and earlier, 'iterative enhancement' [7]. So-called agile development was invented when the eXtreme Programming (XP) designers realized that requirements decomposition allows a very different emphasis on development technology, notably that programming and testing can be brought to the fore, and the customer can assume an important role throughout development.

The slogan that underlies agile development might well be the customer statement, "I may not know what I want, but I'll recognize it when I see it." The focus is on eliciting part of a customer's needs as simply and directly as possible, then delivering a software product that might fulfill those needs and accepting customer feedback about its deficiencies. Once a particular part of what's needed has been developed and accepted, the process continues with another part, and so on until all needs are satisfied.

Requirements of a new kind are needed to drive each piece of an agile development cycle. Precision, accuracy, and comprehensive coverage are not important if the customer is expected to continually change his mind. What is important is that the customer be helped to say something to start the process. The *use case* exactly fills this need. A use case is a sample of what the customer expects to do with the software; it can be elicited by asking, "Suppose you had the software you need. Give us a simple example of how you would use it." Use cases are test cases for the software to be developed, but they have several unusual properties. First and foremost, a use case is almost always a *sequence* of actions, which constitute something that the customer really expects to do as an end-to-end application of the prospective software. As such it includes aspects of the persistent state that will need to be kept, without perhaps explicitly mentioning state. Second, a use case is entirely concrete—it includes only explicit user input actions and so can be executed without the developer supplying any input. The explicit user inputs are loaded with information that might otherwise go unnoticed; for example, whether or not punctuation, spacing, and case are significant in entered strings.

Armed with some use cases, the developer can design and implement software to behave as the customer expects, and the customer is available throughout the process to supply information and correct assumptions. The simplicity of the examples may mean that a separate abstract design is not needed. (After all, if the requirements are likely to change, design time would be wasted.) When things are too complicated to 'just code' then design is appropriate, otherwise it is not. The ability to do only what is necessary, avoiding anything that seems to be busy-work, is a source for the name 'agile.' As each design/implementation decision comes up, the developers check their generalizations with the customer: e.g., "Now this input can't be negative, right? Oh, it can? What should happen in that case?"

In one sense, the tests cases for a piece of agile-development software are its requirements: the use cases. When the code is ready to demonstrate, they will be used, so of course they have been tried before. But testing's real role comes in after that first demo. The customer is encouraged to try out the software "on other similar cases." If there has been a misunderstanding, some of these will fail badly. Thus testing is the primary source of feedback from customer to developer.

5.1.4 Which Model is Best?

As the 'new kid on the block,' agile development is partly a reaction to over-indulgence in the rigidity of the waterfall model, so if a development process seems overly complex for the problem it should solve, and of course if the requirements are unclear, agile development will work better than waterfall development. But for large projects in which software is only part of a solution, agile development would be suicidal. Imagine, for example, developing the flight-control software for a multi-billion dollar aircraft, or an operating system for a supercomputer. In such cases there *are* precise, unchanging requirements and they must be analyzed, then each part of the complicated process documented and verified. Even the spiral versions of waterfall development are unlikely to work well in complex cases, because design decisions must be made in the context of the complete system, or they will have to be done over again and again[6].

---

[6] In the original compiler project that was a test bed for iterative enhancement decisions made about implementation of the symbol table were not initially encapsulated in one module. As new requirements were added, the forest of references to the symbol table got more and more difficult to change. A simple table was a good design choice for the initial compiler of a typeless language on a single machine; an abstract data type would have been an overkill. But for the whole project that culminated in a family of compilers handling modular typed languages on many machines, an abstract symbol table would have been a far better choice.

To discuss software testing in general, as the remainder of this chapter does, imposes an implicit bias for the waterfall model in which its concerns are separated from the other parts of development. Waterfall-like testing can be used in agile development, but the customers who bear the brunt of agile testing are unlikely to learn its arcane details. This argues strongly for automatic tools to do the work.

5.2 Functional/Requirements Testing

Chapter 7 describes many practical techniques for testing a program, particularly for controlling the test coverage of a large input domain. Of these, *functional testing* or *requirements-based testing*[7] is far and away the most important. Requirements-based testing first identifies some action that software should take, then finds and executes test cases that should elicit that action. The 'function' in 'functional testing' is not a mathematical entity, but the isolated action (part of the software functionality). Every functional test serves two purposes: (1) It puts the software through its paces, and may thereby expose a failure. If it does fail, exactly what has failed is known. (2) If a functional test does not fail, it is a sample that developers and users can rely on. Many such examples lead to confidence that the software works (at least for a particular requirement).

5.2.1 Unit Testing vs. System Testing

There are two ways for a person to lose control of a software-testing process: one is to know too little, but the less obvious way is to know too much. One cannot test without clear knowledge of the software requirements, and all too often they are vague or incomplete. Even starting from a relatively good set of requirements for a system, it may be difficult to derive from it precise requirements for the parts that are created by a design. Yet those parts must be tested. These are situations in which the tester knows too little. On the other hand, a well designed part of a system is of limited code size, so it can be studied and understood; but even a 'small' application system (say 20,000 lines of code) defies routine study of its source. Thus testers may know the code for the parts, but not exactly what the parts are supposed to do; they may know better what the whole system should do, but the system code is a mystery. And even this neat dichotomy isn't the worst of it: a 10-line subroutine may defeat extensive study [75], and thousands of requirements may be very difficult to organize into tests[8].

---

[7] Also called "specification-based testing," but this presentation is attempting to avoid the S-word.

[8] It is considered excessive to systematically try each separate requirement as a functional test; yet it is the vast array of *combinations* of requirements [18], pairwise, in triples, etc., that will come up in actual use.

The conventional response to such a hopeless-seeming problem is to muddle through. As parts of a system are implemented, they are tested against whatever vague requirements the developer has. The testers are often the programmer(s) who wrote the code, evidently not a good idea, since those are the very people who may have misunderstood the requirements of their programming assignments. However, this 'unit testing' does find mistakes, which are corrected. In the end, all units have been implemented and (sort of) tested. Then the complete application is assembled from the parts, and 'system testing' starts, a process that makes no use whatsoever of the previous unit tests. To see just how haphazard the whole testing process may be, it is usually evaluated by how much effort was expended: so many hours in test before 'resources were exhausted.' Another evaluation measure is the number of failures detected by tests, which unfortunately confounds the software quality with how well it is tested. If few failures are found, it might be because testing is inadequate; if many are found, it might be because the software is terrible. Combining these two poor metrics gives a poorer one: failures found per test time. There is no outcome measurement that unambiguously means the software quality is good and testing has supported that conclusion.

5.3 Preventing Bugs

Dave Gelprin [32] and the consulting company he worked for in the late 1970s distributed lapel buttons with the slogan "Test, then Code". His message anticipated one aspect of agile development: test (use) cases are wonderful intellectual devices for designing software. Thinking through a concrete test example is a good way to uncover problems before they get cast in the stone of code. It has long been recommended that *all* possible test cases be thought through as programs are created, and there is a technology of program proving in tandem with coding to attempt this.

These techniques to prevent mistakes are valuable in software development, but they are not testing in the sense of this monograph.

5.3.1 Software Inspection

There is solid data (admittedly, from development using the waterfall model) to show that software failures often result from mistakes that can be pinpointed in a particular phase, and early exposure of a mistake makes it far less expensive to find and correct [8]. The language used to describe mistakes is not accurate: it is said that "bugs are injected into the code." Like most intuitive references to "bugs" (or "defects," "errors," etc.), the words bring up a simple picture of something like a typographical error in a programming-language statement. Real software failures, to the contrary, most often result from something (or many things!) missing from code, missing because of poor requirements analysis or design. (In agile development, it might be more accurate to say that failures result from mistakes in generalizing use cases, from lack of understanding in the customer's domain.) A methodology for early detection of mistakes has grown up within waterfall development, which makes intensive use of the intuitive human ability to see something wrong, and relies on each phase producing a formal document for people to study. In *inspection* methods a group of people go over a requirements document (or a design, or code) in a structured meeting that seeks to expose its flaws. Inspection does find problems, earlier in waterfall development than any other detection method, although its cost is often underestimated[9]. An agile adaptation of inspection is 'pair programming,' in which two people work as a team, with one inspecting the other's code.

Inspection's weakness is the twin of its strength. The inspectors rely on intuition and experience, so it is impossible to quantify the results. After rigorous inspection (that is, following the rules about how to structure a meeting) there can be no sound assurance that any single test case will execute successfully. Inspection can be driven by use cases, however. The inspectors work through an explicit case to see what should (or will) happen. The advantage is that most people understand the concrete better than the abstract, yet their intuition is not limited by it. There is an unfortunate side effect of inspecting using use cases, which also arises throughout agile development: The ability of the use case to uncover unexpected failures is 'used up.' Having gone over one explicit example (or designed from that example), it is much less likely that testing with that same example will expose a problem or lead to new understanding. If testing is an adversarial process, the testers against what designers inadvertently hide or omit from code, it is bad strategy to tell the enemy your plan of attack.

5.3.2 Formal Methods

Advocates of mathematical program analysis, notably Edsger Dijkstra and Nicolas Wirth, have argued that programs should be constructed by describing the effect of each part mathematically, then generating code that meets this description. The PRL research group at Cornell University under Robert Constable has developed proof tools for an introductory programming course in which students write programs by developing not code, but mathematics; the tools then help to write the code [5]. If the mathematical descriptions constitute the requirements, there can be no mistakes in code developed this way. Just as inspections and use-case-driven programming force programmers to think deeply about what exactly they are doing, formal mathematical descriptions are the ultimate in forced analysis. Unfortunately, real-world requirements are not in mathematical form, which necessitates a translation step. Opponents of formal methods have correctly pointed out that it is as difficult (or more difficult) to come up with the mathematics as it is to develop a

---

[9] The poster child for inspection is the NASA flight software for the space shuttle, which is said to have only about 1 defect per ten thousand lines of code, and to cost about $1000/line. The raw data supporting these numbers is hard to locate.

program. Equally unfortunately, mistakes in the mathematics mean software that fails (according to the original non-mathematical requirements) [33].

For example, programming mistakes are frequently omissions: some requirement is misunderstood or neglected so that there is nothing in the code to handle it. The same thing happens naturally in translating intuitive requirements to a formal mathematical description. The mathematics doesn't match the intuition, and the program created to perfectly implement the mathematics doesn't either. A pragmatist would say that we might as well get the program wrong directly instead of going to the effort of getting the mathematics wrong first.

There is much more to the debate between advocates and critics of formal methods than the brief description above. Like an inspection overkill, formal methods have been successfully used in practice to help develop safety-critical software, but at high cost.

5.3.3 Creating Perfection vs. Finding Failure

It may be that the debate between those who would prevent mistakes with inspection or formal methods and those who would test afterward to find mistakes, comes down to an underlying optimism or pessimism. Optimists seek perfection and believe it can be attained with hard work; pessimists expect everything to be flawed and to need checking. Software brings out the extremists on both sides because its non-physical nature seems to admit of perfection, yet its unprecedented complication is fertile ground for mistakes.

Historically, engineering is a discipline of learning from error[10] [90]. So if software is just another engineering object, testing is here to stay. But there is the off chance that programs can be treated as potentially perfect mathematical objects, which are not checked by trying examples. Further discussion appears in Chapter 6.

5.4 Testing in CBSD

The unique feature of software development based on components is the one-way nature of the relationship between component level and system level. Whatever techniques are used, they are applied to components without knowledge of systems to be later developed; but in the other direction the systems designer can know everything about the components selected. Thus testing components for CBSD is like testing any software, a process of trial and error to find mistakes and gain confi-

---

[10] The engineer's position was well stated by Isambard Kingdom Brunel, the engineer who designed the Great Western Railway in England. An anecdote (perhaps apocryphal) relates his response when he was called on the carpet by the GWR Board of Directors because a bridge had collapsed: "You should be glad that bridge collapsed. I was planning to build a dozen more to the same design."

dence in component quality, but with the added dimension that something ought to be recorded for later use. Testing a CBSD system could be a trial-and-error process, but there is the possibility of using information recorded about the components used. The goal in system testing with CBSD could be stated: mistakes uncovered and confidence gained at the system level should be in the *system* design, not in its components. *If* the components are OK, *then* is the system OK? A more precise version is quantitative: If the chance of component failure is f, what is the chance of system failure g? If f is large, component testing wasn't good enough and not much can be expected of g; but if f is small yet g is not, then the system design needs work[11].

To summarize, CBSD is all about separating and encapsulating unit- and system testing, and I-CBSD is the extreme in which separation is absolute. At each level, the other is removed. Components are tested knowing nothing about systems; when systems are tested the components are presumed correct. As Chapter 8 will show, it is possible to do much better than that: from information recorded during independent component tests, it is possible to *predict* the results of system tests, which then never have to be conducted at all.

---

[11] See Chapter 12 for details about the probabilistic viewpoint. These questions can also be put in terms of functionality: Assuming the component functions to be correct, is the system function correct? Chapter 17 examines a quantitative version of the functional questions.

Chapter 6
Software Testing Theory

IT is common to talk about the 'functionality' of software, but establishing a rigorous connection between code and a precise mathematical description of the behaviors of that code is a challenging intellectual task. The syntax of code is apparent and well understood—every programmer uses it daily and tools like compilers mechanically exploit it—but the *semantics* that provides execution meaning to code is another matter. Any theory of software testing must be built on an underlying theory of semantics.

6.1 Floyd-Hoare-Mills Semantics

In principle, a precise semantics for imperative code was supplied by Bob Floyd in his 1967 paper "Assigning Meaning to Programs" [25, $\prec A \succ$]. Floyd's idea was soon expressed by C.A.R. Hoare as a logic of programming [61]. For present purposes Harlan Mills's equivalent functional semantics [82, $\prec A \succ$] is more immediately applicable than the Floyd-Hoare theory. Mills assigns to each code statement a functional meaning, and gives rules that combine these meanings when statements are combined to form a program. He symbolized meaning functions by boxing the syntactical entities. Thus the function Mills assigns as meaning for an unconditional statement like a C assignment is written as

$$\boxed{\text{X = X + 1}}.$$

The domain and range of this function are the set of values currently attached to program variables (e.g., X in the example); the example meaning function is 'successor' $\lambda x[x+1]$. That is, whatever value was attached to X before the assignment statement, the value attached afterward is one greater. The function assigned to a sequence is the composition[1] of functions. In the example:

---

[1] Some mathematicians write the 'outer' function first in composition, which is the notation used here; others put the 'inner' function first. If the argument is explicit, that is, if values of the functions are written instead of the function names, then there is is no question about the order.

D. Hamlet, *Composing Software Components,* DOI 10.1007/978-1-4419-7148-7_6,
© Springer Science+Business Media, LLC 2010

$$\boxed{\texttt{X = X + 1; X = X**2}} = \boxed{\texttt{X = X**2}} \circ \boxed{\texttt{X = X + 1}},$$

which composition is the square of the successor function:

$$\lambda x[x^2] \circ \lambda x[x+1] = \lambda x[(x+1)^2].$$

Making the argument explicit, for x attached to X,

$$\boxed{\texttt{X = X + 1; X = X**2}}(x) = \boxed{\texttt{X = X**2}}(\boxed{\texttt{X = X + 1}}(x)).$$

The reader familiar with Turing's definition of TM semantics [94, $\prec A \succ$] will recognize that Mills is doing exactly the same thing—describing the effect of each 'operation' and how to compose them. Turing used the simplest possible programming language, because his purpose was to capture the sense of 'mechanical computation.' Mills chose Pascal, which isn't simple at all, but his purpose was to explain Pascal's complexity to novice programmers.

The same functional composition applies at the program level. If two programs P and Q are arranged into a series system, on input x the first outputs $\boxed{P}(x)$ to the second, which outputs $\boxed{Q}(\boxed{P}(x))$, so the composition rule is literally functional composition. Formally, the meaning[2] is written

$$\boxed{P;Q}(x) = \boxed{Q}(\boxed{P}(x)).$$

Mills taught this theory from his textbook [82, $\prec A \succ$] to beginning computer science students at the University of Maryland for years[3]. The Mills theory went well beyond this simple example—it formalized semantics for most of the Pascal programming language and included a theory of abstract data types [29].

Non-functional behavior of software has a formal mathematical theory, too. Consider the run-time property. It can be described by a function mapping a program's input domain to the non-negative real numbers. Suppose $T_P(x)$ is the execution time of program P on input x and similarly $T_Q(x)$ for program Q[4]. Placing P and Q in series, on system input x, Q receives input $\boxed{P}(x)$, so its run time is $T_Q(\boxed{P}(x))$. Adding the run time for P, the system run time on input x is $T_P(x) + T_Q(\boxed{P}(x))$. The functional behavior of P influences the performance of Q since it supplies Q's input value.

Harlan Mills, and many others following him and following Floyd and Hoare, strongly advocated for so-called formal methods that capture so well the essence

---

[2] Technically, the domain and range of the box functions is different at the program level. Instead of mapping values attached to identifiers, the domain is 'input' values and the range is 'outputs.' But this is really just a shorthand for describing the value attached to special identifiers (which may not actually appear in the program) that are involved in read and print statements. A careful treatment is given in Mills's book [82, $\prec A \succ$].

[3] Many of the undergraduates didn't like it. Comment from the rear of the hall after a heavy lecture (by another faculty member, not Mills, whom most students loved): "I majored in CS because I couldn't do math. Why are you trying to ruin my career before it even gets started?!"

[4] Although Mills didn't attempt to construct non-functional behaviors up from the statement level, it is obvious how to do so: each statement has its run time, and for statements in sequence the run times add.

of composing software components. In the component world, the Hoare theory is called 'design by contract,' well presented in Bertrand Meyer's book [81]. The logical and functional theories are elegant, but despite a great deal of hard work, they have found only limited use in practice. It's hard to formalize even simple programs and components, as the Maryland CS major saw so clearly. In practice, software engineers resort to much less elegant software testing. It is common in computer science and in software engineering to deplore the lack of an underlying theory of testing, and to call for a rigorous basis for this important activity. But there is a well formulated testing theory, grounded in functional semantics.

6.2 Functional Testing Theory

The semantic model used by Goodenough and Gerhart [34, $\prec A \succ$], Howden [64, $\prec A \succ$], and almost all subsequent testing theoreticians[5], is based on the kind of functional semantics that Mills formalized. When the first papers using this model appeared in the 1970s they were startling in their precision and clarity, because until then testing had only been discussed qualitatively in the context of particular practical methods. In a way, the breakthrough has not served the field well, just because it was so dramatic an improvement: theoreticians have been reluctant to complicate a simple, elegant model. But the model's abstractions are far from testing as it is practiced today.

The most damaging omissions from Goodenough and Gerhart's theory are *state* and *concurrency*. A functional theory of state behavior is a straightforward extension of their work, and is presented in Section 6.2.2 below; concurrency is more difficult, and it may be that testing concurrent software should not be modeled as an extension of functional theory. Section 6.2.3 describes a simple case that lends itself to functional treatment.

6.2.1 Functional Testing Theory without State

It was Turing's idea that a program P has as meaning a function mapping its input domain D to an output range R. Mills's notation captures literally the 'blackbox' meaning of P as a mapping from input to output:

$$\boxed{P} : D \to R.$$

The fundamental reason for formally capturing program meaning is to define that most important of program properties: *correctness*. One half of correctness is what a

---

[5] For example, some current exciting work [14, 80, 15], while it goes deeply into some aspects of testing, technically applies only to the case of pure-function programs, no closer to the subjects of real testing than papers from the 1970s. And the problems of testing practice today have unfortunately grown since 1970.

program *does* do—that's its Mills semantic meaning. The other half is what that program is *supposed* to do—its specifications. Formally, a *specification* for a program is an input-output function[6] F:

$$F : D \to R.$$

Thus the *correctness of P with respect to F* is defined by:

$$\boxed{P} = F.$$

A *testset* U is a subset of the input domain, $U \subseteq D$. Members of a testset are called *test points*[7]. For program P with specification F to *fail* on testset U means precisely that $\exists t \in U, \boxed{P}(t) \neq F(t)$. (Also said: the program fails on the test point t.) Test failure of course means that P is not correct with respect to F, but it also supplies the counterexample in a failure point t. When a program does not fail on testset U, i.e., $\forall t \in U, \boxed{P}(t) = F(t)$, it would be nice to believe that a cleverly chosen U would establish something sweeping: ideally, correctness. Unfortunately, it is not always so. There *are* clever testsets that preclude failure for some programs, but in general there is no algorithmic way to find one for an arbitrary program. Bill Howden, in what is arguably the best software-testing paper ever written [64, $\prec A \succ$], thoroughly investigated the subject in 1976. Formally, any general scheme for selecting testsets is *misleading* because it can happen that lack of failure proves nothing about correctness, and only detailed case-by-case creative analysis can establish whether or not this is so for a particular program.

Non-functional properties are captured in the functional theory by associating functions other than $\boxed{P}$ with P. For example, P's run time is a function whose range is the non-negative reals: $T_P : D \to \mathbb{R}$. If desired, correctness can be defined to include non-functional properties by adding them to the specification. For example, it could be required that a program achieve a certain response-time bound B by requiring T_P to satisfy: $\forall t \in D, T_P(t) \leq B$. Although there has been no formal publication of results about testsets that mislead the tester for non-functional properties, at least for run time a result similar to Howden's should hold.

These formal definitions that capture software testing are so natural that they appear trivial. Dijkstra's famous aphorism, that testing can show only the presence of bugs, not their absence, was evidently not derived from a formal understanding of testing. A deeper understanding like Howden's can only come from formalism, however. Howden showed that Dijkstra wasn't quite right: for some programs there *are* testsets that demonstrate correctness. If one wants testing to work (as Dijkstra did not), the deep understanding is necessary.

---

[6] If specification is defined to be a relation rather than a function, it captures the idea that more than one result may be correct, and allows the discussion of 'don't care' inputs. However, the mathematical machinery of relations is less intuitive than functional notation, so functional specifications are used here. Mills's functional semantics is easier to understand than Hoare's logic partly because the basic entities of logic are predicates (relations).

[7] The term 'test' is a good one to avoid. Sometimes it is taken to mean a test point, but often it refers to the aggregate operation of using some scheme for testing, as in "the test required everyone to work the whole weekend." A statement like "the test failed" is thoroughly ambiguous.

6.2.2 *Extending Functional Theory to Include State*

The functional-semantics testing theory of Section 6.2.1 models only programs that do not retain state from test to test. Floyd-Hoare-Mills theory does not concern itself explicitly with persistent external state. At the base of the logical/functional theories is a vector of values for the identifiers of a program P; in the Mills theory, for example, $\boxed{P}$ maps this vector onto itself. Some of the values are 'external' in that their values are established via input statements or their values are printed out. But only the 'standard input' and 'standard output' of read and print statements are singled out for special treatment[8]. To handle testing of programs with persistent state, this section presents a straightforward extension of Mills's theory. The primary motivation behind the extended theory is that it be a natural extension of the pure-function theory of Goodenough and Gerhart and Howden.

The state modeled is *local*, available only to a single program. This choice follows the definition of a component presented in Chapter 3, but the reason for the restriction goes deeper than that. Any sort of global state that can be changed not only by a program P, but by other programs, cannot be formally captured by mappings (like $\boxed{P}$) that are defined on P alone. (State variables could be made external as are functional input/output variables, but as will appear later in this section, such a formalization is wrong in principle.)

The straightforward way to mathematically model state is to add an explicit state set H to the program input domain D and output range R, and to describe the behavior of program P in two parts, each depending on state as well as input. Retaining the box notation for the 'functional' part of P's behavior, but now defining it on $D \times H$:

$$\boxed{P} : D \times H \rightarrow R.$$

A similar notation is needed to describe state behavior, and since the state maps onto itself, a circle notation seems appropriate:

$$\widehat{P} : D \times H \rightarrow H.$$

Thus both the program output and a final value for the state depend on an input-state pair $(d,h) \in D \times H$.

Continuing to follow the stateless treatment, the next thing to do is to define specification, to then define correctness. Private state, local to a program P, has a peculiar abstract aspect in specifications. The *concrete state H* itself is directly manipulated by the code function $\widehat{P}$. The *abstract state J* is an entity that similarly enters specifications. The reason for making a distinction between H and J is that J may be a high-level, intuitive state not available in the programming language of P. It is then necessary to *represent* values of J by some combination of program entities in H. The connection between the two is established by an *abstraction map* $A : H \rightarrow J$. This process of representation and abstraction is the basis for information

---

[8] An explicit logic of state could be constructed by allowing some identifier values to be used without initialization—these would be the 'state variables'—but this is not usual.

hiding, a design technique of the first importance. However, it does no violence to testing theory to identify J with H, a simplification adopted here[9]. The virtue in using J and A is to make explicit the assumption that the states programmers are trying to capture (J) and the ones they are actually using (H) are not the same, and connected only by a mapping (A) that is seldom explicitly captured [6, $\prec A \succ$] or mechanically processed. When a tester attempts to get at J through $A(H)$, there are many pitfalls that can vitiate the effort. For further discussion, see Chapter 10.

In principle, specifications need not concern themselves with software state at all. To describe what is required of a program does not necessarily require a description of persistent storage it will maintain. In so-called *trace semantics* [62] state is not treated as a set of values, but only as history. Specifications in trace semantics use constructions like: "If there was a previous input value $z > 0$, then the most recent such value is returned." However, it is usually awkward and sometimes seems impossible to give a formal description of required actions that depend on previous history without explicitly capturing that history in a set of values. Instead of "...previous input $z > 0$...", people are more comfortable with: "Any input $z > 0$ is stored in a file F, replacing its contents if F exists. If F exists its value is returned." The Z specification language [92] includes explicit state, and the most useful and well defined part of the UML modeling language is the state machines (adapted from David Harel's work [59]) that describe behavior. It seems that the specifications on which state-inclusive correctness is defined must also include an explicit state set:

A *specification* is a (partial) function $F : D \times H \to H \times R$.

The simplest definition of a program meeting its specification is a straightforward extension of the stateless definition:

A program P is *state-blind correct* with respect to specification F iff:

$$\forall x \in D, \forall h \in H, (\boxed{P}(x,h), \boxed{P}(x,h)) = F(x,h).$$

Practical testing explores state-blind correctness by forcing the program under test into particular states, then trying various inputs there. Yet state-blind correctness does not capture the right intuitive notion of a program behaving according to specification, because it accords state the same status as input. It relies on the false idea that state can be independently sampled. In reality, the tester of a program P, and ultimately P's user, does not control state values and cannot set them except implicitly through P's actions. P is completely in charge. P can tell whether or not its state has been initialized, can initialize (and reset) it, can examine its previous value(s), and finally can arbitrarily set state values to be used in the future. Any sampling of state by an outside agency (like a tester) must use only states that the program itself would establish. To assume that certain states exist (say from the specification) is fraught with danger, since it requires that the tester know just how the program works, the very thing that is being probed by testing.

To frame a better definition of correctness, consider what actually happens when a program is run repeatedly and accumulates state. One input after another is supplied; that is, there are *sequences* of inputs. On each input within a sequence there

---

[9] Full details and a revealing discussion of input/output thought of as taking place in the abstract-state values have been presented in the Mills formalism [29].

may be a state change, so there is a corresponding sequence of state values that results from an input sequence. It is usual for a program P with state to have a testable *reset* condition that defines the need for P to initialize. In practice the reset condition is often a missing file that the program creates to initialize[10].

Starting from reset, the behavior of P is repeatable: the same sequence of inputs will produce the same results, namely a sequence of outputs and a sequence of states.

Let P be in a special *initial state* $h_0 \in H$ signifying reset, and consider a sequence of $n+1$ inputs $t = (x_0, x_1, ..., x_n)$. The corresponding states reached by P are:

$$h_i = \boxed{P}(x_{i-1}, h_{i-1}), \ 0 < i \leq n.$$

Successive functional values of the program are:

$$\boxed{P}(x_0, h_0), \ \boxed{P}(x_1, h_1), \ ..., \ \boxed{P}(x_n, h_n),$$

that is, the ith output r_i arises from the $i - 1^{st}$ input x_{i-1} in the state h_{i-1}:

$$r_i = \boxed{P}(x_{i-1}, h_{i-1}).$$

Similarly, the specification prescribes a sequence of states h_i' and outputs r_i':

$$F(x_{i-1}, h_{i-1}') = (h_i', r_i'), \ 0 < i \leq n,$$

starting with $h_0' = h_0$.

There are now formal entities that describe what the program does do on an input sequence, and what it should do, so correctness can be defined:

P is sequence correct with respect to specification F iff for every sequence of inputs $(x_0, x_1, ..., x_n)$ and the corresponding h_i and h_i' as above $0 \leq i \leq n-1$,

$$(h_{i+1}, r_{i+1}) = ((\boxed{P}(x_i, h_i), \boxed{P}(x_i, h_i)) = F(x_i, h_i') = (h_{i+1}', r_{i+1}').$$

That is, the program states and outputs continually agree with the specification as any sequence progresses. The definition requires P to terminate exactly where F is defined so that the domains match.

The intuitive difference between state-blind and sequence correctness is in the states that appear in the definitions. In state-blind correctness, the proof obligation ranges over the whole set H; in sequence correctness only some states in H need be considered, namely those that are specified to occur and actually do occur, in the order(s) they occur. The last clause hides a subtle point: if, for example, state $h \in H$ only appears in one sequence, then the proof of sequence correctness can use any properties that arise in that sequence; that sequence is the only input that can cover state h.

State-blind correctness $\Longrightarrow$ sequence correctness, but not the reverse.

Sequence correctness is essential for correctness proofs, because many intuitively correct programs fail to be state-blind correct. However, it might seem that for testing one should avoid the more complicated definition and just explore the whole

---

[10] A tester may then externally remove the state file to force reset. Taking even this small state action outside the program may be dangerous, however, because the program can have some other state mechanism—maybe another hidden file—that causes it to take special action when the state file disappears.

state set. This intuition, although it is often followed in practical testing, is wrong for four reasons: First, testing over all of H increases the number of tests required, which is already overwhelming. Second, successful testing on states that do not actually occur gives a false confidence in a program's reliability. Third, when a test fails on a state that does not actually occur, a great deal of time can be wasted resolving the spurious problem. Fourth, and most damaging, behavior that occurs frequently in sequences may be rare among all states (and vice versa), so that a tester's overall impression of what the code does can be quite different using the two methods. These points are illustrated in Chapters 10 and 18.

This extension of the Goodenough and Gerhart stateless theory is straightforward and satisfactory because it captures not only what really happens when program use local state, but also what is commonly (and wrongly) assumed to happen.

6.2.3 Testing Concurrent Software

Without concurrency, the semantics of any program and any part of a program are the same kind of functional entity, and the functional operation by which meaning is given to aggregate programs is composition of the functional meanings of the parts. When the parts have local state, this statement is not quite true, as explored in Chapter 10: The state of a system is a cross product of local part-states, and so grows in complexity when there are more parts. Even so, the with-state semantics is functional and composes functionally.

In a concurrent system, functional meaning can still be assigned to the parts that themselves have no concurrency, but the intuitive combination does not seem to be a simple functional composition. Consider the very simplest concurrent situation: Two stateless functional programs P and Q execute in parallel, Q started by P at some point in P's execution (and Q given an input by P). Once Q is started, P continues to execute in parallel with Q. At some (later) point in execution P waits for Q to return a value, which P may then use. Concurrent execution potentially occurs throughout Q's execution, or that part of it taking place before P waits for Q to terminate. For further simplification, stipulate that the parallelism is in no way conditional: P always starts Q just once at the same point of execution; Q always returns a value and they rendezvous at the end of Q and at a single point in P. Although all the parallelism has been described for P, Q is permitted the same ability to start and use Q', etc., provided that there are no cycles in the parallel parts—Q would not be permitted to start P, for example. Ultimately, any succession of n parallel executions ends with a non-parallel program that starts no other and whose return initiates the sequence of n terminations. It could happen that almost the whole of the n-fold execution takes place simultaneously.

This situation abstracts away most of the (complicating and potentially dangerous) features of real concurrency: there can be no race conditions, since P and Q do not interact during their parallel execution, no deadlock since no resources are shared. Despite the restrictions, the important paradigm of N-version programming

(NVP) could be described in these terms—each Q could serve as one of the 'versions' and also start the next version, down to the final Q' that implements the Nth version. The voting procedure could be implemented pairwise back through the chain of returns. (This application is used in the tutorial of Chapter 11.)

Defining correctness of programs executing simultaneously turns out to be easier than the state extension of the previous section, because program meaning itself need not be extended: a concurrent combination acts just like a single program as previously described.

How can a stateless program P that starts another be formally assigned a meaning? P might be given a pair of functional meanings, both of which can can be calculated using Mills's method [82, $\prec A \succ$] without modification. The first, symbolized $\boxed{P}$ as before, is for the intermediate output, the value delivered to Q started in parallel (as a function of P's input). The second, symbolized $\boxed{\boxed{P}}$ captures the output P itself finally returns (a function of P's input and a second 'input' it gets returned from Q). $\boxed{\boxed{P}}$ takes account of what P does while P executes in parallel with Q, as well as what P does before starting Q and after Q is finished. Thus for this simplest simplest situation where Q starts no third program, the output of the parallel combination $P \parallel Q$ on input x is:

$$\boxed{P \parallel Q}(x) = \boxed{\boxed{P}}(x, \boxed{Q}(\boxed{P}(x))).$$

It can be seen that this mapping has the form of the stateless semantics of Section 6.2.1.

At the next level, should Q also be concurrent and start Q' in parallel, the output of the triple combination on input x is:

$$\boxed{\boxed{P}}(x, \boxed{\boxed{Q}}(\boxed{P}(x), \boxed{Q'}(\boxed{Q}(\boxed{P}(x)))))^{11}.$$

As a check on the sense of these multi-function definitions, the meaning(s) of $P \parallel Q$ when both programs are concurrent[12] can be extracted from the last formula above:

$$\boxed{P \parallel Q}(x) = \boxed{Q}(\boxed{P}(x));$$

$$\boxed{\boxed{P \parallel Q}}(x, y) = \boxed{\boxed{P}}(x, \boxed{\boxed{Q}}(\boxed{P}(x), y)).$$

Thus a parallel combination $P \parallel Q$ acts like a non-concurrent program if only P is concurrent, but like a concurrent program if both are concurrent. The definitions appear to make sense. But it will be wiser in what follows (below and in Chapter 11) to ignore this hard-won definition because it creates a new kind of semantic entity

---

[11] This expression approaches what could be called "write-only" mathematics: it is easier to think about the intuitive meaning and write the formalism than to understand the formalism once written. It is common knowledge that a great deal of software has this write-only nature.

[12] The box notation is ambiguous in this case, since if both programs are concurrent it means the intermediate result sent to Q; but if only the first is concurrent it means the final result of the combination. Just as well that the former will not be used.

that would require a new kind of specification. If instead Q does not start another program, it will not be necessary to define what this new kind of entity with two different box functions is supposed to mean.

To capture formally the run time of concurrent P starting non-concurrent Q requires *three* run-time functions: one from input until Q starts, the second from then until the rendezvous where Q returns (both of these are functions of P's input), and the third from Q's return until P's termination (a function of P's input and the value returned by Q). The first and last of these contribute unconditionally to the total run time[13]. For the portion of run time when both P and Q are executing, the contribution is the larger of Q's run time and the second run-time function for P[14]. The run-time formalism when Q also starts another program can be cast in the form of three run-time functions for $P \parallel Q$, but this exercise will not be attempted here.

In principle there is no difficulty relaxing the assumption that the programs are stateless, although the formulas with state are more messy. Intuitively, the easiest case of $P \parallel Q$ for which to define the meaning, is to allow Q to have state, but not P, and to forbid Q from starting another program. As indicated above, there is no loss of generality in that this formalism captures multiple programs running simultaneously. It is only necessary to formalize $P \parallel Q \parallel Q' \parallel ...$ as

$$(P \parallel (Q \parallel (Q' \parallel ...)))$$

rather than as

$$(...((P \parallel Q) \parallel Q') \parallel ...)$$

.

The loss of generality in forbidding P to have state seems worth the simplification. This case is described in detail in Chapter 11, and is the only one supported by tools.

Under the restriction, $P \parallel Q$ is *correct* with respect to specification F iff it is correct as a stateless program (Q stateless) or sequence correct as a program with state (Q has state), with respect to the corresponding kind of specification function.

It is a pleasant surprise that a natural definition of concurrent meaning for programs introduces so little new mathematical machinery. However, this is surely because the parallelism is severely restricted. To capture any more of 'real' concurrent program execution, characterized by interleaved executions that are the arbitrary shuffling of bits of execution from each program, shuffled bits that may have different outcomes depending on their order, would require a different formalism altogether. Similarly, a simple functional formalism precludes more complicated exchanges between the parallel executions, conditional or multiple points of communication, and potential cycles in the programs used. It could be argued that real parallelism should not be allowed to include such 'features,' precisely because they introduce hopeless complication into testing the resulting software. That argument

---

[13] The first and last run-time function could be combined into one in the formalism, which would combine two times: that before starting Q (depending only on P's input), and that after Q terminates (depending on P's input and the value returned by Q). Two is simpler than three, but perhaps three is more straightforward.

[14] The reader might choose to set down a write-only formula.

has been lost over and over again by the side that tries to restrict computing power in the interests of controlling run-away software[15].

6.3 Summary of Testing Theory

Since the primary idea behind testing is *failure* on a test point, the subject must begin with a semantic theory of programs. The semantics of Floyd, Hoare, or Mills assigns to a program a formal, mathematical meaning for its actual behavior. In turn, specifications are similar mathematical entities, but describing what a program *should* do, not what it *does* do. When the two agree the program is correct; when they do not, a test point picks out an input-domain value of disagreement, a failure point. The pure-function testing theory developed in the 1970s can be extended naturally to apply to programs that keep persistent state, and to simple cases of concurrent program execution.

---

[15] If there are to be restrictions, the place to start is not with concurrency, but with 'unlimited' storage: the technology for surely eliminating over-runs in memory has been available for almost 50 years, but it has never been widely used because it has not been enforced. "Giving a programmer a Turing-complete language is like giving a child an AK-47" (source unknown).

Chapter 7
Subdomain Testing

TESTING a program is a daunting task because of the sheer size of the input domain and because of a program's ability to store up state and use it to modify later behavior. It would be bad enough that the variety of inputs is bewildering, but when any one input may produce different results because of invisible state values, it is understandable that testing is poorly done and testers too often believe they have been thorough when they have not. There is only one way imaginable to systematize and organize test points: to group them, defining the groups as *subdomains*, subsets of the program input domain. Systematizing testing is important, one of those rules that engineers require to move beyond craftwork. But two other ideas underlie subdomains:

Can't be missed. The definition of subdomain testing requires the tester to place test point(s) in each subdomain. This guarantees that testing will not neglect any situation described in a subdomain. By delineating the subdomain, the tester forces some aspect of the input domain to be examined.

Same behavior. There must be a (small) finite number of subdomains, each defined by some intuitive aspect of the program to be tested. This makes the number of test points collected in one or more of the subdomains very large, because the input space itself is very large. But the test points in a subdomain are chosen to be 'all the same' in some way—that defines the subdomain. (It should be *homogeneous*.) Therefore, perhaps only a few test points in any one subdomain need be tried. This is a crucial idea, both the main strength and the fatal weakness of the method. If indeed points in each subdomain *are* all the same, then picking one to test suffices, thus reducing the vast potential test domain to a few points. But if points in some subdomain are *not* all the same, then the tester can be completely misled by trying a few.

In effect, a large non-homogeneous subdomain replicates the testing difficulty of the whole large non-homogeneous input space; so it's not only no help, but creates a false confidence that something useful is being done. That's just the trouble with engineering rules. It may happen that engineers dutifully carry out what they've

D. Hamlet, *Composing Software Components*, DOI 10.1007/978-1-4419-7148-7_7,
© Springer Science+Business Media, LLC 2010

been taught, yet their whole effort is a waste of time. Craftspeople, who make up rules at need as they go along, are less likely to fall into a 'busy-work' trap.

7.1 Divide and Conquer (or Multiply and Founder?)

The particular ways in which subdomains are defined, the 'sameness' of the points within each subdomain, determines the quality of subdomain testing. It is all too easy to falsely generalize, to define sameness in some simple way, then to assume it has meaning far beyond the definition. A crucial case in point is to attribute unsolvable semantic properties to algorithmically defined subdomains. The 'sameness' that a tester really wants is with respect to test success or failure: the ideal subdomain would be homogeneous for failure so that if one test point in it fails, then all must fail (and hence if one succeeds, so must they all). A collection of such subdomains that exhausts the input space would enable perfect testing, because one successful test point in each subdomain would establish correctness (all other inputs would necessarily also succeed). Any failed test point would identify a whole subdomain of failing points for debugging. There is no algorithm that can find subdomains homogeneous for failure for an arbitrary program. If there were, it would be possible to solve Hilbert's 10th problem[1] as follows:

> Given any Diophantine equation ϕ, write a program P_ϕ to test integer input tuples to see if they solve ϕ, with output *yes* (the input is a solution) or *no* (it isn't). Given ϕ, P_ϕ can be generated mechanically. Thus ϕ has a solution if and only if there is an input x_s for which $\boxed{P_\phi}(x_s) = yes$. Take as specification for P_ϕ that the output is *no* for all inputs. (That is, its specification function F is the constant function $F(x) = no$ for all x.) For P_ϕ, use the supposed algorithm to find a finite collection of subdomains homogeneous for failure. Select a test point from each subdomain and run P_ϕ on those points. Should any of them return *yes* then ϕ has a solution[2]. Otherwise, all test points in the subdomains return *no*. The correct result (by specification F) is *no*, so every other point in every subdomain must also be correct with value *no*. Hence the program is correct with respect to its specification, and incidentally ϕ has no solution. (After Howden [64, $\prec A \succ$].)

Since Hilbert's 10th problem is unsolvable [20], it must be that subdomains homogeneous for failure cannot be algorithmically found.

Falling short of what's really wanted in the way of subdomains, the various schemes for selecting them have more or less plausibility, but none can avoid the unsolvable problem: no general subdomain collection is always homogeneous for

---

[1] The problem is to determine algorithmically whether an arbitrary multivariate polynomial equation with integer coefficients (a *Diophantine equation*) has integer solutions. For example, an instance of the problem would be: Is there a tuple of integers (x, y, z) such that $x^4 + 3y + 2z^2 + 3 = 0$? In this instance there is: $(1, -2, 1)$.

[2] The input is that solution, and all the other points in its subdomain are also solutions, since the one is incorrect with respect to the specification and so must all the others be.

failure, hence it is always possible that test points selected from a subdomain will succeed, yet others not selected will fail. Any subdomain test is potentially *misleading*. Unless a compelling argument can be made for the 'sameness' being really useful either in the sense of not missing an important test case or of eliminating cases that are redundant, defining and sampling subdomains is just busy work, a kind of wishful thinking that confuses *effort* with *efficacy*. As Section 7.6 will show, the cards may be stacked against subdomain testing from the outset. Dividing a problem isn't always a good idea. Unless the effort pays off in the sense that the smaller problems have solutions whose difficulty together is clearly less than the difficulty of the original problem, the total solution will be harder and harder to find as division proceeds, which might be called 'multiply and founder.'

7.2 History of 'Coverage' Testing

Subdomain testing is surely almost as old as software testing itself, arising from testers grouping inputs that are 'the same.' The original intent was probably to organize testing and reduce the number of test cases. Initially, subdomain testing was called 'partition testing,' beginning with the work of Howden [63] [64, $\prec A \succ$], because if the subdomains are disjoint and exhaust the entire input domain they constitute a mathematical partition in which the subdomains are the equivalence classes. It is usual to insist that a subdomain breakdown be exhaustive—otherwise it is as if there were a hidden subdomain that is not tested—but some important breakdowns are not disjoint, so 'partition testing' may be a misnomer. The accepted definition is:

A *subdomain breakdown* for a program P with input domain D is an effective method of dividing D into n subsets S_i, $1 \leq i \leq n$, called *subdomains* that together exhaust D: $D = \bigcup_{i=1}^{n} S_i$. A *subdomain testing scheme* for P is an effective method for selecting at least one test point from each subdomain of a subdomain breakdown. Executing this collection of tests is said to *cover* the subdomains. A testset T covers the breakdown iff $\forall i, T \cap S_i \neq \varnothing$.

In the definition, 'effective' is an important word: the subdomains may fail to achieve what is hoped for them, but not because they cannot be mechanically obtained and used. Indeed, it is because they are required to be algorithmic that they are subject to the semantic limitations of Howden's result that any subdomain testing scheme is misleading.

In the subsections to follow, common subdomain testing schemes will be described for stateless programs (as they were first defined in the literature; see Sections 7.4 and 7.5 for extensions to with-state and concurrent programs respectively). A brief critique of each scheme will indicate how it can go wrong.

7.2.1 Functional Coverage

One way to understand a particular subdomain testing scheme is to examine the consequences of *not* covering its subdomains. In a functional breakdown of the test domain, each subdomain corresponds to some case with a required result, e.g., "clicking $\boxed{\text{CANCEL}}$ shall clear the screen." Suppose no such test case is tried, that is, this subdomain is not covered. Then the tester has no idea what a user of the program will see on clicking $\boxed{\text{CANCEL}}$, an action very likely to occur. As noted in Section 7.1, trying the button once (and hence covering the subdomain) successfully is no guarantee of discovering every possible failure that might result from this action—$\boxed{\text{CANCEL}}$ might fail under different circumstances—but if the button is never pushed in test nothing is known about what a user might see.

"Functional" in "functional coverage" refers to a program's required 'functionality,' what it should do, not to a mathematical function. Good functional testing turns on culling from the requirements a set of these functionalities that is a good balance between generality (abstraction) and specificity (concreteness). Too far toward abstraction and the subdomains will be too large and each will have too much variation; too specific and there will be too many subdomains, many hardly different from each other. How easy it is to find good functional subdomains depends on how complex the software is and on how well its requirements are organized and presented, as well as on the skill of the test designer. In a very rigid testing plan—for example, to meet a formal test standard for a contract—the functions to be tested may be prescribed. One such standard requires that each constituent requirement be treated as a separate function. Since even a medium-sized software system can have thousands of requirements, this standard imposes a heavy testing burden. In most cases such regimentation will be counterproductive. It will be better for the tester to pretend to be an end user of the software and with the requirements as a guide to run through the functions a user might select. When busy work is legislated, those doing it incline to sloppy work, which can mean that a failure does occur but the tester doesn't notice.

Any functional testing effort will use not only isolated test points, but sequences of tests that build on one another. Users typically have problems to solve, and use the software to solve them in a sequence of related executions. Selecting a sequence of user actions identifies a sequence of subdomains and the test sequence is a test point from each in order. Test sequences will be explored in Section 10.2.2 to follow.

There are some general techniques for gleaning functional subdomains from informal requirements. Requirements isolate cases by describing values of input parameters that define each case. Even the vaguest requirements describe the input parameters themselves and their intuitive meanings. Two examples will indicate how this information can be mined for functional subdomains.

Identify function by conditional requirements. Suppose a requirement reads, "If the temperature goes above 90° C for more than 5 sec, the system shall turn on the pump." The condition defines an input subdomain of values from a temperature sensor and a clock, and the requirement defines the functional result.

Guess function from input parameters. If a program involved in word processing takes a string of characters as an input parameter, it is very likely that certain characteristics of this string are of interest. For example, an empty string may result from a user failing to supply an input field. White-space characters and/or punctuation characters are likely to be significant, dividing the string into intuitive 'words' and 'lines'. Upper and lower case may be significant. Such an analysis leads to identifying cases like "several lines of more than one word each, mixed upper- and lower case"; each such combination defines a functional subdomain.

A breakdown of the test domain using mutually exclusive cases defined by conditional expressions can be organized into tables that allow required results to be read off for each case. Indeed, it has been proposed [60] that tables of this kind should form the requirements themselves, transforming a natural-language document into one that is semi-formal.

Although the situation is slowly changing, even rudimentary requirements for a program may not exist, beyond a few comments in its code. But even in such cases, there is a method for devising reasonable functional subdomains, making use of intuitive knowledge about the problem the code is to solve. The program's potential input values can usually be associated with variable identifiers in the code, and the values of each can be grouped into subsets using common sense. The example above of the possibilities for an input string is typical, and requires almost no knowledge of what the program should do with the string. The *category-partition* method [87] is a way to turn a list of input parameters into a functional subdomain breakdown for testing. Each input parameter is assigned a number of value 'categories,' thus 'partitioning' the multidimensional input domain into subdomains that are cross products of the categories. Each cross-product subdomain singles out an intuitive case in which input variables take those values. The category-partition method is weakest in attaching required results to these subdomains (for use as an oracle), but often choosing a particular set of values in a subdomain will call up an intuitive idea of what the program should do there.

Requirements-based partitions are subject to the general deficiency described in Section 7.1. Subdomains that are too general include multiple functions, and sampling may not try them all. But no matter how well chosen the functions/subdomains, the result of subdomain testing may be misleading. Just because the sampled points succeed is no guarantee that other points in a subdomain cannot fail. The program being tested may act differently on different parts of a subdomain and some of these actions can be correct while others are not.

7.2.2 Structural Coverage

Structural subdomain testing schemes define their subdomains by elements of the code text for the program being tested. What does it mean when a structural subdomain is missed? Suppose no test covers a subdomain corresponding to a block of code that bears the comment "--clear the screen"; that is, this code was never executed. One does not know how this code block might be invoked, perhaps by a user clicking a $\boxed{\textbf{CANCEL}}$ button. But one surely has no evidence that the code does not contain mistakes. In the most benign case the code might be impossible to reach (but might that itself not indicate a programming mistake?); in the worst case it is the only code used to clear the screen in a number of different circumstances (which have not been tried!), and it might fail to do so if it were executed (say because of invoking the wrong operating-system function). Successfully executing the code once (covering the subdomain) is no guarantee that a different invocation will not fail, but if the subdomain remains uncovered the tester knows nothing.

In contrast to requirements-based testing, which is a very subjective and people-intensive activity, structural subdomain testing can be at least partly automated. Each structural method concentrates on some syntactic aspect of the program under test [86]. The input domain is divided by whether that aspect is invoked in execution. For imperative programs, the simplest intuitive structure is the block of code, a group of statements that are executed together under all circumstances. *Statement testing* defines a subdomain for each block: those inputs that cause that block to be executed. Statement-testing subdomains are not necessarily disjoint, since the same input can cause the execution of two or more distinct blocks. Any structural method introduces the possibility of *infeasible subdomains*, ones that are defined for the method but which in fact contain no points of the test domain. For statement testing, a block of dead code defines such an infeasible subdomain. Unfortunately, it is an unsolvable problem to determine if a particular code block is dead; thus statement testing is not a mechanical, algorithmic method. It shares this unsolvable feasibility problem with all other common structural methods. That means structural methods are not technically subdomain testing schemes according to the definition, because the procedure for selecting a test point in each subdomain cannot be algorithmic. (If it were, it would solve the unsolvable feasibility problem.) It is a compensating advantage that structural test coverage can be monitored by instrumenting the program under test.

There is a bewildering array of structural methods, each perhaps invented to improve on the deficiencies of the others. For example, in *branch testing* each conditional statement of an imperative program is used to define the two subdomains of inputs that cause it to take one of the two possible truth values. If a conditional statement has multiple parts formed using Boolean connectives, each of its two branch subdomains can be split into ones that cause just each part to be *true* or *false*. This variant is usually called *multi-condition* coverage. Because of the infeasible-subdomain problem, it may not be possible to carry out a complete structural-subdomain test, which leads to yet another unlimited collection of subdomain-based methods for partial coverage. For example, *85% statement coverage* requires that tests be selected so that no more than 15% of the statement subdomains are not sampled.

The ultimate structural subdomain testing scheme for imperative programs is *path testing*. Subdomains are defined to correspond to each control-flow possibility (execution path) of a program. Achieving path coverage means that each such path has been tried at least once. Path testing is considered the high-end of control-flow schemes, because if paths are covered, so are all other structural control elements. For example, there cannot be a statement or branch possibility missed if paths are covered. Howden [64, ≺A≻] chose path testing for his example, so it is instructive to see why this ultimate structural method failed to establish correctness in 65% of the small programs to which he applied it. Its deficiency is the same as that of all other subdomain methods: Sampling every path subdomain tries all the execution paths, but falls impossibly short of trying all program possibilities. Each path subdomain is comprised of a myriad of input points that traverse that particular path. Some of these may lead to test success and some to test failure. For example, taking a path that clears the user's screen may be sometimes be the correct thing to do, but sometimes a mistake. If the mistaken invocations are few among many correct invocations, any path subdomain test is likely to succeed, missing the failures hidden in the subdomain(s).

Path testing has another deficiency (not shared by branch- or statement testing): Most programs have too many paths. Each conditional statement in a program doubles the path count. A program containing an indeterminate loop (WHILE statement) has in principle an infinity of paths, since iterating the loop body 0, 1, 2, ... times technically each creates a distinct path. Thus true path testing does not satisfy the definition of a subdomain testing scheme, since the number of subdomains is not finite.

Dataflow testing is sometimes motivated as a method that selects a finite subset of the potential infinity of path-testing subdomains. However, it is probably better described as an attempt to add data information to control-flow methods. Among many variants [28], the most common is usually called *all-uses*. An all-uses subdomain for a given program identifier V comprises those inputs on which the value of V is set at a particular location in the program, then subsequently this V-value is used at another particular location (without having been set again between). The pair of locations is said to constitute a *def-use pair*. Intuitively, each def-use pair describes a value stored in V and its later examination. Of all structural coverage methods, dataflow coverage is the closest to functional coverage, since it is often possible to associate a functional result with each particular def-use pair for V. For example, V may be a flag that is used to remember a condition naturally connected to a specific functional case.

All of the structural testing ideas that have been described are based on program control flow. (Dataflow is a partial exception, since it uses variable names to pick out paths.) There is, however, an entirely different kind of structural coverage called *mutation testing* [57, 21]. It imagines distorting a program into variants ('mutants'), and seeking test points that distinguish each variant from the original. Mutation subdomains consist of all inputs that 'kill' each mutant, that is, witness that it produces some result different from the original. The intuition behind the method is that without a test to tell a program from its mutants, a mutant may as well be correct, yet its syntax quite plainly differs from the original. If there were no restrictions on the form of mutants, this method would work perfectly: Unless the original program is correct, some variant (more correct) differs from it, but the original program must fail on tests that would kill this variant. But without restrictions, there would be an infinity of mutations and mutation subdomains. In practice, the mutations allowed are very narrow indeed. It is usual to create each mutant by making only one small change at the expression/statement level, for example, to alter an original assignment statement

    X = (X+1)*Y

to

    Y = (X+1)*Y.

Even drastic restrictions are not enough to control the cost of monitoring mutation testing very well—its bookkeeping is still by far the most compute-intensive of the structural methods. The most difficult part of using mutation testing is its infeasible-subdomain problem: A subdomain is infeasible if the mutant from which it arises cannot be killed; that is, its mutant is a program equivalent to the original. It is much more difficult to recognize equivalence in programs than it is to see that some control transfer is impossible.

The most seductive aspect of structural testing is its potential for automation. Since subdomains and their coverage are defined by the execution of some program syntactical feature, it is in principle possible to mechanically generate subdomains and test points within them, thus eliminating the labor-intensive activity of test generation. Alternately, given a testset that achieves structural coverage, it may be possible to mechanically reduce it to a smaller testset without reducing the coverage. Even without automation, structural testing seems to be more 'systematic' than functional testing, since its goal is to cover items from a finite list (the program syntax); in contrast, functional testing has an open-ended subjective feel. Engineers prefer to engage in tasks that can be seen to be completed by their efforts. "Find a test point that will execute statement 93," fits the bill.

Unfortunately, structural test coverage can turn out to be only busy work, because structural schemes are only surrogates for what testing is supposed to accomplish. It is all too possible to busily attain coverage, yet find few failures and gain little confidence that software works. The underlying reason is that structural subdomains usually do not have a clear connection to the functionality seen by end users. When all structural subdomains have been covered, it is still possible to have missed important functionality. Concentrating on structural coverage diverts attention from the real problem in favor of details in the surrogate problem. For example, one way to achieve statement coverage is to analyze a program's pattern of conditional statements. An uncovered block of code has a chain of guards in the code that lead to it, and will be executed if this chain is satisfied. A systematic attempt to execute such a block naturally concentrates on the conditions leading to it. The tester studies the code and comes up with simple cases that enable all the necessary conditions. However, such cases usually have little connection with the software's functionality. Zero values, empty strings, etc., make it easier to trace and control conditionals in code, but such values are not the common ones in actual usage. Thus the test points that an engineer contrives to achieve statement coverage are then unlikely to expose problems that will arise in real usage of the program.

7.2.3 Combining Functional and Structural Coverage

It seemed obvious to the first testing theoreticians that functional and structural subdomains should be combined and thereby the good qualities of both could be obtained. It's easy enough: define the two breakdowns and take all possible intersections of the two sets of subdomains. In the examples above involving CANCEL and code that clears the screen, one of the intersection subdomains S would be defined by *both* clicking on CANCEL *and* executing the code block with comment "`--clear the screen.`" Assuming that the comment isn't a lie, a test point in S will succeed: the CANCEL is clicked and the code *is* executed. All well and good. But what of other intersection subdomains like F where CANCEL is clicked but the code is not executed? F is evidently a failure subdomain, split off from the functional by the structural intersection. Perhaps F is empty; the failures it describes cannot occur. A tester cannot tell, for it is as difficult to place a test point in F as it is to find a failure point in the original functional subdomain. The intersection subdomain breakdown cannot be used in a subdomain testing scheme because there is no algorithmic way to cover some of the subdomains. Even S may be empty, but how can a tester know? Given the knowledge of which subdomains are empty, no testing is needed: the program is correct if the ones like S are not empty and the ones like F are empty. Without this magical knowledge the intersection subdomains are of no use.

There is, however, a way to exploit the complementary nature of functional and structural subdomain testing, by using structural methods as an *adequacy criterion* [76] for functional testing. The procedure is this:

Functional test. The tester uses the requirements to create functional subdomains and chooses test points for a testset to cover them in the usual way.

Check structural coverage. Using algorithmic tools, the functional testset is used to check for structural coverage. The procedure terminates if the structural coverage is complete. Otherwise:

Add functional tests. Examine each non-tested structural element for clues as to what function it was intended to perform. Then using the requirements, add a new functional subdomain and a test case that covers it. (Don't forget to execute this new case and check its correctness.)

Repeat the structural-coverage check above.

What is essential to this procedure, what allows it to avoid the trap of getting caught up in counterproductive structural busy work, is the third step: Instead of seeking to improve structural coverage by studying the code, one seeks to improve the *functional* coverage, with structure as the clue to functionality that has not been tested.

The proponents of using structural-coverage for judging the adequacy of functional coverage admit that the method is more plausible than rigorous. It is easy to imagine cases in which an inadequate functional test is not caught[3]. In Chapter 19, the plausibility is investigated in more detail.

7.3 Usage Profiles

A primary purpose in the definition of a subdomain breakdown is to capture cases that ought not to be missed in testing. By making a subdomain for each case, test points must be selected to cover it. However, there is evidently more to it than a binary choice of cover or not. Imagine for a moment two subdomains, the first a functional subdomain whose function is broad and somewhat ill-defined; the second a structural subdomain that is very narrow. Perhaps the first results from a functional breakdown using vague requirements and the second from 'multiply and founder.' If these two subdomains are part of a testing scheme, then they must be covered by at least one test point each. But intuition calls for more than one test point in the large functional subdomain, and perhaps none in the small structural one. When the software is used, many variants of the poorly defined functionality are likely to occur, but the peculiar structural aspect might never come up at all. What subdomain testing schemes ignore is the *distribution* of inputs that any program will face when it has been released to its users. Over time, as the program is utilized to attempt useful work in its problem domain, some inputs will be needed more frequently and other less frequently. Any subdomain breakdown will receive more user inputs in some subdomains than in others.

The mathematical device that best captures usage is a probability density function u over the input space D called the *user input profile* (*profile* for short). At input x, profile density $u(x)$ is the probability that x will arise in actual use. As a density, u is normalized so that $\sum_{x \in D} u(x) = 1$. A profile is a wonderful abstraction, but in practice more wonderful than reality ever can be. Over a long lifetime each software system has such a profile, which could be measured by keeping track of every input used and counting the frequencies. But the long-term average may be quite different from what one user does in a week's work on some particular problem, and different users (or even the same user at different times) will generate different profiles. In the short term a profile will be very 'spiky' in that some inputs will get a lot of usage and other inputs none, and 'noisy' in that it will change hour by hour.

Subdomains have been put to use to tame the profile abstraction. In Software Reliability Engineering (SRE) [83], systems are subjected to test sampling that attempts to mimic eventual usage. The system's would-be users are questioned about how often they will invoke each of several functional subdomains. This information is used to sample the frequently used subdomains more often. As test data accumulates, the subdomain breakdown is also refined to match cases the users find natural. A set of rough probabilities are thus obtained that define a coarse input profile $\hat{u}$

---

[3] All that is needed is for a required function to be missed in the functional subdomains, and to be completely unimplemented. Then neither kind of subdomain can see the mistake.

for the system [84] by subdomain, which takes the form of a subdomain histogram, each bar showing the fraction of inputs that are expected to fall in that subdomain. If the subdomains are well chosen and the users who are questioned have experience using similar software, $\hat{u}$ can be stable and accurate. The proponents of SRE make this unlikely data-collection process sound much easier than it is in practice, but they correctly point out that it does approximate the profile, and however questionable the result it is better than nothing.

SRE having provided a practical profile approximation, testers do not have to know or care about SRE to use it. The method not only provides a probability histogram, but also helps to define appropriate functional subdomains. Then the goals of functional subdomain testing will be served best by weighting the testing of those subdomains according to the histogram. Instead of selecting one test point per subdomain, testers should apportion a number of points among subdomains. If subdomain S has a histogram bar of height (say) 0.32 (32% of the inputs are expected to fall in S), then 32 out 100 test points should be selected from S. The choice of total test count can be made so that there are enough test points to cover even the least-likely subdomain, or if resources are limited, unlikely subdomains may not be tested at all. Leaving subdomains uncovered runs contrary to the whole idea of subdomain testing, but Harlan Mills has given a convincing argument [17] that it is better to place test points in high-frequency subdomains, even if this deprives some subdomains of any points at all. Although it is counter-intuitive, Mills's point is that it is not worth finding a failure which is estimated to occur only (say) every 5000 years of operation. Setting a frequency cutoff in this way determines the number of test points needed to cover all subdomains above the cutoff frequency. How should multiple test points within a subdomain be chosen? It makes no sense to impose any scheme based on usage—the profile already goes as far as possible in that direction. The only remaining possibility is to scatter test points in the subdomain at random or use some form of equi-spaced sampling. Section 7.6 shows that it may not matter much how the choices are made.

The SRE profile-approximation procedure naturally works with functional subdomains, since they are the only ones that users can assess. But the functional subdomains that result need not be used directly in testing. The profile histogram can be used to weight any other subdomain breakdown. Subdomain breakdowns other than the functional can also be weighted directly, but with dubious purpose. For example, structural path-testing subdomains might be weighted by the frequency with which programmers believe the paths will be taken in execution. If no user data is available, such a profile might be better than nothing.

The adequacy measure of checking the structural coverage after attaining functional coverage (Section 7.2.3) can be refined to check not only the structural coverage, but the profile over structural subdomains. If one believes that the best structural coverage is uniform, then an infrequently encountered structural subdomain indicates that the functional coverage is not so good as imagined.

Chapter 8 will present a quite different view of profiles for software components. The theory to be presented there is based on profiles, but in the unlikely context that for a software component the profile *cannot be known when the component is tested.*

7.4 Subdomain Testing in the Presence of State

For all that testing theoreticians have not paid attention, most programs do not compute pure functions. On one run they record information, and on another they examine it, so that results on the same input may not be repeated. It has been learned from sad experience that keeping state is a powerful programming device but also a major source of subtle failures that escape detection during testing. One failure situation is that some program function is tested successfully, but in a particular state with which the tester was unconcerned. Then the program gets into a different state where that function was not tested, and the program fails in use. A classic example is an aircraft control program in which the function 'retract landing gear' was tested in the state 'airborne,' but not for the state 'landed,' and was later found to work all too well in the 'landed' state. A more subtle failure situation arises when one execution succeeds, but leaves the program in an erroneous state that will cause a subsequent execution to fail for no apparent reason.

State values are often thought to be 'inputs,' in that a program can examine and use them in its computations just as it can use input values, and hence the 'input' state partially determines what actions a program will take. If state were no more than another input, it could be added to subdomain testing easily: each input subdomain could be split into several state subdomains, each of which would thus be sampled. (It amounts to the same thing to imagine subdomains for the state, each of which is divided into several input subdomains.) Unfortunately, the simple view that state is an input is wrong. Input is not controlled by the program but by its user, and so therefore by its tester. State the program controls absolutely. A user or tester may imagine putting the program in some particular state, but in fact what happens is that the user supplies input, on which the program execution establishes state. The distinction is critical for testing, because the program may malfunction in setting state, making a mockery of what the tester is trying to cover. State thus acts also like output.

There is also a pernicious interplay between state requirements and state implementation. Many requirements describe abstract states and the transitions between them that a program is supposed to make. The very intuitive and powerful notation of the *state machine* [59] is a good mechanism for giving such a description. In coding a program to meet state-machine requirements, the programmer usually tries to work with concrete analogs of the required states, and to implement the required transitions. But as in all programming tasks, mistakes can be made, creating a mismatch between the real states and those that should occur. To follow a sequence of state transitions from the requirements may mean nothing at all to the real program state.

Finally, there is the 'infeasible state' problem. Since the program controls state, it may be impossible to enter a particular state, because no sequence of inputs ever reaches it. The requirements may have such infeasible states (but they are not easy to uncover!); code may have them as well (and the ones from requirements and code may be different!). It is usual that persistent storage has a rigid and peculiar format, which programs maintain as a primary duty; thus in practice almost all arbitrary state values are infeasible. For example, a relational database is a file, but almost all files are not relational databases.

The only correct way to sample behaviors of a program with state is as follows:

1. Adjust the environment so that the state appears 'reset' or 'uninitialized' to the program. To make use of state, a program must know when things are beginning, typically to create and save initial state values. All testing starts from this reset state, and from it testing is repeatable.
2. Select a test point and execute the program. Record the output values and resultant state values.
3. Continue selecting input test points to form a sequence, executing each one and recording output and result state.
4. Each test point involves two pairs: the (input, input-state) pair that begins it, and the (output, result-state) pair that ends it. The input value in the begin-pair is the tester's arbitrary choice, but the input-state value is not—it is the result-state value from the previous end-pair.
5. At some point the tester chooses to end the input sequence. The list of two-pair values (each with a beginning and ending pair) is then a record of the testing activity.

Each time a sequence as described is selected, it constitutes a composite 'test point' for the program with state, a 'point' composed of (input, input-state) beginning pairs in the order they occur. Only feasible state values will occur in the sequences.

Strictly speaking, the input domain for a program with state is a space of sequences of inputs, each sequence being a test point. Subdomain testing over this space would require grouping 'the same' sequences. Intuitively, there may be functional subdomains. For example, in a transaction-processing system, transactions may naturally follow one another, as when a bank customer inquires about a balance, makes a deposit, inquires again, and finally makes a withdrawal. But it seems hopeless to isolate any meaningful sequence subdomains for *components* even if they could be used in such a system. Furthermore, the intuition behind *unit* testing is that of exercising the functionality (or structure) of the component in isolation. The very sparse nature of usage within the state space goes against this idea. Thus on the whole it seems reasonable to deal with subdomains in two separate spaces— the test domain of inputs and the state domain. The former is within the power of the tester to sample but the latter is not—it is under program control. Each space can be independently divided into its own functional or structural subdomains as described above. The (input × state) cross products, however, are not sampled directly. Rather, sequences of inputs are chosen as described above. The pairs of beginning values in a sequence fall into one of the (input × state) cross-product subdomains, which has therefore been implicitly sampled by the sequence composite 'test point'.

Only one question remains: How should the cross-product subdomains be covered? That is, how should a tester choose the testing sequences? Nothing like this question arises for stateless program testing, since there it does not matter in what order test points are selected, so the tester can just systematically go through the input subdomains. To even measure subdomain coverage in both input- and state domains extensive bookkeeping is required. Unless every possible input subdomain is tried at every position in the sequence, some state values may be missed. Furthermore, the particular choice of an input value from an input subdomain may alter the sampling of states. Whatever choices of sequences a tester makes, some of the (input, state) cross-product subdomains will be covered, but most will not, simply because most states are infeasible. It is an open question how to attain wide state coverage. Therefore, when there is persistent state, strictly speaking the definition of a subdomain testing scheme cannot be met because there is no algorithm for covering the state subdomains.

Requirements typically do not provide much guidance in choosing testing sequences or any information on usage profiles for sequences of user inputs. Even when requirements describe how state should influence the results, they may be vague about how state values are established and about usage patterns. Similarly, intuitively useful subdomains are not easy to devise even for the input space alone, since sequences and the states that arise are only implicitly tied to single inputs. However, requirements expressed in a state-machine diagram [59] are an exception to this deficiency. A state-machine diagram not only describes required states, but also the transitions among them. Of course, a programmer may choose not to implement states or transitions from the requirements, perhaps because there is a more efficient way to gain the same results. By and large, however, it is safer and easier to implement a required state machine faithfully. State-machine states form natural singleton subdomains, so there is no state-subdomain sampling problem. More important, there are mechanical rules for state-machine construction that preclude infeasible states in the requirements. It is sufficient to insist that each state in the diagram be reachable from the initial state. That establishes a testing sequence to bring the abstract state to any one of its values. Furthermore, if in every state a transition is defined for every possible input, it cannot happen that the result is unspecified on any testing sequence as described above.

State-machine requirements thus define a number of coverage measures analogous to control flow in imperative programs, with the states themselves analogous to control points, and the transitions of the state-machine graph analogous to execution flow of control. One could ask for coverage of all states (analogous to statement coverage), or all state transitions (branch coverage), or all sequences of state transitions (path coverage)[4]. For a finite-state machine (FSM), all of these coverages are decidable—that is, there is no infeasible-state problem for an FSM. Restrictions on arbitrary state-machine requirements are needed to make the coverage problems solvable, but they are not onerous. Thus in principle all the additional difficulties of choosing state-subdomain-covering test sequences disappear when there are well behaved state-machine requirements. There are no infeasible states and the information needed to achieve coverage can be found in the requirements' transition diagram. This soothing ointment has only one fly in it: a program may fail to correctly implement requirement states.

---

[4] Although it is possible to imagine somewhat far-fetched analogs for dataflow coverage and for mutation, these have not been seriously explored.

Even if an attempt was made to faithfully implement a requirements' state machine, mistakes may have been made. Unfortunately, the possibilities for error can be spread across the input domain, so that each input subdomain is subject to the potential problem that some of its values follow the requirements and some do not. Hence the testing results depend on choices made in input subdomains as each testing sequence advances. Selecting 'good' points that mimic the requirements will lead to testing success; but 'bad' points will carry the program off into state neverland. The worst of it is that 'bad' choices in a testing sequence need not fail; instead they may only put the program in a strange state where some subsequent input will fail, but the testing sequence ends before this happens. This is precisely one way that state leads to obscure failures. The best that a tester can do is to define a careful correspondence between program state values and requirements values, and rigorously check this correspondence at each step in each testing sequence. It can still happen that the program goes state-wrong for untried sequences, but at least the testing actually carried out will not be spurious. It is uncommon to recognize the need to match implementation states with those required—most testers assume without any evidence that they are the same.

7.5 Concurrency

If program-testing practice lags behind programming using state, it falls much farther behind concurrent programming. Concurrency mechanisms range from two processes using operating-system calls to share information in a single memory, to programs running in different computers and communicating across the Internet. The essence of concurrency, from the standpoint of testing a program using it, is that there is an exchange of information between the program and some outside agency that the program does not control except through voluntary observance of some protocol. Information may pass both ways, so the interaction can act like an input or an output. The outside agency can store and retrieve information, so the interaction may act like persistent state. Or, because the outside agency is itself a program, the interaction may be more complicated than any of these. Furthermore, because two interacting programs cannot be sure of each other's execution speed, synchronization may be used (or not used!) to control (or fail to!) when in each execution the interaction takes place.

Subdomains might be defined to subdivide the communication data space between interacting programs, but the situation is so complicated that this is seldom attempted in practice. If subdomain testing is used at all, it will be on the complete complex of programs, and subdomain coverage will be even more problematical than has been previously described, since no execution is necessarily repeatable. To make matters worse, the testing problem doesn't decompose—while testing one partner, assuming that other partners correctly observe interaction requirements isn't safe. Subdomain testing is intended to control input cases so that nothing is missed;

it is hard to escape the intuition that control of that kind isn't humanly possible in the face of concurrency.

In Chapter 6 a very restricted form of concurrent execution was defined, which can be formalized by a functional-semantic model. In that model each program has a two-dimensional 'input' space for which subdomain breakdowns and subdomain testing schemes can be defined. Because more than one program is necessarily involved, it is natural to treat the case using a 'parallel' system construction, in Chapter 11.

7.6 Comparing Subdomain Techniques

Because testing is a precise, even algorithmic activity, it is natural to expect that different testing methods can be accurately compared. Unfortunately, the precision lies with the procedure being followed, not with the results attained. The 'quality' of many testing methods is measured in terms that are really only surrogates. When a method is 'better' it may only mean in its self-defined metrics, not in any real sense of finding software failures. For example, more structural coverage is 'better,' but not necessarily for discovering anything, if what is covered is unrelated to potential failure.

7.6.1 The 'Subsumes' Partial Ordering

Because control-flow structural coverage methods were the first to be invented and are the easiest to support with tools, they have received the widest study. Among these methods there is a natural subset hierarchy called the *subsumes* ordering. Method M1 subsumes method M2 iff any covering testset of M1 is also a covering testset for M2. It was noted above that path testing (strictly) subsumes all other control-flow methods. For another example, 85% statement coverage strictly subsumes 80% statement coverage. (Generalizations of this second example are obvious.)

'Subsumes' is a trickier idea than it seems. First, not all methods are ordered by it. In particular, there is no subsumes relationship between functional and structural methods nor between control flow methods and mutation methods, the ones we would most like to compare. Second, the 'better' method in the sense of subsumes is not always really better. When there is a large gap between two methods M1 and M2 and M1 strictly subsumes M2, it means that the testsets covering M1 are a small subset of those covering M2. It can happen that what should be tested in some program is more frequently encountered by M2; that is, of all the covering M2 testsets, say half have a chance of finding some problem. The very difficulty of achieving M1 coverage may mean that only (say) a quarter of the covering M1 testsets encounter the problem. Then if the tester picks a testset without knowing of the problem being sought (always the tester's situation!), the chance that an M2 testset will find it is twice as high as the chance that an M1 testset will. Furthermore, the M2 testsets are much easier to generate. The fact that any M1 testset selected is also an M2 testset is irrelevant; there is plenty of room in M2 for all of these to miss the problem.

Empirical studies aimed at comparing testing methods are very difficult to do properly [27], and those that have been done have not shown a clear advantage for any method. The choice of method then comes down to what best fits into a particular development methodology. For example, one large advantage of functional testing is that its tests can be devised as soon as the requirements are available; structural testing must wait for the advent of executable code, but it has better tool support.

7.6.2 Random Testing

For most practical testers, functional subdomain testing is their bread and butter; they have never considered its near-opposite, random testing. Serious consideration of random testing is not made easier by the erroneous but commonly held idea that 'random' means 'haphazard' or 'ill-defined' [36, $\prec A \succ$]. Real random testing over a domain is a perfect method with which to compare subdomain testing, since its definition is precisely that the choice of test points uses no systematic relationship among them. Subdomains in contrast are a systematic grouping by 'sameness.' Furthermore, it is easy to assess the effectiveness of random testing probabilistically. Probability analysis of subdomain testing is more difficult, but some surprising results have been obtained.

Given an input domain, (uniform) random testing employs a testset (say of size N) chosen from a uniform distribution[5] over the input domain. Suppose that such a testset succeeds for some program (the usual case for software of good quality and practical values of N). Assuming the failure rate of the program (the probability that it fails on a randomly selected test point) is constant, the upper confidence bound C that the failure rate lies below F is defined by[6]:

$$C = 1 - (1 - F)^N.$$

Setting C, F can be calculated, supporting statements like the following:

Random testing establishes that this program will not fail more one time in 10,000 executions (that is, $F \le 10^{-4}$), with a confidence of at least 90% (that is, $C \ge 0.9$).

It is easy to generalize random-testing theory to a different failure rate in each subdomain.

---

[5] Technically, the choice should be weighted by a user profile (Section 7.3) to apply to that profile, but it is usual to ignore the profile, that is, to assume it is uniform.

[6] Chapter 12 discusses failure rates and confidence in detail.

7.6.3 Comparing Random- and Subdomain-testing

In a seminal 1985 paper, Joe Duran and Simeon Ntafos [22, $\prec A \succ$] published a theoretical comparison between arbitrary subdomain testing and random testing for the stateless case. They used simulation to analyze subdomain testing's probability of finding at least one failure (among other probabilistic measures), to compare with F from random testing. Random testing did surprisingly well, or put another way, it was surprising that subdomain testing did not do as much better than random testing as expected. Their paper led to a flurry of theoretical research with similar results. This research answers a question about testing to match a user profile (Section 7.3): When a subdomain is allotted more than one test point, is it better to use random sampling, or some kind of equi-spaced coverage? The latter amounts to creating new uniform-sized subdomains within the subdomain to be sampled and placing one test point in each. Hence if there is little difference between subdomain testing and random testing, it doesn't much matter how the test-point choices within one subdomain are made. A case study illustrating this is presented in Section 18.1.1.

Comparisons with random testing have provided some deep insights into when subdomain testing works best and why [11]. It remains to explain why there is not a greater disparity between subdomain- and random testing. Recent work has found a surprising bound on the effectiveness of subdomain testing, and in fact on all other forms of testing, in comparison with random testing. It seems that nothing can be done to improve very much on random testing. T-Y. Chen et al. [15] derived a theoretical bound on how much random testing could be improved. The bound is different for different probabilistic measures of test effectiveness, but in all cases the possible improvement is modest (e.g., a factor of 2). Their analysis is limited to stateless programs and rests on assumptions about the description of 'failure do-mains,' shapes of subsets in the test domain where the program fails at every point in the subset. There is no reason to believe that their assumptions are fundamentally limiting, however.

Granting for the sake of argument that further research will confirm Chen's re-sults, the proper interpretation is the one originally suggested by Duran and Ntafos: random testing deserves serious investigation. It's not that subdomain testing isn't a good idea; rather, random testing is also a good idea. The current notion of adap-tive random testing (ART) is an attempt to combine the methods, and it may realize almost all of the possible gain over random testing [14].

Part III
Composition of Components

P ART III presents the original theoretical content of this monograph. It presents a testing-based composition theory for software components, a theory that allows calculation of system functional and non-functional properties that arise when components are combined. Because these calculations are based on testing of the components in isolation, the results are approximations only as good as the testing is thorough. The presentation follows the chronological order in which theory was developed, beginning with series composition of stateless components. Conditional and iterative system constructions are treated next, then state and finally concurrency are added. The SYN tools that implement measurement of components by testing and which perform system-synthesis calculations from those measurements, are described by three tutorials interlaced with the theoretical presentation. The presentation and tutorials use run time as an illustrative non-functional property, but the more difficult reliability property is subsequently discussed at length.

Chapter 8
Subdomain Theory of Stateless Component Composition

ALTHOUGH there are a myriad of ways in which software components can be combined into systems, *sequence* is the most interesting and fundamental. One component's output is fed to another component as input, and the pair constitutes a series system. Intuitively, composition is easily understood in functional terms, because composition is a fundamental operation for functions. But tests do not naturally compose. If there is to be any testing-based theory of component composition, a solution must be found for composing test results.

8.1 Software Testing is 'Non-compositional'

If software is intrinsically different from products of mechanical engineering described in Chapter 2, it is because software obeys no natural laws, and lacks the simplifying organization often imposed by nature [42]. Most natural phenomena are continuous and this continuity allows a brief but precise description of a physical system. For example, a mechanical system often has components that can be described as point masses, and Newtonian mechanics can accurately predict the behavior of complex assemblies from this description alone. Software, in contrast, is usually discontinuous and may have arbitrary human-defined behavior that can only be described explicitly in forbidding detail. This fact explains why software-requirements engineering is so important and so difficult. It also explains why simple descriptions of mechanical components are used to design their assemblies and predict the assembly behavior, while software component (unit) tests are discarded and have no further role in systems development.

The difficulty in predicting software system properties using component test measurements can be illustrated by a simple example. Imagine two software components placed in a series system. The first component C_1 receives the system input, does its calculation and passes its output to the second component. The second component C_2 does its calculation on input received from C_1 and C_2's output is the system output. Consider the performance property of this composite system. To use

D. Hamlet, *Composing Software Components*, DOI 10.1007/978-1-4419-7148-7_8,
© Springer Science+Business Media, LLC 2010

the paradigm that has been successful in other engineering disciplines, one wants to measure the run time of each component in isolation and then (later) calculate the system run time. Suppose that each component is capable of 'slow' or 'fast' performance, depending on its input. The system run time will then depend on two things:

1. The distribution of system inputs over the input domain of the first component. For example, if many inputs lead to the 'slow' behavior of C_1 then the system will be slower.
2. The way in which C_1 sends its outputs into the input domain of C_2. For example, if many C_1 outputs happen to fall on 'slow' input points of C_2, the system will be slower.

The usage of a system can be captured by its input profile: the probability density describing how likely it is that each input will occur. Given this system profile, it would be possible to analyze the series system above by seeing which inputs invoke 'slow' or 'fast' behavior in each component when they are connected together, and make a detailed calculation of the composite behavior. But component developers cannot know the profile and cannot know which components will be used together or how they will be connected—those are all *system* properties that arise long after the components are tested. To use testing as the measurement technique raises another fundamental difficulty in composing C_1 and C_2: their tests will not match at the interface. Since each is tested independently, the test outputs from C_1 are unlikely to fall on the test inputs to C_2. To arrange for a match would again require knowing in advance that the components are to be used together in series. So how can test measurements be made at component-development time that will later be sufficient to calculate the composite behavior?

Subdomain decomposition of testing solves the problem of measuring component properties in isolation, to be later used in calculations that could not be foreseen. Each component input domain is split into subdomains, and each subdomain is separately tested. The test results are subdomain-based approximations to the components' behavior. Suppose that this has been done for the two components C_1 and C_2. Now suppose that a particular system is to be constructed, say the one with C_1 in series with C_2 above. At this time a system input profile is available, which establishes what C_1 will see on input. The profile can be used to weight subdomain test values for C_1, measured earlier in isolation. For example, if subdomain S of C_1 is a 'slow' one, then C_1's contribution to system performance will be determined partly by how much weight the system profile gives to S. This resolves the difficulty that the profile was not known at C_1 test time. The component tester need only measure property values *by the subdomain*, to be later weighted when the profile is known.

Testing over subdomains in components also resolves the issue of matching tests at the interface and how one component will distort the input profile before it reaches the next. Matching is guaranteed because the test subdomains cover the input space of C_2. No matter what output appears in the C_1 test, it will fall in some C_2 subdomain. Brute-force tracing of the profile from C_1 to C_2 is possible because the domain of an intractable number of inputs is reduced to relatively few subdomains. In the analysis, each subdomain is like a single 'point,' which makes calculation efficient and even allows a decidable treatment of iteration.

8.2 Approximating and Measuring Component Properties

Before component test results can be used to calculate system properties, subdomain measurements must be made. The run time of a component C over input space D is a mapping $T_C : D \rightarrow \mathbb{R}$, where $\mathbb{R}$ is the non-negative reals. That is, $T_C(x)$ is the run time when C receives input x. In testing, T_C is sampled by executing the component; at this point subdomains make their crucial contribution. The subdomain division of C's input space is as important to its description as is its code. Finding good subdomains relies on developer knowledge of what the component code is supposed to do and how it tries to do it. But testing skills and techniques are also needed to select good subdomains (Chapter 7); Chapter 17 explores the meaning of "good" for accurate system predictions. For now, suppose that the developer/tester somehow divides a component's input space into n subdomains $S_1, S_2, ..., S_n$.

The simplest way to assign a single value to each subdomain is by averaging over the subdomain. For run time T_C, average values $T_C(x)$ over all x in each subdomain S_i approximate T_C as a step function with constant value t_i on S_i, so that for all $1 \le i \le n$, $T_C(x) \approx t_i$, $x \in S_i$, as indicated in Fig. 8.1. The graph of the approximat-

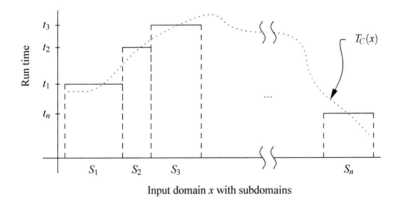

Fig. 8.1 Step-function approximation of a component property

ing step function for T_C is $\{(x,y) \mid y = t_i \text{ if } x \in S_i\}$. For simplicity, Fig. 8.1 shows the subdomains as intervals along an axis, which requires the input domain to be numerical and ordered.

Similarly, component C has an input-output mapping $\boxed{C} : D \to R$, whose values can be averaged to $v_1, v_2, ..., v_n$ over the n subdomains. Approximate $\boxed{C}$ with the step function whose graph is: $\{(x,y) \mid y = v_i \text{ if } x \in S_i\}$.

These step functions are true averages only if all the points in each subdomain are included. But the intention is to make component measurements by more sparsely sampling subdomains, which introduces a further approximation. In principle the number of samples could be increased until their average is arbitrarily close to the exact average[1]. As will be seen in Section 18.1.1, a few samples (1-5) are usually enough.

It is also possible to approximate behaviors across subdomains with non-constant functions. The simplest better approximation in a numerical domain is linear, in which the approximating values on a subdomain are pairs: (slope, intercept), $\boxed{C}(x) \approx m_i x + b_i$, $x \in S_i$, and similarly a(nother) linear function approximating $T_C(x)$. Estimates of slopes and intercepts can be obtained from test samples using a least-squares fit over each subdomain, as close to the true best-fit line as desired[2]. In the sequel, approximating subdomain values by constants will be called the *step-function approximation*, and by linear functions, the *piecewise-linear approximation*. The step-function approximation is just that special case of the piecewise-linear approximation in which all slopes are forced to zero so that the best-fit line is horizontal, but it is treated separately because it is intuitively easier to describe.

Averaging or line fitting requires a numerical input domain. The tools described in this monograph are restricted to floating-point domains and their algorithms depend on the restriction. A step-function approximation can be obtained for any domain by taking a single sample in each subdomain. Furthermore, two of the most important non-functional properties of software (run time and reliability) *are* numerical and their step-function approximation can be obtained by random sampling any kind of input. Chapter 20 explores the apparent paradox that good approximations to non-functional behavior may be obtained using poor approximations to functional behavior.

In any case, the result of a component-developer/tester's measurement effort is an approximate description consisting of subdomains with functional and run-time values for each subdomain. If the subdomains are well chosen, this description may capture accurately the actual software behavior. If not, the accuracy should improve by adjusting the subdomains.

In the discussion to follow, it is often enough to refer to measured approximations as, e.g., "the step-function approximation to run time." But sometimes a notation is needed. When approximating $\boxed{C}$ it seems appropriate to write $\lceil \overline{C} \rceil$, since the approximation is 'full of holes' where it may not agree with $\boxed{C}$. For functions like run time T_C, $\widetilde{T_C}$ will symbolize the approximation. It is left to the context to determine exactly what kind of approximation is under discussion. $\lceil \overline{C} \rceil$ or $\widetilde{T_C}$ might refer

---

[1] Technically, the functions are required to be continuous.
[2] Ibid.

to a piecewise-linear or a step-function approximation; nor do the notations specify which subdomains have been used nor how values have been sampled.

8.3 Calculating Properties of Stateless Systems

The sections of this chapter to follow present a quantitative theory that predicts software system properties from component values measured by testing. The theory applies to many 'composable' software properties such as functional output, performance (run time), and reliability. Some apparently 'emergent' properties like security and memory allocation can be incorporated with a bit more difficulty, while some emergent properties are strictly outside the capabilities of the theory. Chapter 20 discusses these particulars. In order to be concrete, the initial presentation of the theory in this chapter will use stateless components and the non-functional property of program run time. The essential ideas of the theory extend naturally to include state and (a restricted form of) concurrency, in Chapters 10 and 11 respectively.

Section 8.2 above has described component-testing measurements for subdomains. Section 8.3.1 gives the rule for composing two components in sequence that is the heart of the theory. Composition rules for conditional and iterative constructions are given in Sections 8.3.2 and 8.3.3. Section 8.5 describes calculation of the properties of an arbitrary system.

The fundamental ideas behind the theory are very simple:

1. Component behavior can be captured by approximating it as a map from a finite number of input subdomains to output values. This description is finite, but the approximation can be made accurate by careful selection of the subdomains.
2. Subdomain-based descriptions of components can be algorithmically combined into a predicted description of how a system made from them will (approximately) behave. For a series system of C_1 followed by C_2, the algorithm for finding the system behavior on subdomain S is to look up S in the description of C_1; suppose the approximate output of C_1 on S is y and its approximate run time is r_1. Then look up y in the description of C_2; suppose y falls in subdomain S'. For C_2 let the output from S' be z and run time in S' be r_2. Then in the predicated system description, the output for S is approximately z and the system run time is approximately $r_1 + r_2$.

Figure 8.2 illustrates the way in which two component functional maps combine to form a system map. In the figure, the heavy black line at the left represents C_1 (and system-) subdomain S. The subdomain mapping for C_1 sends S to y in a C_2 subdomain S' (middle heavy line). Then the mapping for C_2 carries S' to z. The system mapping W thus carries S directly to z.

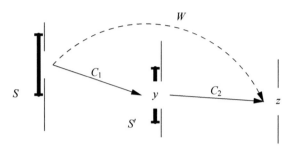

Fig. 8.2 Composing subdomain-defined behavior

8.3.1 Series System

Suppose that two components B and C are to be composed in a series system U as shown in Figure 8.3. The information shown in each shadowed box is a compo-

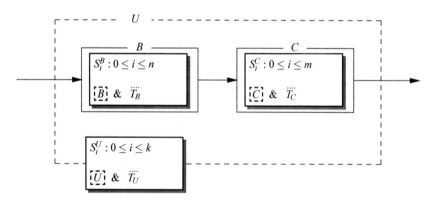

Fig. 8.3 Block diagram of a series system

nent description by subdomains, functional values, and run-time values, as measured for components B and C (Section 8.2), and to be calculated for the composite system U. Figure 8.3 shows the step-function approximation functions, as follows: Let the component subdomains be $S_1^B, S_2^B, ..., S_n^B$ and $S_1^C, S_2^C, ..., S_m^C$ respectively (usually $n \neq m$), and let their corresponding functional approximations be $\lceil \tilde{B} \rceil$ and $\lceil \tilde{C} \rceil$. Let their run-time approximation functions be $\ddot{T}_B$ and $\ddot{T}_C$. It is desired to calculate a set of k subdomains for the system U: $S_1^U, S_2^U, ..., S_k^U$, and to calculate two step functions: $\lceil \tilde{U} \rceil$ for predicted system functional output and $\ddot{T}_U$ for predicted system run time.

The calculation derives an 'equivalent component' for the series system U, a 'component' whose description is in the same form as the description of its constituent components. Thus the calculations can be used repeatedly to synthesize the properties of arbitrary systems (see Section 8.5). To calculate the equivalent component means finding a set of subdomains and predictions on them for input-output and run-time behavior of the system U. The step-function approximation is the most intuitive one to consider.

For the step-function approximation, the system subdomains are those of the initial component B, so $k = n$ and $S_i^U = S_i^B, 1 \leq i \leq k$.

On subdomain S_i^U, B's approximation has constant output value $y = \overline{B}(x)$, where x is any point in S_i^B. Let y fall in the jth subdomain of the following component C. Then the system approximate output value on S_i^U is the constant output of C on S_j^C: $z = \overline{C}(y)$. Since the approximation functions map every subdomain in this way, in summary for all $x \in D$:

$$\overline{U}(x) = \overline{C}(\overline{B}(x)). \tag{8.1}$$

The approximate run time of the system on subdomain S_i^U is the approximate run time of B there plus the approximate run time for C on its jth subdomain as above, that is, $\tilde{T}_B(x) + \tilde{T}_C(y)$, where x is any point in S_i^B and $y \in S_j^C$. That is, for all $x \in D$:

$$\tilde{T}_U(x) = \tilde{T}_B(x) + \tilde{T}_C(\overline{B}(x)). \tag{8.2}$$

It's crucial that the input to $\tilde{T}_C$ be adjusted to account for the functional mapping of B.

Using the piecewise-linear approximation is a considerable improvement because it tracks the way in which outputs from one subdomain of component B disperse into distinct subdomains of component C, as the step-function approximation does not. To see the way in which this happens, consider one subdomain interval $S_i^B = [L, R)$ of the first component, in which the functional behavior is described[3] by a line with slope k and intercept q (that is, this line is $\lambda x(kx + q)$). Then the output range is the interval $S' = [kL + q, kR + q)$. This output may fall into several subdomains of the second component. Let one such intersection be with S_j^C and let the linear approximation of the functional value in S_j^C of the second component be $\lambda x(k'x + q')$. Then the equivalent system component has a subdomain that is a reflection back into S_i^B of part of the output interval: $S'' = S' \cap S_j^C$. If this output intersection is the interval $[L', R')$, then the corresponding part of S_i^B is $((L' - q)/k, (R' - q)/k)$ (if the slope k is 0, the new subdomain is all of S_i^B)[4]. Figure 8.4 illustrates this subdomain construction. The vertical heavy line is a C subdomain and the horizontal heavy line is a subdomain of the calculated equivalent component, formed by re-

---

[3] In the interests of readability the presentation eliminates super- or subscripts on the measured slopes and intercepts that identify the subdomain.

[4] The derivation is correct only for slope $k \geq 0$. When $k < 0$, the end points of the interval in the second component's domain reverse, and there is a technical difficulty because the right end of the interval is open.

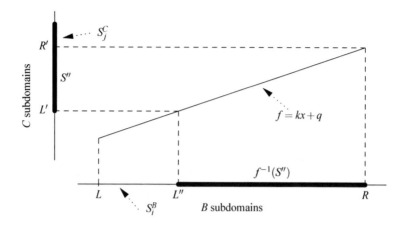

Fig. 8.4 Splitting subdomains in a series synthesis using the stepwise-linear approximation

flecting S'' from the C subdomains into the B subdomains. On this new subdomain the composite functional approximation is the composition of the two lines, that is, it has slope kk' and intercept $k'q + q'$. The composite run-time behavior is similarly obtained for the new subdomain, but it is the sum of the linear run-time functions for the components (say these are: $\lambda x(hx + r)$ and $\lambda x(h'x + r')$), with the second adjusted to receive an input that is the functional output of the first component. This run-time sum line has slope $h + kh'$ and intercept $r + h'q + r'$.

Repeating this calculation for the intersections between each S_j^C and the output ranges of each S_i^B results in a list of subdomains and linear functions on them for the predicted composite functional and run-time behavior. The piecewise-linear approximation improves the subdomains of the calculated system because whenever a linear output from B crosses a subdomain boundary in C (e.g., at L' in Figure 8.4), the equivalent component for the series system acquires a new subdomain boundary (e.g., at L'' in the figure).

In either approximation, the component approximation functions allow calculation of system predictions from equations (8.1) and (8.2) for the step-function case, or from Figure 8.4 and its discussion above for the piecewise-linear case. Predicted system functions define an equivalent component for the system in exactly the same form as the original component approximations. Hence the calculations can be used repetitively to synthesize arbitrary systems as described in Section 8.5.

The quality of the calculated equivalent component—that is, the degree to which it accurately approximates the actual series system—will of course depend on the accuracy of the approximations for the components. The intuition behind the theory is that as subdomains shrink in size, the approximation should be better and the theoretical predictions should improve. For digital input-output data the space is discrete, so each subdomain contains a finite number of points. Hence the smallest possible subdomains are singletons and in this limit the equivalent-component calculations are exact.

8.3.2 Conditional System Control Structure

The sequential construction of Section 8.3.1 can be applied to a conditional:

$$\text{if } B \text{ then } C_T \text{ else } C_F \text{ fi.}$$

Let the three components B, C_T, and C_F have subdomains, functional values[5], and run-time values using the notation of Section 8.3.1. Let B have p subdomains, while C_T and C_F have n and m subdomains, respectively.

The approximation for conditional test component B partitions the input domain D into:

$$D_T = \{x \in D \mid \boxed{B}(x)\} \quad \text{and} \quad D_F = \{x \in D \mid \neg \ \boxed{B}(x)\}.$$

Input $x \in D$ reaches[6] component C_T iff $x \in D_T$ and similarly input elements of D_F reach C_F. The subdomains of the equivalent component to be computed are therefore:

$$D_T \cap S_i^{C_T}, 1 \le i \le n; \quad D_F \cap S_j^{C_F}, 1 \le j \le m. \tag{8.3}$$

On these subdomains, the functional behavior of the equivalent component is that of C_T or C_F respectively. The run-time behavior of the equivalent component is that of B in series with C_T or with C_F respectively.

The calculation of an equivalent system component for a conditional construction is the same for the step-function and piecewise-linear approximations: the split subdomains carry whichever approximation is being used. D_T and D_F are natural subdomains to use for the conditional-test component B because they exactly capture B's functional behavior. For functional behavior it makes no sense to consider B subdomains that cross the *true – false* boundary (that is, a subdomain $S_k^B, 1 \le k \le p$, such that $S_k^B \cap D_T \ne \varnothing \wedge S_k^B \cap D_F \ne \varnothing$), which also means that the piecewise-linear and step-function approximations for functional behavior of a conditional component are the same. However, it may be useful for capturing the run-time behavior of B to break D_T and D_F into smaller subdomains or to use a piecewise-linear approximation for B's run time.

A conditional construction with no **else** part is equivalent to taking C_F an identity component with zero run time, which has a perfect piecewise-linear approximation.

Whenever a synthesis construction uses subdomain intersection, that is: for conditionals, in a piecewise-linear series combination, and in iteration (next Section), the count of synthesized subdomains may be as large as the product of the counts for the components. This means that the subdomain count can grow exponentially in the

---

[5] It is conventional to use the output of B only to determine the branch; whichever of C_T and C_F is selected receives the same input that B received, not B's output.

[6] At least insofar as the approximation to B knows.

number of system components. Fortunately, there are some mitigating factors. First, systems are seldom built with more than a handful of components. Second, whenever a series synthesis has a first component with a step-function approximation, it fixes the synthesis count irrespective of the second-component's count. And finally, since the output range of a first component must be contained in the input domain of one that follows, subdomain boundaries tend to line up so that intersections quickly stabilize.

8.3.3 Iterative System Control Structure

The remaining basic system construct is iteration. Iterative constructions are the bane of program analysis, because in general their behavior cannot be algorithmically obtained in closed form. For this theory things are better than usual. Since there are only a finite number of subdomains, a prediction for loop behavior can be calculated deterministically.

The step-function approximation is easiest to analyze. Begin by unwinding the loop

$$\text{while } B \text{ do } C \text{ od} \quad \text{to} \quad \text{if } B \text{ then } C \text{ fi; while } B \text{ do } C \text{ od.}$$

The trailing loop after the unwound conditional is called the *residual loop*. On any intersection subdomain of the B and C containing y where $[\bar{B}]([\bar{C}](y))$ is *false*, the residual loop makes no contribution; these 'false' subdomains can be eliminated from consideration. If there remain intersection subdomains for which $[\bar{B}]$ is *true* on the subdomain output, the loop can be unwound a second time and further subdomains may disappear because $[\bar{B}]$ is false on them. Continuing, at each unwinding at least one subdomain is eliminated, or none is eliminated. In the latter case, the remaining subdomains are all mapped to one other by $[\bar{C}]$ and this situation cannot change, so the approximation to the iterated behavior does not terminate. But unless this occurs, the residual loop will entirely disappear in at most m unwindings, where m is no more than the product of the number of subdomains of B and of C. Thus the equivalent component for an iterative construction is algorithmically determined in the step-function approximation.

For the piecewise-linear approximation, the series composition of the successive unwound loops can introduce new subdomains as described in Section 8.3.1, Figure 8.4. However, the process is necessarily limited. In the worst case, each of the m intersection subdomains between B and C will be split into m pieces; then no further splitting can occur. The argument for the step-function case then shows that at most m^2 unwindings will either eliminate the residual loop or stabilize on a set of 'true' subdomains that never changes so the approximation loop will not terminate.

If the C subdomains are not fine enough to capture the functional behavior of the loop body well, two difficulties may arise: First, the approximation $[\bar{C}]$ may map out of D_T for some subdomain(s) in equation (8.3), but $\boxed{C}$ does not, so that the loop calculation terminates when the real loop is infinite. The equivalent component will then be erroneous on those subdomains. Second, the value of $\lceil \bar{C} \rceil$ may always fall in D_T for some subdomain(s) but this is an approximation error, so that the calculated equivalent component is undefined in those subdomains even though the real loop does terminate there. The payment for algorithmic loop analysis is that the equivalent-component calculation only approximates the behavior of the iteration construct.

Some care is required in calculating the run-time prediction for a loop, because the unwinding equivalence does not hold for run time—it repeats the conditional B too often, which does not change the functional value but inflates the run time. Proper calculation adds in the B run time only on those subdomains that remain *true* as the calculation proceeds. (In Chapter 10 it will appear that state is not properly treated by unwinding loops, for much the same reason.)

8.4 Combining Different Component Approximations

Although the step-function approximation to component behavior is in general less accurate than the piecewise-linear approximation, steps are sometimes preferred, as in Boolean-valued discontinuous conditional components. In Section 8.5.1 to follow, it is shown that step-function approximations combine easily with components that have been proved correct; linear approximations do not. Furthermore, the input-output (functional) behavior of a component and its non-functional behavior may not be best approximated in the same way. Run time, for example, always has a meaningful piecewise-linear approximation; other non-functional properties like reliability do not (see Chapter 12). Thus there are a number of interesting cases in which components to be combined might have differing approximation measurements. The synthesis theory of the previous sections covers mixed cases without modification.

Input-output functional synthesis makes no use of a non-functional property like run time, so they need not be approximated in the same way. Although run time synthesis does require an input-output approximation, nothing says what form that must take. Hence mixed cases like step-function input-output approximation and piecewise-linear run time approximation require no changes to the synthesis algorithms.

The iteration construction of Section 8.3.3 is presented in terms of conditionals and sequences, so it requires no modification for a mixed case.

The conditional construction of Section 8.3.2, once a set of intersection subdomains has been obtained, only reproduces the behavior of the components in its *true* and *false* branches, which may thus be differently approximated.

In the series construction of Section 8.3.1 the algorithm for piecewise-linear approximation handles both possibilities, which may therefore be mixed. However, if one of two components in series has a step-function approximation, it does determine the prediction for the combination. When it is the first component in series that is a step function, there is no subdomain splitting. No matter which of the two has a step-function approximation, the result will be a step function.

8.5 Synthesizing a Component-based System

At the top level of a 'main' imperative program, any system can be built up inductively using the three elementary structured-programming constructions of sequence, conditional, and iteration. The standard software analysis/synthesis paradigm is to:

- Obtain a general rule for each elementary construction in isolation, then
- Perform system calculations piece by piece, using each construction for a given system.

In this way, the largest system is no more difficult to handle than the simplest—it just takes more applications of the three elementary-construction rules.

The rules for constructing an equivalent system 'component' for each of the constructs are given in Sections 8.3.1 (sequence), 8.3.2 (conditional), and 8.3.3 (iteration). To synthesize an arbitrary system, these rules are applied repeatedly. Each time a part of the system is synthesized, it is replaced by a calculated equivalent component, which then enters into subsequent synthesis[7].

It is convenient to describe an arbitrary system structure in reverse Polish notation, using the operators $\mathbf{S}$, $\mathbf{C}$, and $\mathbf{L}$:

Construct	Polish
$X; Y$	XY $\mathbf{S}$
if Z then X else Y fi	ZXY $\mathbf{C}$
while Z do X od	ZX $\mathbf{L}$

For example, Fig. 8.5 shows the Polish representation for an illustrative flowchart and its reduction to an equivalent component (E_4). In the figure, components are named by integers. The final component (E_4 in Fig. 8.5) has the calculated behavior of the complete system as its functional- and run-time predictions.

8.5.1 Combining Testing and Proving

One of the promises of CBSE and the reuse of components is the prospect that over time it will be possible to prove some components correct, that is, to derive exact mathematical descriptions $\boxed{C}$ and/or T_C for C rather than measuring a testing

---

[7] Although system synthesis was envisaged from the outset, the algorithms given in early published versions of the theory [52, 70] cannot be used with components that result from previous compositions. This was a mistake that came to light only when supporting tools were implemented.

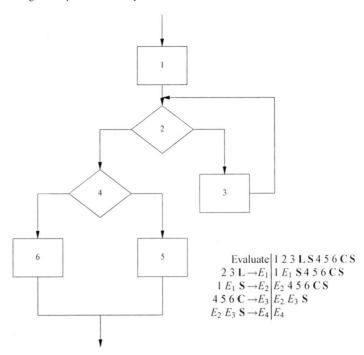

Evaluate	1 2 3 L S 4 5 6 C S
2 3 L $\rightarrow E_1$	1 E_1 S 4 5 6 C S
1 E_1 S $\rightarrow E_2$	E_2 4 5 6 C S
4 5 6 C $\rightarrow E_3$	E_2 E_3 S
E_2 E_3 S $\rightarrow E_4$	E_4

Fig. 8.5 System synthesis by computing equivalent components

approximation. Such a proved component can be incorporated in a system synthesis using the step-function approximation for other components. Suppose that C occurs in a series combination with B_b before and B_a after: B_b; C; B_a. Then in the synthesis algorithm of Section 8.3.1, instead of looking up the values of $\boxed{B_b}$ in C, look up values of $\boxed{C} \circ \boxed{B_b}$ in B_a. That is, the approximation functions 'map through' C. T_C can be used directly in the synthesis formulas in place of $\tilde{T}_C$.

It is disappointing that a similar construction does not work in general for piecewise-linear approximations. The difficulty is that although a constant function is mapped by an arbitrary function to another constant function, the same is not true for a linear function in composition. For example, if across some subdomain of B_b the linear approximation is $\lambda x(mx + b)$, composing (say) $\boxed{C} = \lambda x(x^2)$ gives the non-linear $\lambda x((mx + b)^2)$. Had the B_b approximation been $\lambda x(K)$ for constant K, the composition would be the constant $\lambda x(K^2)$. It's not that a non-linear function's values can't be looked up in B_a, but that the results cannot be recorded in a piecewise-linear form as required for continued synthesis.

8.6 Summary of the Subdomain Testing Theory

The synthesis algorithms given in this chapter take as input: a system description and subdomain test results for the components it uses. They return as output: predictions for system behavior. The predictions are in the same form as the component descriptions, so they might be viewed as test approximations for the system, obtained without any system testing. The sense of 'approximation' is quite different for component measurements and for system predictions, however. On any system subdomain, the synthesis algorithms predict a value (a constant in the step-function approximation, or a slope-intercept pair in the piecewise-linear approximation). But the prediction is not a measurement, and does not behave like one. For example, it does not necessarily have the mean value property one expects of a measurement[8]: The predicted value may lie above or below all actual test values in a subdomain. In no sense is the prediction an average of actual values.

The theoretical results are as they should be. Tests are approximations, and from them one cannot expect perfect predictions. It is a pleasant surprise that the synthesis algorithms exist at all. The ability to make predictions in general, even when there are loops, using only component-test data, is a considerable advance over 'tests are not compositional.'

---

[8] Continuous functions, step-function approximation.

Chapter 9
Tutorial Example – SYN Tools for Stateless Components

T HIS chapter is a virtual tour through the simplest application of the supporting SYN tools described in Chapter 14 and Appendix A—the components used in the tutorial are purely functional, with no persistent state or concurrency. In testing terms, this means that every test of each component is independent and repeatable. Components are completely defined by their blackbox behavior.

In the examples of this chapter (and throughout the book), the presentation is self-contained and can be read without using the SYN software that is provided with the book. However, the examples also serve as a tutorial to using the tools. The reader who wants to learn about the tools can execute them as the text suggests and observe the results, or try variations along the way. When describing tools and their use, the exposition is in the usual Roman font; monospaced 'typewriter' font is used for program input/output and the contents of computer files (boxed and labeled with the file name); A slanted san-serif font on a shaded background marks instructions and comments that are of interest only to someone actually using the tools.

The SYN tools comprise about 8000 lines of Perl scripts. They are 'command-line' tools, lacking any GUI front end. From the beginning, the emphasis has been on devising a 'calculation engine,' whose strength is in its unique algorithms, not its support for pointing, dragging, and clicking. The tools were developed on a GNU/LINUX platform (kubuntu distribution), and there should be no difficulty using them on the popular LINUX distributions, which all include Perl. Current Mac OS X is a UNIX platform and includes Perl. For Microsoft Windows things are a bit more difficult—Perl will have to be installed. The only other support software needed is the graphing package GNUPlot. GNUPlot is not included in some LINUX distributions, but is easy to install, particularly in the Debian-based distributions. The Internet is well stocked with advice about how to install GNUPlot on Mac OS X and Windows. (If you have a choice, get an X-windows version, which has more interactive features.) The software distribution that accompanies the book includes advice on preparing each platform to run its tools.

D. Hamlet, *Composing Software Components*, DOI 10.1007/978-1-4419-7148-7_9,   111
© Springer Science+Business Media, LLC 2010

9.1 Getting Started

Any example of I-CBSD using the SYN tools has the same overall form:

- Component descriptions are created.
- Component-level tools make and record testing measurements (additional descriptions) of each component.
- A system description is created using component descriptions.
- System-synthesis (CAD) tools calculate properties of the system.

The first and third steps are creative operations performed by human beings. The other steps are done automatically by the SYN tools. The entire process always takes place within a single base directory and is controlled by a few files there. The tools themselves reside in the base directory and are executed there. A person using the tools creates files in the base directory[1] (using his/her favorite text editor), then executes SYN commands to process those files. Results are in turn sent to other files and to the screen as text and graphs.

Each component has a 'base name' (for example, comp1), and a description given in a file with that name and extension .ccf (for "component configuration file"), e.g., comp1.ccf. *The extension .ccf is mandatory; the base name must be an alphanumeric string.* This configuration file points to the executable code of the component and lists the subdomains (with sample counts for each) on which it is to be tested. For example, the file:

```
 ── comp1.ccf ──

comp1bin
0  1  3
1  5  7
5  10  2
```

describes a component whose executable code file is comp1bin, to be tested on three subdomains: $[0,1), [1,5), [5,10)$, with 3, 7, 2 test points respectively. *The executable file name must be alphanumeric with no extension.* Suppose that there are two other component descriptions in the base directory with base names comp2, comp3.

A system to be synthesized is described in the base directory by a file with the fixed name system.pscf (for polish system configuration file). This configuration file lists the components to be used by their configuration-file names, and begins with a reverse Polish description of the system control flow among them. For example,

---

[1] Using a single base directory can lead to name-space confusion. If one of the SYN script names duplicates an operating-system command name, the latter takes precedence. The script names were chosen to be unique in most systems. A potentially more frequent problem is a user choice for an executable code-file name that duplicates another command name. However, the simplicity of 'everything under one roof' seems worth the price. If something truly bizarre occurs, the chances are that there is a name confusion.

```
 ┌─ system.pscf ──┐
 │                │
 │ 1  2 S  3 S    │
 │ comp1.ccf      │
 │ comp2.ccf      │
 │ comp3.ccf      │
 │                │
 └────────────────┘
```

describes a system using the three components mentioned above, with the control
flow: comp1 is placed in series (S) with comp2 and the result is placed in series
with comp3. The reverse Polish expression in the first line refers by their line numbers to the components listed below it. (Other Polish operators C for Conditional
and L for Loop are described in the next section.)

Given the files describing system and components, the component measurements
and system synthesis are automatic. The command

COMP

tests the components, while

SYN

synthesizes the system. *The commands given in the text run the scripts with that
name on a UNIX (or Mac) system in which the* PATH *environment variable includes
'.', the current directory. Without this* PATH *the commands must name the directory, e.g., './COMP', although of course there are many other ways to avoid naming
the directory. On a Mac the commands are typed in a 'Terminal' window. On Windows a 'command line' window is required.* Without options on these commands,
the work is done silently and results are stored in files in the base directory where
other tools can display and use them. By adding the option -V to either command,
messages from the tools will describe what is taking place. Adding -G displays
result graphs.

*When trying variations of an example, the safest and least confusing way is to
create and use a different base directory for each change, rather than to edit files
within an existing base directory.*

9.2 A Simple Complete Example

For the remainder of this chapter, a rudimentary example will be used to show
features of the SYN tools for stateless components. The example is artificial: its
components don't do anything very interesting and they are pasted together into
a system without real purpose. The tutorial purpose is to demonstrate the tools
in a way that is easy to understand. *The distribution is located on the Internet
at* http://cs.pdx.edu/~hamlet/bookload.html, *where there are instructions for downloading into your file system. The files for this example are in
the directory* statelesstutorial. *For the demonstration, create a directory
named (say)* mytutorial *and copy all the files from* statelesstutorial

into it. Also copy all the tool scripts to `mytutorial` *from the distribution direc-tory* `tools`. *These operations set up a base directory.*

To keep details to a minimum, only two component descriptions are used in the example. One, with base name `Math`, calculates a Gaussian with a distorting discontinuity to the left of its mean. (`Math` is nearly the same function as the program `Bell` in Chapter 1, but translated into Perl so as not to strain those who are C-challenged, and with a different mean and a different amplitude that makes composition more interesting.) The other component, with base name `Cond`, is a conditional component used to direct the flow of control. The two components are replicated several times and placed in a system control structure that includes sequences, a conditional, and a loop, the three operations of 'structured' system construction [10]. Figure 9.1 is a flowgraph of the example system. Each component in the figure has a unique name (which will be needed to discuss internal profiles in Section 9.5) but C_1, C_3, C_5, C_6, and C_7 are copies of `Math` while C_2 and C_4 are copies of `Cond`. The system structure and content could also be written in pseudocode as:

C_1; while C_2 do C_3 od; if C_4 then C_7 else C_5; C_6 fi

or in a less Algol-like form:

```
C1
WHILE C2 DO
   C3
OD
IF C4 THEN
   C7
ELSE
   C5
   C6
FI
```

Component code can be written in any language. Only executable files are used by the **SYN** tools, but for better understanding of the example, the source code is also displayed here. `Math` and `Cond` are written in Perl so these are the executable files. *Perl files are executed by interpreting the source, which must be made 'executable' for the platform being used. The UNIX command is* `chmod +x Math Cond`; *on Windows there is a trick involving a 'batch' file described in the distribution.* An interval of $[0, 100)$ is arbitrarily chosen as input domain for the example.

Figure 9.2 shows the description of `Math` and Fig. 9.3 describes `Cond`. The `Math` input domain is divided into 24 almost equal-sized subdomains, while `Cond` has 16 subdomains[2]. The subdomain boundaries have been aligned with the known discontinuities in `Math` and `Cond`. For `Cond` these are the points (25.0 and 50.0) where the truth value switches; for `Math` they capture the artificial discontinuity introduced around input 20.0.

---

[2] The subdomain descriptions in `Math.ccf` and `Cond.ccf` were created by hand editing files with 12 and 8 subdomains respectively, then mechanically splitting each subdomain in half using the tool command `splitsub 1` described in Appendix A.

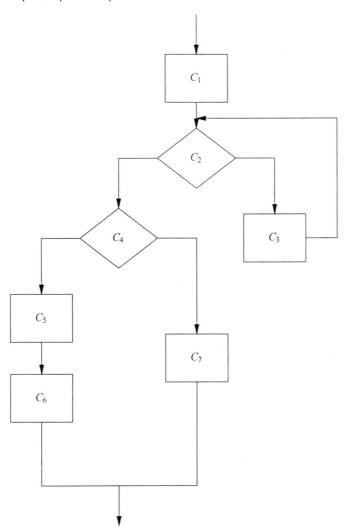

Fig. 9.1 Simple system structure to be populated with two simple components

(As seen in what immediately follows, it isn't necessary to look at the source code to discover these natural boundaries, but the sources would be available to a component developer using the SYN tools.) Each subdomain is to be sampled (tested) 5 times for Math (3 times within the constant region between the discontinuities) and 3 times for Cond. The manual work of creating components is now finished. *All of the files required to run the tutorial have been copied into your file* mytutorial. *The two Perl code files are marked as executable. (The* COMP *command should detect a component whose code is not executable.)* Math.ccf *has been replicated*

```
——— Math.ccf ———
Math
0  5  5
5  10  5
10  13  5
13  16  5
16  18  3
18  20  3
20  22  3
22  24  3
24  27  5
27  30  5
30  35  5
35  40  5
40  45  5
45  50  5
50  55  5
55  60  5
60  65  5
65  70  5
70  75  5
75  80  5
80  85  5
85  90  5
90  95  5
95  100  5
```

```
——————————— Math ———————————
#! /usr/bin/perl
$x = <STDIN>;
$mu = 45.0;
$sigma = 20.0;
$ex = ($x - $mu)/$sigma;
$y = exp(-$ex*$ex);
$z = 2.0 - $x/(1.7*$mu);
if ($z < 0) {
   $z = 0;
}
$gap = 20;
$gw = 4.0;
if ($x >= $gap-$gw && $x < $gap+$gw) {
   $y = 0.6;
   $z = 1.9;
}
$y *= 95.0;
print "$y\n";
print STDERR "$z\n";
```

Fig. 9.2 Configuration description file and code for `Math`

as `C1.ccf`, `C3.ccf`, etc., and `Cond.ccf` as `C2.ccf` and `C4.ccf`. *Now is the time to examine the files in the directory* `mytutorial` *if you like.*

The SYN component-testing tools can now create the step-function approximations to be used in system synthesis. When they do so, in response to the command

    COMP -V -G

they display graphs of behaviors and a table of approximation errors. The latter will be discussed in Section 9.3. Part of the tool output is:

```
Configuration file C1.ccf with code file Math:
  stateless with 24 input subdomains on [0, 100)
Configuration file C1.ccf seems OK
Creating testing-measurements file C1.ccft...
--------------------------------
Configuration file C2.ccf with code file Cond:
  stateless with 16 input subdomains on [0, 100)
Configuration file C2.ccf seems OK
Creating testing-measurements file C2.ccft...
--------------------------------
```

```
┌──── Cond.ccf ────┐
│ Cond
│ 0  10  3
│ 10  20  3
│ 20  22.5  3
│ 22.5  25  3
│ 25  27.5  3
│ 27.5  30  3
│ 30  35  3
│ 35  40  3
│ 40  45  3
│ 45  50  3
│ 50  55  3
│ 55  60  3
│ 60  70  3
│ 70  80  3
│ 80  90  3
│ 90  100  3
└──────────────────┘
```

```
┌───────────── Cond ─────────────┐
│ #! /usr/bin/perl
│ $x = <STDIN>;
│ $y = 0;
│ $z = 1;
│ if ($x >= 25 && $x < 50) {
│     $y = 1;
│     $z = 2;
│ }
│ print "$y\n";
│ print STDERR "$z\n";
└────────────────────────────────┘
```

Fig. 9.3 Configuration description file and code for Cond

(The output for duplicates C3, etc. has been elided.) COMP checks the configuration files, for example to see that the subdomains form a mathematical partition of some interval, and that the sampling count is present. The check includes an actual execution of the code file with a subsequent check on its observance of the input-output conventions required by the tools. In the example above these checks were successful; if they fail, no measurements file is produced, and COMP must be retried after the problem has been repaired.

Figure 9.4 shows part of the graphical output for Math, as component C1. It shows measurements of the functional values and their step-function approximations. The subdomains are marked on the x-axis; notice how they were chosen around the discontinuity. Although the measured values look like a smooth curve, not plotted data points, this is an illusion of using some 72 samples across the entire input domain [0,100); on a printed page the plotted points are only about 0.07 inches apart, and the GNUPlot plotting software joins them with a line.

If this were an actual software development, the component developer would study the smooth curve of Fig. 9.4 to see whether the code is behaving properly, but for present purposes it just describes the output behavior given to the (almost) Gaussian Math. The component developer in an actual case would also study the step-function approximation to evaluate how well the test subdomains capture the behavior. The latter aspect of component testing will be discussed in Section 9.4 to follow. For the purposes of exposition it is helpful to have only a few subdomains. This makes the displays clear, but the behavior capture is not so good[3].

---

[3] But notice in Fig. 9.4 that in the subdomains around input 20 the functional value *is* constant and is perfectly captured.

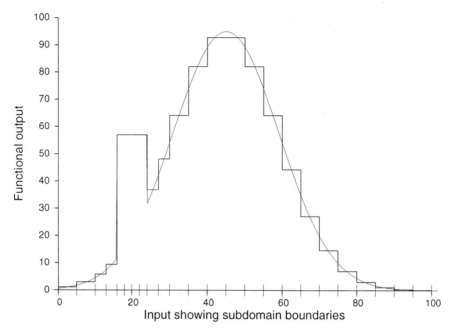

Fig. 9.4 Measurements (*smooth curve*) and approximations (*step function*) of `Math` input-output behavior

The other part of the analysis output from `COMP` captures non-functional behavior of `Math`. Because run time is a natural property of software, that is how the tools identify the single non-functional property that components are permitted. However, the SYN tools are written to allow code an arbitrary non-functional property. What is being called 'run time' is nothing more or less than whatever the code writes to `STDERR`. This could be its actual run time, but often (as in this example) the real run time isn't very interesting, so `Math` creates and sends to `STDERR` a more interesting function. (Discussion of artificial components that report a run time but do not actually run for that time appears in Chapter 14, and non-functional properties are discussed in Chapter 20.) Figure 9.5 shows that the `Math` 'run time' is a decreasing linear function with an discontinuous exception similar to that inserted in the functional behavior.

The other component in this sample system is `Cond` (C2 and C4). Figures 9.6 and 9.7 show the behaviors of `Cond`, whose output is *true* (nonzero) just in the interval [25.0, 50.0]. `Cond` is given a 'run time' of 2.0 when *true*, 1.0 when *false*[4]. Because `Cond` has piecewise-constant behaviors and because the measurement subdomains are aligned with the 'pieces,' the measurements are perfect, not approximations at all.

---

[4] Again, not the real run time, but closer to reality than for `Math`.

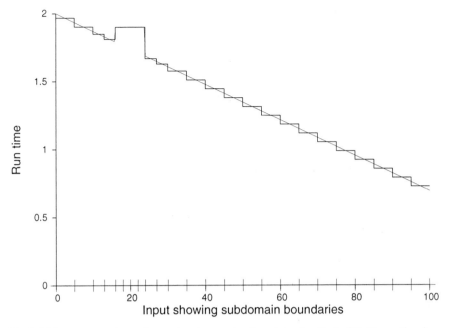

Fig. 9.5 Measurements (*smooth curve*) and approximations (*step function*) of Math run-time behavior

The graphs of input-output and run-time behavior have been separated in this presentation. The tools actually display both behaviors on a single graph using color and dual output axes to clarify a crowded presentation.

The developer could have used the output from COMP shown in these figures to find good subdomain boundaries instead of examining the code.

Because the COMP command tests all components in a system, it makes graphs for each of C1, C2, ..., C7, each a copy of either Math or Comp. These graphs are left in persistent windows so that they may be studied after the component testing is complete. These windows are closed with an enter/return keystroke in the window where the command was issued, allowing COMP to go on to the next measurement and graph.

To calculate the properties of the system in Fig. 9.1, it must be described to the SYN tools. The polish system configuration file is shown in Fig. 9.8; remember that each component name actually refers to a copy of either Math or Cond. The synthesis run is made by the command

```
SYN -V -G
```

with the output trace shown in Fig. 9.9. that describes each step in the synthesis. First the loop is synthesized, which requires three unwindings. In the first, 10 subdomains are eliminated; in the second 4 more; in the third the remaining 3 subdomains. The result is an intermediate 'component' theory1. Now both parts of the first series are available, so the series can be synthesized as intermediate theory2. To do the

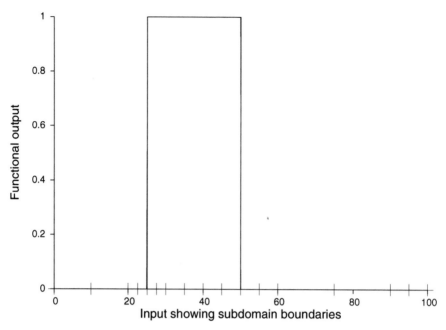

Fig. 9.6 Measurements and approximations of Cond input-output behavior

following conditional, first the series in the *false* arm is synthesized as theory3, then the conditional as theory4. Finally the last series uses two of the intermediate 'components' to create theory5.

The theory 'components' created in each synthesis step are in the same approximation form as those created by the COMP command. The final component theory5 is graphed with an error analysis (Section 9.3 to follow) because of the -G option. Figure 9.10 shows this SYN input-output prediction.

The graphing can also be done by an auxiliary command

    Xcute theory5

since theory5 is the synthesized system. Xcute can be used to display intermediate calculations in the system synthesis; for example,

    Xcute theory3

displays the calculated input-output behavior of C5 in series with C6, i.e., Math with itself (Fig. 9.11).

Running the tools typically produces more information than is displayed in this exposition. For example, SYN -G actually shows both input-output and run-time graphs, also shows graphs measured by executing the system for comparison with predictions, and also gives an error analysis by subdomain. But Xcute shows only the prediction part if explicitly given a calculated approximation file. You might want to look at the behavior of other intermediate synthesis products, for example theory1 for the loop. Xcute also has other useful capabilities. It can select a region of the tested input domain and use more test points in the measure-

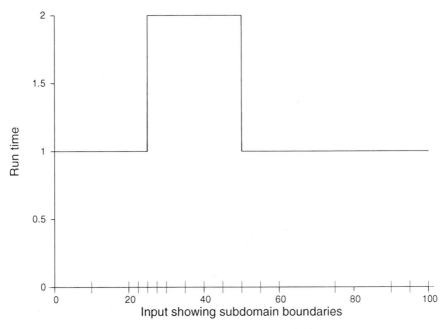

Fig. 9.7 Measurements and approximations of Cond run-time behavior

```
───────  system.pscf  ───────
1  2  3  L  S  4  7  5  6  S  C  S
C1.ccf
C2.ccf
C3.ccf
C4.ccf
C5.ccf
C6.ccf
C7.ccf
```

Fig. 9.8 Configuration description file for the system of Fig. 9.1

ment of actual behavior. For example, Xcute C1 10 60 300 would use 300 test points on [10,60) instead of a default number (72, from adding the test counts in the Math.ccf description file). Sometimes it is necessary to increase the test count because the actual behavior of a function isn't captured well enough by the tests COMP used to create its approximation. When a tool like Xcute has too many options to remember, consulting its script will remind you; the tool scripts each begin with a summary comment describing the options.

SYN predictions are step functions of course, since they are calculated from the measured step functions of the components. As the measurements are approximations, the predictions may be inaccurate. But it isn't quite right to refer to prediction

```
Beginning the system calculation of
    Polish 1 2 3 L S 4 7 5 6 S C S
Loop:  WHILE Cond(C2) DO Math(C3) OD -> theory1
  Conditional:  IF Cond(C2) THEN Math(C3) ELSE (ident) FI
     -> once -> again
  (7/17 active)
  Compose: once o again -> again 3/17 subdomains still active
  Loop terminated (in theory) on 17 subdomains
Series: Math(C1) ; theory1 -> theory2
Series: Math(C5) ; Math(C6) -> theory3
Conditional:  IF Cond(C4) THEN Math(C7) ELSE theory3 FI
     -> theory4
Series: theory2 ; theory4 -> theory5
```

Fig. 9.9 Synthesis trace from SYN -V

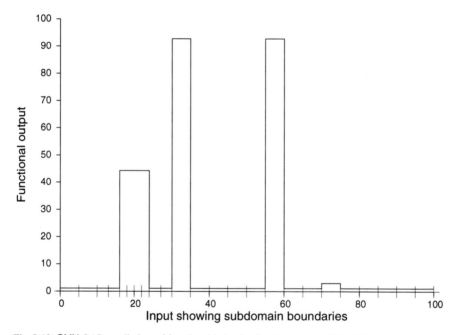

Fig. 9.10 SYN CAD prediction of functional behavior for the system of Fig. 9.1

graphs such as Fig. 9.10 as approximations. The measurement of Fig. 9.4 *is* an approximation obtained by testing Math and setting a step function to the average test values in each subdomain. But Fig. 9.10 is *not* obtained by testing the system and fitting an approximating step function. Rather, the SYN CAD tool *calculates* a system step function from the component measurements. The accuracy of the component measurements depends on the component code and the subdomains selected to test it. The accuracy of the system calculation is something else: if it's close to what the system actually does, then the theory behind it (Chapters 6 and 8) is vali-

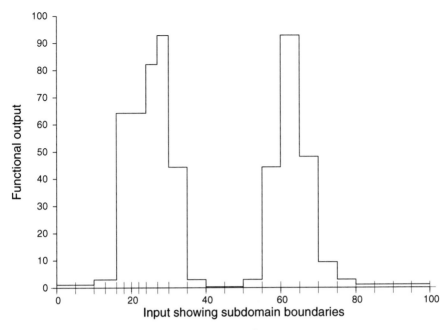

Fig. 9.11 SYN CAD prediction of functional behavior for C5 ; C6

dated; if it's badly wrong, something's wrong with that theory. (For more discussion see Section 9.3 on errors below, Chapter 17 on prediction accuracy, and Chapter 15 on debugging.) Figure 9.12 (really what SYN -G displays) overlays Fig. 9.10 with measurements of the actual system, obtained by linking the components' code and sampling its execution. In this case the calculated result is good in some places and terrible in others. It is easy to improve the predictions—see Section 9.4.

The actual output from SYN -G includes the functional predictions and measured values shown in Fig. 9.12, and two similar graphs for run time, shown in Fig 9.13. The non-functional prediction seems to be better than the functional one. The run-time prediction is of course a step function, and appears in Fig. 9.13 to be a linear approximation, as might be expected from combining components with linear run times. But the measured part of Fig. 9.13 shows that the system run time is *not* linear; the contrary appearance is only an artifact of using crude subdomains. Section 9.4 provides more discussion.

Although the tutorial presented in this chapter is no more than an artificial example that demonstrates using the SYN tools, Figs. 9.12 and 9.13 deserve some comment. First of all, without tool support it would be difficult to imagine how even this very simple system behaves. The system functional behavior has a number of discontinuities that are not simply related to component behaviors. Although the system run time is less complicated, it too is unexpectedly varied. In particular, any attempt to estimate the system run time by combining values from the components is doomed. A worst-case analysis (adding the largest run times from the longest se-

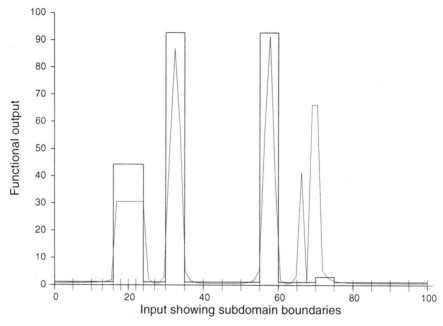

Fig. 9.12 SYN CAD predictions (*step function*) compared with system measurements (*smooth curve*) for the system of Fig. 9.1

quence of components) gives an upper bound of 16; but the bound in Fig. 9.13 is about 13, and for about 80% of the domain the prediction is around 7.

9.3 Approximation and Prediction Errors

Output from Xcute commands (Section 9.2) used to test component execution or the COMP -G command (which uses Xcute) includes an error analysis as well as the measured and approximated graphs (e.g., Fig. 9.4). Figure 9.14 is the error output corresponding to Figs. 9.4 and 9.5. Each subdomain has a line in the error table. The number in curly brackets is the count of measurements that fell in that subdomain. In general, the r-m-s approximation error is larger when the measured functions are changing more rapidly. Within a subdomain, the constant approximation is too high on one part of a rising curve and too low on the other—both errors contribute to the r-m-s error. If the curve is linear, the r-m-s error is nearly the same for all subdomains, as for most of the run-time case in Fig. 9.14. The component developer can thus reduce approximation error by adjusting subdomains. For example, Fig. 9.15 compares a region of measurements from Fig. 9.4 with ones obtained from Math subdomains half as large. The left side of Fig. 9.15 is a part of Fig. 9.14 (24 subdomains) expanded on the interval [20,40]; the right side is for 48 subdo-

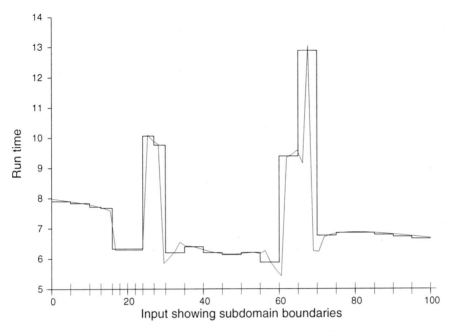

Fig. 9.13 SYN CAD prediction of run-time behavior for the system of Fig. 9.1 compared with measurements

mains. *The commands that produced these graphs were* Xcute C1 15 35 300. *The higher sampling rate improves the graphs.* Subdomains half the size yield approximation errors less than half as large. Figure 9.16 displays errors reported by Xcute C1 15 35 300 for 24 subdomains in a few of those subdomains, with results for 48 subdomains indented after each. Halving the subdomain size roughly halves the r-m-s errors. *An auxiliary tool* splitsub *is provided to make it easy to experiment with subdomain splitting. Executed in a base directory (like* mytutorial *here),* splitsub *creates five new base directories in the parent directory of* mytutorial *named* mytutorial2, ..., mytutorial22222, *in each of which all the subdomains of all components in the system are successively halved, so that in directory* mytutorial22222 C1.ccf *would have* $24 \times 2^5 = 768$ *subdomains.*

Output from SYN -G also includes an error analysis. Figure 9.17 corresponds to Figs. 9.10 and 9.13. The '{count}' at the left of Fig. 9.17 is the number of samples in executing the system for comparison that fell into the listed subdomain. Since the entire domain is sampled with equi-spaced points, smaller subdomains receive fewer hits. These prediction errors are far worse than the measurement errors in any one component. This might be expected in that as components are combined to synthesize the system, their errors might accumulate. This isn't the whole story, but further discussion will be postponed until Chapter 17. It is surprising that the

```
Sampling [0.00, 100.00) for 300 points
normalized rms errors
count    interval           func    run
{15}     [0.00,   5.00)     0.65%   1.34%
{15}     [5.00,  10.00)     1.55%   1.34%
{9}      [10.00, 13.00)     1.67%   0.81%
{9}      [13.00, 16.00)     2.46%   0.81%
{6}      [16.00, 18.00)     0.00%   0.00%
{6}      [18.00, 20.00)     0.00%   0.00%
{6}      [20.00, 22.00)     0.00%   0.00%
{6}      [22.00, 24.00)     0.00%   0.00%
{9}      [24.00, 27.00)     6.21%   0.80%
{9}      [27.00, 30.00)     6.89%   0.80%
{15}     [30.00, 35.00)    11.60%   1.34%
{15}     [35.00, 40.00)     8.96%   1.34%
{15}     [40.00, 45.00)     3.52%   1.33%
{15}     [45.00, 50.00)     3.49%   1.33%
{15}     [50.00, 55.00)     8.93%   1.33%
{15}     [55.00, 60.00)    11.59%   1.33%
{15}     [60.00, 65.00)    11.16%   1.34%
{15}     [65.00, 70.00)     8.73%   1.34%
{15}     [70.00, 75.00)     5.73%   1.34%
{15}     [75.00, 80.00)     3.21%   1.34%
{15}     [80.00, 85.00)     1.55%   1.34%
{15}     [85.00, 90.00)     0.65%   1.34%
{15}     [90.00, 95.00)     0.24%   1.34%
{15}     [95.00, 100.00)    0.08%   1.34%
Weighted ave:               4.60%   1.17%
   Maximum:                11.60%   1.34%
```

Fig. 9.14 Relative r-m-s errors in subdomain measurements approximating Math behavior

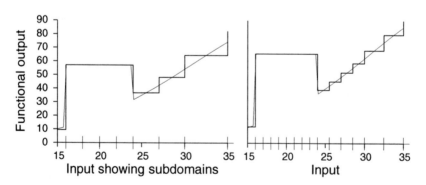

Fig. 9.15 Comparison of measurements around input 25 for two sizes of Math subdomains

run-time prediction is badly off in a few subdomains, since the component run-time approximations are perfect.

The SYN -G *command actually executes a script similar to* Xcute *called* Xcomp *to produce the graphs and error analysis.* Xcomp *can vary the interval dis-*

```
Sampling [0.00, 100.00) for 300 points
normalized rms errors
24 subdomains
  48 subdomains

count    interval            func      run

{9}      [13.00, 16.00)     2.46%    0.81%
  {5}        [13.00, 14.50)    1.23%    0.44%
  {4}        [14.50, 16.00)    1.16%    0.35%

{6}      [16.00, 18.00)     0.00%    0.00%
  {3}        [16.00, 17.00)    0.00%    0.00%
  {3}        [17.00, 18.00)    0.00%    0.00%
....

{6}      [22.00, 24.00)     0.00%    0.00%
  {3}        [22.00, 23.00)    0.00%    0.00%
  {3}        [23.00, 24.00)    0.00%    0.00%

{9}      [24.00, 27.00)     6.21%    0.80%
  {5}        [24.00, 25.50)    3.28%    0.44%
  {4}        [25.50, 27.00)    2.78%    0.35%

{9}      [27.00, 30.00)     6.89%    0.80%
  {5}        [27.00, 28.50)    3.70%    0.44%
  {4}        [28.50, 30.00)    3.02%    0.35%

{15}     [30.00, 35.00)    11.60%    1.34%
  {8}        [30.00, 32.50)    6.26%    0.71%
  {7}        [32.50, 35.00)    5.23%    0.62%

Weighted ave:              4.60%    1.17%
  Weighted ave:              2.27%    0.58%
```

Fig. 9.16 Comparison of approximation errors for two sizes of Math subdomains

played and change the number of sample points used for the measured comparison in the same way as Xcute.

Better-approximated components usually reduce system prediction errors. Halving all the subdomains in Cond and in Math as in Fig. 9.15, (in all the copies C1, C2, ... used in the system), also reduces the prediction error by about half, shown in Fig. 9.18 and 9.19.

This treatment of measurement and prediction errors is very brief, intended only to demonstrate the SYN tools. A more comprehensive investigation is presented in Chapter 17.

```
Comparing on [0.00, 100.00) for 300 points
normalized rms errors
{count} interval            func     run
{15}    [0.00, 5.00)        1.50%   0.69%
{15}    [5.00, 10.00)       1.28%   0.48%
{9}     [10.00, 13.00)      0.69%   0.57%
{9}     [13.00, 16.00)      1.54%   0.76%
{6}     [16.00, 18.00)     52.60%   0.60%
{6}     [18.00, 20.00)     52.60%   0.60%
{6}     [20.00, 22.00)     52.60%   0.60%
{6}     [22.00, 24.00)     52.60%   0.60%
{9}     [24.00, 27.00)    156.50%   1.64%
{9}     [27.00, 30.00)      4.30%  31.52%
{15}    [30.00, 35.00)    197.61%   2.76%
{15}    [35.00, 40.00)      5.37%   0.59%
{15}    [40.00, 45.00)      1.76%   0.63%
{15}    [45.00, 50.00)      1.76%   0.30%
{15}    [50.00, 55.00)      5.15%   0.25%
{15}    [55.00, 60.00)    197.05%   3.24%
{15}    [60.00, 65.00)      4.82%  24.59%
{15}    [65.00, 70.00)    202.34%  64.84%
{15}    [70.00, 75.00)    140.08%   4.33%
{15}    [75.00, 80.00)      0.73%   0.20%
{15}    [80.00, 85.00)      1.27%   0.19%
{15}    [85.00, 90.00)      1.50%   0.59%
{15}    [90.00, 95.00)      1.57%   0.74%
{15}    [95.00, 100.00)     1.59%   0.79%
Weighted ave:              47.37%   6.34%
  Maximum:                202.34%  64.84%
```

Fig. 9.17 Relative r-m-s errors in system predictions corresponding to Fig. 9.10

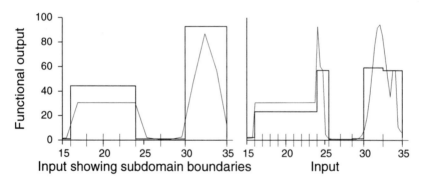

Fig. 9.18 Comparison of functional predictions around input 25 for two sizes of component subdomains

9.4 Better Component Approximations

Step-function measurements are natural for component subdomains, because the very idea of subdomains comes from an attempt to isolate segments of behavior

```
normalized rms errors
24/16 subdomains
  48/32 subdomains

{count}  interval          func      run

{9}       [13.00, 16.00)    1.54%    0.76%
  {5}       [13.00, 14.50)    0.67%    0.32%
  {4}       [14.50, 16.00)    2.35%    0.44%

{6}       [16.00, 18.00)   52.60%    0.60%
  {3}       [16.00, 17.00)   28.17%    0.31%
  {3}       [17.00, 18.00)   28.17%    0.31%

{6}       [18.00, 20.00)   52.60%    0.60%
  {3}       [18.00, 19.00)   28.17%    0.31%
  {3}       [19.00, 20.00)   28.17%    0.31%

{6}       [20.00, 22.00)   52.60%    0.60%
  {3}       [20.00, 21.00)   28.17%    0.31%
  {3}       [21.00, 22.00)   28.17%    0.31%

{6}       [22.00, 24.00)   52.60%    0.60%
  {3}       [22.00, 23.00)   28.17%    0.31%
  {3}       [23.00, 24.00)   28.17%    0.31%

{9}       [24.00, 27.00)  156.50%    1.64%
  {5}       [24.00, 25.50)  144.09%    3.22%
  {4}       [25.50, 27.00)    0.60%    0.87%

{9}       [27.00, 30.00)    4.30%   31.52%
  {5}       [27.00, 28.50)    0.67%    0.50%
  {4}       [28.50, 30.00)    5.68%   27.54%

{15}      [30.00, 35.00)  197.61%    2.76%
  {8}       [30.00, 32.50)  121.93%    1.55%
  {7}       [32.50, 35.00)  104.60%    2.53%

Weighted ave:              47.37%    6.34%
  Weighted ave:            27.17%    3.76%
```

Fig. 9.19 Comparison of prediction errors for two sizes of component subdomains

that are 'the same,' that is, constant over each subdomain. However, even the simple example in Section 9.2 illustrates that things are *not* the same over any old subdomains, which is the source of errors in predictions by the SYN tools. The mathematical study of functional approximation suggests two ways to improve matters: Adjust the subdomains (Section 9.4.1); or, fit more accurate functions than constant ones (Section 9.4.2).

9.4.1 Splitting and Adjusting Subdomains

A nice intuitive justification for testing in subdomains is the limiting case: As sub-domains shrink to singleton sets, subdomain testing becomes exhaustive testing, which works perfectly. This limit is hopelessly impractical, but it can be hoped that smaller (though still large) subdomains will be better. If the functions computed by programs were well behaved[5] then approximation theory assures us that any desired accuracy can be attained using sufficiently small subdomains. Unfortunately, pro-gram functions are *not* well behaved. Chapter 17 studies in detail what happens, in approximating component behavior and in predicting system behavior, as subdo-mains shrink. Discontinuities in component functional behavior cause the greatest practical difficulty, but by placing subdomains boundaries properly the approxima-tion can proceed 'piece-wise.' All subdomain divisions in this chapter are aligned with the discontinuities in Math and in Cond.

A component developer, wishing to publish the best description that testing resources allow, will naturally find points of discontinuity and place subdomain boundaries there. Shrinking subdomain sizes within the piecewise-continuous seg-ments will also reduce the r-m-s error. Both of these operations are labor-intensive, requiring analysis and experimentation, but the COMP component-level tools pro-vide the information to check progress. Figures 9.15 and 9.18 show a sample of the improvement possible when subdomains shrink in size[6].

9.4.2 Piecewise-linear Component Approximation

The second general method for improving approximation is to use more accurate approximating functions. It is common to use polynomials; if the highest exponent allowed is n, the approximation is 'n^{th}-order.' A step function is a '0-order poly-nomial' approximation; higher-order polynomials within each subdomain fit better. Higher-order approximation is little help with discontinuities—subdomain bound-aries must still be chosen carefully. But the piecewise-linear approximation does a much better job of capturing behavior in the 'pieces.'

---

[5] Continuity is enough to force overall approximation improvement, but to really guarantee that nothing important has been missed would require functions of bounded variation, quite out of the question for programs in general.

[6] The astute reader may notice that the 'actual behavior' curve has a different shape at the left and right of Fig. 9.18, yet the system is the same for different approximations of its components. The 'actual' curve on the right is closer to correct, but the one on the left illustrates how difficult it is to test systems. The test samples around input 23 at the left are too far apart to show the peak, which is averaged out with the curve falling to the right. Indeed, the edges of the discontinuity are not captured in the left test, nor are the twin peaks in [30,35). Failure to sample with sufficient density is always a problem for a tester, who of course never knows when enough samples have been taken. The anomaly would have been eliminated by using Xcomp 15 35 300 as was done for Fig. 9.15, but the difference between component approximation and system prediction is that in I-CBSD the system designer does not have the actual system to test and so lacks an error analysis.

To create piecewise-linear component descriptions, the command is

```
COMP -L
```

(`COMP -C` forces the step-function approximation, which is the default). Figure 9.20 shows the piecewise-linear measurement graph and Fig. 9.21 the error analysis

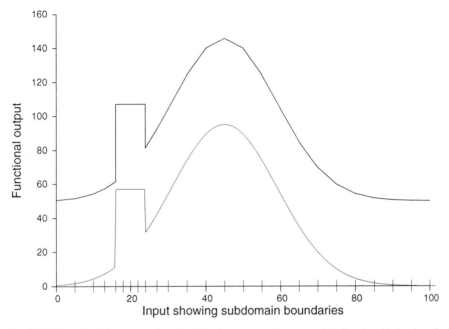

Fig. 9.20 Piecewise-linear approximation (*displaced upward*) compared to functional behavior of `Math`

for the `Math` component produced by `Xcute C1 0 100 300`, much improved over Figs. 9.4 and 9.14 for the same subdomains. (The `C1.ccf` file is unchanged.) The run-time approximation measured for `Math` is perfect, since its run time is a piecewise-linear function. In Fig. 9.20 the approximate and actual curves have been displaced vertically for clarity—when superimposed they are almost indistinguishable. *If components are coded in a language (like C) that allows a choice of floating-point precision, double precision must be used. The tools use Perl's default double precision, and for the piecewise-linear approximation things go wrong near the ends of subdomain intervals when precision is lost.*

With better approximations measured for the components,

```
SYN
```

uses those approximations, with improved accuracy in Figs. 9.22, 9.23, and 9.24[7] compared to Figs. 9.12 9.13, and 9.17. *The system error analysis required a special option* `Xcomp -s` *to sample each subdomain instead of spreading samples uni-*

---

[7] Again the curves have been displaced vertically for clarity.

```
Sampling [0.00, 100.00) for 72 points
normalized rms errors
count    interval            func    run
{4}      [0.00, 5.00)        0.10%   0.00%
{4}      [5.00, 10.00)       0.19%   0.00%
{2}      [10.00, 13.00)      0.10%   0.00%
{2}      [13.00, 16.00)      0.11%   0.00%
{1}      [16.00, 18.00)      0.00%   0.00%
{2}      [18.00, 20.00)      0.00%   0.00%
{1}      [20.00, 22.00)      0.00%   0.00%
{2}      [22.00, 24.00)      0.00%   0.00%
{2}      [24.00, 27.00)      0.14%   0.00%
{2}      [27.00, 30.00)      0.07%   0.00%
{3}      [30.00, 35.00)      0.16%   0.00%
{4}      [35.00, 40.00)      0.64%   0.00%
{3}      [40.00, 45.00)      0.93%   0.00%
{4}      [45.00, 50.00)      1.04%   0.00%
{4}      [50.00, 55.00)      0.67%   0.00%
{3}      [55.00, 60.00)      0.16%   0.00%
{4}      [60.00, 65.00)      0.26%   0.00%
{3}      [65.00, 70.00)      0.42%   0.00%
{4}      [70.00, 75.00)      0.42%   0.00%
{3}      [75.00, 80.00)      0.30%   0.00%
{4}      [80.00, 85.00)      0.18%   0.00%
{3}      [85.00, 90.00)      0.09%   0.00%
{4}      [90.00, 95.00)      0.04%   0.00%
{4}      [95.00, 100.00)     0.01%   0.00%
Weighted ave:                0.29%   0.00%
  Maximum:                   1.04%   0.00%
```

Fig. 9.21 Approximation errors in piecewise-linear approximation of functional behavior of Math

formly over the whole domain. Uniform sampling fails to hit many of the small subdomains created by the piecewise-linear calculation.

Some of the improvement in prediction shown in Fig. 9.22 is the result of better component approximations. The biggest improvement, however, comes from the superiority of the SYN synthesis calculation when the approximations are piecewise-linear, which creates many new subdomains as described in Chapter 8. Although with the step-function approximation there are only 24 calculated system subdomains, there are 209 system subdomains calculated in Fig. 9.22, most of them created by the series synthesis algorithm. For clarity, only a few of these have been shown in Fig. 9.24, concentrating on the larger errors. Notice that although the run-time prediction looks very good in the graphs, there are still substantial errors. As might be imagined, combining piecewise-linear approximation with smaller subdomains produces even better results.

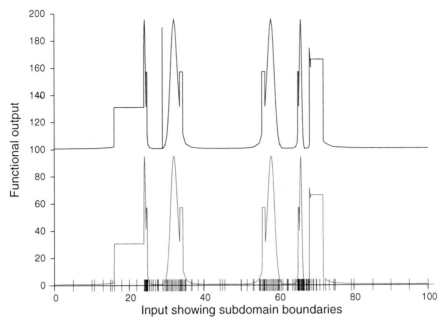

Fig. 9.22 SYN CAD functional predictions (*displaced upward*) and system measurements for the system of Fig. 9.1 (piecewise-linear approximations)

9.4.3 How Well Can a Component Developer Do?

Using tools like Xcute, a component developer can try to get a good approximation to component behavior. However, equally accurate system predictions do not necessarily follow. As described in Chapter 17, system-construction operations unfortunately create new discontinuities which cannot be predicted before the system is designed. At system-synthesis time the component developers have long ago done their testing and gone away; in I-CBSD they cannot be called back to adjust their test subdomains to compensate for new problems encountered, so system prediction errors cannot be bounded for certain. This is one example of *emergent* properties of systems constructed from components—properties that appear *only* in the aggregate, not algorithmically related to isolated properties of the components.

Approximation theory still holds, of course. The actual system functions are piecewise continuous, and can be approximated accurately with step functions. But remember that the SYN CAD tools are not finding a measured approximation to system executions. Rather, they are predicting system behavior from the component measurements, measurements made in isolation before the system structure is known, with knowledge of only each single component. The SYN predictions are useful because they are made without assembling an actual system; there would be no point in approximating a real system once it is built.

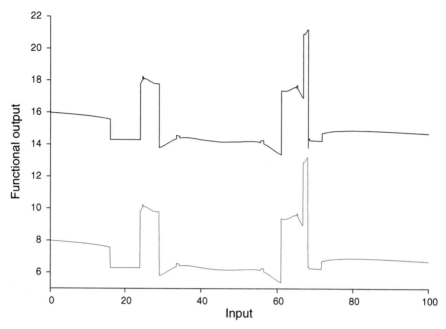

Fig. 9.23 SYN CAD run-time predictions (*displaced upward*) and system measurements for the system of Fig. 9.1 (piecewise-linear approximations)

The best a component developer can do is to produce an approximate description that is as accurate as testing resources allow. By carefully capturing discontinuities and refining subdomains to minimize component-level r-m-s errors, the predictions for many systems will be improved. But it remains true that the best intentions and accurate testing at the component level still produce only poor predictions. In Section 9.5 it will be seen how CAD tools at the system level can give qualitative guidance about the likely accuracy of prediction, but that is no help in I-CBSD—one cannot go back to the component level.

9.5 Internal Profiles

The SYN tools have a number of features and options that help component designers and system designers to understand and control code that is being developed with CBSD. (Many of these are described in Chapter 15 on debugging.) One feature is more important than the others because it arises directly from the idea of subdomain decomposition of testing, which underlies the theory and the tool algorithms. The SYN CAD tool can predict test profiles that exist at the interfaces between components in a system. These internal profiles are not at all obvious and they are

```
Comparing on [0.00, 100.00) for 627 points    (by subdomain)
normalized rms errors
{count}  interval              func      run
{3}        [0.00,  5.00)        0.03%    0.01%
{3}        [5.00, 10.00)        0.08%    0.03%
{3}       [10.00, 10.65)        0.09%    0.01%
{3}       [10.65, 13.00)        0.17%    0.02%
....
{3}       [65.75, 65.86)        2.86%    0.04%
{3}       [65.86, 65.97)        4.27%    0.06%
{3}       [65.97, 66.06)       10.60%    0.15%
{2}       [66.06, 66.06)       12.67%    0.15%
{3}       [66.06, 66.07)       14.03%    0.16%
{3}       [66.07, 66.18)       18.69%    0.21%
{3}       [66.18, 66.28)       22.42%    0.29%
{3}       [66.28, 66.39)       19.74%    0.34%
{3}       [66.39, 66.48)       14.03%    0.35%
{2}       [66.48, 66.48)        9.40%    0.28%
....
{3}       [67.74, 67.88)        0.50%    0.61%
{3}       [67.88, 68.04)        2.40%    0.40%
{2}       [68.04, 68.04)        3.90%    0.20%
{3}       [68.04, 68.06)        4.47%    0.18%
{3}       [68.06, 68.19)      138.22%   70.53%
{3}       [68.19, 68.19)      164.23%   86.37%
{3}       [68.19, 68.20)      162.34%   86.33%
{3}       [68.20, 68.20)       10.57%    0.21%
{3}       [68.20, 68.54)       11.57%    0.89%
{3}       [68.54, 69.03)        0.30%    0.00%
....
{3}       [80.00, 85.00)        0.08%    0.03%
{3}       [85.00, 90.00)        0.03%    0.01%
{3}       [90.00, 95.00)        0.04%    0.01%
{3}       [95.00, 100.00)       0.06%    0.01%
Weighted ave:                    2.52%    0.49%
   Maximum:                    164.23%   86.37%
```

Fig. 9.24 SYN CAD prediction errors for the system of Fig. 9.1 (piecewise-linear approximations)

impossible to assess without tool support; yet, they are crucial to an understanding of how components compose.

The very idea of subdomain testing comes from an attempt to manage the input-spread across its domain that a program sees in actual use. It is evident that to be meaningful, testing must follow the expected input profile. In an extreme case, if test samples are taken only at inputs that almost never arise in use, then little will be learned by testing. Any failures found would seldom trouble a user; little confidence will be gained that the program does not fail; performance data may be wildly inaccurate—in short, the test is worse than useless. In the view taken here that components and their descriptions come to the system developer fixed and immutable, those components were tested without any knowledge of an appropriate profile. By testing in subdomains, information is gained that can later be applied to any profile. Much of the apparently incomprehensible behavior of systems is the result of 'internal profiles' that components present to each other at their interfaces within the system. While the system as a whole sees an input profile that originates with a user, that profile can be seriously distorted at any component interface within the system. For example, it might happen that users present the system with a relatively uniform profile, trying all inputs about equally often. But a mathematical component deep inside the system structure, which can itself operate across a vast range of floating-point input values, might be sent only values in the interval $[-\pi, \pi]$. The uniform system input profile has turned into a narrow spike at this component. As Chapter 19 will show, it is this phenomenon that can compromise the predictions of SYN tools, and that complicates the relationship between unit- and system testing.

The SYN CAD tool invoked with the command SYN -P calculates and stores internal-profile information about the system it is synthesizing. Subsequently, the command

    profile C4

plots (Figure 9.25) an histogram of probabilities at the interface for the component

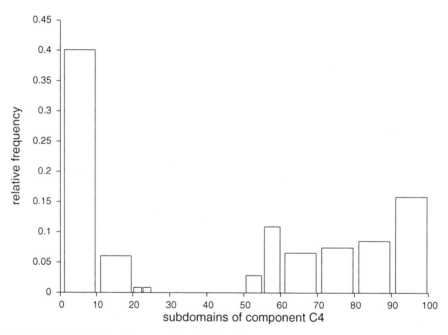

Fig. 9.25 Predicted internal input profile at the interface to C4

described by C4.ccf, the final conditional in Fig. 9.1. The measurement data on which this profile calculation is based is the piecewise-linear approximation shown in Fig. 9.22. The natural profile to assume for system input is uniform across the entire domain and the natural granularity for profiling each component's input is its own subdomains. In Fig. 9.25 the width of each bar is the size of a corresponding C4 subdomain. The subdomains around input 40.0 have zero density because control arrives at C4 from the loop whose test C2 must be *false* for the loop to terminate, and C2 (Cond) is *true* around 40.0. Because C4 itself is a copy of Cond, it therefore never takes the *true* branch to C7. What should profile C7 show? Try it. When component C4 was tested and its approximation recorded, its subdomains were sampled equally (if C4.ccf so specifies, and there is seldom reason to do otherwise), so if the actual profile is roughly uniform, using C4's approximation for prediction calculations is justified. But if the profile has a spike at some subdomain, there may have been too few test points taken there and the prediction is suspect. In this case Fig. 9.25 is close to uniform, except that no test points reached the subdomains around 40.0, and the first subdomain was oversampled.

Internal profiles can also be measured for a system in execution by instrumenting the system code to count the inputs that arrive in each subdomain of a component. Again we emphasize that the SYN CAD tool needs no such measurements[8]: using only the measured-by-testing descriptions of the components produced by COMP and the system structure, it *calculates* internal profile predictions[9].

9.6 Incremental Processing

Based on file-creation times, the COMP command makes an attempt to avoid reprocessing when it would not have new results. It also attempts incremental reprocessing when this might save substantial time. When a designer is testing or synthesizing, it is common to repeatedly adjust the definitions of subdomains in the .ccf files, for example to change subdomain boundary points or to split subdomains. If not too many subdomains are altered, measurements can be confined to those changed, with a large reduction in testing time. For example, in a base file where C1.ccf had 192 subdomains suppose one subdomain is split (so there are then 193 subdomains, two of them new). Suppose that C2.ccf (128 subdomains) and the code files are unchanged since the last testing measurements were made.

```
COMP -V
```

has partial output:

```
Configuration file C1.ccf with code file Math:
   stateless with 193 input subdomains on [0, 100)
Configuration file C1.ccf seems OK
Creating testing-measurements file C1.ccft...
   Incremental measurements: 191 subdomains copied;
      2 remeasured
```

---

[8] A computer science graduate student who was originally assigned to implement this part of the SYN tools gave up, saying it was impossible to get internal profiles without executing the system.

[9] Profile calculations are very sensitive to approximation errors in component measurements. At worst, the prediction in Fig. 9.25 is off by about 14%.

```
----------------------------------
Configuration file C2.ccf with code file Cond:
  stateless with 128 input subdomains on [0, 100)
Configuration file C2.ccf seems OK
Testing measurements file C2.ccft up-to-date...
----------------------------------
```

The C2 (Cond) measurements were not repeated. The new measurements for C1 (Math) took about[10] 0.19 sec of CPU time on a laptop. But when the changed Math.ccf file of 193 subdomains was completely measured anew, it required about 3.0 sec.

In synthesis, if the component-measurement files that go into synthesizing one of the theory files have not changed since the last SYN run, the calculation need not be repeated. For example, in Section 9.2, theory3 can be reused if C5 and C6 are unchanged. If components *have* changed, but the changes were incrementally processed, SYN can incrementally calculate for the changed subdomains only[11].

It can happen that the tools are too clever for their own good, and create a snarl in which the human user has difficulty understanding what has been changed and incrementally processed. (This happens in spades when attempts are being made to validate the incremental algorithms for the tools.) All incremental and time-stamp-based optimizations can be eliminated by using COMP -z, *which will retest all components completely and hence eliminate all incremental processing.*

9.7 Tutorial Summary

This chapter has at least mentioned most of the features of the SYN tools when used with stateless components, and described how to invoke the tool scripts to exercise those features. The examples chosen for illustration have along the way raised issues about testing components and synthesizing systems, and issues about testing in general, despite being intended to be no more than simple cases for the tools to process. When such an issue comes up, it is clearly exposed in the graphs and error tables, and the tools can be used to investigate it further. In the case studies of Chapter 18 such insights are less accidental: the examples are chosen to reveal as much as possible about a particular fundamental issue.

---

[10] The times were obtained with the LINUX times system call, averaging two trials for each situation. The times are not repeatable because of many extraneous differences between apparently identical runs, but here the two runs differed by less than 7%.

[11] Incremental synthesis yields smaller savings than incremental component testing, because the SYN calculation algorithms are fast (they use table-lookup) while COMP testing is slow (it requires actual code execution), and because synthesis using a changed component propagates in such a way that no subsequent synthesis steps can be incremental. Also, in I-CBSD, this kind of incremental change is exactly what is not supposed to happen: system results are not to be used in adjusting the details of component tests. When a component is entirely replaced (which *is* expected in I-CBSD), incremental synthesis doesn't come into play.

Chapter 10
Persistent State

To extend the stateless ideas presented in Chapter 8 to more complicated cases is mostly straightforward. When a component C has local state its behaviors depend on two domains—input and state. Each can be split into subdomains, and the behavioral semantic functions $\boxed{C}$ and $\widehat{C}$ can be approximately captured by sampling executions of C in those subdomains. However, even straightforward extensions of theory often reveal complications and bring insights. The subdomain theory of testing composition and its implementation in tools is no exception. Its complication arises in the way that the additional subdomain dimension of state should be sampled, as described in Section 10.2.2 to follow.

10.1 Extended Subdomain Theory of Composition

Synthesis of more complicated components is a matter of identifying the subdomains that are formed in the combination and finding the way in which values arise from the subdomain values of the parts being combined. In essence, there is not much more to it than in the stateless case: Inputs fall into subdomains, are mapped to other subdomains, and combine to form the output of the synthesized system, expressed in that system's subdomains. Quantitatively, of course, there is a great deal more to it, since the number of subdomains is the product of decompositions in two (or more) spaces. This number grows at least quadratically in the number of divisions in each space.

D. Hamlet, *Composing Software Components*, DOI 10.1007/978-1-4419-7148-7_10,
© Springer Science+Business Media, LLC 2010

10.1.1 Algorithms for Synthesizing Systems from Components with State

For a component with state, the approximate description arises from two sets of subdomains, one dividing the input domain and the other the state domain. The three functions that describe behavior of a component C are $\boxed{C}$ (output mapping), $\textcircled{C}$ (state mapping), and T_C (run-time mapping) as defined in Chapter 6. Each of these functions now depends on two domains: input and state, each with a subdomain breakdown. The (input × state) space is divided into rectangular subdomains by a choice from each space—these are the component's subdomains. To approximate C's behaviors, test points are chosen in each subdomain, the code for C is executed, and the average functional values are recorded for each subdomain. The approximate description thus created consists of three step-plateau functions of two arguments. Figure 10.1 illustrates a simple case in which the run-time function T_C is an inverted parabola rotated about a vertical axis. The figure shows this surface

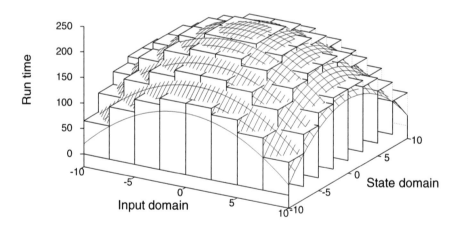

Fig. 10.1 Illustrative run-time function and its approximation for a component with state

with contour lines for visualization, superimposed with the step plateaus that arise from a total of 64 subdomains (8 input × 8 state).

To fit components with state into the theory presented in Chapter 8 requires a re-examination of the three constructs of series, conditional, and iterative composition. Of these, series is fundamental. The simplest case will introduce ideas needed to understand the role of state. Imagine a stateless component C_1 (with a step-function approximation) followed by a component C_2 with state (with its approximate step-plateau description) in series. The two-component system itself has state, and its subdomains are an amalgam of those from the components: the cross product of input subdomains from C_1 with state subdomains from C_2. On such a subdomain, say $U \times V$, how does the system act? U is an input subdomain of C_1 and V a state domain of C_2. Any input in U is mapped by $\boxed{C_1}$ to a value that falls (say) in the C_2 input subdomain U'. Then the system approximate output and state can be read from the plateaus in C_2 subdomain $U' \times V$. The run-time approximate value from a plateau above $U' \times V$ in C_2 is the part contributed by C_2; the other part comes from the run time of C_1 on U. This construction thus supplies a value for the three approximate functions on the arbitrary system subdomain $U \times V$, defining the series-synthesis approximation of $C_1 ; C_2$.

In the simple series case above, the stateless component need not be the result of measurements made on code, but might have been the result of any stateless synthesis, since synthesizing any stateless system results in a 'component' whose approximation has the same form as for measured code. Unfortunately, the same cannot always be said for synthesis involving state. In particular, when both components in a series construct have state, the synthesized system has the cross product of their states. That is, if C_2 has subdomains like $U_2 \times V_2$ and C_3 has subdomains like $U_3 \times V_3$, their series combination has subdomains like $U_2 \times V_2 \times V_3$. Should such a two-state system be composed with C_2, the result has three state dimensions; a two-state system composed with itself has four, and so on.

In the general case a 'component' C_1 with n states is composed with C_2 of m states. (The case $n = 0$ is done above; when $m = 0$ the second 'component' is stateless. If either n or m is greater than 1, the corresponding 'component' must be a synthesized system.) It's easy to extend the construction above. A typical system subdomain has the form $S = X \times Y_1 \times ... \times Y_n \times Z_1 \times ... \times Z_m$, where X is an input subdomain of C_1 and the others are state domains of C_1 ($Y_1, ..., Y_n$) and C_2 ($Z_1, ..., Z_m$). To find what an approximate synthesized system does on S, look up the output of C_1 in its subdomain $X \times Y_1 \times ... \times Y_n$, and find the C_2 input subdomain X' in which it falls. If there is no such subdomain then all the approximation functions are undefined on S; otherwise, take the approximating function values (output and state) for S from C_2 subdomain $X' \times Z_1 \times ... \times Z_m$. Add to the run time from this subdomain that from C_1 subdomain $X \times Y_1 \times ... \times Y_n$.

Anticipating the discussion of infeasible subdomains in Section 10.2.2 below, it may happen that one of the components to be synthesized has some subdomains that can never be reached. Furthermore, the series combination can create new subdomains that cannot be reached in the system synthesized, because the first component in series may have restricted output values that don't fall into some parts of the input domain of the second. In general, the problem of which subdomains can be reached is unsolvable for an actual system, but surprisingly it has a solution for the approximations, which will be explained in Section 10.2.2.

This completes the algorithm for synthesizing components with state in series.

Conditional system synthesis of if C_q then C_T else C_F fi for the stateless case was accomplished by taking some subdomain values from the *true*-branch component C_T and some from the *false*-branch component C_F, depending on whether their subdomains intersected with the corresponding subdomains of the test component C_q. When there is state, in general C_q has k state domains, C_T has n states, and C_F has m states. The difficulty in the algorithm is forming the proper subdomains for the conditional system.

Consider first just the *true*-branch component C_T. It will be invoked only on those C_q subdomains where C_q selects *true*. For each such *true* C_q subdomain S_t, intersect the input-domain subdomain dimension of S_t with the input subdomain dimension of C_T's subdomains. Coupling these intersections with the states of C_q and C_T respectively defines part of the system collection of subdomains. Let Z_t be one such intersection, part of input subdomain X_t on which C_q takes value *true* in state (k-tuple) U. Let Y_t be an input subdomain of C_T which contains Z_t with state (n-tuple) V. Then subdomain $Z_t \times U \times V$ is one on which the approximate values are taken from C_T subdomain $Y_t \times V$. The run-time value for $Z_t \times U \times V$ is obtained by adding the C_q values from $X_t \times U$ to those of C_T on $Y_t \times V$. Filling in the result-state values in Z_t has one further complication. Z_t has a state part $U \times V$, its first k subdomains from C_q and the next n from C_T. The result-state tuples come respectively from $X_t \times U$ and $Y_t \times V$.

Similarly, subdomains can be formed starting with the *false* portions of C_q subdomains, which will select approximation values for the system from C_F subdomains. In the construction, Z_t is replaced by an intersection with C_F subdomains, say Z_t', and the corresponding m-tuple state W for C_F replaces V. Values are placed in subdomains like $Z_t' \times U \times W$.

Finally, results from the two branches of the conditional must be combined. For any of the '*true*' input intersection subdomains like Z_t the system subdomain is $Z_t \times U \times V \times W$, of dimension $1 + k + n + m$. The construction above supplies values for output, run time, and $k + n$ result states, the same for all members of W. The additional m result-state values should retain any states from C_F unchanged—that is, since C_F is not being executed, it has an identity state mapping. Unfortunately, in the approximation being calculated states themselves are not available, only state subdomains. So the algorithm supplies the midpoint of each state subdomain as an identity value[1]. Similarly, on '*false*' input intersection subdomains like Z_t', the construction above supplies values for $k + m$ result states in $U \times W$, and the n values for V are filled in as identity.

The algorithm described finds an approximation to a synthesized conditional 'component' in terms of the approximations that form it. Conditional synthesis with state is the most difficult of the constructions used in the SYN tools. The reader who

---

[1] This expedient introduces a new kind of error into the calculated synthesis approximations, which will be further discussed in describing the SYN tools, Section 14.3.2, an error that diminishes as the subdomain size shrinks and the midpoint better approximates a real identity.

seeks to follow it might be advised to start with the case $k = 1, n = m = 0$, then try $k = m = 0, n = 1$, and finally $k = n = m = 1$[2].

Loops are the final system construct to synthesize. For stateless components the loop was unwound repeatedly, the result being a composition of enough conditionals for termination to occur. The unwinding equivalence holds for the pure-functional case, but not for run time, and neither does it hold for state. To see why, suppose that while C_q do C_b od is to be synthesized. If either C_b or C_q has state, then an unwinding if C_q then C_b else I fi (I the identity component) has $k \geq 1$ state(s), if C_q then C_b else I fi; if C_q then C_b else I fi has $2k$ states, and so on, the state-domain count doubling with each unwinding. But that isn't how iteration works. Rather, the body component C_b has its state, which it reuses each time the loop is entered. Similarly, the state dimension of the test component C_b is reused and does not grow[3]. The synthesis can be worked out by repeatedly composing if C_q then C_b else I fi with itself, but in a slightly different way.

Consider the subdomains of the 'component' if C_q then C_b else I fi. Its state dimension is the combination of states of C_q and C_b as defined in the conditional construction above. Each subdomain can be characterized as *true* or *false* depending on the value that C_q takes there, using only the C_q part of the state. On any of the subdomains with a *false* character the approximation to the loop's behavior is complete: the body has been been executed at most one time there and nothing further can happen to change results on that subdomain. In particular, should *all* the subdomains have *false* character, then the synthesis of the loop is complete with result the approximation of if C_q then C_b else I fi. If not, for each subdomain with *true* character, update the subdomain result by following the input through C_b and taking its output, run-time, and result-state values. This may or may not change the subdomain's *true* character. If it switches to *false*, work is complete on that subdomain. Continue in this way, reaching one of two outcomes: either all subdomains switch to false, in which case the synthesis is complete and the loop approximation terminates; or, at some step no subdomains switch, in which case the approximation loop does not terminate (on those subdomains[4]).

Thus the algorithm to construct an approximation to a loop construct is complete.

---

[2] The SYN implementation was accomplished by breaking out such cases. The danger in that kind of coding is that the simple cases are understood and work, while more complicated cases fail in obscure ways. Some people might be tempted to draw uncomfortable conclusions about 'agile' methods in which a few restricted use-cases as tests guide development.

[3] The final synthesized loop component does have a state-domain count that is the sum of those for C_q and C_b, the same state dimension as that of if C_q then C_b else I fi.

[4] At the point where no subdomains switch, it may happen that there are exchanges among the resulting subdomains of *true* character, but this cannot lead to any future switches.

10.1.2 Verifying the Algorithms

The algorithms given here for synthesizing approximations to system behavior, particularly for conditionals and loops, are considerably more complicated than in the stateless case. The reader probably finds them difficult to understand and more difficult to believe correct. To implement tools as described in Chapter 13 it is necessary to understand; to argue for correctness is more difficult. In mathematics, doubts about an algorithm can be resolved by formal proof, usually by induction. However, it is well known that detailed induction proofs are 'totally uninformative.' This means that understanding must be gained outside the proof in order to follow it; this understanding is much the same as that required to believe in the algorithm without proof. Sometimes mathematicians say that the proof is "by construction," meaning that in describing the algorithm they have already done the best they can to convey understanding.

In addition, proving algorithms has a special character not shared by other proofs. When the algorithm is clearly given, it can be implemented in software. The software can be tested, and insofar as it does not fail, it supports correctness of the algorithm. Unfortunately, the software itself always contains mistakes, the more so if the algorithm was difficult to understand, so each software failure must be carefully traced to its root cause. After a few real failures in the algorithm are observed and the software corrected, the implementer acquires a steadily increasing confidence, not so much in the algorithm or the quality of the software, but in the truth of a meta-theorem something like the following in the case of the system-approximation constructions given above:

> There exists an algorithm for these constructions. The one given may not be correct, but if it isn't, cases will come to light in which the software implementing it fails and each such case can be resolved by making minor corrections to the algorithm.

The meta-theorem doesn't state or imply that a completely correct algorithm will ever be found; it only expresses a belief that the implementing software can be trusted as much as any software can be trusted.

There is usually an additional difficult problem that arises in the process of implementing and testing tool software: it is hard to tell if particular executions of the tools have succeeded or failed[5]. Fortunately, in the case of component-synthesis tools, there exists an unusual means of checking the results of synthesis, which is described in Chapter 13[6]. The algorithm- and tool-development can thus be done in a particularly convenient way: As soon as implementation is possible (that is, when an algorithm is well enough expressed to follow its steps), the tools are written, and

---

[5] This is the *oracle* problem of effectively judging the success of a test case.

[6] It is in this checking that the inaccurate 'identity' states introduced in the conditional case cause trouble. See Section 14.3.2.

their failed testing leads to corrections and confidence[7] as the meta-theorem above asserts.

10.2 Testing Measurements

To make the measurements that describe a component with state requires sampling a two-dimensional cross-product space. One dimension is the component input domain; the second dimension is the state domain. The obvious sampling technique used with stateless input subdomains could also be applied to these two dimensions: if one set of subdomains is sampled n times each and the orthogonal set m times, then each rectangular subdomain is tested with a uniformly spaced grid of nm points. The failings of this method and other sampling techniques are discussed in Section 10.2.2 to follow.

10.2.1 3-D Graphs and Approximation Errors

When measurements of a component's behavior depend on two variables, that behavior has a three-dimensional (3-D) graph: each point of the graph is a triple (input, state, value) for a component with state. To get the step-function approximation, the measured values from each subdomain are averaged to obtain a single value. Thus if the 3-D graph is plotted as a value-surface, it lies above the (input × state) plane. Dividing the plane into rectangular subdomains in each of its dimensions, the value-surface is of constant height over each rectangle, and so constitutes a plateau of steps[8]. For comparison with the approximation, points averaged to compute it can be displayed. Or, additional samples can be taken to obtain a more detailed 3-D surface of actual behavior. It is a good measure of the approximation quality to compute the root-mean-square (r-m-s) deviation of actual points from the average. The average r-m-s deviation over each subdomain, normalized to the r-m-s value of all samples on the whole domain, is a quality metric for the subdomain, and a weighted average of these is a summary quality metric for the whole approximation. Figure 10.1 shows an example of step-plateaus approximating a 3-D function, and a surface plotted for the function itself. The weighted average r-m-s error in Fig. 10.1 is about 8%.

---

[7] It will be no surprise to readers with tool-building experience that failures whose root is software mistakes outnumber failures that come from mistakes in the algorithms by several orders of magnitude. And of course the software bugs have to be eliminated before the algorithm bugs can be seen.

[8] The graph looks like a field of basalt columns like the Giant's Causeway in Ireland, except that for basalt the plateaus are hexagonal.

10.2.2 Equi-spaced vs. Sequence Sampling

It is the essence of subdomain testing (Chapter 7) that test points be placed in every subdomain. Since component measurements are to capture average subdomain behavior, several test points per subdomain are indicated. There seems little to choose between equi-spacing these points across the subdomain, or picking them at random. After all, if there were any structure within a subdomain, it would be reason to divide it further. Since it has not been divided, the choice of test points should not matter. If behaviors within a subdomain are continuous, equi-spaced samples capture them better with fewer tests.

When subdomains become two-dimensional, it is tempting to sample in the same way, with a grid of test points equi-spaced in each dimension. But sampling the state dimension of a component requires more care—state cannot be arbitrarily set outside a program like an input. As described in Chapter 6, states begin as uninitialized, then are set *by the program* in response to a sequence of input values. Hence the dictates of subdomain testing may be impossible to achieve: some state subdomains may never be reached by any input sequence—they are *infeasible*. Unfortunately, nothing stops a tester from directly sampling subdomains with infeasible states and thereby gaining a false impression of how the program behaves. A simple example will illustrate this pitfall.

Suppose a component's run time has the dome-shaped function of Fig. 10.1 in Section 10.2.1, repeated here as Fig. 10.2. That is, the component code performs actions depending on its input- and state-variables that use an amount of time falling off from a maximum in both dimensions. But it is the responsibility of the component code to *set* the state on one execution, then to use that state value on the next execution. Suppose that the code funks this responsibility—because of a programming mistake, suppose the state is initialized to zero, but thereafter is never modified; that is, the state value computed by the program is always zero—all other states are really infeasible. If tested with points systematically chosen from (input × state) subdomains, the approximation plateaus of Fig. 10.2 will be measured[9] for this code. Figure 10.3 shows what happens when the tests are sequences of inputs only. The figures show that systematic state sampling can give a completely false[10] impression of what code actually does. The situation is particularly dangerous because testing may be guided by requirements that prescribe the states to be the dome behavior of Fig. 10.2, which is why a tester is sampling them. Such tests show that the code works perfectly when really it has completely failed to implement most of the required states.

It is most natural to construct random input sequences of random length for testing. Input points within a sequence would be selected at random from the full input

[9] They *are* measured—Fig. 10.2 was obtained by the tools described in Chapter 13 on the erroneous code using equi-spaced subdomain samples. Figure 10.3 sampled the same code but with sequences.

[10] Figure 10.2 is not completely wrong—it agrees with Fig. 10.3 at state zero and the subdomains containing state zero. Systematic sampling gets two kinds of results: ones that are correct and ones that never occur.

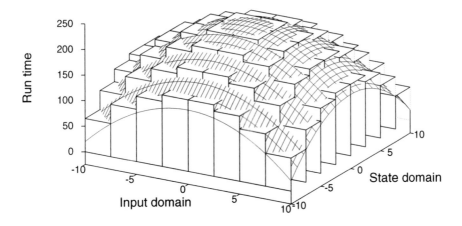

Fig. 10.2 Illustrative state-dependent run-time function and its approximation obtained by subdomain sampling

domain. Although more systematic input choices can be imagined, it is not clear how this ought to be done. For example, choices might be restricted to particular input subdomains at particular points of the sequence, then cycled through all possibilities. It seems more likely that something will be missed by the wrong systematic choice pattern than by sticking with random choices and increasing the sample count.

10.3 System Predictions

From the measured approximate description files of components—stateless or withstate—and a system description of how these components are connected, approximations of system properties can be predicted using the algorithms given in Chapter 8 and Section 10.1.1 above. Each system-construction operation combines some component approximations into an approximation of the composite behavior, and these calculated composites are further combined until the entire system approximation has been synthesized.

The presence of state makes itself felt in synthesis: When a component with state P combines with a stateless component, the result has state that mirrors the state of P. In the more complicated cases when system constructions involve more than

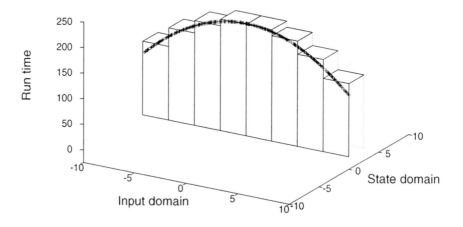

Fig. 10.3 Illustrative state-dependent run-time function and its approximation obtained by input-sequence sampling

one component with state, the system state grows. For example, in a conditional construction where the component in the *true* branch and the test component that selects the branch have state but the *false*-branch component is stateless, the synthesized result has two orthogonal states corresponding to the *true*- and test-component states that go into it. This multiplication of dimension complicates the synthesis algorithms as presented in Section 10.1.1, but more importantly it complicates the presentation and understanding of system predictions, to be further discussed in Section 10.3.1 below.

State does not introduce complications in the prediction of non-functional properties. At each synthesis step the same sort of scalar run-time approximation function arises. However, the domain of this function, which includes the composite system domain, may grow in complexity as the system is synthesized.

10.3.1 Synthesis of Systems with State

Within a system, each component uses at most its own local state, even though the system state comprises the cross product of all component states involved. So understanding of individual component actions is unchanged in a system. But to grasp the *system* behavior, a person must grapple with the composite state both as input and output. The difficulty shows itself in tools as an inability to present results graphically: the system functional properties may depend on tuples of input and states with dimension three or more (an input and two or more states). With a single state, properties depend on only two dimensions and the 3-D graph can be presented in 2-D projection, but there is nothing to be done with higher dimensions[11]. Any display of system behavior must therefore somehow combine multiple state dimensions into one. In general there is no good way to do this, because the cardinality of a multidimensional real-valued space is incomparable with a single real dimension. No matter how the dimensions are combined[12], their orthogonal nature is lost.

One special case has a good solution. If in each state dimension there are only a few state values, then there are few (more, but still not too many) system-state tuples. Each tuple can be assigned a position on a discrete state axis. Plots of the system properties then become 3-D surfaces consisting of parallel curves lined up at each state value, along the input dimension. The result-state curves are discrete points above the input plane. This special case is of interest because it arises when components use state to record 'modes' (or 'preferences'). Then a system state tuple describes each possible combination of preferences. In the general case, perhaps the best composite state is the magnitude of a vector sum of the multiple states.

Presenting properties of a synthesized system with state also raises the problems of how to sample its input spaces and how to present results over a subdomain. Predictions do not have to be sampled—there is one value for each subdomain. But to compare a prediction with actual system behavior, the system must be executed with input samples. The correct way to sample is with input sequences as in Section 10.2.2. For a system, there are even more infeasible-state subdomains than for its constituent components. In a sequence construct, for example, each infeasible subdomain in the first component makes a whole list of cross-product subdomains infeasible. The output values from the first component may also fail to cover the whole of the second-component input domain, creating other infeasible system subdomains.

When there is a single system state (as there is for any one component), predicted system values are constant over each subdomain, so the displayed surface of each prediction is a collection of step-plateaus. However, any scheme that combines multiple states to get a single state value for plotting destroys the plateaus, because more than one pair of component states may combine to the same system state. For example, consider a series combination in which the two component run times are 1

---

[11] A 4-D graph can be presented as a series of 'slices' in which one of the dimensions takes a fixed value and the resulting collection of 3-D graphs are shown in 2-D projection, but this seldom leads to understanding unless the slices are very cleverly chosen. It is a further complication that for the 4-D situation (input and two state domains) there are two result-state values, so each slice has three 3-D graphs.

[12] For integer spaces there at first seems to be a way out: integer tuples can be coded into single integer values in an invertible mapping so that a tuple can be reconstructed from its code. But in practice coding is not helpful: the code value for (say) a pair necessarily maps small integers to a large one, an essential distortion in which invertibility is no use. For example, the usual codings for (1,1) and (10,10) are 4 and 220 respectively, so widely separated that any intuition about the smaller numbers (e.g., that they are fairly close diagonal pairs) is lost.

and 3 for some pair of their subdomains, and 7 and 2 for another pair. If both of these subdomain pairs are mapped to the same composite subdomain, is the approximate subdomain run time of the system to be 4 or 9? Hence when a scheme of combining several states into one is used, predictions can be plotted only as disconnected points. Actual system values obtained from execution must also be plotted as points, so it is difficult to visualize the behavior and also difficult to gauge the accuracy of the prediction. Furthermore, any comparison between two apparently similar points may be confounded because the state tuples from which they arise may not be the same.

10.4 A Tutorial Example with State

It is presumed that the reader who wants to try these examples has been through the stateless tutorial in Chapter 9. As there, these comments in slanted font can be skipped unless you are running the tools.

There is very little operational difference between using the SYN tools on stateless components and using them on components with state. Information about components and system is still placed in a base file along with the tools. COMP measures component approximations and SYN synthesizes a system described in the file system.pscf. The difference when there is explicit state is in code for the components and in .ccf configuration files describing their subdomains. *What is most noticeable in running the tools when there is state, is that everything takes significantly longer to execute than for stateless cases—that's not surprising since the number of subdomains, test points, executions, etc., goes up as the square. The synthesis algorithms are fast, but executions are not. In addition, the presence of state introduces choices about how to sample and what to display, so there are more options available on the tool commands.*

A component configuration file (.ccf) with state has two sets of subdomains with sampling counts, the first for inputs, the second for states, separated by a blank line. For example,

```
 ┌── comp1.ccf ──┐
 │               │
 │ comp1bin state│
 │ 0 .1 7        │
 │ .1 .5 7       │
 │ .5 1.0 7      │
 │               │
 │ 5 6 3         │
 │ 6 7 3         │
 │ 7 8 3         │
 │ 8 10 3        │
 │               │
 └───────────────┘
```

describes an input space $[0,1)$ with three subdomains each to be sampled seven times and a state space $[5,10)$ with four subdomains each to be sampled three times. The code file is comp1bin; "state" is required following the code-file name. For testing components with state, the sample counts are often used only indirectly, but they must be present (more information to follow).

Source code has the same conventions for input, output, and run time (using STDIN, STDOUT, and STDERR) as in the stateless case. A component accesses local state by reading a disk file to get its 'input' state value and overwriting the same file with its result state value. This file has the same name as the code, with extension ".state". In the example above, the state file has to be named "comp1bin.state". States are restricted to a single floating-point value. When "comp1bin.state" does not exist, it signifies a 'reset'—the code is expected to initialize its state. On each execution a component's code must:

Read its input value from STDIN.

Read its 'input' state value from its .state file, or if that doesn't exist, create an initial state value.

Write its output value to STDOUT.

Write its run-time value to STDERR.

Write its final state value to its .state file.

The order and timing of these operations is up to the component code, except that the reads must come before the writes. *If a component fails to observe these conventions, when it is being executed by the SYN tools it may appear to 'hang', since the tools block waiting for the expected action. The most common cause of 'hang'-up is misnaming of the .state file: then the tools are blocked waiting to read it, but the component code is writing elsewhere... COMP checks for proper component behavior, but can't do a very good job of it.*

10.4.1 Tutorial: Modes (Preferences)

The files for this example are provided in the tool distribution in the directory statetutorial. *For the demonstration, create a directory named (say)* my2tutorial *and copy* statetutorial *into it. Also copy the tool scripts to* my2tutorial *from the distribution directory* tools. *These operations set up a base directory. The same toolset handles stateless/state cases, but some of the file names for example components and descriptions (*system.pscf *in particular) are the same in every base directory, so if you want to retain the results of previous work, use a new directory.*

One common use of local state is to record a program's 'mode', a parameter value that influences execution. In interactive software such as a word-processing program modes are called 'preferences', and used to set (for example) the font. This use of 'mode' state is not essential—the word processor could have additional input parameters that would set the font, and on every execution the user could include this additional input. But it is more user-friendly to have a special input set the font mode, which is then assumed on subsequent executions until changed. In a sense, mode values act as modifiers of a program's computed function. Within the program code the mode is tested in conditional statements and different actions taken for different mode values. A somewhat contrived example will illustrate this kind of state and demonstrate the use of SYN tools when components have state.

Figure 10.4 displays a Perl program `Trig` that computes certain trigonometic functions. `Trig` returns phase variants of $\sin x$ on input x and keeps state information that sets the phase. Before anything more is said about `Trig`'s specification, notice in Fig. 10.4 that `Trig` observes the state-component conventions: it has the required input/run-time/output operations near the beginning and end of its code, and it properly manipulates a state file `Trig.state`. The state is initialized to 2.0, a mode that means a phase shift to the cosine (specification details for `Trig` follow).

`Trig` has a floating-point state (mode) value whose integer part describes the phase. Only four phase values are permitted: $0°$, $30°$, $60°$, and $90°$. These are obscurely[13] coded as state values 0, 6, 3, and 2 respectively. Thus state 6, for example, means that for $x \geq 0$, `Trig` is to compute $\sin(x + \pi/6)$. Negative inputs set the mode to the corresponding positive integral value, except that integral values are converted to the adjacent integer, e.g., -7 becomes mode 6. This peculiar requirement makes all inputs in $[-7,-6)$[14] set the mode to 6. If a negative input describes a mode with one of the legal phase values, `Trig` returns -1 and sets the mode; if illegal, no action is taken (the mode remains what it was) and -2 is returned.

Although the `Trig` code actually uses the Perl library to compute its sine functions, it returns a run time that mimics the use of a constant time algorithm near zero-crossings of $\sin x$, linearly increasing run time above $\sin \pi/20$, and a different constant time for setting the mode. The 'real' run time of the code is much less interesting.

This brief description of the requirements for `Trig` can be consulted when the SYN tools are used to approximate its behavior.

The `Trig` implementation comprises its code (Fig. 10.4) but also requires a list of subdomains given in a configuration file to describe its testing, Fig. 10.5. For stateless components it is important to select good subdomain boundaries to capture rapid changes in behavior. When there is mode-state, even more care is required. A change in mode radically alters the component's behavior, so accurate approximations are impossible unless all the points in a subdomain involve the same mode. In `Trig` for example, a subdomain that overlaps two distinct modes (in the state dimension) or two different mode-setting inputs (in the input dimension) will have meaningless 'average' values for approximate output and state. On the other hand,

---

[13] Hint: $\pi/6$ radians is $30°$...

[14] It is usual programming practice to use singleton unique values to trigger program actions. This introduces discontinuities and makes most inputs illegal. In contrast, using ranges makes most inputs legal, and the computed functions piecewise continuous. These features are here introduced to accommodate the subdomains used by the tools, but they are a reasonable defensive coding technique.

```
┌──────────────────────────── Trig ─────────────────────────────┐
#! /usr/bin/perl
chomp($X = <STDIN>); #must read even if reset
$sf = "Trig.state";
if (open(SF, "<$sf")) { #state exists, not reset
  chomp($S = <SF>);
  close SF;
} else { #no state, initialize
  print "-1\n";  #OK output for init
  print STDERR "1\n"; #one unit of run time
  open(SF, ">$sf"); print SF "2.0\n"; close SF;
  exit;
} #not reset, input state in $S, input in $X
if ($X < 0) { #set mode state
  $R = 2; #two units of run time
  $X = -$X;
  $phase = int($X);
  if ($X == $phase) { #integer, move interval
    $phase--;
  }
  if ($phase == 0 || $phase == 2 || $phase == 3
      || $phase == 6) { #legal
    $S = $phase; #set mode
    $Y = -1; #OK return
  } else { #illegal, $S unchanged
    $Y = -2; #error return
  }
} else { #compute proper sin($X) value
  $pi = 3.14159265;
  $phase = $S;
  unless ($phase == 0) {
    $phase = $pi/$phase;
  }
  $Y = sin($X + $phase);
  $mulpi = ($X + $phase)/$pi;
  $imulpi = int($mulpi);
  $delX = $mulpi - $imulpi; #fraction of pi from zero cross
  if ($delX <= 1/20 || $delX >= 19/20) { #cheap near zero-cross
    $R = 3;
  } else {
    $R = 3 + $delX*6.0;
  }
  #(no change in state)
}
print "$Y\n";
print STDERR "$R\n";
open(SF, ">$sf"); print SF "$S\n"; close SF;
└────────────────────────────────────────────────────────────────┘
```

Fig. 10.4 Perl code for component Trig

```
┌──────── Trig.ccf ────────┐
│                          │
│ Trig state               │
│ -10 -9 3                 │
│ -9 -8  3                 │
│ -8 -7  3                 │
│ -7 -6  3                 │
│ -6 -5  3                 │
│ -5 -4  3                 │
│ -4 -3  3                 │
│ -3 -2  3                 │
│ -2 -1  3                 │
│ -1 0 3                   │
│ 0 0.5 3                  │
│ 0.5 1 3                  │
│ 1 1.5 3                  │
│ 1.5 2 3                  │
│ (23 lines omitted)       │
│ 8.5 9 3                  │
│ 9 9.5 3                  │
│ 9.5 10 3                 │
│                          │
│ -1 0 3                   │
│ 0 1 3                    │
│ 1 2 3                    │
│ 2 3 3                    │
│ 3 4 3                    │
│ 4 5 3                    │
│ 5 6 3                    │
│ 6 7 3                    │
│ 7 8 3                    │
│ 8 9 3                    │
│                          │
└──────────────────────────┘
```

Fig. 10.5 Component configuration file for `Trig`

where states are few and discrete, a few test samples per subdomain suffice—in Fig. 10.5 each subdomain is sampled three times. It is better to shrink the subdomain size than to increase the sample count, as the case studies in Section 18.1.1 will show.

`Trig` is complicated enough that it will first be explored by itself using the SYN tools before being placed in any system. The easiest way to approximate it is with the COMP command, but COMP requires a system-description file `system.pscf` listing components to approximate. The file:

```
┌── system.pscf ──┐
│                 │
│ 1  2  S         │
│ Trig.ccf        │
│ Trig.ccf        │
│                 │
└─────────────────┘
```

creates a meaningless system that will let COMP work. When COMP approximates the components for this 'system' it will first approximate Trig, then note that Trig's approximation is up-to-date and need not be done again. *The meaningless system could be synthesized and examined, but that won't be shown in this tutorial because Trig is ill-suited to follow itself. There are other more sensible phony 'systems' that might be tried, for example, one in which the second series component is a stateless identity function that just reproduces its input as output, which can be perfectly approximated with a single piecewise-linear subdomain. Or, COMP need not be used so that no* system.pscf *file is yet needed. The command to just approximate one component in this case (which is what COMP in fact uses), is:* COMPSt -V -U -S Trig.ccf

With a 'system' and its components defined,

COMP -V -U

will create the component approximation for Trig. As Section 10.2.2 above explains, the sampling of state values is a tricky issue. The -U option here forces sampling of Trig to be systematic. The number of samples given in Trig.ccf for each subdomain are taken at equi-spaced intervals across both input- and state dimensions of that subdomain. Systematic sampling is the naive extension of what was done in the stateless case, and observes the purpose of subdomain testing—to make sure no subdomain is missed. -U is not the default because this isn't the right way to sample state, but starting with it will demonstrate why. *Because component measurement for many 2-dimensional input × state subdomains can be slow, the* -V *option displays a progress bar.*

To see the results of these measurements on Trig, use:

Xcute Trig

which displays the functional-output behavior in Fig. 10.6. The figure simultaneously displays the actual output function for Trig and its approximation. The format was chosen to best visualize the approximation in complicated cases. *Try the* Xcute -A Trig *option to see if you like contoured 'surfaces' plots with column-like plateaus better. GNUPlot, which is used to display 2-D projections of 3-D graphs for functions that depend on both input and state, can interactively shift the projection viewpoint—click and hold the (left) mouse button while moving the mouse. Moving the viewpoint and watching the changing shape can help to visualize the surface. The GNUPlot graphs identify the files containing the plot data, so that they can be displayed differently using GNUPlot directly and interactively, if desired. Sometimes this is most easily done by modifying the control file* complot *created by the tools. Displays are repeated with the command:* gnuplot complot *after a tool has produced the display (and created* complot*). The same file is used for every plot, so only the most recent can be repeated in this way.*

It isn't easy to check that Trig is behaving as it should. The sin$x$ curves can be made out[15] at the right of the figure, but the phases (changing across the state dimension) don't separate into the four legal modes. That's because systematic state sampling forces Trig to process any state value, not just the ones it can set. The

---

[15] One reason for choosing a trigonometric example is that the eye can pick out periodic shapes in a welter of data.

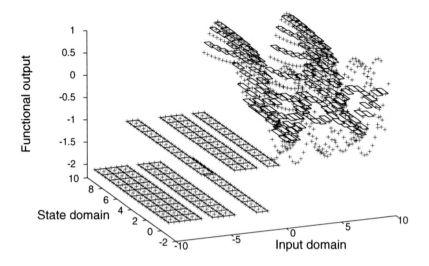

Fig. 10.6 Functional output behavior (*crosses*) of component Trig and its tested approximation (*rectangle steps*)

approximation is great for negative inputs, not so good for positive ones, but the sub-domains were chosen to show up well in graphs, not for accuracy. Xcute provides a detailed error analysis; the weighted average of r-m-s deviations of approximation from actual execution is about 12% in Fig. 10.6. Xcute can also display run time (-T option) or result state (-S option). Figure 10.7 is the result-state graph[16] *from* Xcute -S Trig . Checking result-state behavior in Fig. 10.7 is easier than look-ing at output in Fig. 10.6. The approximation is pretty good (Xcute reports that the maximum r-m-s error is 6.8%) and the two required behaviors are apparent in the figure:

1. For most of the domain, the result state does not depend on the input, and is identity in the state dimension, which appears as planes sloping toward the front of the figure. For non-negative inputs state identity means that Trig is in some mode and stays there, as it should. For negative inputs, state identity represents erroneous attempts to change state which correctly fail, for example on the far right of the figure.

---

[16] In projections of 3-D surfaces, the printed orientation of the graph is chosen to best expose its several features. This may mean reversing or shifting scales and axes. For example, in Fig. 10.7 the state and input axes are swapped end-for-end from the way they appear in Fig. 10.6. In looking at 3-D projections, the rule is to first find a feature of interest, then look at the axes to place it. Don't expect particular coordinates to remain in the same relative place from graph to graph.

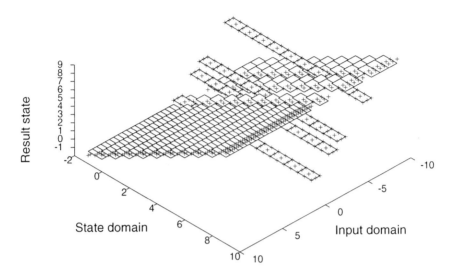

Fig. 10.7 Result-state behavior (*crosses*) of component `Trig` and its tested approximation (*rect-angle steps*)

2. In a few bands (e.g., $[-1,0)$ input interval, the narrow strip nearest the front of
   the figure) the result state is constant across the state dimension. Moving toward
   the back of the figure, these bands rise with more negative input values. Each
   band shows a legal mode change, for example, on all start states for input -0.5,
   the state changes to 0; in the input band $[-2,-1)$ it changes to 1; etc.

Shifting the viewpoint with GNUPlot makes it easy to see these two behaviors.

Close study of Fig. 10.7 reveals something badly wrong, however. `Trig` is only
allowed to have certain modes, yet every input-mode value appears to have a result-
mode in Fig. 10.7 (and the muddle of curves at the right of Fig. 10.6 should be
four distinct curves, one for each legal mode). For example, a state like 1 is illegal
because it does not correspond to one of the restricted phase values. And indeed, in
Figs. 10.7 and 10.6 it can be seen that on input (say) -1.5 which might have selected
this state, the output was -2 (correctly flagging the error) and the state doesn't change
(also correct). Apparently `Trig` is behaving correctly (at least for input -1.5), but
the SYN tools are not clearly displaying its behavior. The fault lies with systematic
sampling. Although `Trig` never goes into state 1, three start states in the $[1,2)$ state
domain were systematically sampled, and when started in those states `Trig` has
behavior that the code implements but which in reality it never exhibits, because it
protects itself from state 1. This phenomenon was described in Section 10.2.2, and
is of great practical significance. If infeasible states are forced on a program, it will

do something, but something that a tester must ignore. The situation is this example is not the worst possible. Trig is correct, and its requirements make state 1 illegal. The worst case occurs when a state is required to be legal, the program does the right thing when tested in that state, but in fact it can never reach the legal state. In that case the program is badly flawed but its tests succeed and the flaws go undetected.

To explore infeasible states further would depart too far from a tutorial, so the issue is deferred to the case studies of Section 18.3.1. However, the correct behavior graphs are obtained by repeating the approximation measurements with

    COMP -V -R

(-R—the default—substituted for -U above), which tests with sequences of random input samples. When COMP tests Trig with sequences, the sample counts in Trig.ccf are used only indirectly to guess at the number of sequences to be tried. It can happen that with too few sequences some subdomains are never sampled; again, the issue is deferred to later case studies. Figure 10.8 is the correct version of the output surface displayed by Xcute Trig, from which it can be

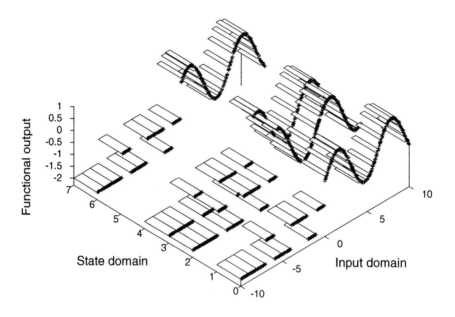

Fig. 10.8 Functional output behavior (*crosses*) of component Trig and its tested approximation (*rectangle steps*)

seen that only the legal states arise. Figure 10.9 is the alternate-format plot from Xcute -A Trig.

The interested reader can try Xcute -T Trig *(for the run-time graph) to explore* Trig's *behavior and its approximation further. Better approximations can be*

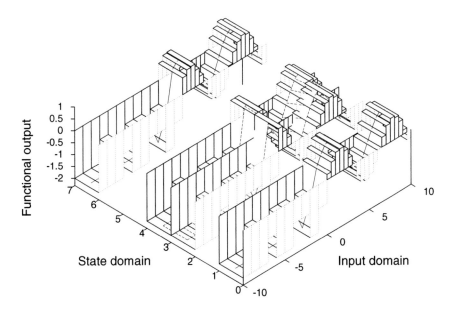

Fig. 10.9 Functional output behavior (*contour*) of component Trig and its tested approximation (*rectangular pillars*)

obtained by splitting Trig *subdomains as described in the the stateless tutorial, Chapter 9.*

In this tutorial, Trig is a vehicle for demonstrating the SYN tools, but a component developer has good reason to go through these same motions. The actual behavior functions of a component being implemented should be examined to see if it meets its requirements. Component testing should be evaluated for thoroughness, which in this context means that the subdomain approximation should be checked to see how well it captures those behaviors. In practice, code and subdomain changes are made until the developer is satisfied. At that point the component and its description might be filed away in a library or repository. In this tutorial, it is now time to synthesize a system using Trig. No other components with state appear in the example, because if they did the results could not be displayed so clearly[17].

A common pattern in CBSD is the construction of a system around one or more components with the intent of restricting their complexity or making them easier to use. For example, a graphical user interface might surround a command-based component. The GUI may not get at all the functionality, but some users prefer that complex features be hidden. A simple system built around Trig will model this kind of modification. Suppose that the desired interface has these characteristics:

---

[17] Chapter 18 includes a similar case study in which two components have state so that one can monitor and control the mode of the other.

- The only phases allowed are modes 0 and 2 (i.e., $\sin x$ and $\sin(x + \pi/2) = \cos x$) for `Trig`
- These modes are to be selected with two ranges[18] of negative inputs:

input	function
(-2,-1]	sin
(-3,-2]	cos

- The output for any negative input is to be 0
- For non-negative inputs, the output is to be 0 unless the input lies in $[0, 2\pi)$ and the output from `Trig` is non-negative

In practice, the reason for this filtering of `Trig`'s behavior might be to adapt it to match some other component. In that case the modifications are called 'glue code'. In the spirit of CBSD, they can be accomplished with stateless[19] components in a system structure described by the system configuration file:

```
— system.pscf —

1 2 3 S 4 S 5 C
Check.ccf
Before.ccf
Trig.ccf
After.ccf
Alt.ccf
```

or in pseudocode:

```
IF Check THEN
   Before
   Trig
   After
ELSE
   Alt
FI
```

These auxiliary components act roughly as follows:

Check decides whether to invoke the sequence of Before, Trig, After (on all non-negative inputs and legal negative inputs according to the new scheme) or the alternative Alt.

Before adjusts the incoming state code to the corresponding values understood by Trig.

Alt is an 'error' routine that returns the newly required zero result.

---

[18] Again, ranges are used instead of particular integer inputs.

[19] Glue code can be much more effective when it has state of its own—see the similar case study in Section 18.3.3.

`After` adjusts `Trig` output to meet the new requirements: it changes all negative values[20] to zero.

Perl source code for one of these auxiliary components is given in Fig. 10.10; the others are even simpler. *The source code from the tutorial file can be examined in the base directory.* Component configuration files (`.ccf`) for the glue components

```
──────────────── Before ────────────────
#! /usr/bin/perl
chomp($X = <STDIN>);
if ($X < 0) { #convert and return state codes
  $XI = int(-$X);
  $Y = 5; #illegal mode change
  if ($XI == 1) {$Y = 1.0;}
  if ($XI == 2) {$Y = 3.0;}
  $Y = -$Y;
  print "$Y\n";
  print STDERR "3\n";   #three units run time
} else { #return non-negative input intact
  print "$X\n";
  print STDERR "1\n";   #one unit run time
}
```

Fig. 10.10 Perl code for component `Before`

also now in the base directory look very similar to the input portion of `Trig.ccf`, although `alt` needs only one subdomain to capture its behavior perfectly. The file `after.ccf`, however, needs to have different subdomains, since its input (from `Trig`) must be reproduced in the range $[0, 1]$ while the positive side of `Trig` deals with inputs in $[0, 10)$[21].

Even this trivial system exposes a couple of important issues about component-based software development.

First, there is the matter of adjusting subdomains to match component interfaces. In this context, its subdomains quantify the testing effort expended on a component—finer subdomains, more testing. In general, adjusting the test effort after a component has been developed isn't kosher, because in I-CBSD components are supposed to be developed and tested in isolation, without any knowledge of how they will be used. Their subdomains must be chosen to capture their behavior, but cannot be tailored to future, unknown use. In synthesizing series constructions, it can happen that the input subdomains chosen for a component like `Trig` fit badly

---

[20] It is fortunate that the negative $\sin x$ values and the -1 from setting the mode in `Trig` are both required to return zero; otherwise it would be necessary to introduce another conditional into the system, to distinguish two paths containing `Trig`, paths on which the component in the place of `After` acts differently.

[21] This mismatch is the reason that the phony system `Trig`; `Trig` isn't interesting. But try it if you like.

with the component that comes before it (Before in this system). However, glue code is an exception. When Before and After are being written, they are expressly intended to surround Trig, and their subdomains (testing) reflects this.

The second issue concerns glue code itself. It may seem silly to write four new components just to make trivial adjustments in input/output values of Trig, and in this illustrative example it *is* silly. It would be easier to modify the Trig code to meet the new requirements. But glue-code adjustments are one of the basic patterns of CBSD. In real cases, it is *not* easier to make modifications to components far more complex than Trig, and more to the point it isn't safe. The code for glue components is simple, easy to get right, and easy to see that it *is* right; but any modification to a complex component is liable to introduce subtle errors that show up only later as obscure system failures.

With the code and description files for components and for the system description in place in the base directory, SYN tools can synthesize a system approximation with first

```
COMP -V -U
```

which will make measurements on the stateless components, but will note that Trig has already been processed (with equi-spaced sampling). *Because there is a choice of how component state-sampling is conducted, it's a good idea to use the -V option and to notice in informational messages the choice that COMP makes (or made in the past when approximation files were created). In this case, if the -U option were omitted, COMP would reprocess Trig with sequence sampling.* To illustrate how easy it is to check glue code, Fig. 10.11 results from running Xcute Before. It clearly shows both aspects of proper component testing: (1) Before meets its specification, and (2) The test approximation is capturing the functional behavior pretty well.

With the component approximations measured and the system structure described,

```
SYN -V
```

does the system synthesis. The trace of synthesis operations for the example system is shown in Fig. 10.12. The order of synthesis in the *true* branch could be altered by changing the Polish description in system.pscf to 1 2 3 4 S S 5 C, which would first synthesize Trig with After. The order doesn't matter—synthesis is associative—but this will be explored later in Section 18.1.2. The final synthesis from the SYN run is placed in the file theory3.ccfc, from which graphs can be obtained using

```
Xcomp
```

for the system output. Figure 10.13 shows the two feasible modes of the system. (This figure and the next were plotted from a modified theory3.ccfc from which some additional infeasible subdomains were removed. Full details are provided in the case studies of Section 18.3.) Similarly, Xcomp -S would display the system result states; Xcomp -T plots system run time in Fig. 10.14. Xcomp also executes the 'real' system formed by linking the actual component code files, and supplies an error analysis for the predictions. It gives information about subdomain usage, which is typical of systems with state: of 330 calculated system subdomains,

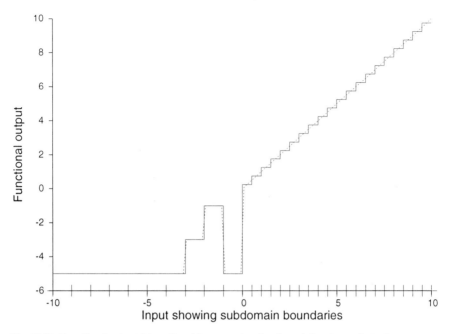

Fig. 10.11 Functional output (*dotted*) and its approximation (*steps*) for glue code `Before`

```
Beginning the system calculation of Polish 1 2 3 S 4 S 5 C
Series: Before ; Trig -> theory1
Series: theory1 ; After -> theory2
Conditional:  IF Check THEN theory2 ELSE Alt FI -> theory3
```

Fig. 10.12 Synthesis operations for a trigonometic system

80% are infeasible (compared to 60% infeasible for `Trig` itself). System sampling always uses randomly generated sequences of inputs, and so does not necessarily match up to the predicted subdomains. If too few measurements were made on `Trig`, the prediction lacks subdomains that are nevertheless executed in testing the real system; or, if too few system measurements are made, none may fall in some predicted subdomain. There are many issues to explore for even the simplest components and systems that use state, presented in case studies in Section 18.3.

The synthesis figures show that the system is behaving as it should. Output is limited as required (and notice how much easier it is to visualize the output behavior in Fig. 10.13 than in Fig. 10.6), speaking to the wisdom of adding glue code. System run time is either constant (when the `Alt` path is taken), or a constant more than `Trig`'s run time for the longer path, because of the constant run times for the glue components.

The subdomains in this tutorial example were selected more for the clarity of figures than for accuracy of the calculated predictions. Nevertheless, the run-time predictions are off by only about 1.8% on average. A full error analysis by sub-

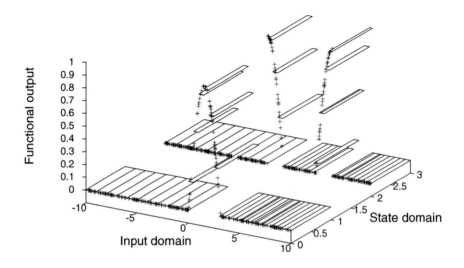

Fig. 10.13 System functional output (*crosses*) and its predicted approximation (*rectangles*)

domain is produced by Xcomp, but its display isn't pleasing because most of the values are not defined (subdomains infeasible) and there are too many subdomains for the error table to fit well on a screen.

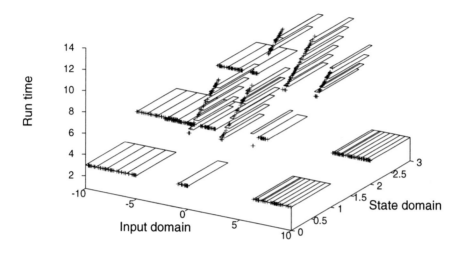

Fig. 10.14 System run time (*crosses*) and its predicted approximation (*rectangles*)

Chapter 11
Concurrent Execution

EXTENDING subdomain-composition theory to include concurrent execution introduces a second domain which influences the behavior of master component A as a result of slave component B executing in parallel. Now instead of state, that second domain is a second input sent back to A from B (that is, values of $\boxed{B}$). The semantic functions to be approximated for component A are a pair of outputs described in Chapter 6: A sends $\boxed{A}$ to B, and $\boxed{\boxed{A}}$ is A's final output. A also has a triple of run-time functions, also described in Chapter 6, which capture A run time before B is started, the run time A uses while executing in parallel with B, and the run time A uses following B's termination.

11.1 Adding Concurrency to Composition Theory

Compared to the complications introduced by combinations of states in Chapter 10, the restricted form of concurrency considered here is easy to handle. In operational terms, concurrency works like this:

1. The 'master' component (concurrent) takes its external input i_1 and may compute for a bit.
2. The master starts a parallel execution of the 'slave' component, (the slave is a regular, not concurrent component) and sends an input value to it. This is output value v_1 of the master.
3. The master clocks a run time t_1 from its inception until the slave begins execution.
4. The slave computes in parallel with the master, and eventually terminates, producing an output and a run time t_2 as all regular components do, and a final state if the slave has state.
5. The master computes in parallel with the slave, but eventually it waits for the slave to terminate. The master's run time in parallel with the slave is t_3.
6. The master receives the slave's output as a second input i_2.

D. Hamlet, *Composing Software Components*, DOI 10.1007/978-1-4419-7148-7_11,
© Springer Science+Business Media, LLC 2010

7. Execution continues in the master as a function of the original input and that provided by the slave. At termination, the master produces a final output value v_2 and another run time t_4 covering the time from slave termination to master termination.

Each of these quantities may depend on the information available when it is produced—for example, the final master output v_2 and t_4 may depend on both inputs to the master, but v_1 can depend on the initial master input only. Thus the master-slave combination is a regular, not concurrent component whose output, on the input to the master, is the final output of the master. Its run time is $t_1 + \max(t_2, t_3) + t_4$, because t_2 and t_3 occur simultaneously.

It is a considerable simplification to forbid theoretical creation of a combination that is itself concurrent, that is, synthesis of two concurrent components. There is nothing conceptually wrong with such a synthesis, but the same result can be obtained more simply by master-slave combinations. For example, to have a concurrent component C start a copy of itself to then start non-concurrent N, instead of treating this system as $(C \parallel C) \parallel N)$, the easier equivalent $C \parallel (C \parallel N)$ has the same behavior: two copies of C will be executing simultaneously with N. In the latter form the second parallel operator yields a non-concurrent (slave) component so all applications of '$\parallel$' are the same form, synthesizing master with slave. It is also a simplification to omit state from concurrent components. Again there would be no conceptual difficulty, but the complications that would be introduced in synthesis don't seem to be worth the generality gained.

11.1.1 Algorithm for Synthesizing Components in Parallel

Suppose now that two subdomain component approximations are given, one for C (master, concurrent) and the other for N (slave, non-concurrent). $\overline{N}$ approximates N as a step function[1] as usual. The description of C is more complicated, since it has two orthogonal input domains, two outputs, and three run times. Each of the five results is a function over the two-dimensional input space, a function that can be thought of as a three-dimensional surface above the cross-product input plane containing points like (i_1, i_2). Three of these functions are constant in the second input dimension—v_1, r_1, and r_3 in the description above do not have the input i_2 available. Each function has a step-function approximation in the C description, although formally defining these five dotted-box functions would get notationally unwieldy. Instead, the functions and their approximations and domains will be named as in the operational description above, e.g.: "C's v_1 output function", "step-function approximation to C's r_4 run-time function", "i_2 input space", etc.

The combination $C \parallel N$ thus has a step-function approximation that can be constructed from the descriptions of C and N as follows:

---

[1] Although a stateless N-approximation may be piecewise-linear, when combined with step functions for C, the linear behavior is washed out, so the linear case will be ignored here.

The input subdomains of $\boxed{C \parallel N}$ are the subdomains of the i_1 input space of C. If N has state, the state subdomains of $\boxed{C \parallel N}$ are those of N; otherwise, $C \parallel N$ is stateless.

Consider one such subdomain S of $\boxed{C \parallel N}$, which is also a subdomain of C's i_1 space. Think first about a stateless N. To get the value of the approximation $\boxed{C \parallel N}$, look up the v_1 approximation value y on S in the C description, then find the subdomain S' in the input subdomains of N in which y falls. Let the N approximate output on subdomain S' be z. Look up z in the subdomains of the i_2 space of C's description, finding (say) subdomain S'', $z \in S''$. The v_2 output approximation value w on S'' is then the final output of $C \parallel N$, that is, the value of $\boxed{C \parallel N}$ on subdomain S. The run time of $C \parallel N$ on S is calculated from the $r_{[1..3]}$ functions of C and the run time of N, on subdomains S for r_1 (say run time t_1), S' for N's run time t_2, and S'' for r_3 (t_3) and r_4 (t_4). The values are combined to get the approximate run time of $C \parallel N$ on S as $t_1 + \max t_2, t_3 + t_4$. If any of the look-up operations should fail because the value sought is not in any of the examined subdomains, then the corresponding approximate value for $C \parallel N$ is undefined.

For the case that N has a k-fold state, its description has subdomains on a dimension-$(k+1)$ hyperspace (N's input space crossed with its k state spaces). When tracing the subdomains as above, S is also in a $(k+1)$-hyperspace, with its input dimension being C's i_1 input space. The necessary values from N are looked up in state subdomains the same as those that are part of S, and a result-state value is also looked up for N in each such subdomain, to be the result states for $C \parallel N$.

The formal concurrent synthesis algorithm, like the one for synthesis with state(s) in Chapter 10, is hard to understand. It may help to imagine the situation without subdomains. If it just happened that tests of C and N 'lined up,' so that outputs could be traced through them, then synthesis is straightforward. The algorithm presented above works because although test points themselves do not line up, subdomains always do.

11.2 Testing Measurements, Behavior Graphs, and System Predictions

To make the measurements that describe a concurrent component requires sampling its two-dimensional cross-product input space. One dimension is the component input domain; the second dimension is the input received from parallel execution of a slave. The systematic sampling technique used with stateless input subdomains is appropriate: if one set of subdomains is sampled n times each and the orthogonal set m times each, then each rectangular subdomain is tested with a grid of nm points. There are no complications like those involved with sampling state, because both inputs are under external control. In principle, any value may occur in either input domain.

For concurrent (master) components, the functional output behavior is a surface plotted above the plane of its two input domains. There are three run-time surfaces, describing the time from starting the master execution until a slave starts, the time in parallel with the slave, and the time from slave termination to master termination. Technically, only the third of these times depends on the second input (from the slave); when plotted above the two-dimensional plane the surfaces for the other two run times do not change elevation along the second-input dimension.

In synthesis, concurrency disappears. Although a concurrent master component has a special multi-dimensional description, it must always be combined with a non-concurrent slave component, and the result has the character of that slave: the composite is non-concurrent; the composite has or does not have state as the slave does or does not. The composite run time is a single value in which the contribution during concurrent execution is the maximum of the slave time and the second part of the master run time. Hence the use of concurrent components in systems does not introduce new system features in synthesis beyond the parallel synthesis of one master and one slave.

11.3 A Tutorial Example with Concurrency

Concurrent components are completely different from those with state, but the two share a .ccf file format. A concurrent component .ccf file has two sets of subdomains with sampling counts, the first for external inputs, the second for input from a slave started in parallel, separated by a blank line. For example,

```
———— comp2.ccf ————

comp2bin concurrent
0 .1 7
.1 .5 7
.5 1.0 7

5 6 3
6 7 3
7 8 3
8 10 3
```

describes an external input space $[0, 1)$ with three subdomains each to be sampled seven times and a second input space $[5, 10)$ with four subdomains each to be sampled three times. The code file is comp2bin; "concurrent" is required following the code name.

Concurrent components must use STDIN, STDOUT, and STDERR as stateless components do, but in a unique pattern. On each execution a concurrent component (here called the 'master') must:

Read its external input value from STDIN.

Write an output value to STDOUT, which signals starting execution of a slave component in parallel, the slave to receive this output as its input.

Write a partial run-time value to STDERR, the master's run time from beginning its execution until starting a slave.

Read (again) from STDIN an input which is the slave's output and signals that the slave is terminating.

Write a second partial run-time value to STDERR, the master's run time from starting the slave until slave termination.

Write a third partial run-time value to STDERR, the master's run time from slave termination until master termination.

Write its ultimate output value to STDOUT.

The order and timing of these operations is constrained by the master component attempting to do something sensible; the input/output read/write operations must stay in order to keep the component from blocking forever when run by the SYN tools. The order constraints dictate dependencies among the parameters available to the master in its computation. For example, its final output might depend on both of its inputs, but the output sent to the slave can depend on its external input alone.

When a concurrent master component observes this pattern it matches with a slave that is a regular non-concurrent component. The slave gets its input (from the first master write), then writes its output (which the master sees as its second input) and writes its run time, which is concurrent with the master's second partial run time. Synchronization between master and slave is accomplished with input/output blocking. For example, the slave blocks on its input, which the master supplies with its first write[2]; then later the master blocks waiting for input from the slave, supplied by the slave's output. Between these two synchronizations the components execute in parallel.

11.3.1 Tutorial: Multiversion Software

The most interesting use of concurrent execution is in multi-version programming (MVP, or sometimes NVP for N-version programming). MVP was invented to mimic the use of redundant independent physical components in parallel for fail-

---

[2] The use of blocking synchronization introduces a slight anomaly: the slave can execute down to its input statement in parallel with the master, but the time for this is not properly accounted for, being overlapped with t_1, not t_3, so that t_2 should technically be divided into two parts. The tools do not do this, so for proper accounting a slave must begin with a read statement, and resist the temptation to do initialization bookkeeping (say involving its state) prior to the read. The slave could similarly continue execution after its final write unblocks the master, but not usefully.

safe systems. Several programs perform computations intended to get the same result, then their results are compared and the majority accepted. Using different algorithms (and independent programmers) seeks independence in the parallel programs, but it is controversial whether independence can be thereby obtained [71]. It is of some importance whether the analogy between mechanical components and software components holds for the parallel-redundant situation, since there is no other known general scheme for increasing reliability. This tutorial constructs a very simple 2VP system to sum integers $1 + 2 + ... + n$ on input n. Two algorithms are used: brute-force addition; and, a quadratic formula[3].

C_2 is a non-concurrent slave component that just computes the sum with a loop. It is written in FORTRAN 66, as befits its pedestrian algorithm[4].

The Perl component C_1 is the concurrent master; it starts a slave component and itself computes the sum in parallel with this slave. When the slave returns its result, C_1 compares the two values. If they agree, it returns that result; if not, it returns -1 as an error[5]. Here C_2 is clearly a component independently developed. C_1, however, seems to know about C_2. This is an illusion: C_1 may use any other independently developed component as slave, but the parallel system will mostly return -1 unless that slave implements the functionality that C_2 expects.

Create a new base directory (say) TutoriaC *and copy the distribution files from* concurrenttutorial *to it, then overlay the tool scripts from the distribution* tools, *as described in the previous stateless tutorial, Chapter 9. The concurrent tutorial contains a* system.pscf *file describing the parallel system, so the* COMP *command can be used immediately.* In the tutorial distribution, C_1 is named Master and C_2 is named Brute, names that will be used from here on. Figure 11.1 displays the two component source files. Note that both programs must be careful to convert their floating-point inputs to integer values, because when tested by the tools, they will be sampled across floating point domains. *The Perl code for* Master *includes a peculiar statement "*$| = 1;*", which the tools require to eliminate buffering. Unless buffers are immediately flushed, the master–slave communication will fail. The symptom of failure will be that attempts to run the real system will hang (with the slave waiting for input that is stalled in a master buffer). Perl has the convenient special variable* $| *to flush buffers; C usually has library routines (e.g.,* flushlbf) *for the same purpose.* Subdomains for each component are listed in corresponding .ccf files, placed on integer input boundaries over the sample input domain $[0, 10)$.

The command

---

[3] There is an apparently reliable story that Gauss derived the formula in school when he was nine years old.

[4] While the component tools can handle executables written in any language, it is surprisingly difficult to correctly resurrect programs that were commonplace 30 years ago but are almost unknown today. The GNU gcc compiler suite, however, does a fine job on the bewildering variety of FORTRAN dialects. The tool distribution for this book comes with C_2 compiled for a Linux platform. The reader may want to simply redo C_2 in Perl or C rather than seek out a compiler. But remember that in a FORTRAN 66 DO-loop the body is always executed at least once...

[5] In this kind of 2VP there is no majority voting, just an added assurance that when a non-error result is returned it is correct.

```
──────────────── Master ────────────────
#! /usr/bin/perl -W
$| = 1;
$X = <STDIN>;
print STDOUT $X; #input->slave
print STDERR ".2\n"; #t1
$X = int($X);
$Y = $X*($X+1)/2.0;
$R = <STDIN>; # value from slave
$R = int($R);
print STDERR ".7\n"; #t3
if ($R == $Y) {
  print STDOUT "$Y\n";
} else {
  print STDOUT "-1\n";
}
print STDERR ".3\n"; #t4
```

```
──────────── Brute.f ────────────
      READ (5,4) X
4     FORMAT (F5.0)
      ISUM = 0
      IE = X
      DO 2 I = 1,X
      ISUM = ISUM + I
2     CONTINUE
      R = 0.12*IE
      WRITE (0,5) R
      Y = ISUM
      WRITE (6,4) Y
5     FORMAT (F8.3)
      END
```

Fig. 11.1 Perl source for Master (*left*) and FORTRAN Brute (*right*)

```
COMP -V
```
creates approximation files for the two components. Brute is a regular stateless component, for which Xcute displays Fig. 11.2. *The command used for this figure and similarly the next three figures was Xcute Brute 0 10 300, a variant that samples the code 300 times over interval* $[0, 10)$. *In the actual tool displays, the curves are slightly displaced and in different colors so both measured and approximated behavior can be seen even though the graphs are the same.* In the figure, the approximation is perfect because subdomain boundaries are at integers, and within each subdomain Brute computes a constant. Brute seems to be correct[6]—for example, it returns $10 = 1 + 2 + 3 + 4$ on input 4. The approximation is certainly good. Run time will be of interest for concurrent execution. For Brute is has been taken to be linear, at 1/10 of the (integer) input value. Again, the approximation is perfect, as the tools show in Fig. 11.3.

```
Xcute Master
```
produces quite different displays, Figs. 11.4 and 11.5. *The alternate display from* Xcute -A Master *is less precise, but better shows the isolated plateaus.*

Master's behavior depends on two input domains, its own, $[0, 10)$, and a second ("Parallel input") supplied by its slave component. Since Master expects the slave to be computing a sum that should range from $0 - 45$ for this interval, Master.ccf contains a second set of subdomains covering $[0, 50)$. These subdomains should be aligned at least with the integer values that Master expects, i.e., 0, 1, 3, 10, ..., 45, but let us suppose that the component developer is lazy, and fails to do this near the right of the interval. In Fig. 11.4, Master's functional behavior seems to be correct. Its most frequent output is -1 (the large plane in Fig. 11.4), meaning that

---

[6] But it is not correct; see what follows.

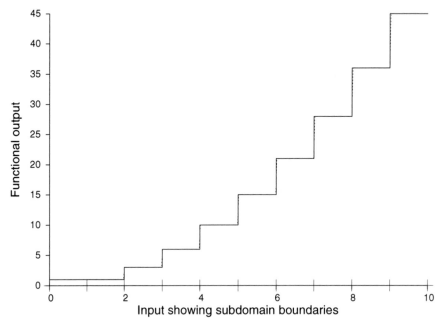

Fig. 11.2 Functional behavior of Brute, measured and approximated

for most subdomains containing input pairs (i, p) (i from its own input, p from a slave), $p \neq \sum_{k=1}^{i} k$, so (i, p) is an error pair[7]. But for a few subdomains (e.g.,, one containing $(4, 10)$), the pairs are not in error, and there Master returns its sum value (e.g., 10). Thus Fig. 11.4 shows a spiral of plateaus above the -1 plane as the measured behavior of Master. The approximated behavior agrees perfectly with that measured, except for the plateau at input 9. This imperfection results from the lazy choice of subdomains for Master, to be discussed in what follows.

Figure 11.5 is the tool output displaying the run-time behavior of Master (obtained from Xcute -T Master)—a constant plane at 1.2 above the two input domains. The run time comes in three parts (which can be displayed with Xcute -T1 Master or -T3 or -T4). Each of these is constant, at .2, .7, .3 respectively. The choice reflects that Gauss's formula takes the most time (.7, which is in parallel with the slave), while setup and comparison take less time. It is of interest that the run-time approximation is not wrong at the plateau near 9 where the functional approximation is wrong.

The command

```
SYN -V -G
```

---

[7] The sum is not really relevant; it would be better to say that p differs from the value that Master computes, which is *supposed* to be the sum. As in all testing work, there is a constant intellectual danger of confusing what a program really *does* do with its required behavior.

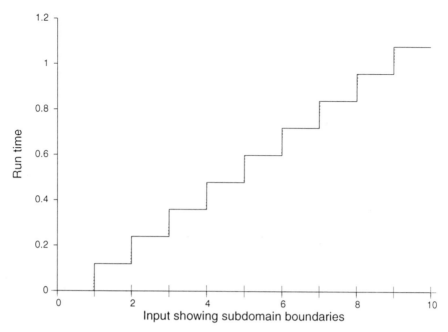

Fig. 11.3 Run-time behavior of `Brute`, measured and approximated

synthesizes the parallel system of `Master` and `Brute`, the result being non-concurrent and stateless, as the tools show in Figs. 11.6 and 11.7, produced by the `-G` option. Figure 11.6 shows that the synthesized approximate system is behaving as expected, except at input 9 where the `Master` approximation is poor. But the careful reader will note that the approximate system fails its requirement to compute the vacuous sum on input 0: the output is not the expected 0, but rather -1. That is, `Master` and `Brute` do not agree on input 0. In fact, `Brute` fails to correctly compute its sum at 0 because of a FORTRAN 66 peculiarity: the loop bounds are $1 \to 0$, no iterations, but it is a feature of early FORTRAN that loops test at loop-end, not -beginning, so `Brute` returns a sum of 1. The mistake can be seen in Fig. 11.2 (now that one knows to look!). Thus in at least this contrived case, 2VP using diverse components did its job.

Concurrency shows clearly in the predicted run-time behavior of the synthesized system, Fig. 11.7. `Brute`'s run time increases linearly with its input, while `Master`'s is constant at 1.2, 0.7 of which overlaps with `Brute`. Below input 6, `Master` has the longer run time in parallel, so the system run time is constant at 1.2. Then `Brute` begins to take longer than 0.7 to run, so its increasing time dominates that of `Master` during the parallel execution, so the system run time is 0.5 greater than the increasing steps of `Brute`.

Because `Master` and `Slave` are approximated using subdomains that match their discontinuities (with the one exception of `Master`'s last subdomain), and both components have constant behavior over these subdomains, the approximations

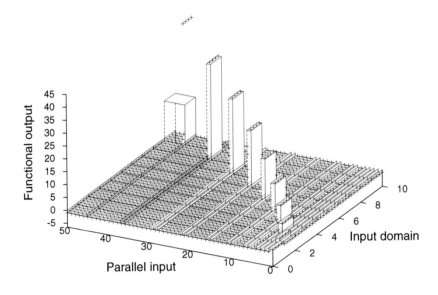

Fig. 11.4 Functional behavior of `Master`, measured (*crosses*) and approximated (*plateaus*)

shown in Figs. 11.2 – 11.5 are almost perfect. `Master`'s functional approximation is wrong only on subdomains around input 9 where the subdomain boundaries don't match. There the approximation includes some values of 45 and some -1 values, which average to about 14.3, the plateau shown at the far end of the spiral in Fig. 11.4. With that exception[8] all of the measured and calculated approximations are perfect, as the tools' error analysis shows.

To convert this example from 2VP to 3VP is easy: make a copy of `Master`, say `Master2`, in which the result is computed in yet another way and the test for non-agreement also checks for a negative return, then form the system:

  `Master2 ∥ (Master ∥ Brute)`

`Master2` will then check that `Master` and `Brute` agree and their common result agrees with its own calculation. In the actual system, all three of the components will be running simultaneously, and this scheme generalizes to NVP for any N[9].

---

[8] The following is wrong, but very seductive reasoning: "The approximate system output on input 9 ought to be -1, not the 14.3 shown in Fig. 11.6, since `Master`'s approximation is computing 14.3 and `Brute`'s approximation is computing 45." Dealing with component approximations adds a new confusion to the usual mixup between what code *should* do and what it *does* do—an approximation does not have code to study, yet it *does* do what it does, which may be nothing like the requirements *or* what's written in the real code.

[9] The simple generalization doesn't do voting or make distinctions based on how many versions agree.

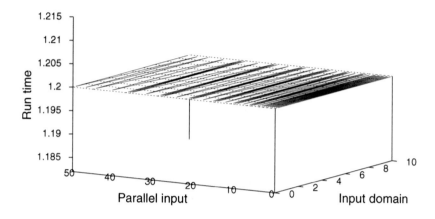

Fig. 11.5 Run-time behavior of Master, measured and approximated

Although this small example was intended only to try out the concurrency features of the SYN tools, along the way it illustrates an important aspect of CBSD: A system prediction can sometimes stand in for testing the real system. The prediction of Fig. 11.6 exposed a problem with FORTRAN loops, and the tool support that produced this graph makes it likely that the problem will be seen. In conventional system testing, isolated failures like this are all too easy to miss.

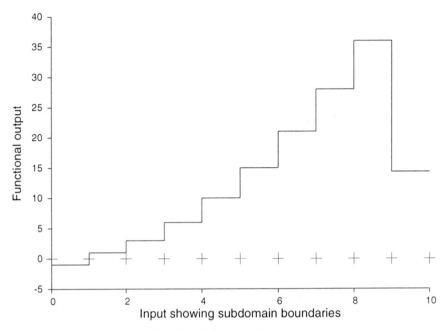

Fig. 11.6 Predicted approximate functional behavior of the parallel system

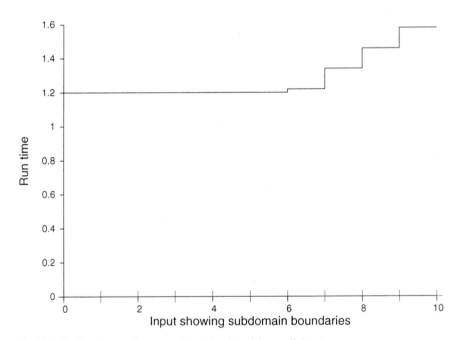

Fig. 11.7 Predicted approximate run-time behavior of the parallel system

Chapter 12
The Other Non-functional Property: Reliability

THE sad state of reliability theory for software can be gauged by noting the failure of the development community to frame a sensible definition of this fundamental engineering parameter and to study it experimentally.

12.1 Reliability in Other Engineering Disciplines

In other branches of engineering, the *failure-rate function* $f(t)$ for a physical object M is defined[1] as the probable rate at which failures occur at time t in its continuous operation, given that M has not failed before t. Thus the units of f are inverse time, and a requirement might be expressed as (say): "The air frame shall have a failure rate of less than 10^{-9} per hour over its lifetime." In a five-hour flight, the chance of failure would then be below 5×10^{-9}. The reference to "lifetime" recognizes that physical objects wear out, so that at best the failure rate can be bounded for a limited time. In the imperfect physical world, meeting such a requirement is the very best that one might hope for, and engineering progress could be justly defined as the ability to control and predict failure rate for the objects that engineers design. In electrical, mechanical, and structural engineering there has been and continues to be excellent progress: extremely complex objects are constructed and can mostly be trusted to work. Planes do crash, computer hardware dies, buildings collapse, etc., but not very often. When there is an unexpected failure it is subjected to obsessive root-cause analysis and design rules are changed to try to prevent its re-occurrence [90].

To design for a failure-rate requirement, an engineer relies absolutely on component-based design, and for component measurement, on statistical life testing. In brief, components are manufactured by a carefully controlled process that limits variability of their properties. The output of each production process is sampled and

---

[1] There is variant terminology to cover whether the failure rate is a limit over a small interval (hence a derivative) or a discrete measure; the term *hazard rate* is sometimes used interchangeably.

D. Hamlet, *Composing Software Components,* DOI 10.1007/978-1-4419-7148-7_12,
© Springer Science+Business Media, LLC 2010

samples are tested to destruction. From this life testing, a failure rate bound for each component is obtained (roughly, the time the samples operate before they fail[2]). Then a composition theory is used to calculate from the failure rates of the parts, a failure rate for the system made from them[3]. The separation into components is essential, since it would be hopelessly impractical to directly life-test an object like an air frame or a skyscraper.

Composition theory for the failure rate of a system synthesized from physical components is based on analysis into subsystems of series/parallel component pairs. Two components A and B are in series if the failure of either causes the system U to fail; they are in parallel if U fails only when both fail. Thus the synthesis formulas are:

$$f_U(t) = 1 - (1 - f_A(t))(1 - f_B(t)) \text{ (series)}$$

$$f_U(t) = f_A(t)f_B(t) \text{ (parallel)}$$

on the assumption that the component failure rates f_x are independent of each other.

Real physical systems eventually fail without fail. The technical *reliability* parameter expresses this better than the failure rate. The *reliability* function $R(t)$ of a physical object M is defined as the probability that M will not fail over a period of normal use[4] t. The restriction to "normal use" is the connection to how life testing must be done: M will be 'normally used' steadily until it fails. In terms of reliability the probability that M will fail at t is $1 - R(t)$, so the rate of failure near t is approximately

$$\frac{1 - R(t + \Delta t) - (1 - R(t))}{\Delta t} = -\frac{R(t + \Delta t) - R(t)}{\Delta t}.$$

The failure-rate function $f(t)$ is conditional on no failure before t, which is just probability $R(t)$, so taking $\lim_{\Delta t \to 0}$,

$$f(t) = -\frac{1}{R(t)}\frac{d}{dt}(R(t)),$$

or integrating both sides

$$\ln R(t) = -\int_0^t f(x)dx;$$

$$R(t) = e^{-\int_0^t f(x)dx}.$$

---

[2] The statistical theory used not only yields a failure rate, but also its *confidence bound*—a probability that the measured failure rate might be wrong—based on the number of samples and the variability of failure times. More on confidence bounds and measuring failure rates follows.

[3] Calculations include safety factors (Section 20.2.3) to cover errors in the component measurements and in the synthesis theory.

[4] The implicit assumption is that M starts out 'fresh,' not having been used before t begins. To capture the situation when there has been previous use, conditional probabilities can be used, e.g., to define the reliability $R(t \mid t_0)$, $t > t_0$, the reliability at t on the assumption that its use started at $t = 0$, and it has not failed up to t_0. The failure rate is already such a conditional probability, so that $f(t \mid t) = f(t)$.

Thus if $f(t)$ is always more than some constant, however small, M is sure to fail eventually:

$$\lim_{t \to \infty} R(t) = 0.$$

Reliability is also expressed as a probability (but of success, not failure) per unit time, but it is *not* the complement of failure rate.

A more intuitively meaningful parameter is the *Mean Time To Failure (MTTF)*, defined as

$$\int_0^\infty R(t)\,dt,$$

a time at which M is likely to fail. MTTF figures both in life testing and in describing M with a single parameter: it is the average of the times at which objects are destroyed in a life test; it is the expected value of $R(t)$.

This summary of reliability theory for physical objects is very brief, and avoids the introduction of random variables. A large literature explores the matter in great detail. The Appendix of Michael Lyu's handbook [74, B], although ostensibly about software, is a good summary of physical-object reliability.

12.2 Software Reliability Theory

A software reliability theory has been constructed by analogy to the mechanical/electrical theory, but the analogy is seriously flawed. Other engineers have empirically studied failure-rate functions for their artifacts and validated life testing; software engineers admit that life testing makes little sense for software but they continue to use its mathematics and terminology[5] [74, Appendix B]. There are two major issues that make the physical reliability theory difficult to apply to software:

Life testing. How can a software component be tested to measure its failure rate? Does 'failure rate' even have meaning for software?

Independence. What does it mean for two software components to be independent? Can independence be measured or checked?

If these issues were resolved, synthesis theory could follow the hardware model. Although as described below the parallel construction is somewhat different for software than for redundant physical systems, the basic combination operation would be multiplication of failure probabilities.

Attempts to examine the analogy and resolve its issues for software have not been very successful. One approach examines the differences between hardware and software, looking for ways to adapt hardware techniques. But the differences are profound and don't immediately suggest what to do. Another approach simply

---

[5] Software engineers have the advantage over other engineers that they *can* test their complex systems without incurring astronomical expense. But perhaps this power is an illusion; perhaps software system tests have as little significance as an aircraft manufacturer towing a new plane out of the assembly hanger and if it does not collapse on the runway saying, "Look! It works!".

assumes the failure rate for software to be constant (or some other simple function), also assumes independence, then uncritically applies the hardware theory. A 'just do it' approach is in the best traditions of immature engineering disciplines. Engineers must have design rules to work with; it is more important that those rules be clear and easy to use than that they be correct [2]. Safety factors and rule-of-thumb experience have saved many a design based on bad theory. But it is also in line with engineering tradition to try to improve theory [97].

12.2.1 Software 'Time' Parameter

There is an important mismatch between programs and physical objects, because in the latter reliability is expressed in terms of a time variable. Some programs—operating systems are the usual example offered—operate continuously and so have time-dependent behavior, for example, they have a sensible MTTF. However, a program's input space is always lurking in the background, and with it an operational profile. What an operating system does depends on its input—the workload of processes it controls. For many operating systems the majority of time is spent executing some kind of 'null job' because no real process needs attention. It doesn't make sense to consider a non-zero failure rate for the system while running the null job, because its few well chosen instructions provably cannot fail[6]. It makes sense to base software reliability theory on execution counts (runs) in place of units of time. A run arises from the choice of an input point (or an input sequence if there is persistent state), and 'normal usage' involves selecting points from the input domain according to an operational profile.

The parameters of software reliability are thus cast as functions not of time, but of execution counts. For example, MTTF becomes MRTF (Mean Runs To Failure), failure rate $f(n)$ is the probability that failure will occur on the nth run (assuming no failure on the previous $n - 1$ runs), and so on.

12.2.2 The Minefield Analogy

The first hurdle to clear in a discussion of software reliability is the very idea that probabilistic analysis is useful, or even possible. Software, unlike objects in the physical world, has the potential for perfection, and a program seems to have more

---

[6] Like all blanket assertions of software theory, this one has exceptions in the real, physical world. A DEC PDP-10 system (c. 1969) mysteriously crashed about twice a week in continuous operation, crashes which when analyzed showed that the null job (a single branch-to-self instruction) had apparently thrown a divide-by-zero (!?) exception. No root cause was ever found—cosmic rays striking the CPU?—but the problem was eliminated by modifying the operating system to terminate and restart the null job. The failure rate was about 2 runs/week; what and where was the 'bug' that was fixed?

in common with a mathematical function than with (say) a toaster. It certainly isn't useful to discuss the probability that some function will fail to meet requirements[7]. However, as experience with large, complex programs has grown, it appears that they exhibit something very like statistical-failure behavior.

A different physical analogy may help to understand why completely deterministic programs appear to follow probabilistic rules. Consider the grounds of an abandoned ordinance facility. At one time land mines were tested there, and the area is fenced off because there may still be live mines in the field. Suppose a person must traverse the field, and decides to follow a particular path. How can the safety of this plan be assessed? One way is by statistical probing. Rocks large enough to set off a mine are thrown into the area at random locations and the number of explosions recorded. From the data one can obtain a probability estimate of stepping on a mine and a confidence bound for this estimate. The location of any live mines is completely determined from the start, yet it makes sense to attribute a failure rate to a crossing. The best way to throw the rocks is at random distances along the chosen path, since one really does not care about mines that are elsewhere in the field. It is possible to be completely safe by throwing the rocks so as to pave the path, then jumping from rock to rock (any mine there will have been exploded). The analogy is remarkably apt:

Mine Field	*Program*
fenced area	input domain
path	user profile
explosion	failure
rock landing locations	test points
mine	bug
paving the path	exhaustive testing
explosions/thrown rock	failures/test execution
steps of a walk	runs in normal use

The analogy breaks down only in equating mines with bugs. Mines reside in the 'input space,' while bugs are in a completely different space of the program text. The blame lies with the very concept of software 'bug' as a unique entity; programs *fail*, but the cause of failure (certainly a deficiency in the program) usually cannot be uniquely localized as a 'fault,' 'defect,' or 'bug.' The analogy with physical objects and their defects is no better. If a machine screw is required but a rivet is supplied, what are its 'defects' and how many are there?

What makes the statistical approach imperative for programs is the size of the 'minefield' and the 'path'—there is no practical possibility of 'paving' it with tests.

The analogy can be extended to cover subdomain testing, analogous to marking off a grid on the field and making sure to hit each cell with at least one rock. If

---

[7] Leslie Lamport has written a clever summary of the mathematical point of view in "How to tell a program from an automobile" [69]. It was never published, but can be found on the Internet. Lamport states that his satire was badly received by his (then) colleagues, so he did not attempt publication. From the statistical-testing viewpoint he was all too persuasive! The program-analysis community was (is?) very intolerant of any probabilistic notions—they said, "A program is either correct or it isn't, and that's that."

there is reason to believe that mine laying was most common near one edge of the field, the grid should be chosen to be finer there[8]. With a grid, one is sure to have some information about all paths, if the test must be done without knowledge of the 'operational profile.'

12.2.3 A Speculative Software Failure Rate

For engineers of physical systems, there is little call to speculate about what the failure-rate function ought to be for some object M. A rate function can be found empirically by assuming different functions, then observing MTTF in life testing and choosing the one with the most accurate prediction. For example, with the *Weibull function* family, the time failure rate is taken proportional to $t^m, m > -1$. Choosing different values of the Weibull parameter m can make the rate rise or fall in a variety of ways [74, Appendix B, Fig. B4], but the mathematical form is simple enough that reliability and MTTF predictions can be derived in closed form. When a particular Weibull parameter gives good predictions, it doesn't seem necessary to seek a theoretical explanation. A safety factor will be used to cover any discrepancies, and continuity of behavior for the physical object M is expected to make the exact form of its failure-rate function immaterial.

The empirical approach has been tried for software, and forms the basis of Software Reliability Engineering (SRE) [83]. The efficacy of SRE is a subject of considerable controversy, which is outside the scope of the present discussion. From a testing-theory viewpoint its deficiencies are three-fold:

1. SRE uses time as the reliability parameter, and neglects the operational profile except to specify that a continuously running program should take its inputs from a profile.
2. SRE improperly handles state, treating it as just another input to be sampled.
3. SRE predictions for MTTF are not definitive and do not distinguish well between assumed failure-rate functions.

The first two difficulties are ones of principle that would be pushed aside but for the third practical difficulty. Here's what often happens in testing a system with SRE:

An SRE data set is obtained by testing with randomly selected data, measuring the MTTF. An initial segment of the data is used to calculate parameters of a particular assumed failure-rate function f_i. The predictions using f_i are then checked against the remainder of the data. Quite different choices for f_i produce essentially the same results. The data is very 'noisy,' that is, the observed values for MTTF do not form anything like a smooth curve, so the predictions are never very good. Worse yet, should the predictions be extended beyond the ex-

---

[8] The subdomain analogy involves the 'fault'–'failure' issue, since information about the input-space location of failures is hard to gain by inspecting the program text. For the mines, there is just the 'input space.'

isting data set, they are inconsistent. That is, two different failure-rate functions, equally good for the given data, have divergent predictions off the data.

It is divergent predictions that call SRE into question in practice; no safety factor will surely cover its errors. For testing theory, SRE's inability to distinguish between failure-rate functions is the important defect of an empirical approach.

Since the empirical approach is so unsatisfactory, it is surprising that there are no speculative theories of software failure rate. Any such theory could be investigated through experiments, which might shed light on its speculations. The speculative approach owes more to physics than to engineering, but again there is ample precedent. When a physical phenomenon is little understood, engineering rules found by trial and error appear inconsistent and confused; fundamental theoretical explanations are first needed to suggest the parameters that must be varied and observed [97]. The remainder of this section speculates on software failure rate in a wholly theoretical way, prompted by a few striking observations about software.

Some suggestive software properties:

Repeatability, no wear. Software can be written to flawlessly repeat behavior under fixed circumstances, unlike physical objects that wear out. It may be difficult to control circumstances in enough detail to make this property hold, but by avoiding inputs from analog devices, race conditions in parallel execution, hidden states, etc., software will 'do the same thing on the same input.'

Perfect duplication. Although software properties may be determined by testing a particular copy of the code on a particular machine, in principle the results apply to any other copy and machine without statistical variation. The manufacturing process that creates multiple physical objects is subject to random fluctuations and these are the source of failures in life testing; not so for software, whose failures come from design and are identically present (or absent) in each running copy.

Trustworthiness after long use. When software has been used successfully for a long time, its users trust it not to fail. This may be no more than a foible of human nature, but it is remarkably independent of the wary attitude that users adopt for an untried software system[9].

These properties can be fashioned into a theory of software failure rate. Imagine a program to be run repeatedly using inputs (input sequences starting from reset where there is state) drawn from some operational distribution, and suppose that $n - 1$ runs have been successful. What is the probability of failure on the nth run? It might happen that the nth input is the same as one of the previous ones, in which case the program will not fail (since it is supposed to have succeeded before). As n increases, this repetition becomes more likely, hence the failure rate decreases with

---

[9] Two examples: (1) No one who has studied run-of-the-mill open-source code has illusions about its intrinsic quality; yet, a stable Debian distribution of the Linux kernel is trusted after a few months of operation. (2) When the first 300-series Airbus aircraft were produced, many reliability experts refused to fly on them because they disagreed with the technical arguments advanced to show the flight-control programs safe. Yet Airbus planes accumulated a good safety record over more than 20 years, and today those same programs are trusted.

increasing n. This scenario *never* occurs with physical objects, because it leads to an unlimited MRTF.

A precise analysis can be given for a program P with finite input domain D and a uniform operational distribution. Suppose that for any untried point of the domain the probability of failure is a constant K, $0 \leq K \leq 1$. If n randomly-chosen points have been tried, where n is expressed as a fraction of the domain size[10] $|D|$, the probability of selecting an untried point (instead of one previously chosen) is e^{-n}, hence the failure-rate function is $f(n) = Ke^{-n}$. Then the reliability is

$$R(n) = e^{\int_0^n f(t)dt} = e^{\int_0^n Ke^{-t}\,dt} = e^{K(e^{-n}-1)}.$$

These functions are shown in Fig. 12.1. This reliability function is unlike any in the

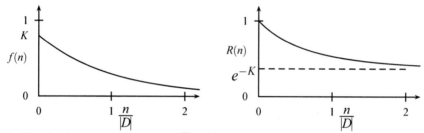

Fig. 12.1 A failure-rate function (*left*) and a reliability function (*right*) for software

physical world, because it does not approach zero as the number of runs n increases; rather it is asymptotic to $e^{-K} > 0$. The MRTF integral therefore diverges—software will not necessarily ever fail.

Expressing the number of runs as a fraction of the size of the input space D removes $|D|$ from the formulas[11], but is a trifle misleading. In Fig. 12.1, unity on the horizontal axis means $|D|$ runs, which for a a program with numerical input is impossibly large. For realistic run counts, only the portion of Fig. 12.1 near the origin is involved, and there the exponential is approximately linear, so for (normalized) $n \ll 1$, $f(n) \approx K$ and $R(n) \approx e^{-Kn} \approx 1 - Kn$. When runs are confined to this region, the failure-rate function is constant[12], because the chance that the nth run is a repetition is very near zero. However, repeated runs can be important in practical cases,

---

[10] Technically, for an arbitrary profile, it is not the whole domain D, but a subset $\check{D} \subseteq D$, the 'effective domain' picked out by the operational profile that is the space from which selections are made. It may not be possible to algorithmically obtain $\check{D}$ from D. The following discussion uses D where $\check{D}$ would be correct, but this is significant only when considering a number of runs r such that $|\check{D}| \ll r \ll |D|$.

[11] It also hides the distinction between D and $\check{D}$.

[12] As in life testing of physical objects, but there a constant failure rate (in time) is not an approximation. The case $t \ll 1$ is not so interesting, so $R(t) = e^{-Kt}$ is not usually approximated as $1 - Kt$.

either because the operational profile emphasizes only a limited number of points, or because the software is written to control the size of its input space[13].

It might seem that when a program has state, the failure rate function is no different, except that there are far more different runs possible. More careful consideration shows that the real situation is much more complicated, because state cannot be directly sampled and its values are not controlled by an operational distribution. When there is state, a 'run' is a sequence of inputs beginning in the 'reset' (uninitialized) state. Such a sequence is very unlikely to be repeated in the course of testing or normal operation. But the observation that software can flawlessly repeat what it has done successfully once might still apply, within the sequence. When a program retaining state receives an input sequence, it creates a corresponding state sequence, each successive state value paired with an input in the original sequence. Among the (input, state) pairs of various sequences, there may be duplications, indeed whole subsequences may be repeated. If a run sequence s_r has within it many pairs that have occurred in a previous successful run, while run sequence s_u has few such repeated pairs, it is natural to assume that the failure probability of s_r is less than that of s_u. As run sequences accumulate, those like s_r should become more frequent, leading to a failure-rate function $f(n)$ that decreases with increasing n. Unfortunately, this analysis is sometimes false. It can happen that although one run succeeds, and a second run contains no pairs that did not occur in the first, the second nevertheless fails. This is an expression of 'coincidental correctness,' in which the state is in error[14] in both runs, but in the first there is an accidental self-correction that the second lacks.

Thus although programs with state may have a decreasing failure-rate function, their behavior is much more complicated than for stateless programs, depending on patterns in the (input, state) pairs and on coincidental correctness. In the remainder of this chapter, derivations that rely on a decreasing failure-rate function may not apply to programs with state.

---

[13] One unjustly neglected design for trustworthiness of life-critical software is to finitely quantize the input space. In an example given by John Knight [67], the input pattern for radiation-treatment software is expressed in bounded integer coordinates rather than the natural floating-point dimensions, and repetition is the rule. However, finite quantization is intended to eliminate profiles and failure-rate considerations by enabling an exhaustive test of the software.

[14] In IEEE standard terminology, 'error' is a technical term that differs from 'failure.' 'Failure' is a disagreement between requirements and implementation for some input sequence; 'error' refers to incorrect internal program properties within such a computation. The notion is obviously vague, since requirements are never given for such internal properties; indeed, they would depend on details of the as-yet undesigned implementation. To add to the confusion, the IEEE standard definition is not universally accepted. A common software-engineering meaning of 'error' is a mistake made by a human programmer.

12.2.4 Measuring Software Failure Rate

On the assumption of perfect software duplication, one copy of a program can be tested to determine its failure rate function[15] $f(n)$—each successive test is a run[16]. When the program is a component, its measured failure rate function can be used in synthesizing a system and predicting the system failure rate, as described in the following subsection.

In measuring component failure rates there remains an embarrassing software difficulty that results from the very success of unit testing: after initial debugging, it is difficult to make a component fail. Indeed, it might almost be taken as a definition of a proper 'unit' that a tester can reasonably convince himself (not always correctly, of course) that no component-level failure is possible. If doubts linger, the tester might say that the unit was too much like a 'system' for proper testing. When testing a component uncovers no failures the only estimate of its failure rate is zero. For such apparently perfect components, only perfect systems are predicted, so the whole CBSD paradigm fails[17]. Fortunately, there is a zero-failure reliability theory.

To return to the minefield analogy, zero test failures is analogous to no explosions in response to rock-throwing and the consequent prediction that there are no mines in the field. But there is a missing parameter: *confidence* in predicting no mines based on no explosions depends on the number of rocks thrown. It's ridiculous (and life-threatening!) to believe anything based on throwing (say) two rocks onto a mile-long path. Furthermore, confidence can be traded off against maximum explosion rate. For the same number of rocks thrown, the confidence should be greater if more explosions are acceptable[18]. There are two limiting cases: the confidence in a ideal prediction, that is, predicting no mines, must always be 0, no matter how many rocks are thrown; and, perfect confidence (that is, probability 1) can only be attained for explosion rate less than or equal to 1 (that is, an explosion every time). In other words, one can be 100% sure that things are no worse than an explosion on every step; it's impossible to believe in perfect safety. Between these extremes, the more rocks thrown safely, the more confidence that things are better than a given explo-

---

[15] Or, multiple copies can be tested in parallel—another consequence of perfect duplication.

[16] It is natural, and quite wrong, to think of program runs as an ordered collection. Each run is independent and repeatable. With state, each test run is itself a sequence, but these sequences have only their internal ordering; there is no sequence of sequences. The order in which test runs are performed may very well influence the successive values of $f(n)$; however, as n increases the difference between different test orders must disappear.

[17] Everyone knows, of course, that the systems are *not* perfect. It is the proper business of CBSD theory to quantify the imperfection at the component level so that system predictions match what's observed. As Chapter 19 suggests, system failures may be mostly an emergent property of combination. Anticipating the discussion of confidence to follow, the confidence in a zero-failure-rate estimate may be low, but that doesn't help CBSD, which still can make no useful prediction. It's little help to say that the predicted perfection isn't very likely to be correct.

[18] It seems cavalier to discuss the field walker's safety so coldly. A person naturally wants 100% confidence that the explosion rate is 0. But if the walk must be taken and there is no time to 'pave the path,' less than perfection must be accepted. For every program this tradeoff is forced on its testers, and the consequences can be as dire.

sion rate. In this discussion, substituting 'test points' for 'rocks' and 'failures' for 'explosions' gives the software version of the theory[19].

When an experiment is conducted, the simplest statistical parameter for quantifying the trust to be placed in its outcome in an *upper confidence bound C*. The experiment being conducted on a program is testing it with N randomly selected points. The outcome is that no failures are observed. High confidence that this result is right means that the probability of a different result is high, yet it was not observed. Thus for example, $C = .95$ means that the probability of success is only 5%, yet success was seen. As $C \rightarrow 1$, success is less and less likely, so if it is observed, confidence in that observation is correspondingly higher.

Expressing the failure-rate function in runs normalized to the program's domain size $|D|$ as above, the probability that the first run succeeds is $1 - f(\frac{1}{|D|})$, and that all N runs succeed is the product of N such probabilities,

$$\prod_{n=1/(|D|)}^{N/(|D|)} (1 - f(n)).$$

So the probability that the no-failure result is wrong is

$$C = 1 - \prod_{n=1/(|D|)}^{N/(|D|)} (1 - f(n)).$$

For the speculative software failure rate function $f(n) = Ke^{-n}$, where $K \leq 1$ is an assumed constant failure rate for untried inputs,

$$C = 1 - \prod_{n=1/(|D|)}^{N/(|D|)} (1 - Ke^{-n}).$$

As the parameter K increases, C increases, so setting a confidence value places an upper bound on K. For a given C, let f_0 be the value of K that satisfies the equation, i.e.,

$$C = 1 - \prod_{n=1/(|D|)}^{N/(|D|)} (1 - f_0 e^{-n}).$$

It is natural to call f_0 a 'failure-rate bound,' even though it is just a parameter of the actual failure rate (function).

Normalizing the number of runs to a fraction of the domain D eliminated $|D|$ from the failure-rate function, but now D reenters the picture unless $N \ll |D|$. Small values of N allow $f_0 e^{-n}$ to be approximated by f_0, so that the confidence is independent of $|D|$:

$$C \approx 1 - \prod_{n=1/(|D|)}^{N/(|D|)} (1 - f_0) = 1 - (1 - f_0)^N. \tag{12.1}$$

---

[19] It will be seen in what follows that a decreasing failure rate alters the limiting case of 100% confidence.

This is the result for a constant failure-rate function, and describes the common case in which the domain size swamps the number of tests. However, the unique properties of software show through at the other extreme, when $N \gg |D|$. If the failure rate were constant, $\lim\limits_{N \to \infty} C = 1$, that is, perfect confidence in any failure-rate bound can be approached arbitrarily closely with enough tests. But for the speculative software failure-rate function, $\lim\limits_{N \to \infty} C = C_{max}$, where $C_{max} < 1$. The value of C_{max} depends on the assumed domain size. For example, for $|D| = 20,000$ and $f_0 = 0.0001$, $C_{max} \approx .86$. In the example, no matter how much random testing is done, no more than 86% confidence can be obtained in a failure rate less than 0.0001. This is the flip side of software reliability that does not approach zero in the limit: more tests cannot improve the confidence in a failure-rate bound without limit, because eventually test repetition becomes overwhelmingly likely. If there are sufficient testing resources to try more random test points than the size of the whole domain, it would certainly be wise to switch to systematic testing and conduct an exhaustive test. In practice this may not be feasible because while any number of random points can be generated mechanically, the domain[20] may not be algorithmically defined.

In the case of a large input domain relative to the number of tests, how much confidence in what failure-rate bound is enough? The two parameters are intertwined, but not symmetrically. The cases of most interest are those of high confidence (C near 1) and low failure-rate bound (f_0 near zero). In this situation the number of test points is large. For a given number of test points, confidence changes greatly with failure-rate bound, but not the other way around. The following table is calculated from equation (12.1) for constant failure rate and a million test points[21]:

failure-rate bound	10^{-5}	6.9×10^{-6}	4.6×10^{-6}	2.3×10^{-6}	10^{-6}	10^{-7}
confidence	99.995%	99.9%	99%	90%	63%	10%

In the table, to improve the failure rate by two orders of magnitude requires a sacrifice of all confidence; but to gain more than three '9s' in confidence the failure rate need only be worsened by half an order of magnitude. Thus it is usual to choose an arbitrary confidence in the top decile and then look at failure-rate bounds. The example in the table might be summarized, "To achieve high confidence that the failure rate is below 1 in 10^5 requires executing about a million test points without failure." This ratio of about ten times the test points to the denominator of failure-rate bound holds in general—high confidence in a rate below 1 in 10^6 will require about 10^7 test points, etc.

It is discouraging that so many test points are required for confidence in a failure-rate bound. For 'ultra-reliable' safety-critical applications where $f_0 < 10^{-8}$ is required, the number of tests needed is simply infeasible, and there seems no way to circumvent the unfortunate statistics [13, $\prec A \succ$]. The underlying cause is software's failure to be continuous. Physical engineering objects do not need to be probed so closely because their behavior can be interpolated between observations.

---

[20] or the effective domain $\hat{D}$

[21] The implicit assumption is that the input domain is much larger, $|D| \gg 10^6$.

To establish a failure-rate bound f_0 for a program is entirely straightforward: Using random input samples from the operational distribution execute the program for N failure-free runs, and calculate the confidence from equation (12.1). If testing resources (that is, N) are limited, it may be necessary to relax the bound or accept low confidence.

12.2.5 Failure Rate in Subdomains

Non-functional software properties like run time were modeled in Chapter 6 as functions from an input- to an output domain (e.g., $T : D \to \mathbb{R}$). In Chapter 7 the dependence on D was approximated by a step function constant on each of several subdomains, $\tilde{T} \approx T$. The SYN tools measure values of T and average them in subdomains to find the approximate values $\tilde{T}$, each of which is in error to the extent that T is not constant in a subdomain. The error values indicate which subdomains are poorly chosen and help a component developer to improve them before placing the approximate description in a repository. Failure rate, however, is not a point-wise mapping of the input domain D. It is an inherently statistical property defined only on sets like D itself. By assuming the failure rate to be a constant f_i in each subdomain S_i for a fixed confidence, a step function $\tilde{f}(x) = f_i, x \in S_i$ is obtained in the same form as the run-time approximation $\tilde{T}$, but $\tilde{f}$ does not approximate anything, and no error estimate applies to its values f_i. Unfortunately, the values may very well be erroneous. For example, if a subdomain should have been split because failure is unlikely in one part of it but likely in another part, no value f_i is correct for the whole. As subdomains shrink, there is no assurance of improvement.

In making the application of reliability to components and their synthesis into systems, some of the same issues arise as for any non-functional 'composable' property like run time (Chapter 8). A measured failure-rate bound for a component program is a domain-wide worst case, so the issue of distortion of input as functional output to a second component in series does not seem to arise. In this regard reliability is like a worst-case run time: the worst case for a series system is no more than the sum of the worst cases for its components. But the issue of input profiles has only been partially hidden. The operational profile used to select test cases determines the range of 'worst.' If the profiles used in testing its components are quite wrong relative to a system's operational profile then the measurements may miss the real worst case, so synthesis predictions cannot be trusted. As in the case of run time, the 'right' profile for testing a second component in a series depends both on the system profile and the choice of first component, neither of which can be known when that second component is being tested in isolation. As in the case of run time, using subdomains in testing components goes a long way toward solving the problem of unknown profiles. By testing each subdomain separately, enough information is obtained to approximate any profile that will subsequently be encountered.

A subdomain breakdown of a component's input space has two purposes. First, it forces testing in each subdomain so that whatever the subdomain captures cannot be completely neglected. Second, it provides the tester a measure of intellectual control by grouping 'same' inputs. This second purpose for the non-functional reliability property is of some interest. For any subdomain breakdown, the primary 'sameness' is functional, to account for the way in which one component distorts its input profile to pass on to another component. For the run-time parameter, there may be a further secondary 'sameness' in run time that splits functionally defined subdomains because the same output does not necessarily mean the same run time. For reliability, a secondary subdomain split should occur if different parts of one functional subdomain have different failure-rate bounds. In the zero-failure theory for which equation (12.1) was derived, there is a paradox of subdomain splitting. Take any subdomain S and any fixed confidence bound C. Then N random tests without failure establishes failure bound f_0 for S, from equation (12.1). Split S into $S_1 \cup S_2$. The same reliability bound for each will be obtained with N random tests *of each*, or $2N$ test points. But if $2N$ points were used on the original S, higher confidence in f_0 would be obtained[22]. It would seem that random testing over the full domain is always superior to random testing in any subdomain decomposition. What's missing from the zero-failure theory is any idea of the cardinality of the (sub)domain being sampled.

There is a reliability notion of 'sameness' for subdomains that goes back to Howden's initial investigation [64, $\prec A \succ$]: the ideal subdomain for testing is homogeneous *for failure*. That is, if one test point in the subdomain fails, all fail. In such a homogeneous subdomain, a single successful test point constitutes a proof of correctness, so Howden's result that although these subdomains exist they cannot be algorithmically obtained, is not surprising. Reliability theory is as close as it is possible to come: no confidence in a zero failure-rate bound can be obtained by testing, but enough tests can establish high confidence in a bound arbitrarily close to zero. Dijkstra's famous aphorism that testing finds only failure, not success, could be similarly modified to say that testing can establish only confidence in the probability of success.

12.3 Component Independence

Multiplying probabilities for components in series is correct if their failures are independent[23]. In special cases of redundancy, independence is essential and not

---

[22] Or equivalently, the same confidence in a better failure rate.

[23] Technically, the product may overestimate the probability of failure because there can be a coincidental correctness: a component could fail, but another component in series could happen to give the right composite result on this erroneous input (by itself either succeeding or failing). Since this error lies in the direction of safety, it will be ignored in the discussion to follow.

easy to attain [71]. For example, it evidently will not do to use several copies of the same component in MVP—all will fail on the same inputs[24].

In general, do two unrelated components placed in series fail independently? Intuitively, they do not, because the first determines the input profile seen by the second. The failure-rate bound in the second is valid only for the profile used to measure it, which may be different than the profile supplied by the first. Measurements with a uniform profile in subdomains partially compensate for a profile mismatch, but within one subdomain the uniform profile can be wrong, invalidating a prediction based on independence. For a simple example, consider C_1 in series with C_2, and a particular C_1 subdomain D_k on which its output is (correctly) the constant k. Let C_2 fail only on input k. k lies in a C_2 subdomain that was uniformly randomly sampled without failure, therefore k was not chosen as a test point. Testing without failure on C_1 and C_2 gives a certain confidence in a failure rate bound of (say) 10^{-3} for each, and the product formula predicts a system failure-rate bound of $1 - (1 - 10^{-3})^2 \approx 0.002$ for D_k with the same confidence. Yet the system fails on every point of D_k.

'Independence' is a tricky idea for software. The argument of the previous paragraph has nothing to do with a code-based or related-failure relationship between C_1 and C_2. Supposing them entirely unrelated, the prediction is still wrong; or, they may be intuitively 'dependent' without compromising the prediction. As an example of the latter, consider putting a component C_0 in series with itself. Let $\boxed{C_0}$ map a subdomain D_0 roughly uniformly onto itself. Then if uniform-random testing C_0 without failure on D_0 gives a certain confidence in failure-rate bound f_0, the prediction of system failure-rate bound $1 - (1 - f_0)^2$ will be accurate because in the second position C_0 is receiving inputs that approximate the distribution on which it was tested. It is irrelevant that the identical components fail at the same points. All that counts is the way in which outputs from the first component are distributed to the second. In special system configurations like MVP, the independence issues are completely different, because it is stipulated that several components receive exactly the same inputs and the majority output is correctly determined. In that case, what counts is coincident failures among the components, and it is obvious that using the same code for them all will be of no avail.

12.4 Reliability Synthesis

As for non-functional run time, component synthesis requires first measurements, then a theory to compose them.

---

[24] Just such a failure occurred in an Ariane 5 satellite launcher [73]. A design mistake in one component caused a failure, which was detected with a switch to the backup computer system. It was running the same software and immediately failed in the same way.

12.4.1 Difficulties in Component Measurements

At the component level the only available measurement theory assumes a constant failure-rate function for each subdomain and a failure-rate bound obtained by observing no test failures, as in Section 12.2.5. It is straightforward to estimate failure-rate bounds for subdomains as follows: The input test profile is taken to be uniform on each subdomain; for a given confidence value, uniform random testing yields a table of failure-rate bounds, one table entry for each subdomain, a better bound for more test points. It is not inconsequential that testing cost rises with the number of subdomains. To gain a certain confidence, each subdomain must be probed as often as the whole domain[25]. Some subdomains may be small enough to test exhaustively; in using automatic measurement tools this must be recognized, the sampling method changed, and a failure-rate bound of zero recorded by hand.

During component testing, it is assumed that the component developer finds and fixes any failures that are detected, so that in the end each component test is a success characterized by a failure-rate bound at the given confidence level. A considerable burden is thus placed on the human component tester, since test outcomes are judged by hand. If subdomains are badly chosen, and bad functional behavior is not excited (or excited but not noticed, always a problem in testing), then the component failure-rate bounds will be too optimistic. Unfortunately, in a zero-failure test the tester can gain no information about possible failure-rate variation across a subdomain. For run time, approximation graphs can be compared to actual run-time measurements, exposing poor subdomains. But there is no 'actual' reliability in a zero-failure test. The best a tester can do is to adjust subdomains to minimize approximation errors in the component's functional values, and carefully compare functional results to requirements. Failure-rate bounds are just theoretical deductions from assumed zero-failure testing.

A final testing problem is that the component test domain may be two-dimensional. For a 'master' component in a concurrent construction uniform sampling the the (input × parallel-input) domain is straightforward, but as noted previously there are difficulties in properly sampling a state domain. It does not seem enough to simply choose random input sequences, but there is no evident alternative.

12.4.2 Synthesis Rules

As addition is the basic rule for composing run time, for reliability the rule is multiplication. Any subdomain S_1 of a series system is a subdomain of the first component. A point in S_1 is carried to some subdomain S_2 of the second component.

---

[25] It seems contradictory that for a fixed number of test points, the confidence in a certain failure-rate bound is the same no matter what domain is sampled. Intuitively, the subdomain measurements should be better because they take account of parts of the input space having different failure rates, but the theory fails to capture this. As described in Section 12.2.4, the independence of domain size is really only approximate, a consequence of assuming a constant failure-rate function.

The system succeeds in S_1 only if the two components succeed in S_1 and S_2 respectively[26]. Hence the probability that the system will succeed in S_1 is the product of the two independent component-success probabilities. Using component failure-rate bounds f_1 (in S_1) and f_2 (in S_2), the system failure rate bound is

$$1 - (1 - f_1)(1 - f_2).$$

Conditional and iterative synthesis take care of themselves[27] because they use the series construction. However, the analog of redundant physical components is not straightforward. In mechanical and electrical systems, a component that fails can often be designed to disappear from system operation. For example, a failing power supply ceases to produce its required voltage, but another connected in parallel silently takes over[28]. The formula for composition of success rates in parallel is the complement of a product of the parallel-component failure rates—system failure requires all the redundant components to fail together. Software parallelism in the form of concurrently executing components is, as usual, more complicated.

First, in software it is clear that nothing happens or fails to happen except by explicit design. A software component cannot 'drop out' without other parts of the system hanging up waiting for it. Its failure must be detected and explicitly handled. Physical components can be designed to 'fail safe' on their own; for software, safety rests with other software. This is not a bad thing, since it gives the system designer more control and forces explicit consideration of potential failure modes. The corresponding downside is that the very safety-checking code might itself fail. In order to make progress in understanding the situation, it is necessary to outlaw certain bizarre failures, which can plausibly be done. Assume:

- Each execution of a component terminates in a standardized way. Conventional operating systems routinely do part of what's needed, but in addition there must be a provision for timing-out a misbehaving process. It is not required that the termination mechanism identify failure, because in general this is impossible. Since an operating system cannot tell that (say) a sine routine returning 3.14159 has failed, it need not be careful about what is returned for (say) an attempt to divide by zero. But *something* must be returned. The point is that the mechanism of invoking a component and providing it with input and access to its state must always yield an output and result state (which may be erroneous).
- Certain control components do not fail. Again, part of this requirement falls on the operating system mechanism for initiating and monitoring processes; part falls on tools that manage component connections, e.g., in the SYN tools the construction of the SystemCode script (Appendix A); but part may involve the working components in a system. The most important example of a component that must be assumed not to fail is one implementing voting in an N-version

---

[26] Ignoring an accidental correction of a first-component failure by the second component.

[27] The identity component used for an IF with no ELSE and in iteration synthesis now has success rate 1 instead of run time 0.

[28] Of course, things can go wrong. Instead of just obediently dropping out, a power supply could fail by producing a burst of high-voltage oscillation that damages other components and/or causes the system to fail.

system. This assumption is reasonable because the code that must work is of limited size and can be carefully tested or proved to be correct[29]. Analysis of voting-algorithm reliability universally assumes a perfect voter (and usually fails to make the other necessary assumption that the conveyance of identical input to each component is also perfect).

These assumptions still leave wide latitude for components to fail, but restrict failure in the mechanisms of component interaction. For example, in concurrent execution as implemented in the SYN tools, the rendezvous between master and slave is assumed to always take place, but without constraint on the data values exchanged. Such restrictions are necessary for there to be an effective relationship between measured component failure rates and system failure rate, because otherwise synthesis would introduce its own failure modes unrelated to the components.

The peculiar form of concurrency implemented in the SYN tools involves a 'master' and a 'slave' component. The slave is non-concurrent, and so is characterized by a single failure rate. The master M can fail in several ways:

1. M may send the wrong value to the slave.
2. While the slave is executing in parallel, M may do the wrong thing.
3. M's response to the slave's returned value may be wrong.

These are the failure-rate analogs of three distinct master run times in Chapter 11. For reliability the master's code is better thought of as three executions and their failure rates: one maps master input to an output sent to the slave (this is $\boxed{M}$ in Chapter 6) with failure rate f_1; a second maps master input to internal results available when the slave terminates with failure rate f_3; the third maps master input and parallel input from the slave to final master output (concurrent $\boxed{\boxed{M}}$ in Chapter 6) with failure rate f_4. Parts of the master's code are shared in these executions, but potential failure of the shared code can be different for each one. Let the failure rate for the slave be f_2. How do these rates combine into a failure rate of the parallel system? The chance that a correct result is returned by the slave is $(1-f_1)(1-f_2)$— this is just a series combination of the slave following the first part of the master. In general, the master's third mapping is also a series connection that can fail, so the combined failure probability is $1-(1-f_1)(1-f_2)(1-f_4)$. If there were no more to it, the concurrent combination might as well have been coded as three separate components[30] in series. The possible failure (rate f_3) of the concurrent part of the master's execution is of no especial interest; it is subsumed by f_4.

However, special redundant cases are important. In multi-version programming (MVP), for example, an odd-length chain of masters has the intent of computing a value using different implementations. The last master in the chain invokes a slave, and as each master-slave combination returns its value it enters into a vote, the final returned value being the majority. The rate f_3 for each master describes its failure

---

[29] Parts of an operating system are not so easy to verify!

[30] Of course, concurrency might be used solely to gain the overlap in execution time between master and slave, for example, to divide the computational task between them.

to compute a correct value for use in the vote. Again stipulating that the input-distribution code is correct (that is, each $f_1 = 0$) and each part of the voting code is correct (that is, the executions described by f_4 and f_3 could fail only in the parallel part so $f_3 = f_4$ in each master), the failure rate of the combination contains only products of terms like $(1 - f_3)$ for masters and $(1 - f_2)$ for the final slave, so as more independent implementations enter the vote it should be possible to gain a combined failure rate approaching zero. For a two-out-of-three vote where the three independent component failure rates (two masters a and b and a slave c) are f_{3a}, f_{3b}, f_{2c}, two or three will agree and the majority result will be correct in a number of cases, for example if a and b succeed but c fails, probability $f_{2c}(1 - f_{3a})(1 - f_{3b})$; or, all three succeed, probability $(1 - f_{3a})(1 - f_{3b})(1 - f_{2c})$, etc. Collecting all possibilities and simplifying, the system failure rate is

$$f_{3a}f_{3b} + f_{3a}f_{2c} + f_{3b}f_{2c} - 2f_{3a}f_{3b}f_{2c}.$$

For component failure rates of 10^{-4} the system failure rate is about 3×10^{-8}.

Some failures included in this rate are those in which no two components agree. It is reasonable to stipulate that the perfect voting code excludes this case[31]. In an output range R of cardinality $n = |R|$, the fraction of triples in which at least two values agree is

$$1 - \frac{(n-1)(n-2)}{n^2} = \frac{3n-2}{n^2},$$

which falls to 0 asymptotically from 1 at $n = 2$. So the system failure rate conditional on there being a majority is $f^2 \frac{3n-2}{n^2}$, where the two agreeing components each has failure rate f, hence the system fails at rate no more than f^2. Furthermore, since a majority result is a rare event in a large range, small system experiments can provide high confidence that majority will occur. The confidence that majority will always occur when it has been seen in N system tests is

$$1 - (\frac{3n-2}{n^2})^N.$$

For $n = 2$ confidence of about 99.9% in majority is obtained when $N = 10$.

In the tutorial example of 2VP in Chapter 11, the only possibility for success is that both master and slave succeed, so the system failure rate is

$$1 - (1 - f_3)(1 - f_2) = f_2 + f_3 - f_2f_3$$

if they are independent. This value is worse than either component alone because it includes failures in which the components do not agree. If it is stipulated that correct code detects agreement, the system failure probability conditional on agreement is no more than $0.5 f_3 f_2$, since for two output possibilities agreement occurs half the time and the multiplier decreases asymptotically to 0 as output-range cardinality increases. Thus the system failure rate is always better than the product of the component rates. As in the 3VP case, a few system experiments can establish a high confidence that agreement is likely.

---

[31] An MVP system must do something when there is no majority, perhaps return the value from the most tested component. But this case is special because it can be trivially detected.

Part IV
Supporting Tools

TUTORIALS in Part III give an implicit functional description of the SYN tools that accompany this monograph. In Part IV, tools are themselves the subject. Appendix A gives detailed documentation of the SYN code, but in Part IV more general tool issues are raised and illustrated using SYN as an example. Because stringent restrictions are placed on components the SYN tools are able to attain ambitious goals. The context of 'debugging' is ideal for showing off what the SYN tools (and by implication good tools of any kind supporting CBSD) can do.

Chapter 13
CBSD Support Tools

I$_{\text{N}}$ any particular case of software development, introducing 'components' and
CBSD has an importance that falls on a spectrum from 'trivial' to 'central.'
As with any software technology, it is always possible to "write FORTRAN"[1]
while ostensibly using a new technology. Components can be used as if they were
nothing more than FORTRAN library subroutines. At the other extreme, a development project may attempt to make essential use of a component model, relying on
middleware to implement essential parts of the system, so that the project could not
be carried out in any other way. This section explores the role that supporting tools
play in shaping development.

13.1 Component Developers and System Designers

The fundamental principle of CBSD is the separation of design/implementation into
two levels—components and systems—and connections between those levels. Much
of the promise of CBSD comes from this separation, because isolating component
development allows designers to concentrate on different issues. Designing a component stresses its generality and quality; designing a system is concerned with interfaces and application-domain detail.

There is a cost associated with separation. If a system and its parts were designed
together, without the separation of I-CBSD, the components could be tailored to the
system. This would make them easier to design, implement, and test; it would eliminate adaptation needed to make general components fit a particular system. Despite
these advantages of integrated component/systems design, the usual argument sup-

---

[1] The reference is to persistence of a programmer's first language and resistance to new ideas.
Old FORTRAN programmers may be writing in C++, but making no use of object-oriented or
information-hiding concepts. In a high school science talent contest c. 1986, a winning entry was
a program written in Modula III, but which made no use of Modula's class facilities. When asked
why they had not just used Pascal, the students replied that Modula was cool, but Pascal wasn't.
They were programmers who still thought in BASIC.

D. Hamlet, *Composing Software Components*, DOI 10.1007/978-1-4419-7148-7_13,
© Springer Science+Business Media, LLC 2010

porting separate development falls back on reuse: however awkward it may be to make and use independently constructed components, the savings in taking them 'off the shelf' should more than compensate. Reuse is important, but a compelling argument for CBSD can be made without it: CBSD has the potential to produce systems of higher quality. Separating out the bulk of implementation detail allows everyone to do a better job—component developers on their code and its testing, and system designers on their customers' arcane requirements.

Component- and system developers always share a number of concerns that need tool support. Both need database and version-control tools to record and track information, and of course implementation and verification tools. What's new for I-CBSD is that component-development tools measure and record properties that will later be available to system-development tools; these properties must not be peculiar to one application, because the system development to come later is unknown when they are measured.

13.2 Ideal Tools for I-CBSD

Formal methods (FM) of software development seek an ideal that has not (yet?) been realized in practice. From a set of requirements for a software system that are expressed in some precise, mathematical form, FM mechanically generate an implementation that is guaranteed to meet those requirements. Components and CBSD do not necessarily enter the picture, but if they do, FM are applied at the component level, and a predicate-logic composition theory (see Chapter 6) is used to obtain and check system properties. Testing is unnecessary at any level[2], but if it is employed the FM provides a mechanical oracle to judge test results.

Although FM underlie testing theory and component test composition, this monograph is not about FM as a practical development method, but rather about testing. Without FM, tests lack a mechanical oracle, imposing a large burden on the human tester—to detect a software failure when a test exposes it.

13.2.1 Ideal Component-level Testing/Measurement Tools

Without an oracle, the best that component testing tools can do is to generate test data, record results, and display them for human examination. Graphs are the best display mechanism. Subdomain decomposition of the component input domain helps with test generation and provides a measure of test quality: a test is better if its composite subdomain values closely approximate actual test results of the component.

---

[2] The strongest advocate of FM must acknowledge that mistakes get made in stating requirements, in typing program text, etc., mistakes that testing often finds immediately [33].

Every test point and its outcome could be recorded; subdomains reduce the volume of data if only averages within them are recorded.

13.2.2 *Ideal System-level Synthesis (CAD) Tools*

Chapter 8 explains the difficulty of composing test results and how subdomains solve that problem. The composition algorithms of Chapters 8 and 10 – 11 are the basis for tools that deserve the name "computer-aided design (CAD)," because they predict behavior of systems from behavior of their parts. Unfortunately, without an oracle, there is no way to assess the predictions in practical development. By actually executing a system, the prediction accuracy can be judged, but this operation properly belongs not to development tools (certainly not to CAD tools), but to some independent observation of the system. Without an oracle, neither prediction nor actual execution can be compared with original system requirements, except by human judges. Tools can make the comparisons easier by presenting results graphically.

13.2.3 SYN *Tools: An Existence Proof*

Practical testing-support tools today do little more than extensive bookkeeping to keep track of test actions performed by hand. The difficulty of passing from these primitive tools to something like I-CBSD seems insurmountable. A useful investigation of component-testing measurements and their synthesis can only be carried out by starting over. The SYN tools described in this monograph provide an 'existence proof' of the ideal, obtained by sticking to immutable components and strict separation of components and systems. When implementation difficulties arise, SYN tools restrict the generality of the components rather than compromise the ideal. For 'real' components, there seems no way to achieve powerful tool support; the SYN tools can achieve I-CBSD support because they apply only to simplified components and systems.

Chapter 14
Tool Implementation

'RESEARCH tools' is a name given to a peculiar kind of software written to aid in experimental computer science. An analogy is implied with more usual scientific equipment like microscopes or spectrometers, tools used not to construct, but to probe and study. There is also an implied disclaimer: research tools are often throw-aways. Only the experimenter can use them, and when the experiment is finished, they are very difficult to use again[1]. Thus research-tool software is fragile, hard to use, poorly documented, and full of failures waiting to happen. Part of the reason is that the tools, like Topsy, "just growed." The experimenter starts out needing something simple and writes a quick-and-dirty program to do it. As the work continues, the program is augmented and modified, its deficiencies papered over, until it is a rat's nest of bad code. There is never time to document or to rewrite. Failures appear each time the tools are used in a new situation (or even in attempting to repeat an old experiment because they've changed since it was first run), leading to further 'development' that makes things worse.

The SYN support software that accompanies this monograph is not quite so bad, but it is research software.

The SYN tools are written in Perl, which was chosen for two reasons. First, Perl allows easy access to operating-system services in a platform-independent way; second, its learning curve is shallow (at least for pedestrian coding) so that an ever-changing group of students could make significant contributions. But Perl and many short-term programmers only exacerbate the problem of bad code.

The overall 'architecture' (to give it a name that implies more planning than there was) of the SYN tools is a collection of stand-alone programs (Perl scripts), of the sort that are often combined in UNIX 'shell scripts.' Each program is controlled by its command line of options and parameters, and each can be run (hence tested) in isolation. When one program needs another, it uses Perl's system() command to

---

[1] In the attic of Rockefeller Hall at Cornell University in the 1960s, there was a jumble of research tools that were thought too good to throw away—WW II RADAR equipment, for example. But although each jury-rigged device had been important, some in famous experiments, it was clearly impossible to reuse any of them. Even the original physicists would not remember the collection of tricks needed to employ them.

D. Hamlet, *Composing Software Components,* DOI 10.1007/978-1-4419-7148-7_14,
© Springer Science+Business Media, LLC 2010

execute it. The scripts can execute code for components being studied in the same way. Many SYN scrips have a file parameter, a file used to communicate with other programs. These files usually contain a component description of some kind; they are easy to manipulate with a general-purpose editor because they are character files divided into lines. This architecture makes it easy to write each program in isolation and to test with files created or examined by hand, and for several programmers to work on different scripts simultaneously.

The scripts are run from a current 'base directory' containing all necessary files as well as the program scripts. In the rare cases where recursive invocations are needed, the programs create a subdirectory as a fresh base. The most commonly used scripts communicate through files that are not named on the invoking command line but rather have fixed names known to the scripts. Of these fixed-name files, system.pscf is the most used; it contains the description of a system to be synthesized and pointers to files (with extension .ccf) describing the components needed. system.pscf is created by hand to describe a system, and when it is present, two commands can do everything: COMP tests components; SYN synthesizes a system. These two scripts communicate by creating and using component approximation files, whose names are variants of the names in system.pscf.

Using a current directory that contains all tool commands and all files can lead to name-space confusion. Should any file inadvertently use a name that is already taken, strange and incomprehensible things will happen. Most difficulties are automatically avoided by choosing user file names in the base directory to have no extensions, since all the SYN tools' files do have extensions. However, executable file names are required to be extensionless (because Windows cannot deal with executable extensions), so a user could pick a conflicting executable name. For example, on a system with an existing sort command, creating a component named sort will cause COMP to complain about the code file misbehaving, because the system command is being executed instead of the user's code[2]. Things are worse if the user inadvertently selects an executable name that duplicates one of the SYN tools script names. For example, creating a component named Calc would destroy the script with that name, after which no synthesis would work[3].

Appendix A gives the format of the three files most important to SYN operation: system.pscf describing a system, xxx.ccf (one for each component xxx) describing the subdomains and pointing to executable code, and the table file describing the approximation of component xxx, xxx.ccfc. Most other files used are plot data used by GNUPlot, consisting of data-pair (or -triple, etc.) records.

Some utility routines are collected into Perl module (.pm) scripts, and called as subroutines by other scripts. Most of these calls do not use the object-oriented mechanism provided by Perl, but two utilities, sampling.pm that returns a sequence of test-point values, and component.pm that runs component executable files, make essential use of O-O because several distinct instances are active at the same time.

---

[2] More incomprehensible things happen if the system command should happen to follow the SYN tools conventions so that it passes COMP checking!

[3] The SYN command would 'hang' on the first synthesis step, since the user replacement for Calc would be waiting for input that is never supplied.

14.1 Component Conventions

A deeper reason why research tools are flaky is that the environment they probe is itself unstable and evolving as the work proceeds. This environment may have been hastily conceived by the experimenter, perhaps with the intent of getting quick preliminary results. But once tools are implemented and begin to take on a life of their own, they constrain changes in the environment by their design. Tentative experimental choices get hard-wired into the code, and by the time it is apparent that some choice is dead wrong, it is difficult to go back without losing everything.

In the beginning of the component research described in this monograph it was decided to first attack the case of components with single numerical input/output domains. The decision was grounded in simplicity, and anticipated the use of random testing, both of which turned out to be sound reasons for the restriction. However, another rationale was spurious: in the theory of computation using natural numbers, single values for input/output suffice because multiple values can be coded into one. As the SYN tools developed, natural numbers were abandoned for a variety of reasons and coding of multiple values turned out to be awkward and counterintuitive, but by then the single-value restriction was thoroughly entwined in the SYN tools. Another early decision was to avoid persistent state and concurrent execution, permitting only 'pure-function' components. Here it proved possible to later modify the tools and include these characteristics, but not without a certain mess in the scripts. Stateless synthesis is of course only a special case of the more general algorithms that were later added, but it remains encapsulated in the tools with its own special file formats and algorithms. These expedients kept stateless cases working while development went beyond them, but are responsible for many strange duplications and conditional statements (bearing equally strange comments) in scripts.

Another far-reaching early decision was to begin with just series composition as a system-construction mechanism. Generalizing to systems built using also conditional and iterative mechanisms was relatively easy, but the choice precluded consideration of more general 'connector' architectures than 'pipe and filter.'

Without further historical explanation ('justification' would be an unjustified description), here are the restrictions imposed on components and systems by the SYN tools:

1. Components are executables arising from any source.
2. Components have single-variable finite floating-point input, output, and state domains.
3. Components have a single non-functional property (called "run time") with a floating-point value.
4. On each execution, a component must read a single input value from SYSIN, then later write a single output value to SYSOUT and write a single 'run-time' value to SYSERR.
5. A component with state must initially read a single value from a special state file, and finally overwrite that file with a result-state value.

6. A concurrent component may not have state. In the interval between reading input and writing output, it must include another write-output/read-input sequence and two additional run-time writes.

7. The system architecture may use only the three 'structured' operations: 'pipe and filter' composition, conditionals, and iteration, plus a limited form of concurrency. These may be arbitrarily nested.

One way to evaluate these choices after the fact is to take note of how difficult it is to devise an example that observes the restrictions, yet the example probes some important situation. On this criterion the results of case studies (Chapter 18) are mixed, but mostly positive. The examples needed often required trial and error to make them work, but work they did. Examples making significant use of persistent state posed the greatest difficulty: state is by its nature multi-dimensional and discrete, so a single floating-point value can be very awkward.

14.1.1 Artificial Components

There are components everywhere in many large software systems. Furthermore, it is not difficult to start with a monolithic application program and convert its subroutine parts to separate executable components [101]. Yet finding real components to use in even simple experiments is surprisingly difficult. Real software is written to do a job, not serve as a subject for experimentation. Strangely enough, initial experiments with the SYN tools were *too* successful. Programs used as introductory exercises—for example, a Java implementation of vending-machine control—didn't tax the tools' capabilities, because they had a few natural subdomains with constant behavior, so approximation and synthesis were trivially perfect. When an attempt was made to complicate their behavior, there were intellectual conflicts between making the code 'do something sensible' and at the same time exhibit interesting behavior.

Most difficulties in implementing the SYN tools were in the functional synthesis algorithms. Program run time was early chosen over reliability as the non-functional property to study, and given the functional synthesis algorithms, run time is an easy add-on, for example in the series synthesis algorithm given in Chapter 7. But when it comes to *measuring* run times of components and systems, things are more difficult. System measurements are not part of the ideal CBSD in which system properties are calculated from component approximations; but measurements are required for validation. In a general-purpose operating system (as opposed to one specifically intended for real-time applications), timing is inexact for many reasons, starting with sophisticated hardware caches and virtual memory whose performance is not repeatable, and ending with variations in run time for a process because the operating system time-slices the CPU and is always running hidden processes in the background. When gross variations like the unexpected starting of a resource-hog background process have been controlled, there remains the large granularity of the system clock (often 1/60 sec), which does not count short bursts of CPU activity accurately. It is not unusual to see a 20% variation in an attempt to repeat a run-time measurement, even when a dozen runs are averaged.

The factors described in the two previous paragraphs combined to suggest that although the SYN tools could handle any executable components that obey their input-output conventions, and their actual run times could be measured, revealing experiments might be better conducted with artificial components. For example, discontinuities to study could be created directly using conditional statements. If a component with rapidly varying functional output was needed, its code could just print values of (say) an exponential formula. The programs for such components were real, but they did contrived things. Systems formed from such artificial parts are even more contrived. For example, it is of interest to study the way in which component discontinuities act in series, but an example system linking two artificially discontinuous components would never be designed in reality because it doesn't 'do' anything sensible.

Artificial components really shine when it comes to measuring their run time. In pilot experiments each component was expected to time itself using system services like UNIX's (and Perl's) `times`, and to report the result to STDERR as required by the SYN input/output conventions. To improve repeatability, 'busy loops' were sometimes inserted to make the CPU times longer, so an experimenter had lots of time to think while an experiment was in progress. Here's a thought: "Why am I waiting for the time that I artificially inserted to elapse and be sent to STDERR when I could just as well have sent the same value directly?" This insight allowed arbitrary run times using arithmetic formulas to be fabricated by artificial components. There is no difference in principle between a component that uses and measures time and one that just fakes that same time, when only the value sent to STDERR can be observed. The real difference is that a complicated arbitrary time is easy to artificially create, it is repeatable, and the experimenter doesn't have to wait for it to elapse.

The `Math` component displayed in Fig. 9.2 of the stateless tutorial is a typical artificial component. Its code uses arithmetic formulas to calculate output and run-time values, then writes these values to STDOUT and STDERR. It contains an arbitrary discontinuity inserted to study its interaction with subdomain boundaries.

Using artificial components whose behavior is so easy to contrive is addicting. An experimenter begins to view a component as a graphical generator, not as software with a sensible purpose. For many experiments, particularly when studying capabilities of the SYN tools, the artificial viewpoint is valuable and appropriate. But its danger is that components and systems with purpose are the reality, and they may exhibit unsuspected characteristics that artificial studies omit or misrepresent.

14.2 Underlying Algorithms

Apart from the implementation of the synthesis theory presented in Chapter 8 and extended in Chapters 10 and 11, the SYN tools are just an exercise in careful bookkeeping. Of the roughly 8000 lines of Perl code, Calc, the script that does the synthesis, takes a bit over 2000; the rest of the SYN code does obvious things in straightforward ways.

COMP executes the code for each component named in system.pscf, over a domain described by its .ccf subdomains, and records the results in a .ccfc table file. The samples taken can be equi-spaced across the domain, or may be sequences of random values. The only slight difficulty arises because results must be averaged across each subdomain, which for random sequences requires collecting and sorting.

SYN performs the synthesis in steps described in the Polish of system.pscf, using Calc to calculate a sequence of synthesized-table files, one for each system-construction operation. Each step results in a .ccfc composite file, which may then enter into subsequent steps. SYN also constructs a Perl program SystemCode which is a script for executing the complete system, constructed from linked invocations of the actual code for components that comprise it. SystemCode is built using the operator/operand code-generation algorithm driven by a list of Polish tokens.

Displaying the results of COMP and SYN is done by auxiliary scripts Xcute and Xcomp. Xcomp must run the SystemCode script to compare the SYN calculation with actual system execution; this is done in the same way that COMP executes each component. Xcute may also have to re-execute a component's code, if the sampling requested is different than that used by COMP to create its approximation file. These two comparison scripts also produce r-m-s error tables by subdomain and graphs of the measured/calculated functions. GNUPlot has proved more than adequate for displaying graphs. Any calculated results (without measured comparison) can be graphed by Xcute using only a .ccfc file; in particular, the result of each synthesis step is available.

All of the SYN scripts are described in more detail in Appendix A, and each script begins with a comment something like a UNIX man page.

14.3 Execution by Table-lookup

Each .ccfc file, whether it is a measured approximation to the behavior of a component (measured by COMP), or an approximate prediction from a synthesis step (calculated by Calc), consists of tables indexed by subdomains. The simplest case for stateless components has a one-dimensional list of subdomains and two table values (output, and run time). The most complicated cases are predictions for systems with composite state, an N-fold cross product of local states. For $N = 3$, which might arise from synthesizing a conditional component with state and a component with state in each of its branches, or from three components each with state in series, the calculated .ccfc file has four lists of subdomains (over an input domain and the three state domains), and comprises five values indexed by these subdomains: functional output, run time, and three result-state values.

These table files can be used to look up result value(s) for any given subdomain, and hence can be used to find approximate result(s) for any given input value(s). For example, in the stateless case, to find an approximate run time on input x, find the subdomain S_x with $x \in S_x$, index the value-table at S_x, and read out the run-time value. For the 3-state system, to find the result value of (say) state 2 on input x and starting state (s_1, s_2, s_3), look these values up to find the corresponding four sub-domains, index the result table, and take from it the second result-state value. So long as $N \leq 1$, the tables can be displayed as step-graphs, which is exactly what Xcute does. Adding a small amount of wrapper code to one of these tables creates an executable program that accepts inputs, looks them up, and returns the output. The wrapped program, when the table is a component approximation, does the same thing as the component executable, but only approximately. In the notation of Chapter 6, where a component C computes functional output $\boxed{C}$, its table-lookup code computes $\lceil\!\lfloor C \rfloor\!\rceil$. These 'table-lookup components' play an important role in I-CBSD.

First, they capture the descriptions recorded by component developers in repositories, the descriptions used by system designers to design and synthesize systems 'on paper.' The SYN tools work with them, but a designer can also use them directly. Anything that could be done with a real component's executable can instead be done with the table-lookup code, but only approximately. Approximate is sometimes better than exact. Component developers may be unwilling to release executable files before purchase, but they presumably don't need to protect approximations. It can happen that approximate behavior, being simpler than the full details of the exact, is easier to understand. And certainly the execution of table-lookup code can be faster than some exact computations.

Second, they allow any tool that works with executable files to be used on the approximation. The SYN tools attempt to provide a number of useful features, but in addition a system designer might like to use other sophisticated testing and analysis tools based on execution[4]. For example, test cases generated by a requirements-analysis tool can be used on the approximations. Trace monitors can be used at the component level. (The SYN tools do have a trace facility.)

Finally, table-lookup code provides a way to validate that the hard part of the SYN tools (that is, Calc) is working, to expose tool failures, as described in the next subsection. Without this oracle, the tools would have been far harder to debug and impossible to trust in complicated cases.

14.3.1 Validating Tools

Suppose that the system-execution script SystemCode that links together the real executable components for a system into runnable code, instead linked together their

---

[4] An analyzer that examines execution at too low a level won't work, however. For example, a memory-leak detector could not detect leaks in a system resulting from mistakes in its components' code; any leaks it detected would come from the wrapper code that is the same for all components. In the same way, structural-coverage test generators will be uninformative.

table-lookup approximation codes—call this script `SystemCodeA` (for Approximation). When `SystemCodeA` is executed, it will carry out the proper system constructions: Its conditionals will test their arguments and select one branch or the other, its loop guards will test and repeat loop bodies, its sequences will feed one output into the next input. But all of these operations will be only approximate, because the code that performs them is looking up subdomain average values in tables. The system results will thus also be only approximate, but here's the crucial insight:

> *The result of executing a table-lookup system `SystemCodeA` should agree exactly with the result calculated by `Calc` on a `SYN` command to synthesize that same system.*

Like many insights, this one is obvious once it has been stated. What `Calc` is doing, after all, is collecting together all the possible subdomain combinations in a synthesized approximation. To execute `SystemCodeA` is exactly like following through this synthesis subdomain by subdomain, for a single point.

Thus the tables created by `SYN` for a synthesized system are an oracle for tests of `SystemCodeA`, or put the other way around, every test of `SystemCodeA` is a check on the correctness of `Calc`'s synthesis. In practice, the command `SYN -X` 'compiles' `SystemCodeA` in place of `SystemCode`, and the check is accomplished by making a comparison between calculation and execution using `Xcomp`. Zero r-m-s error in every subdomain means that no mistake in the tools has been exposed by the current example. Without this check, it would have been extremely difficult to tell the difference between a synthesis that is in error because of an imperfect approximation and one which exposes a mistake in `Calc`.

It is very unlikely that `Calc` will calculate the same incorrect result as an erroneous `SystemCodeA` execution, much less likely that there will be many such nasty coincidental agreements when `Xcomp` samples over the system domain to make the comparison. The only thing the two have in common is the tables measured by `COMP`; these are obtained by straightforward brute-force sampling, and each example in which `Xcute` compares graphs of the measured approximation with the real component code (for example, see Figs. 9.4, 9.15, and 9.20 in Chapter 9) is a validation of `COMP`. Given correct tables, there is no overlap in the algorithms[5]. When there is a disagreement, `SystemCodeA` is almost always right, because the linking of wrapped tables is simple and straightforward. The only conceptual mistake made in `SystemCodeA` during tool development was a failure to properly save environments in nested conditionals, found and corrected early on.

It's instructive to give examples of subtle failures[6] in `Calc` exposed by comparison with `SystemCodeA`.

---

[5] Even the table lookup is done differently; `Calc` uses binary search, the execution wrappers in `SystemCodeA` use exhaustive search. (The latter reflects a lazy programmer who didn't take time for efficiency.)

[6] The following subsection describes a systematic error involving the arms of conditionals that was exposed by comparing `SystemCodeA` executions with calculations, which is difficult to fix in the existing tool design.

Off-by-one run-time calculation. The basic iteration calculation in `Calc` uses loop unwinding. `Calc` synthesizes a single conditional with the body, then repeatedly composes this with itself. While this produces the correct functional output, it distorts the run time. The guard is *false* in the last composition, but is used once more in the residual, so its run time is added in when it should not be. Without the check of `SystemCodeA`, the `Calc` mistake might have appeared to be an approximation error (particularly when the total run time is large because of many iterations).

Data-structure maintenance error. When state was added to the capabilities of the SYN tools, the format of approximation tables had to change to include a count of the number of times each subdomain arises in sampling using random sequences. (For infeasible states, this count is zero.) A count field was added to the record and checked before any use is made of each subdomain. As noted above, the stateless case was not incorporated in the more general, but left intact within `Calc`, including its table records lacking the new count-field. At one point in `Calc`'s code, a test that was meant to look at the count-field was mistakenly applied to a stateless table where the corresponding field stores the functional output value. So long as the output was not zero, the record appeared valid and was correctly used. But output zero caused a legitimate record to be ignored. This case did not come up for more than two years after the mistake in `Calc` was made, in an example published in TOSEM [48]. When it did surface in the `SystemCodeA` comparison, finding and fixing it was not the usual maintenance nightmare of not knowing exactly what is wrong nor where to look for it in a large program.

14.3.2 A Nasty Mistake

Many times in the course of developing and experimenting with the SYN tools, disagreements arose between the execution of table-lookup code in `SystemCodeA` and results calculated by `Calc`, and each failure (almost always in the relatively complicated algorithms of `Calc`) was eliminated, with one (known!) exception. When `Calc` was extended to include state, it was decided not to implement the piecewise-linear approximation, largely because of bad experiences with roundoff errors in the stateless case, and because it is unclear that a plane fitted to component measurements in two or more dimensions would be meaningful. In retrospect, the decision was a wise one—the algorithms to handle state are themselves complicated enough in the simpler step-function approximation. However, without linear approximations, there are necessarily two peculiar approximation errors in synthesis, errors in which `SystemCodeA` executions are closer to real system behavior than is the `Calc` synthesis.

The simpler of these errors involves a conditional without an `ELSE` part. In the basic algorithms presented in Chapter 8, this case is treated as a full conditional in which the *false* branch contains a stateless identity component with zero run time.

What was not recognized is that only a linear approximation to such a component is perfect. When a step-function approximation is used for identity, the synthesis algorithms of Calc produce a stairstep approximation to identity when the conditional is *false*. But SystemCode and SystemCodeA, in which the conditional test is actually made, do nothing whatsoever when the test is *false*—that is, they compute a perfect (linear) identity for the missing ELSE branch. Thus Calc and SystemCodeA do not agree as they do in all other situations. As subdomains shrink, the difference also shrinks, but the number of subdomains needed to make the error negligible may be much larger than those needed to approximate the rest of a system, and because the identity component is not explicitly provided by a component developer, its error can dominate all others. The worst of it is that loop synthesis is implemented as repeated composition of ELSE-less conditionals, which compounds the error.

Something similar occurs in the more difficult error case, which involves the calculation of result-state values in a conditional branch when it is not taken. For a concrete example, consider a stateless conditional component with a stateless component in the *false* arm and a component C_S with state in the *true* arm. In the Calc synthesis, the equivalent approximate system has the behavior of C_S on those subdomains where the conditional is *true*, including the result-state behavior. But the system state is identical to the C_S state. What is the system result-state value when the C_S branch is *not* taken? It should be identity; that is, since C_S is not executed, its state (and hence the system state) should not change. Indeed, that is how SystemCode and SystemCodeA behave. But Calc has only a step-function approximation available, not the correct linear one, so synthesis does not agree with execution of SystemCodeA. The two error cases both arise when a loop has a body component with state.

Short of rethinking the decision not to implement linear approximations with state, which is THTC[7], the errors introduced by using an imperfect identity can only to reduced, not eliminated. The expedient chosen for the SYN tools is to replace numerical values in the calculated tables with I when the result should be identity. When an I value is to be used as output, in some cases the input is known and so can be replicated for a perfect identity. In the prediction graphs this turns a rectangular plateau into a plane tilted to the horizontal in either the input or the input-state dimension (but not both at once, since the identities occur in different graphs—the functional output graph may have input slope; the result-state graph may have state slope).

Figure 14.1 is an example of output behavior from a system contrived to exercise the I feature. A component B is given a dome-shaped output ranging from about 1 to 10, much like Fig. 10.2 in Chapter 10. B is made the body of a loop, with a loop guard that is true for input less than 5. Thus in Fig. 14.1, there can be no output

---

[7] Too Horrible To Contemplate. This expression might have been coined by the developers of DEC 10 systems (c. 1965), when it was suggested that they modify the operating system to store four eight-bit characters in each 36-bit memory word, instead of the five seven-bit characters of the original design, which included special hardware-instruction support. This would have entailed rewriting not only the operating system, but all other programs, many of which had strange and wonderful uses for the left-over 36th bit. Not the least consideration in a THTC decision is the

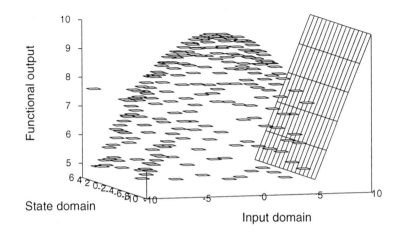

Functional output

State domain

Input domain

Fig. 14.1 Approximation graph showing tilted output-prediction rectangles

values below 5, since B has been repeatedly invoked to eliminate them. The body B is never invoked for input above 5, producing the predicted plane at the right of Fig. 14.1—the output table contains I for these subdomains and the approximation is perfect there. Furthermore, the output approximation calculated by Calc agrees perfectly with the table-lookup system SystemCodeA. However, I table entries are an imperfect expedient. When Calc must create a series table from another table containing an I, as it does when synthesizing the composition of a loop body for more than one iteration, it cannot just use the I, since this 'value' may be moving to a new subdomain and the 'identity' applies only to its original subdomain. The result-state behavior of the iterated dome system shows the flaws of the I expedient in Fig. 14.2. At the right of Fig. 14.2 are the inputs for which the loop body B is never invoked, hence the predicted system state is linear (an I in the calculated tables), and there is no prediction error. However, over most of the remainder of the input domain in Fig. 14.2, the result-state from executing SystemCodeA is linear in input, but the calculated approximation is the step plateaus shown, so the prediction differs from SystemCodeA execution by an average of about 2.2%. In the center of Fig. 14.2 there is a diagonal line of tilted rectangles. These come from the peculiar situation that two I values are composed, and thus even though the I is moved, it can be retained. But SystemCodeA produces a constant, not linear

number of mistakes that would arise in re-implementation. Embarking on such a change almost guarantees that the software will never work again.

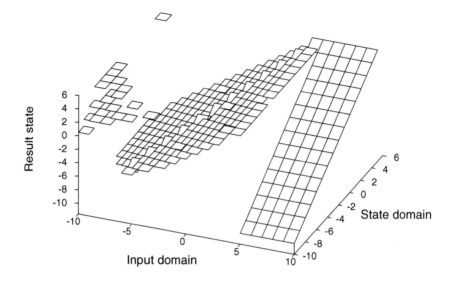

Fig. 14.2 Approximation graph showing tilted result-state-prediction rectangles

result for this case. The calculation using the I expedient is closer to correct (that is, it agrees better with execution of the real system SystemCode), but it does not check with SystemCodeA. Expedients are like that—they behave strangely.

The scattering of subdomains to the left of Fig. 14.2 are those for which several compositions of the unrolled conditional are required for termination; as in almost all result-state graphs, it is difficult to intuitively grasp what the code is doing to the system state.

14.4 Tool Performance

The natural standard by which to judge performance of the SYN tools is a comparison with the alternative: the time to test a real system. The approximations may have some intrinsic merit—they solve the problem of trying proprietary component code, for example—but experimenting with a designed system is the bottom line. If the SYN command can synthesize and display the behavior of a reasonably accurate approximate system very quickly compared to real-system execution, it may be worth putting up with the imprecision of approximation.

Cutting to the bottom line entails omissions and value judgments on both sides of the issue.

- The time required to measure and record approximate properties for components is ignored. The rationale is that this is but a small addition to the component testing that should be done in any case.
- The substantial work of actually testing a system, assembling it and selecting test points, is ignored.
- Support features of the tools like easy access to functional graphs, are ignored.
- Approximations, even good ones, may not be usable in making judgments about whether requirements are met, since requirements are themselves precise.

Some of these favor the tools, some favor actual system execution.

Using the SYN tools, it is easy to make a rough comparison between synthesis time and system execution time. For the simplest cases, it takes about five times longer to obtain system graphs by testing than it does to get the approximate graphs from synthesis. But such a comparison reflects mostly the difference in the overhead of processing fewer subdomains with table-lookup algorithms, versus more test points with heavyweight process initiation. Unfortunately, the parameters that determine performance for synthesis calculations and actual executions are different, making a precise theoretical comparison impossible.

For synthesis using the step-function approximation with n system subdomains, the time required is proportional to the number of synthesis steps (roughly the number of components K in the system). Series synthesis uses an $n \log n$ algorithm (for table lookups by binary search). The intersections required for conditional synthesis can be done in $n \log n$ (but the tools do not use the sophisticated algorithm with this performance). Loop synthesis by composing conditional unwindings takes $n^2 \log n$. The conditional and iteration times are worst case; there is a further complication in that these algorithms can increase n. For an arbitrary system of unknown structure, perhaps

$$T_s = c_s K n \log n$$

is a compromise formula for the synthesis time T_s, with the proviso that if loops dominate there should be an additional factor of n. The proportionality constant c_s reflects the overhead of the algorithms, which can be estimated by measuring the time for one case; it is about 1.4 ms for a modest laptop, a small overhead because the algorithms are lightweight.

Test executions of a system, on the other hand, require a time proportional to the number of test points N and to the average execution time t of a component and to the number of components executed A. If all the K components are in series, $A = K$; each conditional replacing two series components with three (of which only two are executed) introduces a factor of 2/3; a loop multiplies by an arbitrary average number of iterations, say R. So a compromise formula analogous to the above for system execution time T_e might be

$$T_e = c_e N K t,$$

with again dominant loops treated as a special case by introducing an additional factor R. c_e is the proportionality constant, estimated from one case as about 1.8 s, a much larger overhead reflecting the high cost of initiating a process.

To compare T_s and T_e requires a relation between the independent parameters that occur in each. In general there is no such constraint, so either time can be made to dominate and by an arbitrary amount. However, if system testing is to produce graphs comparable to those of synthesis, N must be a small multiple of n, the ratio being the average number of times a test falls in each subdomain. With $N/n = 3$, the comparison is

$$\frac{T_e}{T_s} = \frac{3c_e t}{c_s \log n} = \frac{3960t}{\log n}.$$

There seems no plausible way to link the average component run time t to the number of subdomains n, but for $t = 1.3$ ms and $n = 32$, $T_e/T_s = 1.0$. As both parameters increase, synthesis is relatively faster; for $t = 42$ ms and $n = 2048$ (a 32-fold increase in each) T_e/T_s is about 16. For many components, t has an input dependence, typically increasing at least linearly as the component input grows. Since n does not depend on input, synthesis would eventually be arbitrarily faster than execution. When loops dominate, the additional factors R and n enter, again with no plausible relationship. But again if R increases with larger input, synthesis is eventually arbitrarily faster. On the other hand, if components are very efficient but it takes many subdomains to gain a good enough approximation, system testing is faster. For $t = 0.1$ ms and $n = 1024$, T_s/T_e is about 23.

Another way to look at the performance of tools is to judge the time they take absolutely: Is it possible to do the calculations for enough subdomains to get reasonable accuracy, yet keep the execution time under (say) a minute? The answer is 'yes' when K and n are reasonable, on the order of 10 and 1000 respectively, for then $T_s \approx 2$ sec.

Chapter 15
Debugging Components, Component-based Systems, and Support Tools

TESTING can be described as a technique primarily used to discover that software fails, but finding a failure is only a first step toward improvement. To eliminate a software failure once it has been uncovered is called 'debugging.' Debugging, like most software terms involving 'bug,' is often misleading, because it suggests a minor correction to the code source. In reality the cause of failure is frequently an omission—the code fails because its author failed to provide for some circumstances, under which it failed. To search through source code looking for something that is not there is a good way to find nothing. It would be better to look at those places in the code where action should be, with an eye out to discover it is missing. Unfortunately, the code correction for an omission is not unique, seldom localized, and seldom small. This is another way of saying that many 'bugs' have no real existence: the failure is real and real work must be done to eliminate it, but the only localized cause is in human incompetence, impossible to 'squash.' One thing people are really good at is fastening a simple, misleading name on something complex, and 'debugging' is one of the best.

CBSD ought to make debugging easier, since each component is relatively small and their interactions are constrained. CBSD tools can help.

15.1 Debugging Components

In I-CBSD, the primary testing of real code takes place at component level. The evolution of a testset that starts the debugging process could be thought of as debugging the testset as well as debugging the program. A poor testset is one that does not fail yet failures are possible[1]. A testset's 'bugs' are all omissions; time wasted on poor test cases is important only if it contributes to leaving out good ones.

---

[1] It has been suggested that "success" of a testset should mean that some test point within it fails. Even within a jargon-rich technical article, this reversal of terminology is too confusing to seriously consider. The question of what constitutes a good or bad testset when the program being tested is correct has never been resolved.

D. Hamlet, *Composing Software Components,* DOI 10.1007/978-1-4419-7148-7_15,
© Springer Science+Business Media, LLC 2010

15.1.1 Checking Tests Against Requirements

Recognizing a test-point failure for a component is sometimes easy—perhaps the execution throws an exception or fails to terminate in a reasonable time. Otherwise, 'failure' is only defined by requirements that serve as an oracle. Functional test points and functional subdomains arise from requirements, explicit or assumed. When there is a functional test failure, the principle behind debugging is straightforward: look in the code for necessary work to see that it is or is not being done. Here the manageable size of a component's code is critical. Starting with the failing test input, the steps can be followed by hand, looking for code actions that are needed in that case (and also for actions that seem unnecessary). The hand execution usually doesn't require hand arithmetic. There can of course be mistakes in the formulas used for calculation, but more likely the failure is at a different conceptual level[2]. At some point in the hand execution, the tester thinks, "Aha! It can't work without using that table" (or whatever); or, "Why is that extraneous value being changed?". What has been found is evidence of a mistake the programmer made. The final step is to generalize to other inputs ("That will happen every time...?"), other test points that can be checked and will inductively falsify or support the generalization. Furthermore, the functional subdomain breakdown may be called into question: The failure cases themselves often comprise a subdomain. Thus the 'bug' is found—it is the programmer's mistake in handling a functional case.

Making code changes to eliminate a found failure are usually included in debugging. Perhaps these are small, if the conceptual programming mistake was small. A common mistake is failure to detect a special-case input and make an exception calculation for it; that can be fixed with a conditional and a bit of new code. When it comes to modifying a component's code, a tester tries to get inside the original programmer's head, because the ideal 'fix' is one that does the least violence to the existing design. It is seductive to think: "This is all wrong," and make sweeping changes, but that is usually a mistake. If the design was mostly good and the programmer competent, a big change will introduce more failures than it fixes. One way to accomplish a minimal change is to find a subdomain that exactly captures the failing cases, and make sure that changes affect only that subdomain. On the other hand, it may be clear that the component programmer has made a serious or fatal mistake that cannot be fixed with changes whose effect can be predicted and controlled. Then a new implementation from scratch is called for, its requirements including an explicit note about misconceptions in the failed code.

---

[2] It's a little like checking a bank statement: very likely the bank's software has done the arithmetic correctly, but the human check is to see that all items are present and correct (and that there are no spurious ones).

15.1.2 Executing Code Outside the SYN Tools

Powerful software-support tools can themselves fail. Nothing is a bigger waste of time than 'debugging' that starts from a false failure that is really in the tools[3]. Fortunately, Szyperski's definition of components as executables allows direct execution with no tools involved . When the SYN tools show a result that the component tester considers to be a failure, the component can be run by hand using only the operating system[4] to check if it is real. The reverse situation is not so satisfactory. If support tools should happen to *hide* a component's failure, the tester has no clue that anything is wrong. Fortunately, tool implementation is mostly simple bookkeeping, which means that it is difficult to make such a mistake. When there is a serious mistake in the tool code, it usually appears in application as universal (false) failure.

15.1.3 Finding Good Subdomains

The SYN tool COMP creates approximation files for components, in which approximate execution values can be found by table-lookup indexed by subdomain. These files can be 'executed' as described in Section 14.3. But with real code on hand, why would a component developer want to execute an approximation? Table-lookup is faster, but that's seldom important. It is sometimes helpful that the approximation behaves more simply, is easier to understand. But the only compelling reason for approximation execution has to do with the quality of subdomains used to test, that is, with debugging the testset. The I-CBSD component designer is building not only code, but descriptive subdomains. The best way to improve those subdomains is to compare the approximate executions with the real ones.

When a component is selected for use in some system, in I-CBSD its source and executable code are unavailable, so the approximation tables are all a system designer can use. A system failure can be traced to some component (approximation) in system design (see Section 15.2 to follow) only if the table-lookup code standing in for real component code is reasonably accurate. At the system level, subdomains in the approximate predictions are not independently devised, but come from the component approximations. For example, the subdomains in a series prediction are exactly those of the first component[5]. Thus finding good subdomains at the component level is an important part of testing.

For debugging a component, a failure in subdomain S immediately suggests that S's description might be a generalization of failing cases. That is, S might be homogeneous for failure. If not, then it is a debugging plan to refine S to home in on the

---

[3] Unless of course the tester is testing those tools. But tool users don't like it when they are put in that position.

[4] You have to trust something!

[5] Except in the stateless piecewise-linear approximation, where they also reflect boundaries in the second component's subdomains.

problem. Normally, testsets assembled from points that failed are useless once the original failures are fixed—at best they stand on guard against future maintenance that reintroduces an old problem. But if the result of debugging is partly to adjust subdomains, then after fixing code the refined subdomains remain as a useful part of the component's description.

15.1.4 Graphical Aids

Tools like the SYN script Xcute produce graphs that cover the entire test domain, but can zoom in to show the comparison between actual and approximate execution in a single subdomain. The close-up graphs are helpful in refining a subdomain to isolate a failure. Often code exhibits discontinuities that point to the problem, which went unnoticed in the larger domain. But the most dangerous part of changing code to eliminate a test failure is the possibility of introducing unexpected new failures. Displaying behavior over the whole test domain is a way to catch an ill-advised change, and noting the subdomain in which some new failure pops up can be a great help in correcting it.

At the syntax level, a source comparison between original code and fixed code is invaluable for checking that unintended changes have not been made. Tools like UNIX diff localize comparisons in a way that makes editing mistakes stick out like a sore thumb. The SYN tools can do something similar for test executions. The script subddiff compares two approximation files, listing only the subdomains on which they differ. When the subdomain containing a failure has been refined to S and the code fixed, subddiff should show that the original code's approximation and the fixed code's approximation differ only on S. subddiff is a kind of 'semantic diff' that is useful because the subdomain approximations are defined for a larger granularity than individual test points. The subdomains of a component approximation are semantic analogs of 'lines' of the source text.

15.2 Debugging Component-based Systems

Conventional system testing is not part of the I-CBSD paradigm. At system level, the designer works instead with predictions from tools like SYN and their analysis using tools like profile, subddiff, and (to follow immediately) tracer. Thus a system failure occurs in synthesized behavior when the prediction for an input X_f appears wrong to the system designer. It could happen that the approximation is at fault[6], but imagine that X_f really fails. In order to learn more, the failed prediction must be brought down to the subsystem- or component level.

---

[6] There is no way to check without purchasing the actual components, assembling the real system, and testing it on X_f, but often peculiar system behavior is quite distinct from approximation errors.

The SYN tool `tracer` displays the progress of an input through an approximation. It shows the component(s) and subsystem(s) involved, the subdomains used in the approximation, and the approximate outputs. To illustrate the use of `tracer` in debugging, consider a system of three series elements, the middle one a conditional:

$$C_a; \text{ if } C_q \text{ then } C_t \text{ else } C_f \text{ fi}; C_z$$

Take a domain of $[0, 100)$ divided into ten equal-sized subdomains for each component. Component descriptions have led the system designer to believe that:

- C_t returns *true* just for the first half $[0, 50)$
- All the other components compute identity functions

The designer therefore believes that the system will compute an identity function, but its components are invoked hither and yon in the process. Figure 15.1 shows the predicted approximate functional output obtained from command SYN -G for this

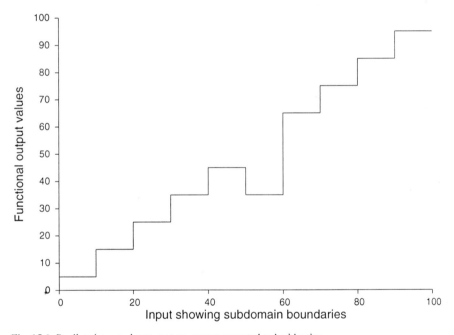

Fig. 15.1 Predicted approximate system output expected to be identity

system. Even this coarse subdomain granularity shows that something is wrong—the stairsteps are not uniform as an approximation to identity would be. It looks as if the prediction is failing in subdomain $[50, 60)$[7].

Figure 15.2 is a typeset version of output from the command

---

[7] Debugging would be easier with refined subdomains to pinpoint the failure, but the system designer is stuck with those provided by the component developers.

```
tracer -D 0 55
```
that examines the predicted system behavior on input 55. The -D 0 option stops

$$\xrightarrow{55}\ \boxed{\begin{array}{c}\text{theory3}\\ [50,\,60)\end{array}}\ \xrightarrow{35}$$

Fig. 15.2 Trace of system input 55

the analysis at the top level (recursion depth of 0; more to follow). In tracer's display a system or component appears in a box with the subdomain in which that input falls, input to the left and approximate output to the right. In Fig. 15.2 the system is theory3, the final synthesized system (the default if no name is given to tracer as final argument). The tracer tool uses no system executions[8], but rather uses measured/calculated table-lookup files. It can recursively invoke itself until it reaches the component level[9].

Figure 15.3 shows the complete tracer output[10] down to the component level, from the command tracer 55. Figure 15.3 identifies two failures: First, the C_q

$$\xrightarrow{55}\ \boxed{\begin{array}{c}\text{Ca}\\ [50,\,60)\end{array}}\ \xrightarrow{55}\ \boxed{\begin{array}{c}\text{Cq}\\ [50,\,60)\end{array}}\ \xrightarrow{\textit{true}\ 55}\ \boxed{\begin{array}{c}\text{Ct}\\ [50,\,60)\end{array}}\ \xrightarrow{32.5}\ \boxed{\begin{array}{c}\text{Cz}\\ [30,\,40)\end{array}}\ \xrightarrow{35}$$

Fig. 15.3 Complete trace of system input 55

approximate value is *true* on $[50, 60)$ where it was expected to be *false*. The wrong branch is selected in the approximation there. Second, the C_t approximation is not getting close to identity on $[50, 60)$—its value of 32.5 on input 55 is too low to be explained as an approximation error[11].

Without access to the component code, system debugging can go no farther. It is possible to look back at the approximations of the two components that have failed, however. Xcute will display their problems and would have done so at the

---

[8] As SYN and tracer are currently implemented, only components and systems with at most one state dimension can be traced.

[9] Loops are a special case. tracer does not step through the series of approximations in the iteration-synthesis algorithm (it's possible, but was judged too confusing to display), but gives only the final result from the synthesized loop approximation. The -D option sets the recursion limit; if missing, tracer recurs all the way to component level.

[10] The double output/input between C_q and C_t means that output *true* from the conditional C_q selects the C_t branch, but the branch receives the input that came to C_q. A diagram on one line gives all the information, but doesn't always correctly show what goes where.

[11] If it were not for the error in C_q, this error in C_t would not appear. In this system, what C_t does at 50 and above should be irrelevant. We don't know whether C_f, were it used as it should be on $[50, 60)$, would fail. Some questions can be answered with tracer using other inputs, but not this one.

beginning. But at the outset the system developer may not have known where to look. If the system developer chooses to replace C_q and C_t, it will be helpful to run subdddiff on the replaced pairs to see that only the values in subdomain $[50, 60)$ have changed. Since the difficulty in this example seems to be within the conditional that is synthesized as theory1, tracer 55 theory1 will look at only this subsystem.

15.2.1 Component Mismatch

One kind of system failure in CBSD is special: the output from a series component falls outside the domain of the following one. When this happens in executing a real system, there is usually a catastrophic system failure. The Ariane 5 flight-control software failed [73], for example, when a subroutine sent a symbolic error code to a routine expecting a short integer. In the Ariane 5, the root cause was a complicated mistake in real-time processor scheduling, but many simpler scenarios are possible. Perhaps the intermediate output needs only to be scaled to fall in range[12].

The SYN tools, since they calculate predictions for all system-input subdomains, report any range/domain problem[13], as a synthesis error. The algorithms cannot proceed if subdomains cannot be traced through composition. There is a difficulty, however, in presenting the failure information. In a sequence composition of two components CA and CB, SYN might issue a message like:

```
Output 103.6 from CA subdomain [10,20)
    does not fall in any CB subdomain
```

The system designer can then examine the situation to discover whether CA is producing the wrong value on $[10, 20)$, whether CB should have been able to handle 103.6, or whether the design itself is wrong, e.g., CA should not be in series with CB.

The same difficulty can arise between two subsystems that are themselves the result of calculation. In illustration, the tutorial system from Chapter 9 is repeated as Fig. 15.4, but a domain/range mismatch is created by replacing subdomain $[0, 5)$ of component C5 with $[0.5, 5)$. In the SYN synthesis this change causes the domain-error message:

```
Output 0.365 from theory2 subdomain [90,95)
    does not fall in any theory4 subdomain
```

---

[12] Again, the system designer can't alter either offending component because in I-CBSD the components' source code is not available. As an alternative to replacing one or both, a 'glue' component could be added between them to adjust the range.

[13] As usual, since the predictions are only approximate, it is wise to check that the actual system behaves as predicted. There may be a false positive—a reported mismatch that does not actually occur. A false negative—a predicted match when the real system would fail with a domain violation—is less satisfactory because the prediction does not exhibit any dramatic effects.

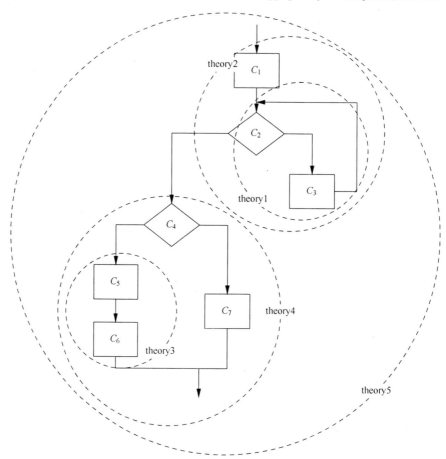

Fig. 15.4 System used in the stateless tutorial showing synthesized subsystems

The error arises in the last step of the synthesis of Fig. 15.4 when the subsystem consisting of components C1, C2, and C3 (previously synthesized as `theory2`) is being composed in series with the subsystem of components C4, C7, C5, and C6 (`theory4`). The `tracer -D 1 92` diagram of Fig. 15.5 presents the situation at the next-to-top level. The error message has identified the offending system subdo-

$$\xrightarrow{92} \boxed{\begin{array}{c} \text{theory2} \\ [90, 95) \end{array}} \xrightarrow{0.365} \boxed{\begin{array}{c} \text{theory4} \\ [?, ?) \end{array}} \xrightarrow{??}$$

Fig. 15.5 A domain error resulting from interface mismatch in system synthesis

main as $[90, 95)$, so a value there (92) was selected to trace. When there is a domain mismatch question marks replace numerical values.

Figure 15.6 shows the complete `tracer` 92 output for the system of Fig. 15.4 for input 92. The synthesized `theory2` and `theory4` predictions have been de-

$$92 \xrightarrow{} \boxed{\begin{matrix} \text{C1} \\ [90, 95) \end{matrix}} \xrightarrow{0.36} \boxed{\begin{matrix} \text{theory1} \\ [0, 10) \end{matrix}} \xrightarrow{0.36} \boxed{\begin{matrix} \text{C4} \\ [0, 10) \end{matrix}} \xrightarrow[\text{true}]{} \xrightarrow{0.36} \boxed{\begin{matrix} \text{C5} \\ [?,?) \end{matrix}} \xrightarrow{??}$$

Fig. 15.6 Analysis of a system domain error down to component level

composed into their components, showing that the domain error occurs in C5, but also showing the full surrounding context. The example was created by artificially distorting C5's domain, but the root cause of failure might be anywhere in Fig. 15.6. For example, C1 might be improperly producing the near-zero value or the loop `theory1` failing to modify it.

In I-CBSD the components' source code is not available, so the system designer can do nothing more than ask for help from component developers or replace (say) C5. But the SYN tools provide an excellent trouble report in that they pinpoint exactly what fails in the test. The example demonstrates detection and analysis of a system design problem (mismatched component interfaces) "on paper," without system execution.

15.2.2 Interface Profiles

However good the testsets for its components are, synthesis of a system can be in error because in I-CBSD those testsets must be defined and used before any system is even conceived. Details are provided in Chapter 17 on synthesis accuracy, but intuitively the difficulty is that in series composition the first component distorts its input distribution in providing output to the second component, which has not been properly tested[14] on the skewed distribution. The SYN tool `profile` (Section 9.5) displays interface profiles using the subdomains of any component in a system. When a second-component subdomain dominates its interface input profile, that subdomain should have been split—splitting it would level out the profile to match the component tests that are uniform across subdomains.

The information a system designer gets from `profile` would contribute to debugging component testsets (through the subdomains used), but it comes too late. As usual, all the system designer can do is to replace a poorly tested component with a better one[15]. In this case 'better' means one with a better subdomain breakdown,

---

[14] It is not entirely untested, because its subdomains cover the whole domain unless there is a domain error as described in the previous section. But because of how many values actually arrive in one subdomain relative to another, the test emphasis might have been quite wrong.

[15] Or consult with the component developer and suggest better subdomains, feedback more likely to be quickly accepted because to correct matters the component developer need only retest the original code. In SYN terms, code need not change, just the subdomains of the .ccf file.

more subdomains where the interface profile peaks. There may be nothing wrong with the old component, but trusting a poor testset that has shown no failure is a fool's game.

15.3 Debugging of Support Tools

There is a large software-engineering literature devoted to writing good code and to the impossibility of 'testing quality in' to bad code. The most compelling part of this position is cost and resources: it is undeniably more expensive and difficult to diagnose and correct a software mistake the older it is. First there is the human difficulty of remembering the details surrounding it; second there is all the subsequent work that may have been based on it and hence must be redone. Testing-time comes at the end of development, maximally separated from mistake-making-time.

Unfortunately, exploratory programming spread over many years, in a research effort competing with other responsibilities, and which employs an ever-changing student programming team, has to choose between producing bad code and not creating much code at all. For the SYN tools, the choice was bad code. Fortunately, there is a natural decomposition of the requirements into a half dozen relatively independent functions, and the powerful technique of iterative enhancement [7] is ideally suited to the circumstances. Token obedience is even paid to CBSD itself in that the component scripts of the SYN tools are separately executable.

15.3.1 Problem Decomposition

Exploratory programming is an intrinsically chaotic process, but looking back on the order in which the SYN tools were implemented and debugged, there is a pattern.

First: component execution. Components are executable programs, so to control their execution with SYN scripts is a short step from just typing the operating-system 'run' command. Graphing component results makes it easy to see if the SYN executions are correct.

Second: component approximation. Once SYN can execute a component, it is easy to record its approximation, and graphing makes it easy to check. Varying the subdomains used makes it easy to locate problems.

Third: system linking and execution. Since the system structure is provided in reverse Polish form, parsing it is trivial. The 'code' into which it is compiled is an ordered collection of component executions, each passing its output to the next (or determining the flow of control), expressed as a Perl script SystemCode. SystemCode can be executed like any program, and the execution mechanism for a component previously developed within SYN can be used to run it. Exactly the same compilation, if it is expressed in the table-lookup 'executions' of the component approximations instead of the components' actual code, can be run as an approximate system. Graphing the results, trying trivial systems of just one construct, and comparing table-lookup with actual code are good techniques for detecting and fixing failures.

Finally: synthesis algorithms. Calculation of an approximate system's behavior from its components' approximations is the most difficult part of the SYN tools. This task can be decomposed into the four system constructs, beginning with series. As described in Section 14.3.1, synthesized results can be checked quantitatively by comparing with the table-lookup executions. Debugging the synthesis-algorithm script is far more difficult than for the simpler scripts previously described. At times the only technique that worked was to trace the algorithm by hand for a simple example.

Along the way, utility scripts were implemented when they seemed useful. Perl is designed for extracting data from files and printing reports[16], so most utilities were 'designed' on the fly as the header comments were entered in the source-code file.

15.3.2 Iterative Enhancement

As described in the literature [7], iterative enhancement is a top-down process that begins with a complex set of requirements, selects a small subset of them, implements that subset, then expands to implementations of larger and larger requirements' subsets until the original full requirements are implemented. So-called agile development is sometimes described in a similar top-down way, although the 'full requirements' are vague and kept in the background as the abilities of the implemented system expand. It would be more accurate to describe these processes as bottom-up, because each implementation is complete in its own right, and the succession may wander away from any preconceived end product[17]. In the academic setting where the SYN tools were developed, research activity takes place under strong constraints. Most researchers are under pressure to publish their work year by year—it is professional self-destruction to pursue a research program that has a long period without publications, even if that is needed to create software. The additional pressure of required teaching (usually unconnected with research topics) puts a premium on getting software to work quickly and with minimal effort. Student 'slave labor'[18] is an immense help—research often could not be done without it—but students graduate just as they become trained. These constraints almost

---

[16] It's the Practical Extraction and Report Language.

[17] The SIMPL compilers that were Joe Turner's vehicle for iterative enhancement are a good example. A conventional statically typed language SIMPL-T was his goal, attained by first implementing a typeless SIMPL-X. But after Turner was finished, others created further compilers he never imagined: SIMPL-R for mathematical computation on a minicomputer, a PDP-11 systems-programming language SIMPL-XI, and SIMPL-D with user-defined abstract data types.

[18] So called because the pay is terrible and the slave has almost no say in what he or she works on.

guarantee that software supporting academic research will go through a series of quick-and-dirty enhancements, each just enough to support a research paper.

Here is the progression of SYN tool enhancements beginning in 2001:

- The initial implementation handled only two stateless components in series, with integer domains and a step-function approximation, for the non-functional reliability property.
- Run-time replaced reliability.
- Conditionals and loops were added to series as system constructions, and the system structure could nest these.
- Piecewise-linear approximation was added and almost immediately the integer domains were expanded to floating point.
- State was added.
- Incremental processing was implemented for stateless components.
- Internal profiles were calculated for stateless components, replacing an original implementation using run-time instrumentation.
- Concurrency was added.

In each enhancement, at attempt was made to freeze the previous version so that it could be executed for comparison should some major failure arise. Since enhancements added functionality to the tools, the older versions could not always be used on new examples, but comparisons were invaluable. For example, adding state considerably complicated the algorithm for synthesizing conditional constructions. When the new version failed on an example with state, comparing it to the previous version for a stateless case eliminated the possibility of many simple editing mistakes. However, since each enhancement and new examples also exposed old failures that were fixed only in the enhanced tools, the old versions gradually drifted away from usefulness.

Proper use of iterative enhancement requires that an enhancement step be of reasonable size so that it is easily seen to be correct on the assumption that the previous step was correct. This was true for each of the SYN enhancements except for the addition of piecewise-linear approximation and of state.

15.3.3 Components and Debugging of SYN Tools

Software researchers who propose a new idea and support it with software tools are often asked an embarrassing question: "Did you use your wonderful idea when you wrote your own software?" The answer is almost always, "No." The question is a bit unfair—when the tools were being written they were not yet available to use[19]—but usually it's their limitations and restrictive assumptions that make them impractical. The SYN tools found no application in their own development for apparent reasons. One of the major data types involved is 'executable code file,' hardly

---

[19] Self-compiling compilers surmount this seeming paradox. Perhaps their technique of bootstrapping through a series of increasingly powerful languages deserves wider application.

a single floating-point value. However, some ideas from CBSD were important in SYN implementation and debugging.

Independent executable parts. The parts of SYN tools are Perl scripts, started from within each other by Perl `system()` statements. Each such script is independently executable. Information that scripts need to exchange comes from command-line input parameters and shared files. Most files are persistent state for the system of SYN tools. All files contain only plain text. This organization has important advantages for coding and testing, and debugging:

- Scripts can be written in parallel by coders who need not talk to one another, because each script's function is easy to describe independently. The only connection between scripts is the format of a shared text file.

- Scripts can be tested in isolation because input file information can be created by hand when another script that normally creates the file is not available. If a script creates an output file, it can be examined by hand, so a script that will eventually use the file need not be ready.

- When scripts are ready to be tried together, the hand-made files used for isolated testing can be compared to those actually written by other scripts. Any difference exposes mistakes made in one script or the other, and catches any misunderstanding of the shared file format.

Narrow interfaces. Limiting the volume of data that passes between scripts decreases their interdependence and makes isolated testing easier. Using files to communicate, as the SYN tools often do, is a little better than passing data directly. The text files can be simpler, converted into more complex and efficient data structures within a single script[20].

Local state. If the SYN scripts are thought of as components, their primary defect is that their state is global—permanent files. However, it is some mitigation that these files are of two kinds, one created by people to describe a system and its components for experimentation, the other created internally but shared among only a few scripts. The formats of human-created files (the `.ccf` subdomain descriptions for components and `system.pscf` describing a system) are designed to make hand editing as easy as possible, and so are simple and stable. SYN-system created permanent files are used only to pass component-level approximations (made by the COMP scripts) to system-synthesis level (the SYN script). But these `.ccf[tc]` files are not stable, and their complexity is an important source of failures. Comparison of file creation times is important in deciding which parts of the state are valid.

Components 'Invoke' rather than 'use'. It is characteristic of components developed and tested independently that their connections with other components are *not* like conventional subroutine call/return. The subroutine mechanism is what

---

[20] In Parnas's terminology [89, $\prec A \succ$], an internal data structure is a 'secret' of the script that makes it. It is a foolish economy to pass these secrets across an interface just to avoid multiple conversions.

Dave Parnas [88] calls a 'uses' relationship: the caller depends on the callee, and fails if the subroutine fails. In Parnas's complementary relationship, 'invokes,' the caller is responsible only for starting the callee and is indifferent to what it may do, even if it fails. Evidently, 'invokes' is best for independent components, and in the model supported by the SYN tools, each component executes entirely in isolation[21]. In the SYN tools themselves, both mechanisms are employed. SYN 'uses' Calc, calling it like a subroutine, waiting for and storing its result. But COMP -G and SYN -G 'invoke' Xcute and Xcomp to display graphs and calculate r-m-s errors.

These component ideas were important in getting the SYN tools to work under difficult deadlines.

---

[21] The 'master' component in a concurrent pair is an exception, since it receives a second input from the slave it starts. That's why reliability calculations for concurrent components are so problematic (Chapter 12).

Chapter 16
Unfinished Business: Volunteer Tool Makers

T HE software distribution that accompanies this monograph includes Perl
scripts for the SYN tools, tutorial examples described in previous chapters, and data for replicating some of the research case studies to follow in
Chapters 17 and 18. Using the tools on this 'canned' data is not likely to expose
any serious failures[1]. Variations on the data provided should also work dependably.
Varying the given subdomains, or making small component code changes, or trying modified system structures, are easy and safe. For example, the Bell stateless
component used in the Introduction Chapter 1 and the tutorial Chapter 9 could have
its 'bump' modified; a more complicated system structure could be tried in Chapter 9; the subdomain refinement in the accuracy study of Chapter 17 could be done
differently, etc. Making minor changes is a good way to learn how the tools work.

But to use the SYN tools in new research is more problematic.

16.1 Unstable Algorithms and Code

Many parts of the algorithms used to test components and synthesize system properties are straightforward and the code dependable. At the component level, the task
of recording subdomain-based approximations is completely routine. The idea that
underlies synthesis is tracing one subdomain into another from tabular descriptions,
also routine. Routine bookkeeping, when it is seen to be correct for one case, is
likely to be correct overall. However, some parts of the SYN code are error prone.

Loops. The SYN tools make deterministic loop predictions, because there are a
finite number of cases for a finite number of subdomains. However, detection
that an approximate loop does not terminate is complicated by the possibility
that subdomains and their functional values change on each composition of the

---

[1] The Windows version is the least tested. It relies on Perl modules to compensate for the deficient
Microsoft environment, and runs in the command-line mode that isn't the best part of Windows.

D. Hamlet, *Composing Software Components,* DOI 10.1007/978-1-4419-7148-7_16,
© Springer Science+Business Media, LLC 2010

conditional and the body. The patterns of non-termination can be complicated and may not be properly detected.

Piecewise-linear approximation. Composition of two piecewise-linear component approximations has the desirable property that the synthesis subdomains are refined to reflect where output from the first component crosses subdomain boundaries in the second. But finding boundaries of the new subdomains requires calculating the inverse of a linear function, and when the slope is large it magnifies the uncertainty of floating-point approximation. Points near the boundary may fall is the wrong subdomain, or subdomains of near-zero length may be created.

State cross products. Every time two components with state are synthesized, the system state becomes a cross product of their states. Hence the state-space dimension grows as a system is synthesized, and the tables that describe its approximation become first three-dimensional, then four-, five-, ... Manipulation of multi-dimensional tables is error prone, and it doesn't help that the results cannot be graphed for examination.

These dubious implementation features can interact; it would be particularly unwise to trust synthesis of a loop whose body or conditional component is a synthesis with a high-order state dimension, for example.

16.2 Improving the SYN Tools

Software that has changed and been extended over a long time period can always be improved by retrofitting better code that appeared late in the cycle. Many of the SYN tools have common tasks that could be moved to a Perl module, with an improvement in consistency. The processing of command-line options would be an obvious place to start—each script has its own peculiar way of handling options. Some scripts have been modified so often that they are close to incomprehensible and could profitably be restructured from scratch—Xcute and the scripts it invokes come to mind.

Numerical instability problems in the piecewise-linear synthesis calculations could be eased by using an arbitrary-precision package in place of Perl's default floating point.

The stateless versions of the SYN tools are so fast that there was little reason to consider efficiency. Even with a dozen components and hundreds of subdomains, none of the calculations take more than a second. Clever and efficient algorithms are typically more difficult to get right than brute-force trial and error, which favored the latter under time pressure. Table look-up is frequently used throughout the SYN scripts, because the approximation tables are indexed by subdomain, and it is frequently necessary to find the subdomain index of an input value. In component-processing that creates the tables and in synthesis of the sequence construction, binary search is used for table look-up, but there are many places where the index is found by linear search (e.g., in finding profiles at component interfaces).

By far the slowest part of the SYN scripts is the overhead of repeated component/system executions. Each test point is sent to a newly started copy of the executable, repeatedly using the heavyweight operating-system run mechanism. It would be a dramatic improvement to run the executable just once and feed it one input after another. This could be done by establishing conventions for input and surrounding each executable with a wrapping loop that feeds one input at a time to the body[2]. If this were done, the overhead of writing and reading disk files for state could also be eliminated: the wrapper could keep state in a global variable accessible to the wrapped code through another convention. However, to make the change to a looping wrapper would compromise the ability to write component code in any language—the wrapper would have to have a version for each language. Components observing the needed conventions could not be executed without the wrapper.

Table look-up files that describe the approximations for components exist in two distinct formats (with extensions .ccft for stateless components and .ccfc for those with state), as a consequence of keeping stateless processing unchanged when state was added. The only reason not to replace the stateless files with the more general ones is the way these names are spread throughout the tools and the sad consequences of missing a reference. If the two formats were combined, it would also be wise to extend the .ccfc format to encompass piecewise-linear approximations for both output and result-state. (But see Section 14.3.2 for a discussion of the complications.)

Incremental component testing (described in Section 9.6) and calculation of interface profiles without system execution (Section 9.5) are implemented only for stateless components. These features were incorporated only to demonstrate that they can be implemented; neither is necessary. The support scripts subddiff and tracer that are useful in debugging are implemented for only the stateless case; extending to cases with state is just a matter of more complex bookkeeping.

Finally, the most ambitious change in operation of the SYN tools would be conversion from a command-line user interface to a graphical user interface (GUI). The existing Perl scripts provide the calculating engine that would underlie an environment-based implementation, and there would be many opportunities for interesting tricks. For example, when Xcute displays a component's functional output beside its approximation, clicking on a subdomain of the graph could automatically refine that subdomain and show the result. Changing to a GUI is a nontrivial extension, and not the least of the difficulty would be the need to write and maintain multiple versions that interface to different windowing environments. The command-line SYN tools are very nearly platform independent, relying on Perl modules to handle operating-system differences. The development tools for a GUI are not as powerful or easy to use.

---

[2] The code file created to execute a system for comparison with calculations (SystemCode, see Appendix A) is written in this way.

16.3 Who's Next?

Many of the changes suggested in this chapter are exercises for anyone who wants to understand and use the SYN tools. However, the original tool developers have probably picked all the ripe fruit: the reason that the existing scripts have long-standing problems is that it wasn't much fun to fix them, particularly when experiments could be conducted using workarounds.

In a more formal setting, a computer-science Master's student could modify and use the tools as the basis for a thesis. Perl programming isn't enough to make a respectable MS thesis, but it would not be hard to raise and solve interesting problems along the way. For example, the subject of debugging components that fail within a system (Section 15.2) could be studied using the SYN tools. Or, an MS student could repeat or extend experiments such as those presented in Part V, or devise a new experiments along similar lines. At the PhD level, perhaps it would not serve a student well to get involved with software tools. The effort and time required are all out of proportion to the quantity of respectable research that can result. But a student with a strong software background, who wants to indulge in exploratory programming, might make the gamble. Chapter 22 suggests some open research issues. Certainly the most difficult, which goes far beyond the SYN tools, beyond CBSD, to testing in general, is the issue of sampling non-numeric domains and their reliability theory (Section 22.1).

Part V
Case Studies

C ASE studies hold a special place in experimental computer-science. They do not aspire to generality—each is just one case. Yet they can go beyond the singular if the case chosen is representative. The SYN tools are powerful within the narrow scope of restricted components they can process, so they can be used to investigate large questions through revealing examples. Choosing the examples to capture the essence of an interesting issue yet stay within SYN restrictions is a challenge. Part V begins with a systematic investigation of accuracy in component approximation, and its connection with accuracy of system predictions. Some technical issues involving sampling, subdomains, and synthesis are next resolved. These issues come up in almost any example. Finally, Part V presents a number of examples that are simplified versions of common component-based systems, each of which yields insight when investigated in detail. These examples are a more-or-less accidental sample of cases that might be studied.

Chapter 17
Accuracy of Component Measurements and System Predictions

I N the Introduction and the tutorials of Chapters 9, 10, and 11 the subdomains for
component testing were not chosen to obtain accurate approximations or good
predictions of system properties. Subdomains were chosen instead to clearly
illustrate features of the SYN tools. In the theoretical limit as subdomains approach
singletons, the approximations and predictions should be exact, perfectly accurate.
This chapter investigates the relationship between subdomain choice and accuracy
for cases between those extremes. In general, better accuracy can be obtained by adjusting subdomains, and the SYN component-measurement tools can help to make
the right adjustments, but there are a few surprises. The underlying reason for studying accuracy is to investigate the possibility of predicting and using safety factors in
software development.

17.1 Better Component Approximation, Better System
Prediction

The stateless-component tutorial example in Section 9.3 illustrated how splitting
subdomains in half affects accuracy (on average, functional accuracy improved by
better than two times for component measurement and by about 1-1/2 times for prediction, but there were some anomalies). In this section the same system structure
(Fig. 9.1) will be investigated more thoroughly. One deficiency in the tutorial example has been corrected: Using copies of the same conditional component for C_2 and
C_4 in the example system causes the latter to always take the *false* branch. Now the
original Cond code is used only for C_2 while C_4 is a conditional component that
changes its value from *true* to *false* at input 35. The descriptions of the (now) three
components in this system initially have ten equal-sized subdomains on $[0, 100)$.
The system and components have thus been described in full detail, but the reader
need not look back to Chapter 9 for the details—suffice it to say that a representative
system structure has been populated with representative stateless components, for

D. Hamlet, *Composing Software Components*, DOI 10.1007/978-1-4419-7148-7_17,
© Springer Science+Business Media, LLC 2010

the purpose of clocking systematic improvements in subdomains[1]. Table 17.1 shows the results of repeatedly dividing all components' subdomains in half. Even without

Table 17.1 R-m-s relative errors (%) in component approximation and in system prediction as subdomains are refined

Number of Subdomains	Component measurements				System predictions					
	Function		Run time		Function			Run time		
	Ave	Max	Ave	Max	Ave	Max	> 5	Ave	Max	> 5
10	10.98	97.59	3.56	36.16	62.02	161.53	10	9.19	29.28	3
20	4.29	18.47	1.69	10.93	36.43	148.24	13	5.88	39.40	3
40	2.10	12.02	0.81	8.16	26.16	168.95	19	1.38	38.74	1
80	1.06	12.34	0.44	10.48	14.53	157.96	27	1.13	39.02	2
160	0.51	7.86	0.21	10.51	6.06	128.74	35	0.51	29.21	2
320	0.26	11.19	0.11	10.42	3.41	122.02	49	0.32	26.88	3
640	0.13	10.83	0.05	8.32	1.90	139.53	45	0.17	27.74	3
1280	0.06	10.85	0.03	10.39	0.88	139.85	32	0.11	29.17	4
2560	0.03	7.61	0.01	10.39	0.37	95.82	23	0.04	29.17	3
5120	0.01	10.78	0.01	10.39	0.25	134.80	10	0.01	26.90	1

the detailed description of Table 17.1 given below, it is clear that as subdomains are refined in successive lines, the "Ave" component approximation errors decrease and so do the "Ave" system-prediction errors, but some measures do not improve.

R-m-s (root-mean-square) relative errors between actual and approximate curves are calculated by squaring pointwise differences, averaging the squares, taking the square root, then normalizing to the full r-m-s value of the measured curve. With this error measure there is no error cancellation when signs differ, and fewer difficulties with normalization when the values compared are near zero. "Ave" error is obtained by sampling at equi-spaced points of the input domain, using three times as many points as there are subdomains. The component-measurement errors at the left of the table are averages over all seven components that comprise the system[2].

But two error measures do not steadily decrease: The maximum error over all subdomains ("Max") for components and for system predictions, and the number of subdomains with at least a 5% prediction error ("> 5"). These measures pay attention to bad subdomains even when good subdomains swamp the average. Xcomp and its error analysis reveal why anomalies occur. Figure 17.1 shows the actual and predicted functional values for the system within subdomains where the error remains large. The lower curves come from the seventh line of Table 17.1 while the upper ones are from the eighth line[3]. In Fig. 17.1, the anomalous errors occur in a

---

[1] The example is similar to one published in TOSEM [48]. Although the TOSEM example is more complicated, using different components for each of $C_1, ..., C_6$ in Fig. 9.1 and evaluating both step-function and piecewise-linear approximations, the results are similar to those presented here. Indeed, many experiments with more complicated system structures and components have qualitatively similar outcomes.

[2] Except for the first line of the table, components C_2 and C_4 are perfectly approximated, so the component averages really reflect just the behavior of Math, the code for all other components.

[3] The ordinate scale has been omitted and the curves separated vertically.

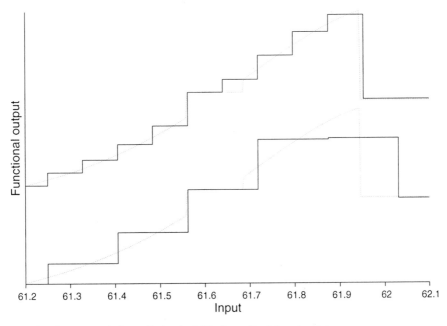

Fig. 17.1 Error anomaly in prediction (*solid line*): small subdomains, large error

subdomain whose left edge is at 61.88 (just before the drop at the right of Fig. 17.1).
The error is large in the lower curves because the actual system discontinuity occurs
within the subdomain, where it is impossible for the calculation to track it. Things
look better in the upper curves, but the discontinuity is still within a subdomain. The
size of the error depends on the accident of where the subdomain boundary falls; at
the next halving the error will actually increase. A similar anomaly occurs around
the discontinuity near 61.7 in the figure.

In this experiment, the SYN tools made system predictions, then the actual system was executed and compared with the predictions in Table 17.1. The purpose is
to validate the tools and the theory behind them. But in I-CBSD, actual system execution is not available. The system developer has not purchased the components and
cannot assemble the system. Only the SYN-tool prediction is available. So no system accuracy measure is available to the system designer—only those of component
approximation. The question is: Can system prediction errors be controlled by controlling component-measurement errors? Section 17.2.2 to follow investigates this
issue quantitatively[4], but Fig. 17.1 already shows that in principle there can be no
guarantee. The system functional variation responsible for the anomalous system-
prediction error *is itself not predictable from individual component data*. None of
the components has poor behavior in the troublesome region; there is nothing to

---

[4] The same problem of discontinuities within a subdomain shown in Fig. 17.1 can arise in measuring component approximations, but the component developer *can* control them by adjusting
subdomain boundaries.

suggest that their tests should be improved. The poor prediction arises not from any component, but from their interaction, which also depends on the structure of the system. Thus, each component's approximation error might be made arbitrarily small, yet the system-prediction error remain large in some subdomain(s). And inserting a safety factor (say by halving each component-measurement subdomain once more than seems necessary) may actually make things worse. This discussion is continued in Sections 17.2.2 and 17.2.3 to follow.

When components retain state, the effect of refining test subdomains is similar. As an example, a system modeling some aspects of a command-driven editor is investigated. Full details of this system are presented as a case study in Section 18.3.3; here it is enough to describe its gross features as a system with state. The structure is:

$$\text{if } C_c \text{ then } C_a; C_e \text{ else } C_d \text{ fi.}$$

Components C_c and C_e have state; the others are simple stateless glue code. Roughly, C_c is a control component for a complex C_e, whose actual functional behavior is shown[5] in Fig. 17.2. C_e has two distinct modes (back and front of Fig. 17.2) sep-

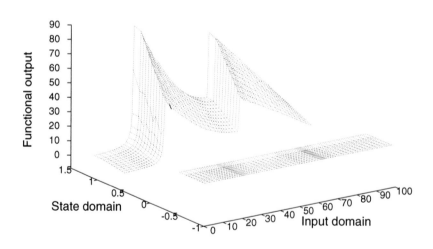

Fig. 17.2 Functional behavior of C_e

arated by a band of infeasible states; in its more complicated mode there are two discontinuities in the input dimension and a downward slope in the state dimension.

---

[5] The grid drawn in Fig. 17.2 is contours of the surface plot, not connected to subdomain approximation.

The system state is two-dimensional, a cross product of states from C_c and C_e, so the four-dimensional system behavior can't be sensibly displayed[6].

Initially, each component is described by about 20 subdomains, selected not to cross discontinuities. These are systematically refined[7] and Table 17.2 displays the r-m-s error data[8]. As in Table 17.1 the average prediction errors ("Ave") decrease

Table 17.2 R-m-s relative errors (%) in component approximation and in system prediction as subdomains are refined

Number of system subdomains			Component measurements						System predictions					
			Output		Run time		State		Output		Run time		State	
Total	Feas	Exec	Ave	Max	Ave	Max	Ave	Max	Ave	Max	Ave	Max	Ave	Max
4.3K	170	143	2.77	46.68	0.08	4.64	2.77	9.87	5.78	87.28	1.07	43.41	2.13	9.05
10.6K	276	211	1.69	41.04	0.04	2.77	2.08	8.73	3.76	58.49	0.65	30.44	2.34	6.18
30.2K	528	234	1.10	34.08	0.02	1.48	1.64	9.62	2.88	39.14	0.13	14.50	3.45	7.82
242K	1280	663	0.59	23.60	0.01	0.75	0.90	5.47	1.36	43.68	0.02	0.36	1.50	3.69
1935K	2560	2225	0.29	15.12	0.01	0.39	0.45	2.85	0.37	23.45	0.01	0.19	0.15	0.70

smoothly with decreasing component-measurement errors, but the maximum prediction errors fall more slowly. The explanation for persistent errors is probably the same as in Table 17.1, but the difficulty of displaying 4-D graphs makes it harder to visualize the cause.

Table 17.2 also provides information about state feasibility. The number of potential states increases by about eightfold each time subdomains are halved (each of two components with state increases fourfold), but the feasible number ("Feas") falls to a tiny fraction, from about 4% (first row) to about 0.1% (last row). Even with a large number of sampling sequences, not all feasible subdomains are reached in actual system executions ("Exec"); the reverse also occurs in that near the end of the table no calculation is available for some subdomains because the component approximations did not sample densely enough. The number of subdomains with these difficulties is a tiny fraction of the whole.

---

[6] A display of state behavior would require five dimensions, since there are two result states. In the case study of Section 18.3.3, it is seen that there are really only eight composite system modes, so that a display of the eight kinds of behavior they exhibit is possible.

[7] The first two refinement steps use the automatic tuning procedure described in Section 17.1.1 to follow.

[8] Although the system predictions would require four-dimensional graphs to display, it is mostly the independent-variables space (three-dimensional) that causes the difficulty; in each 3D subdomain there is a single functional and run-time value with an r-m-s error. The system state is two-fold, so to get the state errors in Table 17.2 the two states' errors are combined as if they were the magnitudes of orthogonal vectors.

17.1.1 Tuning Subdomains with Tool Support

In the stateless example of Section 17.1 the initial subdomains were selected blindly, then repeatedly divided in half. The experiment illustrates that subdomain refinement improves the testing approximation to components and the prediction of system behavior. However, a conscientious component developer would follow a different plan in practice. The SYN tools provide information about the quality of testing and the accuracy of component approximations, which can be used to good effect. The tools allow a component developer to study the testing approximation and purposefully adjust subdomains to improve it.

Figure 17.3 shows the functional and run-time behaviors and the error analysis produced by Xcute C1 0 100 500 for the component Math from Chapter 9. The upper curve is for run time, the lower for functional output[9]. This approximation to C_1 was part of the first line in Table 17.1. It is obvious that a different subdomain boundary is needed for the 'bump' at the left, and that it would help if subdomains were smaller where the Gaussian is changing more rapidly. Making these adjustments in C1.ccf results in Fig. 17.4. Figure 17.4 (again from Xcute C1 0 100 500) shows that the subdomain boundaries are now aligned with the Math discontinuities, and the measurement errors are roughly the same in the handful of subdomains. This process of hand adjustment can be repeated, running Xcute and shrinking subdomains with the largest errors. Sometimes it may be convenient to use splitsub to halve all the subdomains.

The hand process is tedious and becomes more so as the number of subdomains grows, so it makes sense to automate it. Xcute's error analysis can be mechanically examined to split subdomains with the largest errors. Repeating this process indefinitely uses only machine time. The result is an improvement in approximation and prediction using fewer subdomains, as shown in Table 17.3[10]. Compare (say) the second-last lines of Table 17.3 and Table 17.1. Although there are 23% fewer subdomains (1962 vs. 2560), the average component approximation errors and average prediction errors are about the same, the worst-subdomain component measurements are far better, and predictions in the worst subdomains are improved (there are fewer, although their errors are still large).

This exercise in careful adjustment of component-testing subdomains reinforces the lesson of Fig. 17.1: however carefully components are tested, on a small part of the system input domain system properties may still be badly predicted. As the component testing improves, the fraction of the domain on which the prediction is

---

[9] The functional graph differs from Fig. 9.4 only because the subdomains are slightly different. The ordinate scales are not shown and the run time curve is shifted to appear above.

[10] A Perl script smartsplit was written to examine the output of Xcute for each component, split the subdomains whose error was in the top 50%, and repeat. If the fraction split is set low (say splitting only the top 20%), more iterations are needed to reach a better approximation because the number of subdomains increases slowly; for a large fraction (say splitting the top 80%), soon all subdomains are being split. Starting with subdomain errors roughly balanced avoids splitting just one worst subdomain repeatedly. Other algorithms for deciding which subdomains to split may perform even better.

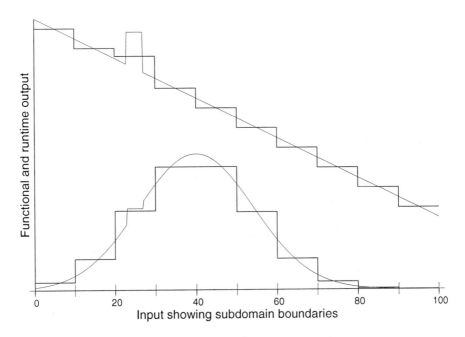

```
Sampling [0.00, 100.00) for 500 points
normalized rms errors
{count} interval          func     run
{50}    [0.00,  10.00)    5.05%    3.16%
{50}    [10.00, 20.00)   15.26%    3.16%
{50}    [20.00, 30.00)   23.41%   10.26%
{50}    [30.00, 40.00)   13.82%    3.15%
{50}    [40.00, 50.00)   13.77%    3.15%
{50}    [50.00, 60.00)   24.05%    3.15%
{50}    [60.00, 70.00)   15.28%    3.15%
{50}    [70.00, 80.00)    5.06%    3.16%
{50}    [80.00, 90.00)    0.95%    3.16%
{50}    [90.00, 100.00)   0.10%    3.16%
Weighted ave:            11.68%    3.87%
  Maximum:               24.05%   10.26%
```

Fig. 17.3 Actual behaviors (*smooth curve*) and approximations (*steps*) for component C_1, with errors by subdomain

erroneous falls, but poorly predicted subdomains may never disappear. For example, in Table 17.3 the run-time error is above 5% on about 0.1% of the domain in the second-last line, but only on about 0.05% of the domain in the last line.

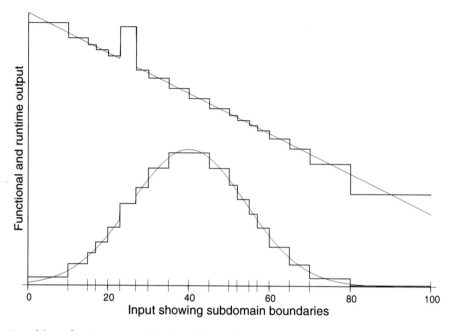

```
Sampling [0.00, 100.00) for 500 points
normalized rms errors
count          interval      func     run
{50}        [0.00, 10.00)    5.06%    3.16%
{25}        [10.00, 15.00)   6.01%    1.58%
{10}        [15.00, 17.00)   3.28%    0.63%
{15}        [17.00, 20.00)   5.85%    0.95%
{15}        [20.00, 23.00)   6.79%    0.95%
{20}        [23.00, 27.00)   0.00%    0.00%
{15}        [27.00, 30.00)   7.13%    0.95%
{25}        [30.00, 35.00)   9.37%    1.58%
{25}        [35.00, 40.00)   3.77%    1.58%
{25}        [40.00, 45.00)   3.74%    1.58%
{25}        [45.00, 50.00)   9.35%    1.58%
{10}        [50.00, 52.00)   4.66%    0.63%
{15}        [52.00, 55.00)   7.37%    0.94%
{10}        [55.00, 57.00)   4.84%    0.63%
{15}        [57.00, 60.00)   6.78%    0.94%
{25}        [60.00, 65.00)   9.14%    1.58%
{25}        [65.00, 70.00)   6.02%    1.58%
{50}        [70.00, 80.00)   5.07%    3.15%
{100}       [80.00, 100.00)  1.08%    6.31%
Weighted ave:                4.87%    2.62%
  Maximum:                   9.37%    6.31%
```

Fig. 17.4 Actual behaviors (*smooth curve*) and approximations (*steps*) for component C_1, with errors in subdomains adjusted by hand

Table 17.3 R-m-s relative errors approximations as subdomains are algorithmically refined

Number of Subdomains	Component measurements				System predictions					
	Function		Run time		Function			Run time		
	Ave	Max	Ave	Max	Ave	Max	> 5	Ave	Max	> 5
19	5.69	97.59	2.67	36.16	32.57	201.90	18	3.94	44.32	2
34	1.70	6.01	0.99	3.41	13.63	92.93	25	0.46	1.78	0
63	0.90	3.35	0.49	1.67	7.82	78.57	27	0.88	35.73	2
123	0.45	1.73	0.25	0.85	3.97	74.23	32	0.36	35.72	1
222	0.27	0.85	0.15	0.42	2.36	65.81	26	0.21	31.41	1
430	0.14	0.48	0.08	0.22	1.55	107.82	30	0.06	3.88	0
608	0.10	0.38	0.06	0.21	1.20	118.79	31	0.09	25.64	1
1007	0.06	0.27	0.03	0.11	0.47	33.46	19	0.06	35.73	2
1962	0.03	0.15	0.01	0.05	0.30	110.88	12	0.04	31.39	2
3688	0.02	0.07	0.01	0.03	0.15	112.04	5	0.02	35.72	2

17.2 Predicting Prediction Accuracy

In Chapter 19 to follow, it is suggested that system testing can be eliminated from CBSD, to be replaced by predictions of CAD tools like SYN. To justify such a plan, it is essential to know how component measurement/approximation errors are related to system-prediction errors. Should a system developer decide to use predictions, it is a decision *not* to assemble and test the system during design, so no system comparison between prediction and actual behavior like that of Table 17.3 will be available. The alternative is to predict the error in the CAD predictions.

17.2.1 Prediction Error is Linear in Measurement Error

Data from Tables 17.1 and 17.3 and 17.2 relate component errors to system errors. Figure 17.5 shows four possible relationships from Table 17.3. A straight line is fitted to data for each relationship[11]. For example, the top curve ("Function: Ave vs. Ave") plots column 6 of Table 17.3 against column 2. The fitted slopes are shown along the curves in Fig. 17.5, e.g., 8.9 for the top curve, meaning that the average functional system prediction error is about 8.9 times as large as the average functional component measurement error. The functional predictions fit the linear relationship better (about ± 6%) than the run-time ones (about ± 14%), but their slopes are larger. Using component maximum error as the independent variable in place of component average error changes the slope but not the fitting error[12].

---

[11] In the line fitting, points are weighted inversely to the component functional average error (column 1 of Table 17.3), which gives them closer to equal effect on the log-log plot. If true equal weighting is used, the least-accurate, larger-error points dominate.

[12] If the data from Table 17.1 is used, maximum component error does not have any sensible relationship with prediction errors. Without the iterative process that explicitly reduces component maximum error, component max values do not decrease. However, data from the "Ave" average

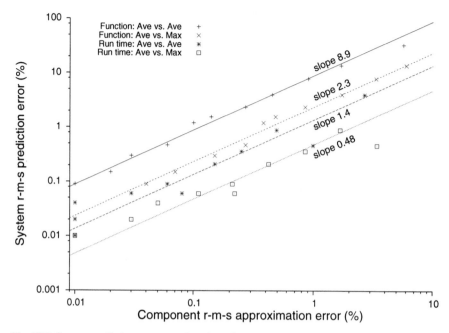

Fig. 17.5 System prediction errors as a function of component measurement errors

Figure 17.5 is evidence that controlling component approximation errors controls average prediction errors.

17.2.2 Theory of Error Propagation

Subdomain-testing theory of stateless component synthesis is simple and explicit. It can be used to analyze the propagation of component errors into systems and to understand how prediction can go wrong. In each synthesis step[13] functional errors combine as follows:

Series composition $C_1; C_2$. Consider any subdomain S of C_1, which is also a sub-domain of the synthesized system. Let y_S be the functional approximate value assigned to S in the C_1 approximation, and S' be the C_2 subdomain in which y_S falls. If every point of S is actually mapped into S' by $\boxed{C_1}$ (that is, actual execution results), then the prediction error for S is just the C_2 error for S', for which

---

columns of Table 17.1 still produce a linear relationship with about the same fitting error, though with larger slope (13 for the function-averages case).

[13] The exposition to follow is written as if it were always real-component approximations being combined, while in actuality the combination may involve previously synthesized approximations. But subsystems are indistinguishable from components in the stateless case.

there is an estimate from C_2 testing. On the other hand, if points of S are mapped by C_1's actual code to other subdomain(s) S'' of C_2, then the prediction error is the difference in C_2 values for S' and S'', which is likely to be more significant than the measurement errors in these values. That is, the correct system value should come from S'', but instead it is taken from S' in the prediction. Should it happen that the values of C_2 in S' and S'' are close, then its measurement error comes back into play. Thus the measurement error for C_1 never enters directly into the prediction error, but only through the distorted action of C_2. When subdomains shrink, as in the experiments of the previous section, two factors can improve the prediction: C_1 may really map S entirely into S'; but even if it does not, the difference between C_2 functional values in S' and S'' may decrease[14]. Exceptions occur when either component has a discontinuity within the relevant subdomains, cases considered in the subsection to follow.

Conditional if C_c then C_t else C_f fi. Again consider subdomain S of C_c. If $\boxed{C_c}$ is constant (either *true* or *false*) for all of S, then the prediction error is just that of either C_t or C_f respectively, on its subdomains that intersect[15] with S, for which there are estimates from their measurements. On the other hand, if C_c is not constant across S, then the prediction error is the difference of C_t and C_f values on S, with the perhaps minor errors in their estimations, as in the series case. But for a conditional, prediction improvement can come only from C_c becoming more homogeneous: there is an intrinsic discontinuity between the values of C_t and C_f which is the very reason a conditional is used.

Loop while C_c do C_b od. Loop synthesis is repeated composition of a conditional subsystem with the body in its *true* branch. The *false* branch is perfectly approximated by an identity. The simplest case in which there are no errors in subdomain mapping occurs only when the loop conditional has homogeneous subdomains and when each application of the body does not cross subdomain boundaries. As more composition steps in the synthesis are required, the latter becomes less and less likely.

The prediction error in run time is only slightly more complicated to explain. For example, in series composition, synthesized run times are off by the run-time error in C_1 combined with the error in C_2 (there may be cancellation if one is too large and the other too small). But furthermore the C_2 run-time value may be completely wrong because it is taken from the wrong subdomain, as in the discussion of functional values above. Run-time predictions may be better because of cancellations, and also because run-time functions are more likely to be smooth and of limited variation.

As in other aspects of component combination, the series-synthesis construction is the fundamental one. To study it, a system can be constructed by cascading a component with itself once, twice, etc. Choosing a suitable component is unexpectedly difficult: If its function is too far from identity, a few composition steps lead

---

[14] Furthermore, for more refined subdomains the r-m-s component errors are more accurate estimates.

[15] These intersections are the system subdomains.

to a spiky system function that is not predicted well with a few subdomains; but an identity component won't do because the midpoints of subdomains have functional values that agree with the subdomain average, and the prediction error is constant. A compromise component C_w selected for repeated series composition is shown in Fig. 17.6. $\boxed{C_w}$ is identity with a sinusoidal 'wiggle' of about 5% added. The iden-

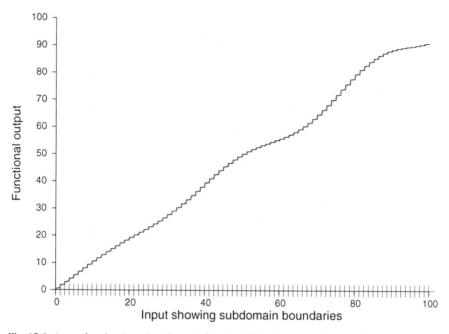

Fig. 17.6 Approximation (*steps*) and actual functional behavior (*smooth curve*) for a component C_w to repeatedly compose

tity keeps the total r-m-s value roughly constant for any number of compositions; the wiggle introduces enough variation that there are increasing prediction errors for more compositions[16]. The test domain is $[0, 100)$ and there are 80 equal-sized subdomains[17]. As C_w is composed with itself, its 'wiggle' is exaggerated. Figure 17.7 shows four series compositions.

Table 17.4 shows the result of composing C_w with itself n times from two components ($n = 1$) up to five components ($n = 4$). In the last two rows of Table 17.4, the normalization (the total r-m-s value varies by about 10% over the compositions) has been removed to give an absolute error. The straight line $e = 0.09n + 0.33$ is a good fit ($\pm 2\%$) to data in the second-last line.

---

[16] The functional behavior of C_w is continuous and of bounded variation, the simplest theoretical case.

[17] Figure 17.5 indicates that any reasonably refined subdomain set will give the same results.

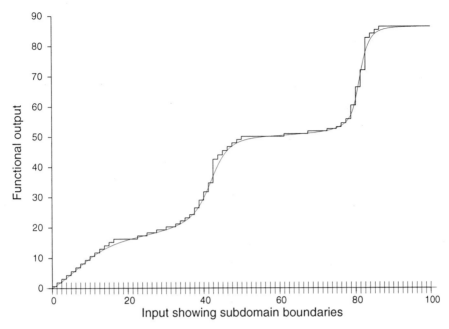

Fig. 17.7 Approximation (*steps*) and actual functional behavior (*smooth curve*) for a series system of five copies of C_w

Table 17.4 R-m-s functional prediction errors cascading C_w

No. components	C_w	2	3	4	5
Relative error	0.59%	0.79%	0.99%	1.19%	1.38%
Ave error	0.325	0.421	0.514	0.604	0.688
Max error	0.557	1.18	1.87	2.66	3.95

Thus there are two factors entering into average prediction error: the number of synthesis steps and the component measurement error. Both effects are roughly linear, as shown by Table 17.4 and Fig. 17.5. It remains to explain the residual "Max" errors in system prediction and the quantitative relationships represented by the slope of the lines in Fig. 17.5 and Table 17.4.

17.2.3 Prediction Error is an Emergent System Property

Imagine a worst case in series composition. A slight error in the functional approximation of the first component sends one of its subdomains to the wrong input subdomain of the second component. The subdomain boundary that is incorrectly crossed happens to fall on a system discontinuity. The system prediction falls on the wrong side of the discontinuity, which is all out of proportion to the size of the small error in the first component. As subdomains shrink, this prediction error persists, but in a smaller and smaller system subdomain. This is exactly what seems to be happening in Table 17.3. Assuming that all component subdomains are properly aligned with local discontinuities, the component-measurement error will be roughly halved with every subdomain split. The average system error will also be halved, because it is proportional to the size of the discontinuity (unchanged by the split) weighted by subdomain size (halved). This explains the linear relationship displayed in Fig. 17.5; the proportionality constant (e.g., 8.9 for the top line in Fig. 17.5) reflects mostly the size of the discontinuity. The subdomains in which the "Max" error does not decrease are those surrounding the discontinuity.

The same thing happens for continuous functions in a region where the function value changes rapidly. A mistake in subdomain mapping between series components adds an error that depends only on the value change across the mismapped boundary. In Table 17.4 this is apparently 0.09 for each synthesis step; the intercept 0.33 is the contribution over most of the domain, which is just the component error of C_W acting as the last component in the cascade.

Recall that the goal in analyzing system prediction errors was to control them by controlling component test-measurement errors. Behind this goal is the crucial one of choosing a safety factor in component testing measurements: a systems designer needs to know the proportionality constant between component measurement errors (known) and errors in predicted system values (unknown). For example, in the system described in Table 17.3, average predictions will be off by about 8.9 times the component error. Unfortunately, the analysis above shows that the goal is unattainable. The size and location of system discontinuities and of regions of rapid change that determine the slope of the prediction-error curves are emergent system properties, so this slope cannot be exactly calculated from component measurements and system structure. Measurements for the particular systems of Table 17.3 and Table 17.4 cannot be applied to other systems or to other components in the same or similar systems. Thus a safety factor seems to exist for any given component-based system, but it cannot itself be accurately predicted.

However, safety factors by nature need not be exact. It is often immaterial[18] how large a safety factor is needed—what's crucial is that it be enough to surely encompass the predicted error.

17.2.4 Approximating System Prediction Errors

The analysis of Section 17.2.3 can be made quantitative, which allows a rough safety factor to be predicted from the approximation curves alone in graphs like 17.7, in the

---

[18] In physical systems, cost can require safety factors to be trimmed. A stronger beam costs more. Equally important, adding more safety than necessary can invalidate a design. A stronger beam is heavier, and the whole structure may not be able to support it. In software, if safety is achieved by adding code, both factors can come into play: more code costs more, and increasing code complexity can lead to more mistakes.

absence of 'actual' curves not available under I-CBSD. The idea is to use changes in approximate functional behavior to guess regions of the largest error and to bound that error. Suppose that the actual curve being approximated by a step function is linear within a subdomain. Then the (unnormalized) r-m-s error e is a fraction of the step height h, the fraction determined only by the shape of the deviation, which is a sawtooth: $e = h\sqrt{12} \approx 0.289h$. Since component measurements are fitted, this analysis should be close to exact for them if the subdomains are small enough that the function is close to linear over each subdomain. In Table 17.4, for example, the worst subdomains for C_w (on both sides of input 76.25) have a measured r-m-s error of 0.557, while in Fig. 17.6 their largest step height is 1.94, $1.94\sqrt{12} \approx 0.560$. System predictions are *not* fitted, but their worst errors occur in regions of rapid change. In Fig. 17.7 for example, the variation is largest near 82.5 where there is a change of about 16.3 across the two nearest subdomains. $16.3\sqrt{12} \approx 4.70$, which bounds the 3.95 shown in Table 17.4.

Estimating the average error rather than the maximum in a system prediction is more difficult. For most subdomains the contribution will be a value that arises from measurement error in the components, but for some in regions of rapid change the step height will introduce a larger contribution. A very rough estimate can be obtained by substituting the component error in its worst subdomain for all subdomains except those whose step height exceeds this error. For Fig. 17.7 the result is an average r-m-s error of 0.697, which bounds the 0.688 shown in Table 17.4.

These calculations indicate that it is possible to estimate the prediction error for system synthesis with the SYN tools. The system designer can thus obtain a bound on the inaccuracy of the prediction in terms of the accuracy of component measurements.

17.3 Approximation Accuracy as a Component Test-quality Metric

When a system is designed using components, each with a description that includes the accuracy of its tested approximation, predictions of system behavior are accurate in direct proportion to the component accuracy. Therefore, it is a better component that is better tested, and the error analysis supplied by a tool like Xcute is a direct measure of component quality. It is a no-brainer to select the better tested of two otherwise similar components. Because each synthesis operation increases the system prediction error, a component with less approximation error can be accurately used in systems with more components. It is more difficult to assign a quantitative value to better component testing. Is half the approximation error worth double the price? Probably not.

Almost all testing-quality metrics are surrogates based on some form of coverage. The best ones measure functional coverage, since that is directly relevant to software usage. The worst measure only some kind of structure whose connection with usage is dubious. But it is confounding that the functional measures are necessarily vague (just what is a 'function' and how is it 'covered'?) while the structural ones can be made precise (e.g., "85% branch coverage" sounds quantitative and objective). The SYN tools approximation metric has the best of both worlds: it is precise and objective, but it measures real semantic content that enters directly into the accuracy of system predictions.

When the non-functional property measured for components is reliability, it clarifies test accuracy as a quality metric. For the common case that no failures are detected, estimates of component reliability cannot be checked by the component developer as can run-time measurements. But the functional measurements still provide a precise quality metric with the usual significance in system predictions. When a series system is synthesized, the predicted system reliability will be accurate only if one component maps its subdomains correctly into the next component's input domain. The quality of this mapping is exactly what gets measured for each component. A reliability prediction for a system will be in error if a subdomain is mapped incorrectly, *and there is a substantial reliability difference between the subdomains into which the mapping goes.* The latter cannot be investigated until a system is designed; but the component functional quality metric quantifies the possibility of mismapping. Happily, for reliability the component tester can arrange that there are no large differences in reliability estimation across subdomains.

17.4 The Right Subdomains for Component Testing

For describing and measuring (testing) a component, the choice of a subdomain breakdown is second in importance only to the component code itself. Subdomains are to group 'same' behavior, which for the numerical domains used by the SYN tools largely means selecting regions in which the variation of functional and non-functional values is small. The tools' error analysis can be used to adjust subdomain size to equalize approximation errors. A few other obvious rules:

Non-functional behavior. It is unusual for a large variation or discontinuity in run-time behavior to occur at a place in the input/state domain(s) where the functional behavior does not have a similar change. But in concentrating on the component's function, keep an eye on the run time, too. It may be necessary to split a perfectly good functional subdomain because it encompasses too much variation (or even discontinuities) in run time.

Discontinuities. Each discontinuity in behavior must fall on a subdomain boundary for accurate synthesis. Unexpected discontinuities will appear in synthesis; there is nothing to be done about them at component level. But failure to capture a component discontinuity will introduce synthesis errors that could have been prevented.

Singular points. It is always possible that within a subdomain a singular point or group of points can hide from probing by test cases. The only defense is knowledge of the source code, since odd behavior usually requires explicit code to implement it. The limited size and complexity of component code helps. But the inherent discontinuity of software behavior is always available to trap the tester, and missing something in testing a component invalidates accurate synthesis of systems that use it.

There can be no rule in component testing about how much approximation accuracy or subdomain refinement is enough. Errors in synthesis predictions are controlled by errors in component approximation, but their extent can only be approximately learned after synthesis of a particular system. Since better component approximation with the SYN tools is a largely mechanical process, it is reasonable to push it as far as testing resources permit.

The theoretical explanations of prediction error in this chapter have been confined to stateless components. Although the broad outline of this theory can be expected to apply to situations with state and with concurrency, the extra dimension(s) make everything much more complicated, particularly for state, which is sampled only implicitly in testing.

Chapter 18
Case Studies of I-CBSD

I NVESTIGATION of I-CBSD issues and questions with the SYN tools has unique
advantages, but also characteristic difficulties. The tools allow an experimenter
to learn exactly what happens in component testing and system synthesis, because they provide graphs and analysis automatically. The difficulty comes in finding example components and systems that address a real issue of interest, yet fall
within the severe restrictions the tools impose. For example, Section 18.3.3 studies
the way in which two components with state are synthesized into a system with a
cross-product state. A real example of this situation is a command-line editor component (with its state modes) invoked by a front-end control component whose state
keeps track of what the editor will be allowed to do. The real example might use
as components the UNIX 'vi' editor and a control program with a GUI. But these
real components are far beyond the capabilities of the SYN tools, so in Section
18.3.3 they have simple stand-in components that roughly model editor- and control
features. Finding and tuning these stand-ins so that SYN can handle them yet they
retain the intuitive character of the real situation is not easy.

Each section in this chapter begins by stating a question or issue to be investigated, then describes components and systems whose study can illuminate it,
and concludes with an analysis of results from the tools. Most of the examples
can be repeated using data supplied with the software distribution that accompanies this monograph. In a few cases data collection was facilitated by using one-
off Perl scripts to conduct the experiment, for example, using a modification of
`smartsplit` to create subdomains, or a script to pull numbers from the output
displays of `Xcute` and `Xcomp`.

18.1 Fundamental Questions about Subdomain Testing

In any example using components that meet the SYN tools restrictions, there are
common issues in the experimental design. A few preliminary studies supply gen-

D. Hamlet, *Composing Software Components,* DOI 10.1007/978-1-4419-7148-7_18,
© Springer Science+Business Media, LLC 2010

eral answers to what should be done. These studies use stateless components; it is
expected that results for state and for concurrency will not differ essentially.

18.1.1 How to Sample Subdomains?

If each subdomain truly captured some 'same' behavior, then any single point would
suffice to completely test it. In particular, when seeking to find failures, if all inputs
in a subdomain fail or all succeed, then failure cannot be missed no matter what test
point is chosen in that subdomain[1]. Howden's theorem that all algorithmic subdomain breakdowns are misleading (Section 7.1) establishes that subroutine behavior
can never be counted on to be 'the same.' The tester's only weapon is multiple
probes, in the hope of stumbling on a variant behavior if there is one. Given the
huge cardinality of the input space and the small number of subdomains, it would
take spectacular luck to hit anything interesting with a practical number of samples.

  For components satisfying the restrictions of the SYN tools, 'the same' has a
clear meaning: functional output is homogeneous on a subdomain if it is constant.
Then the average (that is, the step-function approximation value) is that same constant and the r-m-s approximation error is zero no matter how many test samples
are taken to obtain the approximation. There is reason to take care with the sampling, however, and to use more than one point per subdomain, because a single
test point might hit the average of a non-constant function and thus miscalculate
the r-m-s error as zero[2]. When the actual output function varies non-linearly across
a subdomain, the contribution to r-m-s approximation error can be very different
for different sampling; too few samples can emphasize or miss large error contributions[3]. A fundamental fact of SYN subdomain sampling for a component is that
the cost of testing N points is the same no matter whether they fall one in each of
N subdomains, or all N in the same subdomain. Because execution time is often
the limiting factor in testing, and since better predictions result from smaller subdomains, it is worthwhile investigating the tradeoff between more samples in each
subdomain and fewer samples in more subdomains. The method of choosing the
samples can also be varied.

  A good experimental component has rapidly changing and discontinuous behavior. The component ClipTan has an output $\tan(x)$ function with the central behavior asymptotic to the vertical line $x = \pi/2$ limited to about ± 15. Its run time is
taken to fall off cubically on each side of $\pi/2$ with a notch corresponding to the
function's clipping. Figure 18.1 shows the behaviors of ClipTan in the interval
$[0, \pi)$, as graphed by Xcute ClipTan 0 3.14 1200. With 1200 samples the

---

[1] Care is required in locating subdomains relative to *requirements*, of course. If a requirements distinction is glossed over because it falls inside a single subdomain, the 'sameness' only guarantees
that some result(s) in the subdomain are incorrect.

[2] An important example is a function linear across a subdomain that is sampled at the midpoint.

[3] The worst case occurs when there is a discontinuity in the actual behavior. Then the error depends
on the magnitude of the discontinuity but also on which side of it the samples fall.

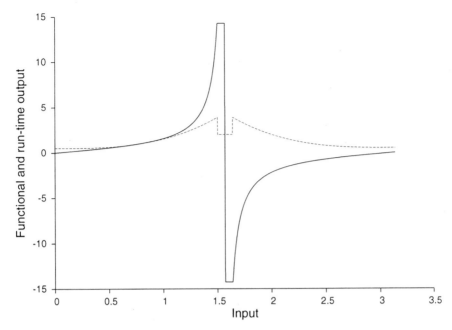

Fig. 18.1 Actual functional (*tangent-like solid curve*) and run-time behaviors (*central dotted curve with notch*) of component ClipTan

measured curves appear smooth. The functional behavior has a discontinuity at $\pi/2$; the run-time has two discontinuities at the edges of the notch. Beginning with three roughly equal subdomains, a variant of the smartsplit script (Section 17.1.1) is used to split subdomains with the least accuracy until there are 32 subdomains, enough for a fairly accurate approximation. Table 18.1 collects some error data.

Table 18.1 R-m-s approximation errors for ClipTan with different sampling

Number of subdomains	Samples per subdomain	Error sampling	Functional Ave	Max	Run time Ave	Max
32	1	equispace 1200	15.7%	479%	5.96%	72.6%
32	3	equispace 1200	12.8%	360%	5.23%	55.5%
32	6	equispace 1200	12.5%	346%	5.13%	53.4%
32	13	equispace 1200	12.4%	346%	5.12%	53.2%
32	3	random 1200	12.8%	349%	5.14%	57.0%
32	3	random 2400	12.8%	355%	5.17%	55.4%
32	3	subdomain 21	13.1%	360%	5.35%	55.8%
32	3	subdomain 43	15.9%	482%	6.00%	72.5%
58	3	equispace 100	1.98%	20.1%	2.30%	36.7%
58	3	random 200	3.15%	234%	2.13%	39.2%
58	3	equispace 1200	3.76%	275%	2.50%	45.5%
58	1	equispace 1200	3.68%	261%	2.49%	45.3%

The first four rows of the table show the effect of taking 1, 3, 6, or 13 samples/subdomain to average for the step-function approximation. The maximum errors, which occur in the subdomains with discontinuities, are large and vary substantially[4]. For these subdomains there is no meaningful average—the error depends entirely on which side of the discontinuity is sampled. However, it appears that 3 samples/subdomain is enough to get stable average errors. So instead of approximating with 6 samples/subdomain in 32 subdomains, it will require the same execution time to use 3 samples/subdomain in 64 subdomains. The last two rows of the table are the closest to 64 that smartsplit produced. The maximum errors are still large and variable, but the average has been improved by $12.5/3.76 > 3$ times (line 3 vs. line 11). The last line suggests that it might be even better to use a single-sample approximation, which would reduce the test time by a factor of three.

The conclusion from these six lines of Table 18.1 ("equispace 1200") is that there is no point in taking many samples/subdomain to approximate a component's behavior—it is a better use of execution time to sample more subdomains. The error estimates are more accurate with three samples/subdomain than with one, however. Furthermore, where discontinuities fall within a subdomain, sampling rate causes large variations in the subdomain error, but all its values are inaccurate: for approximation accuracy a subdomain boundary has to be moved to coincide with the discontinuity.

"Equispace 1200" identifies rows of Table 18.1 measured with 1200 equi-spaced samples. Xcute has two other sampling options: equi-spaced in each subdomain (-s option), which is the sampling used by COMP to construct approximations in the first place, and random on the whole input domain (-r option). These two techniques are also displayed in the bracketed middle rows of Table 18.1, which can be compared with the default sampling of the second row. Results from random sampling are little different, but it takes more points (1200 and 2400 samples are shown) to get stable values. The Xcute -s option takes the number of equi-spaced sample points for each subdomain from the .ccf description file. For both "subdomain" rows shown in the table the counts were 3 when COMP calculated the approximation. They were then altered to 21 and 43 equi-spaced subdomain samples to get the row measurements. Because the errors are largest in small intervals that other sampling techniques do not emphasize, the "subdomain" rows exaggerate the maximum error, but they cannot miss a bad subdomain as the other options can. In the fourth-last row of Table 18.1, the default option missed 11 subdomains with 100 equi-spaced samples; in the third-last row, 200 random samples hit the functional discontinuity but missed 9 subdomains including one with a run-time discontinuity. Both these rows substantially misestimate the actual error values.

When comparing error values using options of Xcute, care must be taken to retain a single interval size, since the values are normalized to the total r-m-s value over that interval. If the interval shrinks, the total r-m-s will decrease and the relative errors will appear to rise.

---

[4] The variation in average errors is itself mostly due to inclusion of the maximum value(s) in the average.

In summary, for error analysis it is suggested that the component developer start with Xcute -s, which will identify subdomains whose boundaries and sizes need adjustment. Then the default sampling with a large sample count is indicated. The count is large enough when no subdomains are missed, or more stringently, when each is hit (say) three times or more[5]. The default error analysis is the one that should be published with the component description. Xcute -r is useful only as a check that nothing has been missed, since it could by chance concentrate test points in any part of the input domain.

18.1.2 Is Series Synthesis Associative?

Intuitively, because a system synthesized from two components in sequence has calculated system subdomains identical to those of the first component[6], a more accurate synthesis would seem to result when the first component has more subdomains; too few in the first component would wash out a finer breakdown from the second. One way to check this intuition is to experiment with three components C_1, C_2, C_3 in series and to compare the predictions of two systems *Front* and *Back*:

Front: $(C_1; C_2); C_3$ (Polish 1 2 S 3 S)

and

Back: $C_1; (C_2; C_3)$ (Polish 1 2 3 S S)

If the intuition is correct, the synthesis order should be chosen to avoid a first component with few subdomains in its description. Variants of the almost-identity component code C_w devised in Section 17.2.2 seem good choices for an experiment. The frequency and amplitude of the 'wiggle' were doubled from C_2 to C_3 to C_1 to make the components more difficult to approximate, and correspondingly more subdomains were used in their descriptions. Table 18.2 gives the component data, and the functional behavior of C_3 is shown in Fig. 18.2. In this configuration, the first

Table 18.2 Parameters for three components to be used in series

Component	Subdomains	Relative wiggle	Ave error	Max error
C_1	40	4	5.4%	16.5%
C_2	10	1	4.9%	8.0%
C_3	20	2	3.6%	9.6%

synthesis of *Front* has the 40 subdomains of C_1, while in *Back* the first synthesis has the 10 subdomains of C_2.

---

[5] The somewhat awkward alternative is to use Xcute -s with a modified .ccf file whose test counts are set to cover the subdomains more densely. With 10 samples in (say) 20 subdomains, Xcute -s could be compared to a default run with 200 total points.

[6] In the step-function approximation. In the piecewise-linear approximation there is an effect from second-component subdomains, but the first still dominates.

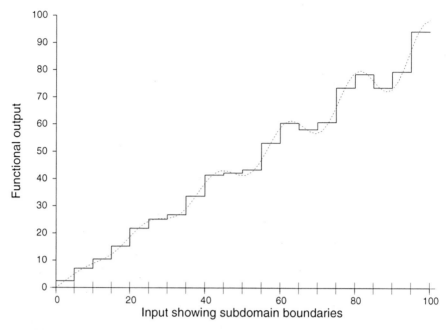

Fig. 18.2 Actual functional behavior (*dotted*) and test approximation (*solid*) of an almost-identity component similar to C_w in Section 17.2.2

Contrary to the intuitive expectation, *Front* and *Back* synthesize to exactly the same system, shown in Fig. 18.3, with 40 subdomains and an average prediction error of 9.5%. (But notice that the actual granularity of the approximation is only that of C_2.)

Thus series composition is associative for **SYN** synthesis, and the system designer need not consider which of several series constructions should be done first.

18.2 Moving Control Structures between Components and Systems

The **SYN** tools restrict components to single output-input values, which sometimes makes it awkward to combine components in a natural way. For example: sequences normally pass along a whole complex of values; conditionals modify the input passed down the *true/false* branches; loop bodies pass out one value to be tested for termination, another for what they have computed thus far. None of these natural patterns can be used at the interfaces in **SYN** -synthesized systems, but of course they may appear within the code of components themselves. The experiments in this

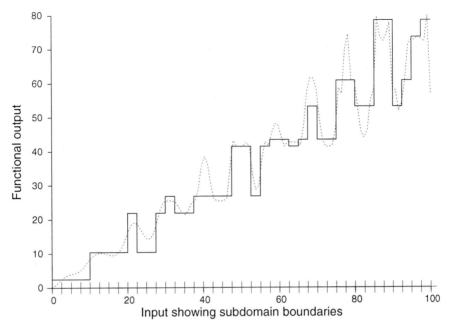

Fig. 18.3 Actual functional behavior (*dotted*) and test approximation (*solid*) of both *Front* and *Back* system

section[7] compare structured-programming constructions within a component (at the programming-language level) with elevating a construct to system-level where it is synthesized.

18.2.1 Series Composition within a Component

The limitations of the first FORTRAN compilers encouraged a style of programming[8] in which values are passed from one assignment statement to another something like this:

```
X = A+B
Y = (X+1)**3
Z = SQRT(Y-1)
```

---

[7] Discussion of iteration is deferred to Section 18.4.

[8] Today 'FORTRAN style' is denigrated. However, it suits not only Backus's seminal code generator but the thought processes of human programmers, by assigning names to parts of a complicated calculation. Perl's quoting convention in which variable values, but not values of expressions, can be easily combined, encourages FORTRAN style today.

As less pedestrian parsing algorithms were developed, this could be more elegantly[9] written:

$$Z = SQRT((A + B + 1)**3 - 1)$$

Components placed in series mimic the FORTRAN style; each computes and passes its result to the next. Or, the series could be accomplished within a single component with a sequence of programming-language statements. Is there any reason to prefer one to the other?

Approximations measured by the SYN tools are inaccurate in subdomains where a component's functional variation is large. If two components have large functional variation, there can be cancellation in their composite function that reduces its variation. It will then be better to code the composite function as one component than to synthesize it from two pieces. A series synthesis would be working with poor approximations whose errors exacerbate each other at the interface; a single component would not have large approximation errors to begin with. The exact opposite is also possible: two components' variations can reinforce each other rather than cancel, so their composite function has even greater variation. Then a single component would be less accurately approximated, so it will be better to use a synthesized pair[10]. Separate components always have one subtle advantage. The SYN tools display their separate functional behaviors, which may help a software developer to discover mistakes that would be hidden in a composite. In the FORTRAN example above, suppose that the subtraction of 1 were forgotten. Would it be easier to see this in a graph of the composite function or in a graph of just the square-root part?

For complex components, it would be silly to think about combining their code instead of using them as components—the point of CBSD would be lost[11]. But the lesson is that there is a limit to how far 'componentization' should be carried.

18.2.2 Conditionals in Code and Conditional Components

If the boundaries of subdomains that describe conditional behavior can be made to match exactly the points at which the code function switches between *true* and *false*, then conditional synthesis introduces no synthesis error beyond the errors of components in the branches. If the three components of a conditional system were combined into a single component using a programming-language conditional statement to make the same decision, the approximation measurement error for this single piece of code would be the same as the prediction error for the three-component

---

[9] But less clearly? Aided by its definition using a context-free grammar (in which John Backus also had a hand), Algol 60 seemed to encourage elaborate expressions. By assigning operators precedence values, parentheses were never required in Algol 60 expressions. It became something of a game to write expressions that no human being could comprehend but even the first compilers could easily translate. Fortunately, it's a game seldom played today.

[10] Because series-synthesis prediction error is usually a multiple of the component error (See Chapter 17), there is a built-in bias for using a single component in place of a series pair.

[11] Not to mention that they may be written in different languages...

synthesis. However, if the subdomains cannot be aligned with the intrinsic discontinuities of a conditional, it not obvious whether it is better to have the conditional at system- or programming-language level. Subdomain alignment may be difficult for two reasons:

- The *true/false* transitions occur too frequently or at points difficult to calculate. In principle the boundaries could be perfectly adjusted, but it is too much trouble.
- The conditional component itself is synthesized from other components, so that its subdomains are an emergent property of the system not subject to adjustment.

An experiment can be constructed with a conditional that changes from *true* to *false* at several arbitrary points of its domain, and in the *true* branch the component computes constant value 1, in the *false* branch constant 0. The conditional system then has the behavior of a square wave with 'high' 1-values alternating with 'low' 0-values over any domain that includes the discontinuities. The conditional itself computes the same function as the system because of the choice of 0-1 values, so its measured approximation can be compared to the system prediction. The smartsplit script was used to refine subdomains for the conditional until there were about five near each discontinuity; only the one containing the discontinuity had an approximation/prediction error. In this experiment the error values themselves are not meaningful, since they occur in infrequently sampled subdomains. But there is a qualitative difference between error behaviors. In the conditional code itself, there are large errors at each discontinuity; in the synthesized system several of these have disappeared[12]. The explanation lies in the Calc synthesis algorithm, which during the SYN run issues a warning message for each discontinuity subdomain, e.g.:

```
test component does not have clear binary value on
    subdomain [0.33593, 0.33691) -- 0.857 replaced by 1
```

Calc must have a 0 or 1 value to take its intersections, and for an ambiguous value it substitutes the majority result. In the example this choice was good enough to hide the subdomain error. As subdomains get smaller and more sample points are taken in each, these replacements are more accurate and more discontinuity-containing subdomains are predicted (nearly) correctly[13]. Nothing like this happens in approximating the conditional component itself; indeed, when it is approximated there is no way to know that later it will be used as a conditional. Thus predictions for a synthesized conditional construction will be better than approximation for a component in which the same conditional is used in the interior programming language. It would, of course, be silly to artificially split conditionals out of perfectly good components into system constructions.

---

[12] For example, with seven discontinuities, only three subdomains in the synthesis have errors while the conditional code itself has seven bad subdomains. The run-time errors are identical in both cases and occur in all seven.

[13] The prediction can never be perfect, because there *is* an interior discontinuity. But one side or the other can be so dominant that points on the other side will never be sampled, making the error appear to disappear.

18.2.3 Raising the Level of Programming

Better results are obtained when conditionals are in system structure instead of within programming-language code; for sequences it can go either way. But simple examples don't really support moving control structures in and out of components, even when this can be easily done. The primary characteristic of a helpful component is its encapsulated functionality—the way in which a programmer can begin to think of it as an elementary action in system design. The SYN tools help with this necessary shift in viewpoint by displaying component behaviors as a whole. By looking at components in isolation, it is easier to catch mistakes before they are hidden from testing within a more complex whole. It would be foolish to alter a well designed component, whose intuitive meaning would be lost.

18.3 Persistent State

The components-with-state Chapter 10 introduced the idea that the state space of a program—the collection of values it preserves from run to run—has peculiar properties. The state space is something like an input domain in that program actions may depend on the values there. At the same time, state is entirely unlike input in that it is completely controlled from within a program, not supplied by an arbitrary external agent. For program testing, this property is crucial: it is fundamentally wrong to externally supply state values in testing a program P. *Input* values are supplied by the tester; P creates a sequence of state values in response to a sequence of inputs. The state that influences P's behavior on some input in a sequence is one that P created on earlier input. One important consequence is that many or most state values are infeasible—they will never be created by P. But should a tester create them in violation of good sense, P may very well use the impossible values to generate nonsense.

The SYN tools have sampling options that facilitate experimentation with the state space, COMP -R and COMP -U introduced in Section 10.4.

18.3.1 Infeasible States

The component Trig introduced in Section 10.4 (Fig. 10.4) is a good example for further investigation. Trig computes sin functions with one of four phases; it codes the phase as 0, 2, 3, or 6 and stores it as persistent state. Figure 18.4 is a reminder[14] of the functional behavior of Trig. The four feasible states are evident in the figure.

---

[14] Similar to Fig. 10.8 but stripped of approximation plateaus. 120 random-length sequences of random inputs were executed by Xcute -r Trig. Recall that these figures are *measured* values

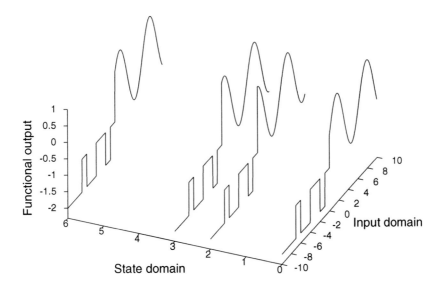

Fig. 18.4 Functional output of component `Trig` sampled with input sequences

Positive inputs return the phased sin functions; negative inputs are used to change state with output -1 for success, -2 for failure.

Because the issues raised by different sampling methods are crucial to the approximation of components measured by COMP, the approximation for `Trig` will now be considered in place of the actual code. Figure 18.5 shows the approximate result-state behavior of `Trig` measured with random input sequences (COMP -R[15]). Again the four 'mode' states are evident. For example, look at mode 6 at the right. For most inputs in mode 6, the result state is also 6—`Trig` mostly stays in the current mode. But some negative inputs switch modes: just below input -0 mode changes to 0, just below -2 it changes to 2, and just below -3 it changes to 3. These are the legal mode switches; all other negative inputs represent illegal mode switches, so `Trig` stays in mode 6[16]. The other mode curves are similar, each at its own elevation. Only modes 0, 2, 3, and 6 appear in the figure. Those are the only result-state values and the only input-state values at which the state behavior is defined. Approximation errors are 0, since the subdomain boundaries are aligned with discontinuities and the result-state behavior is constant over each subdomain.

---

from code executions. They appear as smooth curves only because the data points are joined by line segments imperceptible at the display scale.

[15] 240 random sequences were used in the measurements over 80 × 40 subdomains. With `Xcute -S -A Trig.ccfc` the approximation alone is displayed.

[16] Strictly speaking, below -6 is a legal (but invisible) change to mode 6. Figure 18.4 shows which mode switches are legal/illegal by displaying the -1/-2 return values for negative inputs.

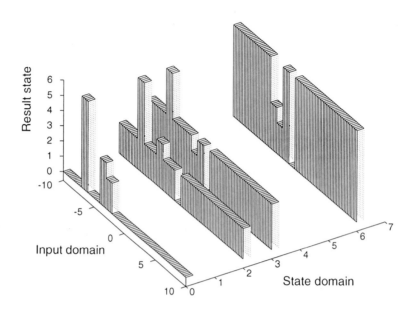

Fig. 18.5 Approximate result-state behavior of component `Trig` sampled with input sequences

If `Trig`'s input × state domain is systematically sampled, however, quite a different picture appears (Fig. 18.6). There now appear to be many more modes (even some negative ones!), and the dominant impression is that the result-state function is linear in the input state (the large sloping planes of the figure). The constant 'troughs' in the figure still show values 0, 2, 3, 6, but now across a range of input and input-state values. The figure demonstrates that when `Trig` is artificially placed in a state, its code acts even when that state could not result from any input sequence. A vertical slice through Fig. 18.6 at (say) input state 6 (at the far right) would reproduce the mode-6 curve from Fig. 18.5, but this real behavior is lost in the noise of Fig. 18.6.

It is a paradox of state sampling that in the feasible parts of Fig. 18.6 the samples are different in principle from those in Fig. 18.5. In the random-input-sequence sampling, only feasible subdomains are hit, but how often each is hit depends on the sequences used to test. If a feasible state is hard to reach[17] (perhaps because it is necessary to pass through a number of other states to reach it), that state may be missed altogether by input-sequence sampling. In systematic sampling each feasible subdomain receives a fixed number of equi-spaced samples specified by the `.ccf` description file (it was nine samples for each subdomain in Fig. 18.6). Unfortunately,

---

[17] For `Trig` the random sequences do an excellent job of hitting feasible states. 60 is the fewest samples in any subdomain for Fig. 18.5. Subsequent examples do less well.

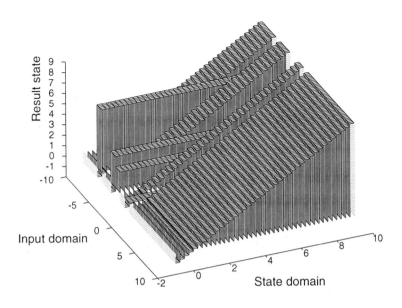

Fig. 18.6 Approximation of result-state behavior of `Trig` sampled 9 times in each of 80 input ×
40 state subdomains

all the infeasible subdomains also receive their systematic quotas and they contribute
only confusion to the behavior displays.

It is an unsolvable problem to decide if an arbitrary state value is or is not feasible. The sequence of states hit by an arbitrary sequence of inputs may vary arbitrarily and in general no sequence however long is sufficient to show that some state
will *never* be hit. However, for component approximations the problem is solvable!
In the approximation table-lookup file `Trig.ccfc`, for example, it is possible to
trace through the states starting with the initial one, marking those that are reached.
Because the table is finite and cycles in it are cut when a state is reached more than
once, the tracing process always terminates[18]; unmarked states are infeasible. Just as
it is sometimes easier to visualize approximate behavior from its plateau graphs than
to grasp the full graph of what a component actually does, so the feasible-state analysis of component approximations can be helpful in understanding a component. It
cannot be performed at all for the actual code. As usual, unless the approximation
errors are small, working with approximations can be misleading. For a poor choice
of subdomains, some will wrongly be infeasible in the approximation. For example, a large state subdomain S may approximately map to itself when the real state
mapping splits part of it out to another subdomain S'. Then although S' is feasible
(because it can really be reached from S), in the approximation S reaches only S.

---

[18] The reason is similar to why loop unwinding always terminates for an approximate system: the
finite number of subdomains changes an infinite problem into a finite one.

The SYN tools have a script `infeas` that performs the marking algorithm and creates a modified approximation table with only feasible subdomains. Starting with the systematically sampled approximation shown in Fig. 18.6,

    infeas Trig.ccfc

creates a new approximation `Trig-feas.ccfc` in which 36 states (2880 subdomains) have been eliminated, and `Xcute -S -A Trig-feas.ccfc` produces an exact copy of Fig. 18.5. The `infeas` script also creates a modified description file `Trig-feas.ccf` in which the sampling counts of infeasible subdomains are reduced to 0. If this description is used in place of `Trig.ccf`, systematic sampling will not hit any infeasible states, and again Fig. 18.5 will result.

In subsequent examples where some feasible states are difficult to reach through input sequences, it may be necessary to uniformly sample with a few test points in each subdomain, then run `infeas` to create a feasible-only description, then finally modify the measurement counts on feasible subdomains so that they are uniformly sampled often enough.

18.3.2 Modes and Storage in State

Component `Trig` uses its mode states to select one of four related behaviors. The mode value acts something like an input parameter that chooses a function for `Trig`[19]; or, four different components can be imagined, each with one of the modes 'hardwired.' Modes are called 'preferences' in interactive programs like web browsers, and there they save users from repeatedly having to answer questions about (for example) screen format. A finite set of modes is an important programming device, but at the same time represents only a trivial use of persistent state. The more significant use is for long-term storage of computed data: A program puts arbitrary information away in its persistent state, then retrieves it on a later run.

To experiment with more complicated states, consider the following system requirements:

> Each input x is a noisy 'digit' ($x \in [n-0.5, n+0.5)$ is 'digit' n), but the only legal 'digit' values are: 2, -2, 4, 3 -3, 6. The system is to count uninterrupted sequences of digit 2s and 3s. Runs of successive 2s are interrupted only by 4; runs of 3s are interrupted only by 6. On the two negative values the largest run-count seen thus far for the corresponding positive digit is returned. Other 'digit' inputs (in [-9.5, 9.5)) return -1; illegal inputs return -2. Finally, sequences may be no more than 6 long; should a longer sequence occur, the return value is -3 and all subsequent negative inputs for that digit return 7.

This contrived set of requirements models a remote-sensor application in which a system (call it `Tally23`) is started each time the sensor is activated, and the

---

[19] But to emphasize that state values are *not* inputs, but program-determined values, there would be no use in asking `Trig` to go into (say) mode 9.

accumulated counts can be read out. The size limitation to 6 simplifies everything without losing the point of the example.

The core of a system design is a component `Count1s` that does almost what is needed: It counts 'digit' runs, but 1s rather than 2s and 3s. Any negative input reads out the largest run count so far; any non-negative, non-1 input interrupts a digit-run. The system designer conceives of using two identical copies of `Count1s`, say renamed `Count1s2` and `Count1s3`, with conditional glue code to separate inputs into {2,-2,4} sending 1s to `Count1s2`, and {3,-3,6} sending 1s to `Count1s3`. Five trivial stateless glue components are used[20] in the system structure with pseudocode:

```
IF Sel2or3 THEN
  IF Choose THEN
    Div2
    Count1s2
  ELSE
    Div3
    Count1s3
  FI
ELSE
  Error
FI
```

`Sel2or3` sends illegal inputs to `Error` which returns the required -2; `Choose` makes the 2/3 separation; `Div2` and `Div3` change all the values to 1s[21].

The requirements for `Tally23` do not explicitly describe its state, but it has one related to the states kept by the two copies of `Count1s`. Here's the state description that comes with that component:

> Each value of the `Count1s` state stores two counts: the maximum run length since reset, and the length of a current run if one is in progress. The format of state K is $K = 10m + c$, where $0 \leq m \leq 7$ is the largest previous run length and $0 \leq c \leq 6$ is the current run length. The initial 'reset' state is 0. One additional state is needed to record that a sequence longer than 6 occurred; let it be $K = 70$.

Thus for example, starting from reset on the input sequence -5, 1, 1, 5, 1 the local state should be 21 (two 1s seen, currently a run of length 1 in progress). Evidently, in order to accurately capture the state behavior, state subdomains must separate states like 20, 21, 22. But many nearby states are infeasible, e.g., 23 (because a continued run would lead from 22 to 33). Figure 18.7 shows part of a state-machine description[22] of how `Count1s` could behave. State names in the diagram are values

---

[20] The distinction between using `Count1s` unchanged with glue code to adapt its functionality and altering the `Count1s` code itself is important. Altering code is chancy, the more chancy the more extensive the code. Glue components are so simple that one can tell at a glance they are correct.

[21] Some details have been glossed over; the complete example is provided with the SYN tools.

[22] The figure is concerned only with state changes, and does not capture outputs. In a complete state-machine diagram, every state in Fig. 18.7 would have transition arrows to itself for negative

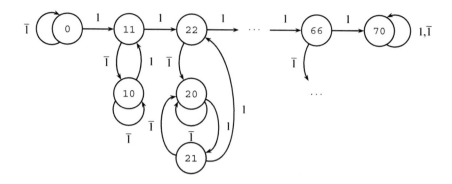

Fig. 18.7 State machine description of Count1s states and transitions

K described above; state transitions occur on positive inputs that are ones (1) or non-ones ($\overline{1}$). There are 22 feasible states in the complete state machine.

Component Count1s must first be tested to obtain its approximate description. It is of interest to observe what happens if the state subdomains are inaccurate, so begin with 24 state subdomains that evenly divide domain $[0, 80)^{23}$. Count1s is a component in which some states are hard to reach by testing with random sequences since larger states require that there be unlikely long uninterrupted runs. The SYN command COMP -R uses 96 random test sequences, in which there are only two runs of length 7 and none of greater length. Fewer than 20% of the feasible subdomains for states larger than 55 are sampled.

The output behavior graph (from Xcute -O Count1s) in Fig. 18.8 looks good from both viewpoints:

Correct functional behavior. Count1s seems to be meeting its input-output requirements. This is best seen by studying negative inputs for different state values. When the state is in $[30, 35)$, for example, negative input returns 3 as it should.

Accurate approximation. With a single exception, all measured points fall exactly on the approximation plateaus so the r-m-s errors are all zero. The exception is a 61% error in subdomain $[0.375, 0.75) \times [75, 80)$ in which measured values of -1 and -3 are combined.

However, something is wrong: Fig. 18.7 does not show any states beyond 70, but larger states appear in Fig. 18.8. State behavior will be discussed next.

In contrast to output, the state behavior of Count1s is more difficult to observe and not so well approximated (Fig. 18.9, from Xcute -S Count1s). Many states in Fig. 18.9 are correctly infeasible, for example those in state subdomain

---

or error input. For example, in state 11, input -5 should produce output 1 but the state should not change.

[23] There are 32 input subdomains over $[-2.5, 3.5)$, but it is the states that are central to this case study.

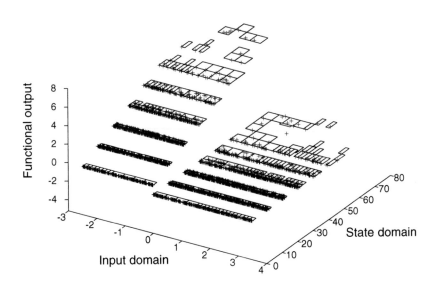

Fig. 18.8 Output behavior of Count1s measured (*crosses*) and approximated (*rectangular plateaus*)

[45, 50). The 'non-1' inputs (greater than about 1.5) are fine: In any input state with tens-digit d, the result state is $10d$, perfectly approximated (for example, all input states 31, 32, 33, ... have result state 30, showing that the sequence has been interrupted). Inputs in [0, .5) are also in the 'non-1' case, but a poor choice of input subdomain boundaries mixes in some '1' inputs, so the step behavior is not perfectly captured in the approximation. For negative inputs the state does not change, so the state mapping is identity, a plane of unit slope. The approximation is a stairstep plane with an r-m-s error of about 2 – 5%. But the interesting state behavior occurs for inputs in [0.5, 1.5) where the counting is going on. Here the result state goes up 1 for each '1' input, e.g., $41 \rightarrow 42$, $42 \rightarrow 43$, etc. It is easiest to see this behavior in state subdomain [40, 45). States like 45 are infeasible because $44 \rightarrow 55$. The approximation subdomains are too coarse to track this increasing behavior well, except for larger states where the coverage is too sparse to see much. States above 70 deserve special comment—they do not exist in Fig. 18.7, but they are evident in Fig. 18.9. Further study reveals that the implementer of Count1s did not follow Fig. 18.7 and use a state 70, but rather used a collection of states 70, 71, ..., 76. That is, Count1s actually treats the error count of 7 in the same way it treats other previous-maximum counts[24]. At the back of Fig. 18.9, the approximation plateaus

---

[24] Whether or not this is a failure is a moot point—Count1s meets its input-output requirements, which strictly speaking don't include the details of state K in Fig. 18.7. One might just as well say that the part of Fig. 18.7 showing state 70 is an over-specification, which the implementer chose

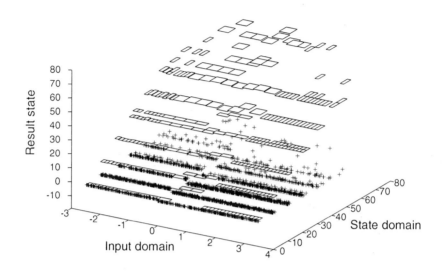

Result state
Input domain
State domain

Fig. 18.9 State behavior of `Count1s` measured (*crosses*) and approximated (*rectangular plateaus*)

are spotty, because no test sequences were long enough to reach some of the feasible states. The state approximation could be improved with finer state subdomains; it would be perfect if the boundaries fell on successive integers. To cover feasible subdomains for large states would require either many more test sequences, or using systematic subdomain sampling. Missing subdomain data in the approximation will cause difficulties in system synthesis to follow.

With this better understanding of the `Count1s` component, the system designer again turns to `Tally23` to be built from it. Since there are two copies of `Count1s` in `Tally23`, the system state is the cross product of their local states: the first part is remembering runs of 2s while the second part is remembering runs of 3s. Thus for example the system input sequence -1, 2, 3, 2, 2, 4, 2 should produce a system state of (31,11), and the additional inputs 6, 2 lead to state (32,10).

`SYN -V` synthesizes the `Tally23` system. For comparison, the actual system was executed with 90 random sequences. Because the behavior functions of this system are defined over a 3-dimensional space, there is no general way to visualize them[25]. However, r-m-s errors in the prediction can be obtained for each 3-D sub-

---

not to follow. (More likely, the implementer simply neglected to deal specially with a 70 state, and found that the code worked anyway. Most implementers do not consider it their business to change documentation like Fig. 18.7.)

[25] The SYN tools calculate a composite state that is the magnitude of the vector sum of states as orthogonal vectors, but this scheme, though it preserves the rough magnitude of local states, also

domain. The functional output for `Tally23` is predicted perfectly. Some statistics of interest: 21,266 of the 36,864 system subdomains were calculated to be infeasible. Execution of the actual system code hit 96 subdomains for which no value was predicted—these arise because no calculation can be made that involves a subdomain of `Count1s` not covered by its random-sequence tests. If the component approximations are taken systematically with `COMP -U` instead of with random input sequences, the apparent `Count1s` behavior is almost unrecognizable (compared to Figs. 18.8 and 18.9) because many spurious infeasible states appear[26]. However, using equi-spaced component sampling fills in the predictions for those 96 subdomains[27].

In contrast to the output prediction, the result-state prediction for `Tally23` shows substantial errors. The prediction is perfect on about 66% of the subdomains but the average r-m-s error is still 1.8%, with a maximum of 35%. Without graphical support, it is difficult to understand what's happening. `Xcomp` has a feature that helps a bit. `Xcomp -D 1 1`[28] selects the first state (counting 2s) and displays functional output behavior (the default) above a plane of input × first-state.

Figure 18.10 (from `Xcomp -S -D 1 1`) displays the way in which the result state 1 (the part from `Count1s2`) depends on state-1 as input state. In most of the figure, the state mapping is identity (a plane of slope 1) and the prediction is accurate. However, at inputs around -2, 2, and 4 the state behavior forms a series of plateaus, and (particularly around 2 where the counting is going on) the approximation doesn't accurately track the actual system state. The worst case is transitions like $33 \rightarrow 44$ which are missed altogether. These account for most of the state errors. Figure 18.10 also clearly shows the region in which there are no predicted values, around input state $60 - 70$. Similarly, `Xcomp -S -D 2 2` would show the depen-

---

confuses them. In contrast, 1-1 invertible mappings like pairing functions nicely separate states but inflate the magnitude alarmingly. At best what can be seen in a general display is the range of possible output or run-time values as the input varies, but the state behavior is inscrutable.

[26] In the simpler example of Section 18.3.1, the `SYN infeas` script could correct the state errors of equi-spaced sampling. For `Count1s` and `Tally23`, `infeas` is no help. Because states are imperfectly approximated, `infeas` cannot reach many states that are actually feasible and its approximations cover fewer states than random-sequence sampling.

[27] A subtle point is that sometimes random-sequence samples reach feasible states that systematic sampling misses. If there is a long chain of related state changes (for example, using state to count how often some input feature occurs, as in Section 18.3.3 to follow), then a sequence test has a chance of reaching states far along the chain. But systematic testing may be unlucky in the input values chosen to probe subdomains whose states lie along the chain, so that a gap is introduced and later states in the chain appear infeasible.

[28] The two state numbers following the -D option are an input state and a result state. The input state number chooses a state independent variable; the result state number is used only to graph the dependent state variable in (say) `Xcomp -S -D 1 2`, which would graph the second-state result values as a function of the first-state (and input) values. These graphs can be shown in two-dimensional projection no matter how many system states exist. However, the error analysis that accompanies the graphs is less meaningful than without the -D option, since each 'subdomain' with -D comes from many real subdomains in the higher dimensional state space. The very fact that only one approximation rectangle appears for each of these composite subdomains shows that the two system states are independent of each other. Each of the many choices for the unseen other state replots the same rectangle. (That's why GNUPlot takes a long time to show a simple graph.)

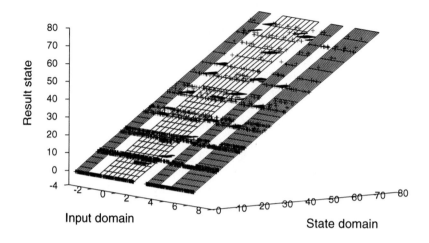

Fig. 18.10 First-state behavior of `Tally23` measured (*crosses*) and approximated (*rectangular plateaus*)

dence of the second state on itself. It has exactly the same form as Fig. 18.10, but with the interesting behavior around inputs -3, 3, and 6, since the second state comes from `Count1s3`. `Xcomp -D 1 2 -S` and `Xcomp -D 2 1 -S` are completely uninformative (Fig. 18.11) because the two states that make up the system have no interdependence at all[29].

In summary, this example illustrates the many difficulties of using state for data storage, particularly when the system state is a cross product. It is hard to choose good state subdomains, difficult to pick a sampling method to avoid infeasible states, easy to confuse 'required' states with those actually implemented, and above all, impossible to visualize the system behavior. In the example, the system functional output behavior appears to be perfectly synthesized, but this is an accidental consequence of the way state is defined—the state synthesis is inaccurate. The example certainly suggests that systems with persistent state are a real challenge to test.

The example does clarify the use of random-sequence sampling vs. equi-spaced systematic samples. Sequences avoid infeasible states and make the behavior of components expressed in functional graphs easier to understand. But they miss hard-to-reach feasible states and if used in synthesis there will be feasible states missing from the system predictions. Perhaps component developers in this situ-

---

[29] Unlike the `-D 1 1` case, multiple rectangles are plotted at each of the composite 'subdomains,' making an incomprehensible display.

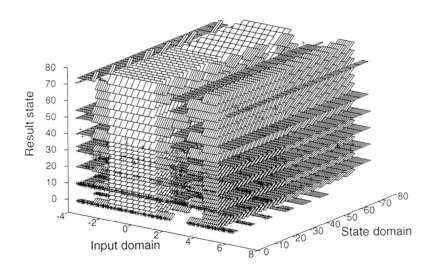

Fig. 18.11 Cross-state independence of `Tally23` measured (*crosses*) and approximated (*rectangular plateaus*)

ation should provide both kinds of approximations, sequence-sampled for human study and systematically-sampled for synthesis using the CAD tools.

18.3.3 A Controlled 'Editor' System

A final example of systems with state models an editor-like component that is controlled and restricted by a front-end component[30]. The 'editor'[31] component Ed has features to stand in for those of a command-line text editor:

Two basic modes. Command-line editors are either in the 'input' mode where they simply store everything, or in 'command' mode where they perform actions on what has been stored. Editors maintain a kind of transitory collection of preferences, complex modes that apply for awhile, then change. For example, when an editor begins a search for some string in its stored text, it remembers the string so that a subsequent search need not repeat it. But the stored string changes more frequently than the usual preference mode.

---

[30] This system is the one used for the accuracy study presented in Table 17.2 in Section 17.1, line 2 of the Table to be exact.

[31] Although the Ed component is thoroughly artificial and nothing like a real editor (not even the rudimentary UNIX one of which it is the namesake), the quotation marks will be dropped.

Complex input/output behavior. In input mode the editor output does not vary—
it's just an acknowledgment that the input is stored. But in command mode the
output may be acknowledgment, a variety of error messages, or tailored repro-
duction of stored data (for example, in response to a search-and-print command).

These features are crudely modeled in the component Ed whose functional-
output behavior is shown[32] in Fig. 18.12. The flat plane in the foreground is the

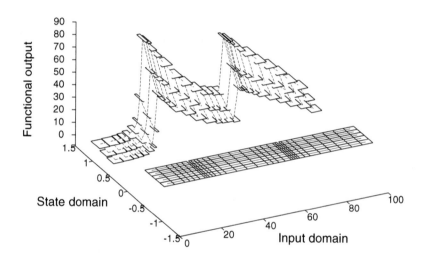

Fig. 18.12 Measured (*contoured surface*) and approximated (*rectangles*) functional behavior of
Ed

'input' mode with constant output; to the back is the complex 'command' mode,
in which output depends on input (modeled by peaks and discontinuities in the input dimension) and on state (modeled by the falling off from peaks in the state
dimension). Ed's state behavior is shown in Fig. 18.13. For most feasible states the
result-state mapping is identity, the plane rising linearly from front to back for inputs
greater than 20. A band of infeasible states in [-0.5, 0.5) interrupts this plane. Negative states signify 'input' mode (foreground); positive (back) are for 'command'
mode. The identity function means that for larger inputs, the editor stays in its current mode. Inputs in [0, 10) effect a mode switch; this is most easily seen in Fig.

---

[32] This and the following figure are composites from Xcute -A Ed (measured curve) and
Xcute Ed (approximation). The grid lines on the former are provided by surface-fitting algorithms in GNUPlot. The functional values are not defined at two feasible points in the 'input'
mode because random-sequence sampling did not reach the corresponding subdomains—these are
barely visible along the inner edge of the flat plane near inputs 20 and 60.

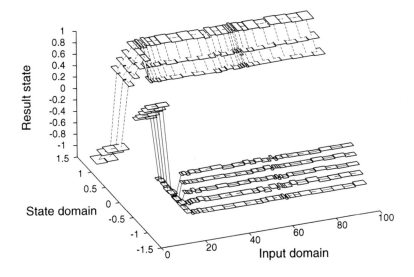

Fig. 18.13 Measured (*contoured surface*) and approximated (*rectangles*) result-state behavior of Ed

18.13 in three plateaus at the far left descending toward the rear, which approximate a plane of negative slope, e.g., state 0.7 → -0.7, state 1 → -1, etc. A similar ascending group appears at the left end of the foreground surface, mapping -1 → 1, etc. For inputs in [10, 20), the result state rises linearly (rear) or falls linearly (front) with the input. This behavior models storing values other than the mode in the state without changing the mode.

In the figures, the **SYN** tools approximate Ed using random-sequence sampling with 32 input subdomains and 17 state subdomains. Approximation errors are mostly those of step-plateaus for a linear plane, 4% – 5% on average; errors in functional output are larger near discontinuities in the input dimension.

Now suppose that Ed is to be used in a system LimEd where Ed's functionality is restricted. The component Control is a front end to invoke Ed in limited ways. In contrast to the example of Section 18.3.1, Control has its own states:

- With the sign ($\pm$) of its state Control shadows the mode it expects Ed to be in if invoked (+ command, - input).
- States 0, 1, 2: In these states Control uses negative inputs that are not sent to Ed. This models a separate dialog with Control's user.
- States 3, -4, 5, -6: Ed is forced to change mode here, and has been requested to do so one, two, three, or four times respectively.
- State 7: Ed may not subsequently change state (four changes have already occurred, so the ultimate Ed state should be 'command').

Control is written specifically for LimEd in which Ed is the primary component. Its functionality relies on Ed fulfilling its own requirements. For example, if Ed should fail to switch modes when requested, then the sign of Control's state will not meet requirements. Thus the study of LimEd raises the issue of checking mode combinations.

LimEd uses Control as a conditional component. It needs stateless glue code Adj in front of Ed (since a conditional cannot adjust the input Ed will receive). Adj filters out the Ed inputs [0, 20) that would cause state alterations other than the mode change, so in the system Ed is allowed only two states (1 and -1). A stateless component Talk is invoked when Ed is not. The structure of LimEd is:

```
IF Control THEN
    Adj
    Ed
ELSE
    Talk
FI
```

For the SYN tools, Control is given an input domain of [-100, 100). Figures[33] 18.14 and 18.15 show respectively the measured state and output behaviors of

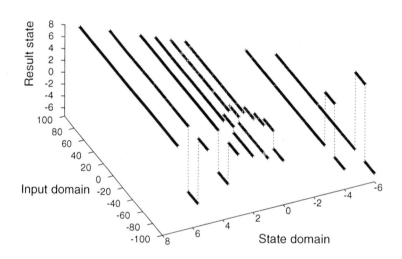

Fig. 18.14 Measured result-state behavior of Control

---

[33] In these and subsequent figures the graphs produced by the SYN tools are slightly modified by hand to connect points that fall in each mode.

`Control`, when sampled with random sequences on 10 input subdomains and 15

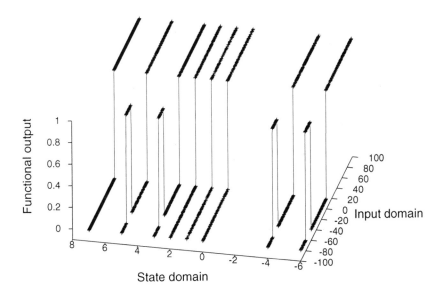

Fig. 18.15 Measured functional output behavior of `Control`

state domains. The measured approximation is perfect, because `Control`'s subdomains are aligned with the points at which it changes output- and result-state values. Using these figures the required behavior of `Control` can be checked. For example, look at input state -4 in Fig. 18.14 (second curve from the right). `Control` stays in state -4 except for input in [-80, -60) which switches to state +5. Figure 18.15 shows that in state -4 `Control` selects the *true* branch for positive inputs (where `Ed` should take 'input' action) and also for [-80, -60) (forcing `Ed` to switch to 'command' mode; `Control` enters state +5 as part of counting the number of switches; similarly, state +5 next goes to state -6 in the second curve from the left in Fig. 18.14).

Synthesizing `LimEd` with the **SYN** tools, the system functional errors average about 5.5%, system state errors about 2.3%. The state maximum error is about 5.5%, but there are many subdomains with large functional errors, the worst near 100%. Once again, the inability to display results in terms of 3-D system subdomains makes detailed study of the system hopeless. The trick of using just one of the state dimensions (with, for example, `Xcomp -D 1 1`) as in Section 18.3.2 fails—the states of this system are intertwined. However, the system should have a limited number of cross-product modes, since `Ed` and `Control` have only a few each. A special script `modes` checks system modes. `modes` searches the synthesized approximation prediction file (which here is `theory2.ccfc`) and a measurement file (like `state.datt` for system result-state values), for mode pairs, giving each pair found a standard integer name $1, 2, ..., M$. In the prediction, all floating-point state values are replaced by subdomain indices, so at most M can be the product of state-space sizes (here, $M \le 14 \times 17 = 238$)[34]. For this system, `modes` finds eight modes from both sources, which in terms of measured state pairs are:

```
1:(0 1)  2:(1 1)  3:(2 1)  4:(3 1)  5:(-4 -1)  6:(5 1)
   7:(-6 -1)  8:(7 1)
```

The list itself is informative: the paired states are of the same sign, showing that `Control` is correctly sussing out Ed's state, which is correctly limited to ± 1.

The files produced by `modes` have just one state dimension, so they can be meaningfully displayed and analyzed by `Xcomp`, in Figs. 18.16 and 18.17. In Fig. 18.16

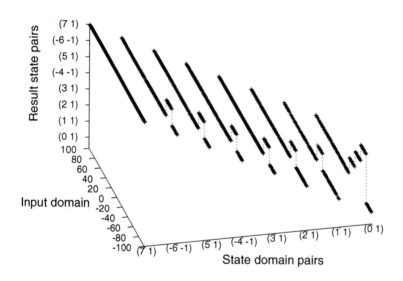

Fig. 18.16 Measured result-state behavior of system `LimEd`

the approximation is perfect—the small errors in the 3-D subdomain predication have been eliminated by standardizing the states, which removes a small floating-point variation in state predictions. The figure clearly shows (for example), the sys-

---

[34] The composite modes are no help in displaying results unless there are fewer than ten. System measurement files, since they could contain a wide range of floating-point state values, can appear to have a vast number of modes. These could be standardized into subdomain indices, but it may be little improvement. In the Section 18.3.2 `Tally23` example, `modes` is no help: the prediction there exhibits just 9 modes, which don't capture `Tally23` behavior well; the state measurement shows 264 modes, too many even when reduced by standardization (83 modes).

tem mode passing from (-4,-1) → (5,1) → (-6,-1) → (7,1) (curves at the center and moving left).

Functional output prediction in Fig. 18.17 is not much improved, but the Xcomp

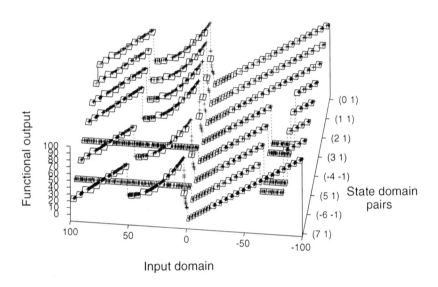

Fig. 18.17 Measured functional-output (*crosses joined by dotted line*) and prediction (*rectangles*) of system LimEd

error analysis now shows that this is nothing new. The large errors are in subdomains whose input values fall near system discontinuities, visible near the center of Fig. 18.17 for small positive inputs. Most of the functional-output errors are just the usual step-approximations to the smooth curves. Similar predictions have been seen in many previous examples, and should be improved by adjusting the subdomain sizes and boundaries in the approximations to Control and Ed[35]. Figure 18.17[36] can be used to check that the system meets its requirements. For example, in state (7,1) at the front of the figure, all negative inputs are shunted to Talk but Ed displays its 'command' behavior for positive inputs. In state (-4,-1) (fifth curve from the back), Ed is in its 'input' mode, and negative system inputs in [-80, -60) cause a mode-switch command to go to Ed and return a success code (zero output shown at the right).

In studying LimEd, a tester must grapple with state graphs such as Figs. 18.13 and 18.14 for the components, and the predicted Fig. 18.16 for the system. These

---

[35] As indeed Table 17.2 in Section 17.1 shows that they are.

[36] Strictly speaking, in I-CBSD only the prediction rectangles would be available to the system designer, but they are quite good enough.

graphs are difficult to understand, but precisely because interacting states are inherently complex. Testing the components and studying the system cannot be properly done without confronting state details. Any easier path to understanding must rely on wishful thinking; for example, trusting that the system cannot change state once it is in (1,7) because in a few cases it does not[37]. In this presentation, coarse subdomains were chosen to make the approximation graphs easier to visualize. The quality of measurements and predictions can be greatly improved by adjusting the testing subdomains for Control and Ed.

18.4 Iteration at System Level

A loop is repeated series composition, but more, since its control aspect is all-important: the number of compositions is not static, but may vary under program control. Restrictions imposed by the SYN tools make the construction of loop examples difficult, because one-in-one-out values make it hard to separate the composition aspect from the control aspect. In the simplest accumulating loop like this C program for finding the mean of a list of 10 numbers in an array daTa:

```
Sum = 0;
for (index=1; index<=10; index++) Sum += daTa[index];
Mean = Sum/index;
```

the values of Sum and index must be kept separate. To use conventional loops in SYN systems requires circumlocutions involving state, which makes a straightforward comparison between programming-language loops and system-control loops impossible. The compositional aspect can be expected to act like an exaggeration of Section 18.2.1 above, but what of the control aspect?

At the outset of explaining the construction of a loop experiment, it must be acknowledged that the example does not provide the hoped-for insights. System-level loops can be constructed, but they reveal more about restrictions of the model than about iteration. This is the sole case in this monograph where an example was not found to model a general situation within the capabilities of the SYN tools.

In order to separate loop computation from loop control, it is natural to use a loop-body component Body and a loop-conditional component Iter and give each a state. A glue component Fix with state will also be needed to filter inputs to Body. Here are the component requirements for an accumulating loop in which the count is an input:

Body. Retains in its state whatever has been accumulated in previous iterations, and on each execution adds a value that depends on its input, which is expected to be the loop index. At reset the accumulation is set to its base value.

---

[37] Of course, the best testing is still only testing, and subject to misleading omissions. But in Fig. 18.16 a large number of random input sequences that place LimEd in state (1,7) have result state (1,7), far more convincing than artificially setting the system state to (1,7) and trying a few inputs, which is the usual system-testing procedure.

`Iter.` Retains the remaining count in its state, which on reset is initialized from
the input. Except for reset, ignores its input, counting down the state by one on
each execution. Returns *true* until the state reaches zero, then *false*.

`Fix.` Mimics `Iter` in retaining and counting down a input value received at reset,
but provides this stored count as output.

These components are placed in a system design as follows:

```
WHILE Iter DO
    Fix
    Body
OD
```

In a format similar to the one used by `tracer`, Fig. 18.18 shows part of the required computation where `Body` accumulates 0.3 on each iteration[38], starting from

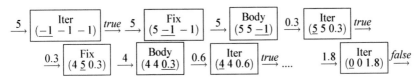

Fig. 18.18 Part of the iterative computation required on input 5

reset with input 5. In the figure, the system state is shown as a triple inside each
component box; the local state for that component is underlined. For example, in
the last invocation of `Body` shown in Fig. 18.18, its state is 0.3, which it modifies
to 0.6, returning this value to `Iter`.

To model this simple counting loop requires three components, each with local
state. This makes the loop system an eight-dimensional object in which the input
and three states are mapped into output and three states, so system visualization
is hopeless. Furthermore, since the local state values must be coordinated, each of
the components is unnatural, more concerned with its state than with the substance
of the iteration. Finally, the number of system subdomains grows far too rapidly to
permit good approximate predictions. In the synthesis to follow, each component has
16 input subdomains and 18 state subdomains, so the system has $16 \times 18 \times 18 \times 18 =$
93,312 subdomains, and if the component subdomains are halved, the system total
would rise by a factor of 2^4 to about 1.5 million. The required coordination of local
states means that the accuracy of state approximation must be almost perfect for
any hope of accurate prediction. Although the SYN tools are still fast at testing and

---

[38] The example only accumulates a small constant on each iteration because of a peculiar domain-
matching problem between `Body` and the other two components. Since `Body` returns the accumulated value, the input subdomains of `Iter` and `Fix` must accommodate whatever values arise,
even though they ignore the inputs that come back from `Body` during the iteration. If their domains are extended, they in turn feed larger values to `Body`, which returns yet larger values. The
domains cannot be matched for synthesis. The problem underscores the unnatural nature of these
components and their system interactions.

approximating the components, the huge four-dimensional tables created in loop-synthesis quickly exhaust high-speed memory, slowing the calculations by several orders of magnitude.

Despite this gloomy prospect, the components were written in Perl and the system synthesized. Figure 18.19 shows the measured and approximation behavior of `Fix`, where the average r-m-s approximation error is about 2.7%. To the right of

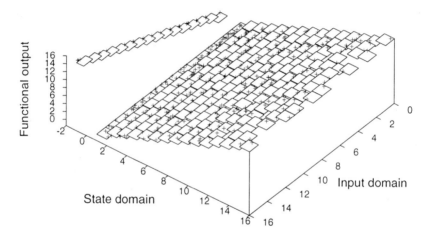

Fig. 18.19 Functional behavior of `Fix` measured (*crosses*) and approximated (*rectangular plateaus*)

the figure, `Fix` ignores its input and returns what's in its state. But at the left of the figure (negative state, signifying reset) the output is instead a copy of the input[39].

The loop synthesis requires 16 unwindings for termination. In the first, the conditional is true on 49,637 of the 93,312 subdomains; on the final unwinding, the last 42 subdomains change from *true* to *false*. The calculation illustrates well the difference between synthesis and actual loop execution. In these 16 compositions of the body and conditional, an approximation (stored in `theory2.ccfc`) is obtained for the complete loop behavior for all inputs. On one particular input (say 5) the actual system would execute `Body` six times and `Iter` seven times. The approximate prediction takes a single table-lookup in `theory2.ccfc`. On input 10 the actual execution takes five more iterations; a single table-lookup still suffices.

---

[39] The state behavior of `Fix` is very similar, because its functional output is obtained by reproducing its state.

It isn't meaningful to simply use Xcomp to judge the predictions for this system against its actual behavior. The first reason is that the descriptive graphs would have five dimensions. Secondly, the system employs state in a peculiar way. On one input after reset, the system uses its state to obtain the accumulation result. Subsequent inputs in a sequence are not of interest[40]. So to compare predictions to actual system execution, Table 18.3 was obtained by running actual code for comparison with the table-lookup values. Despite all the adjustments to accommodate the SYN tools, the

Table 18.3 Comparison between actual iteration and loop synthesis

	Functional Output			Run Time		
Input	Actual	Predict	Error	Actual	Predict	Error
0	0.3	0.3	0.0%	1.0	1.2	20%
1	0.6	0.83	38%	2.0	2.2	10%
2	0.9	0.83	7.8%	3.2	3.5	9.4%
5	1.8	0.83	54%	8.3	8.9	7.2%
10	3.3	1.92	42%	21.8	23.3	6.9%

results are poor, and of course the calculation involving nearly 100,000 subdomains is far slower than any of the actual iterations.

Accumulating loops are an indispensable device of imperative programming, but iteration comes into its own with a recurrence relation, for example a Perl square-root routine using Newton's method:

```
$x = <STDIN>;
$y = 0.5*$x;
$dy = 1;
while (abs($dy) > 0.001) {
   $newy = 0.5*($y + $x/$y);
   $dy = $newy - $y;
   $y = $newy;
}
print "$y\n";
```

Of course, the virtue lies not with iteration, but with rapid convergence of the recurrence[41].

Modeling a test for convergence is even more convoluted than for the counting loop above, but can be done with three components. Roughly, the loop-body component computes both the recurrence value and the information needed to check for termination, and returns these values alternately. The other components use their state to keep track of which value is coming from the loop body, and to see that

---

[40] The actual code returns to its reset state (-1 -1 -1) at the termination of the accumulation loop, so given a sequence it computes a sequence of results, but the approximation doesn't capture this perfectly.

[41] For example, $\sqrt{10^7}$ to within the accuracy of double-precision floating point requires 15 iterations.

when the loop terminates it is on the final recurrence value. Such a system is even more difficult to approximate than was the counting loop, because the test-condition component must make distinctions accurately between values over a wide range. For example, when computing $\sqrt{1000}$ with Newton's method, the successive values of the error term are about 249, 123, 60, 26, 8, 1, 0.02, 0.000006; for $\sqrt{10}$ they are about 1.5, 0.3, 0.02, .00004. An approximation to capture this behavior in a loop-conditional component would require a vast collection of subdomains[42].

The unsatisfactory experiment reported in this section speaks more to the restrictions of the SYN tools than to the subject of iteration at the system level. However, some of the difficulties are inherent in the separation of the loop-test and body-calculation into separate components. Separation of concerns is what CBSD is all about, but it seems to be counterproductive in iteration. Intuitively, neither of these components has behavior that makes sense in isolation, so their independent testing and display isn't helpful. The relevant subdomains in each component are two-dimensional, but intuitively iteration does not require four dimensions to describe. Most of the cross-product subdomains are infeasible and irrelevant. Comparing a component C_L with an internal loop to a system with the loop separated into two components C_{test} and C_{body} can also be viewed from the reliability perspective. A reliability estimate for C_L, as for any program, depends entirely on the number of test samples taken in its subdomains. The same goes for independent reliability measurements of C_{test} and C_{body}. But if there are actually M iterations, the system reliability will be an M-fold product of the latter two, falling to zero as M increases. The assumed independence of the two components is no advantage.

18.5 Component and System Reliability

(For more than enough information on software reliability theory, see Chapter 12.)

To use reliability as the non-functional property in place of run time is a trivial change of synthesis calculations in the SYN tools. All that is required is to replace sums of times with products of reliabilities. However, assessing the base reliabilities of components is not like approximating run times. Run time is a point-wise property of component execution that can be measured externally, or the component itself can supply the values. The SYN tools expect component-supplied run times to be written to STDERR on each input; this allows artificial components to lie about their times as described in Section 14.1.1. It does not make sense to treat reliability in the same way. The essential difference is that while run time is a function whose values can be sampled across a subdomain, reliability is a property of the subdomain itself, a single value that is estimated from the number of samples and their outcomes (success or failure), not accumulated from point measurements at different

---

[42] As indeed it did in a published experiment [48]: in an even simpler recurrence, to get roughly 5% prediction accuracy, more than 3 million subdomains were needed.

places. Furthermore, sampling for reliability must be random[43]. Finally, there will never be any measured estimate of reliability except 1.0. If a failure should occur, the component developer is expected to eliminate it, so that when the subdomain measurements are ultimately published, the observed failure rate must be 0. The zero-failure theory presented in Section 12.2.4 can be used to assign a failure-rate upper bound at any given confidence, but this is less satisfactory than observations of real failures with their confidence bounds[44].

Reliability measurements for a component are therefore conducted by sampling each subdomain N times from a uniform random distribution, and as usual examining the functional results to be sure that no failures have occurred. That being so, for a given confidence bound C, the recorded reliability-lower-bound value r_0 for the subdomain is $r_0 = e^{\ln(1-C)/N}$ (solving equation (12.1) for $(1 - f_0) = r_0$). The confidence bound is supplied to COMP as an option, e.g., COMP -F 95 for $C = 0.95$. Values of N come from the sample-count field of lines in the component .ccf file. Component executions are needed in computing r_0 only to check for the absence of failures; the formula requires only their number N. Execution is also needed to approximate the functional-output behavior of components, which must be available in order to find the inputs sent to a second component in series combination. There is a disparity between the number of test points needed for these two purposes: A handful of points in each subdomain suffices for graphical accuracy of output approximation, but (say) five test points gives reliability only better than 0.63 with 90% confidence. So the tools cheat, and use a .ccf test count of n to perform n executions, but count N as $10n$ for the number of points in computing a reliability bound. This dishonesty lifts the reliability numbers into a more practical range without increasing COMP execution time unnecessarily; the example above goes from 0.63 to 0.95. In describing examples, the counts given are the smaller ones (that is, the ones for test executions, not the inflated reliability counts).

For a simple example demonstrating reliability synthesis, the tutorial stateless system of Fig. 9.1 will serve. Recall that all its unconditional components have the same code file Math that computes a bell-like curve, and its conditionals switch from *true* to *false* only a few times on the test domain of $[0, 100]$. In Chapter 9 most subdomains of a component were sampled the same number of times (5 times for the unconditional components in the tutorial). But to see the effect of different reliabilities in different subdomains, the description files C1.ccf, etc. are altered to have a variety of sample counts[45]. Thus in the reliability example to follow, the approximations for components C1, C3, etc. are no longer the same. Although they share

---

[43] Strictly speaking, samples should be taken according to a (perhaps non-uniform) usage profile across each subdomain. But the very definition of subdomains is intended to separate out all distinctions within the input domain. If there were any reason to believe that one part of a subdomain should be weighted differently than another, it would be cause to refine it into two new subdomains. There being none, a uniform distribution within each subdomain is the only possibility.

[44] In life testing of physical objects, failures of individual units are the basis for measurements. But once a software component has been fixed to eliminate a failure, it is a new object to which previous data does not apply.

[45] An auxiliary script sampcounts creates these files from those used in Chapter 9, assigning a random count in the interval $[3, 11]$ to each subdomain.

an executable code file and a subdomain breakdown, the subdomains are sampled
differently, and so have different reliability bounds. The values chosen are different
enough that subdomains can be distinguished, but not so different that the random-
ness swamps the effects of the synthesis calculations.

One graph created by COMP -F 90 -G for component C1 is shown in Fig.
18.20. The functional approximation graph and error analysis for C1 are much the

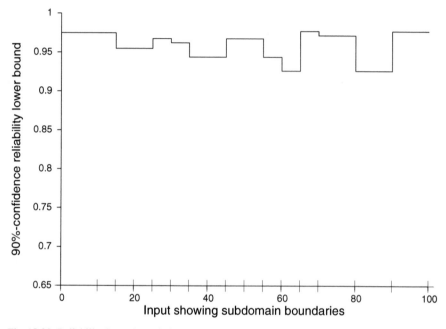

Fig. 18.20 Reliability lower bounds for C1

same as in Chapter 9, but the reliability measurements vary from 0.93 to 0.98. (Reliability would have been constant at 0.95 if all the sample counts were 5.) Synthesizing the system with SYN -G yields the reliability graph of Fig. 18.21, in
which the system reliability prediction varies from about 0.67 to 0.85. The calculated values are lower as the result of series compositions in which the component reliabilities multiply. Despite the variation introduced to distinguish subdomains, prediction of the worst reliability (0.67) can be seen to occur in subdomain
$[60, 65)$. The tracer script introduced in Chapter 15 carries non-functional values along with its functional trace[46], as indicated in Fig. 18.22. In the figure, component subdomain reliabilities are shown following each output, e.g., "$25.8\langle0.93\rangle$"
means that C1 had predicted output 25.8, and its subdomain reliability bound was
0.93. The product of reliabilities in the trace is the predicted system reliability, e.g.,
$0.93 \times 0.88 \times 0.94 \times 0.94 \times 0.93 = 0.67$, the value for system subdomain $[60, 65)$ in

---

[46] Feature suppressed in Section 15.2.

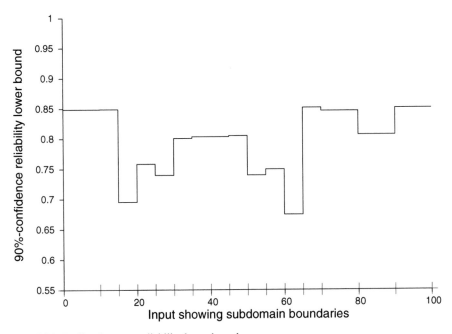

Fig. 18.21 Predicted system reliability lower bounds

Fig. 18.22 Trace of reliability bounds at input 62

Fig. 18.21. The low system reliability in $[60, 65)$ partly comes from the loop subdomain reliability prediction of 0.88. If the developer of this system wants to improve reliability, it might be wise to replace the two components C2 and C3 that synthesize to theory1 with a new single component in which the loop is embedded. This substitution, if the new component has a reliability bound of 0.98 in all subdomains, improves the predicted system reliability bounds to a range of $0.74 - 0.90$.

Reliability-synthesis calculations are trivially different from run-time synthesis in the SYN tools, but there is a profound conceptual difference between these non-functional properties. For reliability, there is no way to estimate component measurement error except in the confidence bound of the zero-failure theory. Hence there is no non-functional quality measure of component testing—who is to say that 90% confidence in a reliability bound of 0.93 is good enough[47] for C1 in $[60, 65)$? The component functional-output approximations still have their r-m-s error anal-

---

[47] According to equation (12.1), the same data ($N = 30$) supports 26% confidence in a bound of 0.99, or 99.9% confidence in a bound of 0.79, etc.

ysis, but there is no reason why non-functional behavior should be linked to functional. The other important difference between reliability and run time is that only the latter is a functional, point measure. It makes no sense to talk about the reliability of one test point: the result is either correct or it is not. Without subdomains, sampling the entire input domain would assign it only a single reliability bound. Subdomains are a way to split the domain into pieces, to refine the reliability measurement. For run time, the situation is reversed: it is perfectly sensible to speak of a component's run time on one test point, and subdomains only approximate the real situation as blurred averages.

18.6 Substituting one Component for Another

When a system designer discovers that a design-in-progress fails, the design itself may be at fault. For example, the interface between two components placed in series may not match, not because of some component implementation blunder, but because the two don't belong in series[48]. A more subtle design flaw involves non-functional behavior: the system may fail to meet a run-time or reliability requirement. Anyone can blunder, and instantiating particular components in a design, even when they are only approximations drawn from a catalog, can expose system-design blunders. Since overall functional behavior, and even more so overall non-functional behavior, are not easy to conceptualize even for simple systems, the only way to check a difficult design may be trial-and-error component placement. The SYN tools make it easy to approximate system behavior for a chosen set of component approximations.

On the other hand, component developers blunder, too, so perhaps a system design is sound yet fails because some of its component(s) fail. Chapter 15 describes the process of tracing a system problem to its cause in a component, and the way in which SYN tools and subdomain testing support this process. A component failure means that its implementation does not satisfy the requirements which the system designer used to select that component. There is one insidious way this can happen, which could be called the Achilles heel of CBSD: a component catalog description does not match the executable component. Then the system designer is being lied to, and CBSD goes wrong. It is not so bad if the actual component is as needed, but its description is mistaken. Such a component will not be selected, so there is no more than an opportunity lost. But when a misleading catalog description *is* what's wanted, that component is selected and the later system failure seems inexplicable. With the SYN tools, the scenario would be that the approximate component, used to synthesize an approximate system, hides a fatal flaw in its inaccuracies. The system designer will then observe that the approximate predictions are (approximately) as desired, buy the real component, and at best be disappointed.

---

[48] An inverse sine function, for example, can't legitimately follow an exponential function without range restriction on the former.

Suppose then that a component fails in a sound system[49]—what's to be done? A subdomain breakdown may pinpoint the problem; perhaps it is too long a run time in a particular subdomain, in turn caused by a slow component. Knowing just what's wrong isn't much help in I-CBSD, where components are taken as inviolate and immutable. The disappointed system designer can report the problem to the component developer[50] but a fix might be a long time in coming. The system designer would be better advised to make a component substitution, which is easy to do with the SYN tools: Obtain an approximate description file for a new component, and with it synthesize the same system structure. Mechanical comparisons can be made between the new and old approximate descriptions and between the new and old predictions from synthesis.

A particularly interesting case occurs when failure is observed in an actual working system whose real components have been purchased and linked together. A failure means that some system input X excites unacceptable behavior. In locating the cause, it might be helpful to revert to the approximate system so that SYN tools like tracer can be used with X; or, conventional debugging methods might locate the faulty component C_f. An ideal test bed is available for a replacement component: the system itself. Again, it might be helpful to test a replacement for C_f by substituting its approximation into the original approximate system and using SYN to predict the behavior. This scheme has the advantage that the SYN tools display the behavior not just at X, but for a whole input domain. Or, the new component's approximation can be wrapped with a table-lookup routine and this executable linked into the working system in place of C_f. Using mostly actual code along with one approximate component has the virtue that most of the values in system execution will be exact. In either case, candidates to replace C_f can be tried easily before purchase.

18.6.1 Meeting a Non-functional System Requirement Bound

For a concrete example of component substitution, consider performance requirements for a system during its design. The constrained trigonometric system used in the tutorial on components with state (Section 10.4.1) has predicted run time shown in Fig. 18.23[51]. The largest run times[52] about 13; one occurs at $[2.5, 3) \times [0, 0.5)$, for example, where the tracer 2.7,0.2 output is shown in Fig. 18.24. In Fig. 18.24 the values are pairs of (input,state) shown with the run time in angle brackets

---

[49] In the case of the SYN tools, suppose also that the approximation matches actual execution in also failing; that is, a valid system prediction disagrees with system requirements.

[50] Subdomain information vastly improves a software-failure report: "Your component Trigon from your Internet catalog appears to be running far too slowly on inputs in the range 180–190."

[51] This is the same data shown in Fig. 10.14, but plotted with Xcute -A -T theory3.ccfc and a different projection view to make it easier to see the numerical values.

[52] Recall that the run times used with SYN tools are without units because they are artificial—supplied arbitrarily by the component code through STDERR. But an attempt is made to use sensible or interesting values in examples; for instance, Trig's run time is chosen to be constant when

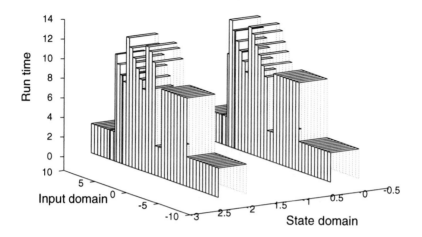

Fig. 18.23 Predicted run-time behavior of trigonometric system

$$(2.7, 0.2) \xrightarrow{} \boxed{\begin{array}{c} \text{Check} \\ [2, 3) \end{array}} \; true\langle 2 \rangle \; (2.7, 0.2) \xrightarrow{} \boxed{\begin{array}{c} \text{Before} \\ [2.5, 3) \end{array}} \; 2.75\langle 1 \rangle \xrightarrow{}$$

$$(2.75, 0.2) \xrightarrow{} \boxed{\begin{array}{c} \text{Trig} \\ [2.5, 3) \times [0, 0.5) \end{array}} \; (0.37, 0)\langle 7.9 \rangle \xrightarrow{} \boxed{\begin{array}{c} \text{After} \\ [0.35, 0.4) \end{array}} \; 0.38\langle 2 \rangle \xrightarrow{}$$

Fig. 18.24 Trace of run time at (2.7, 0.2)

"$\langle\ \rangle$". Although components like Before do not have state, the system state is carried along since it must be supplied to Trig^{53}. The run times add to the system value: $2 + 1 + 7.9 + 2 = 12.9$.

If the performance requirement is (say) run time below 15, the predicted values are OK. But can these run-time predictions be trusted? As described in Section 17.2.3 and anticipating discussion in Sections 20.2.3 and 20.3.3 to follow, errors in predictions are themselves an emergent property of a system, and cannot be determined with certainty short of executing the real system, not possible under I-CBSD. However, it is plausible to reason along the lines of Section 17.2.4 as follows:

In this system the average functional r-m-s approximation error for the components is about 1.2% (maximum 12%); the glue components have zero run-time

---

it is switching modes, but when computing the sine, to be different for different inputs, modeling a faster algorithm at one part of its domain.

[53] tracer is not designed to cope with more than a single system state because of the difficulty of sorting out which component gets which part.

error, but `Trig` averages 5.8% (maximum 62%). The longest series path in the system has length four (`Check`; `Before`; `Trig`; `After`). The functional error (which might accumulate along a path) is irrelevant except that it might throw `Trig` into a wrong subdomain, where the prediction could be too small. But since this would not be worse than the longest `Trig` run time (about 8), it can be discounted as unable to lead to a larger total time. What remains is the error in `Trig` run time itself, which is a maximum of 62%, so that instead of 8, it might be $1.62 \times 8 = 12.9$. With the constant addition of $2 + 1 + 2$ for the glue components, the result would be 17.9, violating a requirement of 15.

For a particular subdomain, it is possible to make an accurate error analysis—for example, it is important just where the large run-time errors in `Trig` occur, and they are not in fact in the region where the system run times are largest. But the system designer cannot be expected to perform an exhaustive analysis[54]. What's needed is a quick overall estimate of whether the prediction is safe.

If component(s) of a trial system much be replaced, it is certainly best to begin with glue code. The implemented functions are typically simple, and often glue components are tailor-written to go with a more complex component. Hence substituting for them is easy, whereas it may be impossible to find a substitute for something like `Trig` that does not occasion redesign of the whole system. If the total run time for `Check`, `Before`, and `After` could be brought below 2, the same rough error analysis shows that the worst case is $12.9 + 2$, which is within the performance bound of 15.

In Section 18.5, a similar replacement was imagined—substituting a loop within one component for a conditional/body pair of components. As noted there, this substitution improved the predicted reliability bound. The crucial difference between predictions of reliability and of run time is that in the latter, a component-level error analysis permits a rough engineering estimate of error in the system run time, so the system designer can have confidence—from the SYN predictions alone—that the system will meet its performance requirements.

---

[54] Tools could do the complete analysis subdomain by subdomain, but the result would still be somewhat problematical, since any of the subdomains selected by approximation could be wrong.

Part VI
Implications for Software Testing

INVESTIGATING a particular form of CBSD in full detail from the testing viewpoint and with the support of the SYN tools throws light on all three subjects: components in system development, support tools, and testing itself. The insights gained are summarized in Part VI. Two topics emerge as of special interest, because they arise over and over in software development, yet have proved difficult to study in a general context. One is the relationship between unit- and system testing; the other is the treatment of non-functional software properties. Part VI ends with a brief list of open problems.

Chapter 19
Unit vs. System Testing

THE testing perspective on CBSD reflects a stubborn bias toward unit testing of software. Testing small programs is such a satisfactory process under such good intellectual control, in strong contrast to testing large systems, as to suggest that only unit testing can be made to work. Behind this hypothesis is the belief that testing is intrinsically no more than a craft, which talented people can successfully accomplish in limited circumstances, but which lacks a satisfactory engineering basis, which will never 'scale up.' There is no solid evidence supporting this belief that testing will never become routine engineering. It hasn't happened in almost 60 years of trying, but of course there might be a breakthrough tomorrow. (Or, less exciting but with many historical precedents, the advance of technology may provide a brute-force 'solution' that isn't a breakthrough but works well enough that system testing ceases to be a real problem.)

Throughout this chapter, 'unit testing' and 'component testing' will be used almost interchangeably. The latter is just an example of the former in a more restricted setting.

How does unit testing work in the hands of a talented tester? Successful unit testing seems to be a peculiar combination of functional testing with structural checking. The tester starts with a good functional testset (that is, a set of subdomains that isolate most cases of interest; it is probably important that there be relatively few such cases). Next the code coverage is checked and functional tests are added to make sure that all the code is used, in the manner described as 'structural adequacy testing' in Section 7.2.3. Adequacy checking is easy for a tester who knows what each part of the code is supposed to do. The author has this knowledge; for a small unit of unfamiliar code, it can be gained by study. Now comes the creative part. The tester looks for evidence that the functional and structural coverage is adequate in a way that has much in common with program proving. The working testset contains points that cover each functional and structural subdomain, but do these points guarantee that the subdomains are homogeneous for failure? That is, could the test point(s) in some subdomain succeed, yet others in that subdomain fail? There is no better example of the analysis required than Howden's paper on path testing [64], in which he carefully analyzes a set of textbook examples. The process has been

D. Hamlet, *Composing Software Components*, DOI 10.1007/978-1-4419-7148-7_19,
© Springer Science+Business Media, LLC 2010

studied off and on, but not much has been added to what Howden knew. Matthew Geller wrote a seminal paper [31] in which he exploited linear properties of common integer constructions, for example to prove informally that a loop bound cannot be wrong if it passes a certain pair of tests. It may be that so-called metamorphic testing [16] is the generalization of Geller's insight.

The process described in the previous paragraph may not be the only way to conduct a sound unit test. Creative people work in many and various ways and cannot always describe what they have done. But it should be clear that whatever the process, it relies heavily on code analysis that is not mechanical and probably not humanly possible beyond the unit level. If it is so that only software units (components) can be properly tested, then testing theory of CBSD should seek to leverage component tests up to the system level. In contrast, current software-engineering practice treats unit- and system testing as two independent activities: no use whatsoever is made of unit test results in system testing.

The form of I-CBSD being investigated seeks to be analogous to mechanical-engineering design: components are described, tested, and certified, then their descriptions are used in systems design and prediction/analysis. When a mechanical system is actually assembled its properties are already well understood, so it is expected to work with no more than a few checks on the predictions.

19.1 Components Make Ideal Software 'Units'

Unit-testing theory cannot be satisfactorily abstract so long as the definition of 'unit' involves details of a programming language. Most natural 'units' are some form of procedural abstraction, quite different in different languages. In particular, the procedure parameter/argument mechanisms differ widely among languages, yet arguments play a central role in functional testing theory. Szyperski's definition of a software component as nothing more than executable code supplies just the right degree of abstraction. The input, output, and state spaces of an executable are arbitrary abstract domains that can be matched and connected to create (and hide) similar domains in a system. Whereas programming-language units are entities rather different intuitively from systems—they are intuitively sources that can be modified and must be compiled and linked—a Szyperski component is a miniature system. More important, a system itself is a larger Szyperski component. The intuitive essence of 'unit' is that it be a part, and as Szyperski defined 'component' it is just that and no more. Thus CBSD is an ideal setting in which to study the relationship between unit- and system testing.

19.1.1 Solving Unit-testing Problems

Testing and approximating component behaviors as the SYN tools do has advantages over the usual unit testing (say with subroutine units). Some ideas are suggestive for the more general situation.

Testers are often 'flying blind' in their work, because the software under test does not have an adequate set of requirements, and so lacks any oracle to decide if the result of a test execution is success or failure. The oracle problem is at its worst in unit testing, because units are invented in the software design. While what each unit should do may be clear to its designer/implementer, there may be little recorded documentation. It has often been said that unit code sources are 'self-documenting,' meaning that the code itself is its only description. This is no use to a tester looking for where the code might go wrong. Components in themselves do nothing to attack the oracle problem, but because they are intrinsically functional (in the sense of mappings of the input domain), they encourage more abstract, general descriptions. The SYN tools exploit components' functional nature by displaying graphs. Although a behavior graph is also only 'self documentation,' it is superior to studying code, because anomalies stand out visually and often point to mistakes. Conventional unit testing could benefit from a more functional approach.

Poor documentation of unit requirements makes it impossible to judge functional adequacy of a test collection. But the SYN tools do provide an adequacy measure of the testing-approximation match to the actual function computed by a component[1]. Again, it would be worthwhile to add functional error analysis to conventional unit testing.

Testing components as units has a tremendous advantage over other kinds of software unit test: components need no stubs. In conventional unit testing, if a subroutine (for example) calls another subroutine then it cannot be tested in isolation: Some mechanism must substitute for the missing routine. The simplest substitute is a dummy that does nothing but return—a 'stub.' There are no satisfactory stubs: a dummy will almost always seriously distort the subsequent actions of the caller. Two other schemes and their drawbacks are:

Interactive human stubs. A call to a missing routine can be replaced by an interactive interchange with a person. Instrumentation inserted in the unit being tested prints for the person the routine called and arguments sent to it; the person then provides an appropriate result to return to the unit. The practical drawback of this scheme is that it slows testing to the speed of human thought and typing, making it impossible to use many test points. And of course the person may supply inappropriate values.

---

[1] The two meanings of "functional" are particularly easy to confuse in this setting. "Functional (requirements) testing" is impossible without requirements; the SYN tools report on "functional" errors, i.e., deviations of the test approximation from the function (graph) that a component computes. A large error does not mean that requirements are not being met, only that the test does not capture the function. On the other hand, approximation error may point to an unexpected anomaly which in turn may indicate incorrectness.

Aggregating in dependency order. In the absence of recursion, a collection of routines can be ordered into those that call no others, then those that call only routines previous in the order, continuing until all routines have been placed. The routines can then be tested in this order without the need for stubs, using instead the previously tested routines themselves. This is the practical procedure commonly used to test a collection of units that form a system. Its drawback is that except for the routines that call no others, the tests are not really unit tests, but rather subsystem tests. That is, the software being executed may not be understood by the tester because it becomes large and complex. The difficulty is compounded by potentially inadequate testing at each stage. Because the tests get progressively less trustworthy as the subsystems grow, the behavior when testing routine X may really be untested behavior of routine Y that X calls.

Components need no stubs because they do not by definition make explicit use of other components[2]. If they did, they would not be executable. Instead, the connections among components are supplied externally by a system definition, so each component can be unit tested in isolation.

The SYN tools treatment of 'master' concurrent components suggests a new way to handle stubs in conventional unit testing. A master component is tested without its slave (Section 11.2) by giving it a second input domain (whose values would be supplied in system execution by the slave). The same trick will work for unit testing a subroutine X (with one parameter, say) that calls another subroutine Y (which returns say one value). Test points for X can be drawn from a two-dimensional cross-product space of its input domain D and a second orthogonal input domain D' for what Y would return. Sampling $D \times D'$ eliminates the need for Y altogether—anything it might return would have been tried in the X unit test. The drawback is that a quadratic space requires much more sampling than does D alone. However, subdomains on D' could reduce the number of test points at the possible expense of missing some strange aspect of Y's behavior. Since D and D' are being sampled independently, they can be divided into subdomains using different criteria. For example, a functional breakdown might be good for D, while a dataflow breakdown for D' (on a variable sent to Y as an argument) might be more revealing. If there were conventional testing tools using this two-dimensional idea, it would open the murky idea of stubs to experimentation.

---

[2] It would be a generalization of the SYN model to allow one executable to start another directly, send it command-line arguments, and wait for a result, much like subroutine call and return. The SYN tools themselves often work this way. Mason and Woit [78] showed that any system using such a component C that calls B has an equivalent system using only independent components that invoke one another. Their proof splits C into the code C_1 before the call and C_2 after the call; the equivalent system is $C_1; B; C_2$. The technical difficulty in the proof is that C_1 must pass its internal state through B for C_2 to use.

19.1.2 Choosing Unit-test Subdomains

Many general software units are stateless, as are the simplest components. For testing stateless units, functional subdomains defined by requirements are the ideal choice. Each subdomain is independent of the others, the order in which test points and subdomains are selected is immaterial, and executions are repeatable. What makes functional testing work so well for units may be an implicit use of structural adequacy (described in Section 7.2.3). The tester who is familiar with a unit's source code can easily have an insight something like: "Wait a minute—no collisions in that hash table have been tried...", which suggests a subdomain refinement that can expose a coding mistake[3]. In contrast, while testing a large system the tester is unlikely to know that a hash table is even being used and its use will not be easy to connect to a subdomain of the system input domain. The error analysis supplied by the SYN tools also provides pointers to good functional subdomains, because when the finite-support function defined by testing does not capture the real execution function well, chances are that anomalous behavior is not being given its own subdomain. This kind of error analysis is not usual in conventional unit testing, but it could be. When requirements for a unit are vague or unknown, it is a starting point to form subdomains that try to evenly divide the input domain. Technically, such a division is neither functional nor structural, but this straightforward technique is often useful (especially in conjunction with an error analysis to detect poor subdomain boundaries), and too little used.

In the more complicated case that a unit has local state, functional subdomains are harder to devise, because requirements seldom describe cases of 'same' state values, and when they do, the required states may not have been implemented correctly. Proper repeatable testing requires sequences of input values starting with a 'reset' state. These sequences could be grouped into subdomains, but again there is unlikely to be any requirements guidance. For systems whose intended application is not too specialized or arcane, a human tester finds it relatively easy to think of natural sequences based on common sense, but these are not available at the component level. Thus it is very unlikely that input-sequence subdomains can be described and covered in unit testing. Perhaps proper input-sequence subdomains make sense only for systems testing. The subdomains used by the SYN tools for unit testing do not divide an input-sequence space, but rather use the much simpler (input × state) space. This choice is partly a consequence of the intuitive difficulty of grouping points in a sequence space, but is also forced by the difficulty of displaying behaviors. Two-dimensional graphs depending on (input, state) pairs are hard enough to grasp; there is no good way to map sequence points into one or two dimensions as an independent variable. Furthermore, using a sequence space would hide the dependence of unit behavior on its local state, which seems to go against the very idea of exploring unit code in its own terms.

---

[3] Not the least likely mistake is one of omission—the implementation gives no proper consideration to hash collisions at all.

It is instructive to compare the SYN treatment of local state with the treatment of input received from a concurrent process. In both cases a two-dimensional space determines unit behaviors, but in different ways that dictate different test sampling. For (input × state) the state dimension is strictly determined by past inputs in a sequence; state is a *dependent* variable. In contrast, a master concurrent component receives input both from the outside environment and from values returned by a slave. Both dimensions of the (external-input × slave-input) space are independent and there is no necessary dependence on previous values.

It could be argued that a concurrent master controls the slave-input space like a local state, because inputs appear there only if the master starts a slave. Such a view is supported by sparse coverage of the slave-input space: usually the slave provides only a few values so most values sampled for the alternate input space of the master would never occur[4], just as most local-state values never occur. Nevertheless, it is the independent slave that controls the master's second input space, and when testing the master in isolation, that space must be directly sampled. It may be that most values are not what the master expects, but to assume they do not occur would be worse than failing to try 'invalid' inputs to any program. 'Slaves' misbehave at least as often as human operators. It is only a *system* requirement that the concurrent communication work as desired; the best time to discover that the master fails to provide for error cases is when unit testing it. Of course, valid and invalid inputs expected from the slave are a primary means of defining subdomains on the slave-input space. In contrast, the infeasible values of a local-state space are not 'error' or 'invalid' values. There is no point in trying infeasible states because the component *never* reaches them[5] no matter what other components may or may not do.

The lesson for unit testing in general is clear: the 'second' space that determines a unit's behavior must be seriously and correctly sampled. For concurrent communication that means covering the whole second input domain; for local state it means using enough input sequences to cover feasible states. The tester's enemy, as ever, is implicit assumptions about what need not be tested, confusing "should not" happen with "cannot" happen. To paraphrase the old proverb about horses and beggars, "If wishes were programs then software would work."

In testing conventional units, the constraint to strictly local state is often not observed. Global variables in programming languages have fallen out of favor[6], but global persistent state is still the rule. When there is global state, isolated unit testing is simply impossible. It is as if the unit contained a variable never assigned a value, yet its value is referenced in the code. The only option would be to treat that

---

[4] In the concurrent-tutorial example of Section 11.3.1, the master component expected its slave to return a very special value, so most of the space was an error plain (Fig. 11.4).

[5] There can, of course, be states that are in error according to a component's requirements, and states that seem infeasible but are only infrequent. Careful unit testing can reach and expose these states.

[6] With good reason. The use of globals intertwines pieces of code that a designer means to be strictly separate, and leads to unexpected behavior. At the same time, there is no easier fix to unusual communication difficulties between units than to introduce a global flag. Putting a global value into persistent state is a way to get around language restrictions on variable scope, but it causes even more difficulty in testing and understanding than would a global variable.

variable's value as an input, but this is wrong in principle. The hard fact is that a unit referencing global state does not have independent behavior: its actions may be completely controlled by an outside agency setting the shared state. Testing without knowledge of what that agent will do is wasted effort. If there is one thing a designer can do to make unit testing productive and meaningful, it is to eliminate global state.

19.2 Unit Testing Is More Than it Seems

If units (components) are no different in principle from systems, there might seem to be no essential difference between unit testing and system testing. So there is not, except in scale, but scale makes all the difference. Craft methods, which work for those talented enough to use them, require an intuitive grasp of the entire situation. Many people can completely master (and hence adequately test, without necessarily knowing how they do it) a straightforward 100-line component; no one can begin to really understand a million-line operating system. So whatever it is that good testers do, they can do it only at the unit (that is, small-scale) level.

19.2.1 Saving and Using Unit-test Results

For mechanical and electrical components it would be unthinkable to discard the results of testing and certifying component units. Indeed, it is these results that make up component catalogs, handbooks, or data sheets, and which enable the whole process of system design to be done 'on paper' before any component is acquired in tangible form. Yet in software engineering, unit testing is a process carried out in isolation, its only record a 'done' check-mark in a configuration-management database[7]. At the very least, there should be information flow between unit and system testing, seeking to establish procedures that make each work better as a result of the other. Capabilities of the SYN tools suggest possibilities of doing much better.

19.2.2 Unit Tests the Only Tests

The goal of the subdomain testing theory presented in this book is to enlarge the role played by unit testing in software development. Behind this goal is the belief that testing craft works pretty well at the unit level, but does not scale up. It follows that testers should apply their skills to components, and tools should carry the burden of extrapolating these tests to systems using those components. Throughout the book examples have been presented in which components are tested, the test results

---

[7] True, sometimes process statistics are saved. A unit that failed inordinately often in unit testing may later be examined as a possible source of system failures, or be replaced instead of reused.

examined for accuracy, then subdomains and tests adjusted to improve the approximation[8]. There is no practical limit to this refinement process—subdomains can be adjusted until they are singletons and the testing is exhaustive. But when finite resources and skill give out, the component description (approximation) has gone as far as craft can take it.

The whole point of adequate unit testing is to make it possible to trust the units after they are placed in a system. Conventional wisdom is that additional 'in-place' testing is needed, because the units are seeing a new environment within the system. Subdomain testing tries to forestall this argument. At component level every aspect of the unit's functionality has a subdomain, and an adequate unit test closely approximates behavior on each of these narrow environments. Then within a system nothing can come to the component that has not been tried[9]. The best reason not to try probing units in place is that it's very difficult. Looking at a component through the lens of system inputs that reach it is problematic because the tester never knows if enough system inputs have been tried. Too often when a system test point does reach the component (after a good deal of testing effort), it is only in one of several possible ways; the untried ways can later show up as failures.

If it is stipulated that components work in every possible context, then system tests take on a new, more productive role: they can probe for system-design mistakes[10]. For example, freed from checking whether or not a sorting component indeed sorts, attention can focus on whether sorting is taking place where it should be. When a system test fails, analysis is vastly simplified if the only root causes to be traced lie in the system structure. Furthermore, adequate component testing buys an important new capability: predictions of system behavior by a CAD tool. The SYN tools scripts `SYN` and `Calc` compute, from the unit-tested approximations for a system's components, an approximation to system behavior. This prediction, instead of actual system testing, can be used to check requirements. The tools are fast, but speed is not their primary advantage. The system designer need not acquire any actual components to gain the predictions, because they require only published approximate component descriptions. Thus the goal of system design and analysis 'on paper' is realized for software, as it has long been available to mechanical and electrical engineers.

In the end, when a system designer can find no fault with a design, it will be time to acquire its real components and to augment approximate predictions with real system tests. Real testing will be directed by previous study of predictions, since points where the accuracy was in doubt are ones to try. Once the actual code is in

---

[8] An apogee of such schemes occurs in Section 17.1.1, where feedback from errors in component approximation is used to automatically adjust subdomains to reduce the error. The drawback of automation is that it hides most of the unit testing from view, and that subverts the important dual purpose of subdomain testing: the component tester should be checking that a component's functional behavior is correct and using subdomains to help.

[9] Section 19.3.2 to follow explores this point in greater depth.

[10] Just as von Neumann is said to have thought that his first program could only fail because of hardware failure, so the system designer naturally blames components (her 'hardware instructions') instead of her design. Freed from this misconception, von Neumann and the designer look for the real bugs.

hand, a tool like Xcomp can be used to expose points at which the predictions were wrong.

.

19.3 Trusting Unit Tests

In I-CBSD, the operational difference between component- and system level is that component code is fully accessible to its developers. They are required to produce approximations in a form that system-design CAD tools can use[11], but can use a variety of other methods and claims to make their products attractive.

19.3.1 Trustworthy Component Testing

Using the SYN tools, approximate component descriptions have a creative, human-made part, consisting of subdomain definitions and a sampling plan; and, a mechanical, tool-made part, consisting of the test results expressed as an approximation (from COMP), with its functional graphs and deviations from the actual code behavior (from Xcute). The developer is required to publish (catalog) this information, which can be objectively evaluated by anyone thinking of acquiring the component. Comparing descriptions is easy: First, the graphs are examined to see if the output and run time are what's needed. If so, the approximation errors are checked, which includes an implicit judgment on the subdomains used. It is easy to see which of two competing components is the better.

A component developer cannot misrepresent the required catalog information except by bald-faced lying, which is called 'fraud' in the commercial marketplace. But it is permitted to tout a component's quality in additional ways. Its developer might brag that a process at CMM level 4 was used in development, or that it used a formal method for requirements analysis and proof, or that mutation testing was used, or cite a large user base with beta testing, etc. Should the developer indeed use these methods, they would be validated if they are truly helpful in creating the required objective description.

19.3.2 Matching Interface Profiles

When a system is assembled from components, it becomes possible to evaluate the unit testing those components received. If the subdomains in component descrip-

---

[11] For the SYN tools, they have to use COMP so that the system developer can use SYN.

tions were well chosen[12], the resulting subdomains in the system prediction will be adequate to handle its user profile. In I-CBSD, adjusting component approximations to better fit the system being synthesized is forbidden, but they can be evaluated for fit using the `profile` script, as follows:

> Let `Deep` be a component of system P. Run `profile Deep` after synthesizing predictions for P[13]. The `profile` graph is a histogram of subdomain usage in `Deep` at its interface within system P, if P were executed with a given operational profile (uniform by default). If the histogram is itself uniform, then `Deep` is being subjected within P to usage that matches its testing, since the unit-test measurements of `COMP` treat each `Deep` subdomain the same. However, if any `Deep` subdomain has a usage spike, then P is emphasizing that subdomain, and it would have been better to similarly emphasize it in unit test. A subdomain spike does not necessarily mean that `Deep` has been inadequately tested—that subdomain *was* covered in its component approximation—but it could have been better tested. When the `profile Deep` histogram is uniform, one knows that unit testing was as good as it could be.

> The system designer who distrusts `Deep`'s testing might decide to substitute another component `Deeper` for it in P. In selecting `Deeper`, one should look for better subdomains and more sampling in the region of the `profile Deep` spike.

The suggested evaluation is a good example of the way in which details of unit-test results should be carried forward to aid in system testing.

19.4 Comparing System Predictions to Requirements

In the simple, numerical-domain examples that appear in this monograph it is often possible to evaluate and use predictions made by the SYN tools even though those predictions are only approximate. In the very first example of the Introduction, Chapter 1, a chopping component and a Gaussian-function component were combined. The prediction of a chopped Gaussian (displayed in Fig. 1.3) seems to meet the system requirements; from the figure it is possible to estimate pretty accurately the width and spacing of the chopped interval, the Gaussian mean and standard deviation, etc. Of course, when the components have been purchased and the real system assembled, the properties that were close to right in the prediction should be checked. But this check is very unlike conventional system testing; it has more in common with the "smoke test" of a new electrical assembly: turn it on and if you

---

[12] Keep in mind that the component tester *cannot* make perfect choices in principle, since what are 'good' subdomains is not known until this particular system is designed and its user profile determined.

[13] Recall from Section 9.5 that `profile` does not require actual system execution, although its current implementation realizes this only for stateless components.

don't see smoke, it probably works. The design calculations carry the brunt of the proof that requirements will be met.

Software requirements are usually very precise and can be forbiddingly detailed. It might seem that they cannot be checked "approximately" because no matter how good the approximation, it will disagree with detailed requirements and the check will fail. But the hard part of system testing, what makes it such an intellectual challenge, is not accurate checking of a myriad of test results. Rather, system testing is hard because the larger purpose gets lost in the detail—all the results are exactly correct, but the tester is uncomfortable because their sum does not seem to add up to a system that can be trusted[14]. For example, consider a type of requirement common in control systems:

> If the temperature stays above 90° C for more than 5 sec, the pump shall go on and remain on until the temperature is below 75° C for at least 5 sec.

The hard part of testing this requirement is not the exact check for temperatures and times, but to be sure that there are no circumstances when an elevated temperature will not be dealt with. An approximate graph of pump activity as a function of inputs *and of system state* captures this larger intuitive requirement, and qualitatively shows the pump going on (and off!) as required. It is of less importance that the switch points in the approximation might not be exactly right—they can be checked later. Indeed, study of the approximate graphs can yield a list of detailed system tests that must be conducted with the real system.

Qualitative features of a system's behavior are often points of discontinuity. It is characteristic of subdomain-based approximations that they may miss discontinuities by smoothing across subdomain boundaries; however, they seldom create false discontinuities. In the pump example, the approximation may fail to predict the pump going on or off, but it does not fabricate a spurious activation. Thus an approximate prediction is usually conservative in the sense of being pessimistic: at worst a prediction may miss actions that the real system takes. If the qualitative behavior of a prediction appears correct, it can be trusted; if it appears wrong, the real system may have to be tested to see what really happens.

Anticipating the next chapter on non-functional properties, their subdomain-based approximations are typically more accurate than functional predictions. Furthermore, non-functional requirements are often imprecise, expressed as bounds rather than exact values. For example, run-time requirements are usually given as upper bounds on response time[15]. Even a relatively poor approximate prediction of system run time can be seen to meet such a bound, and if the prediction error can be bounded, the approximation may be all that is ever needed. In the worst case, an approximation can point to particular subdomains which are likely to be the worst performers, for detailed checks of actual system performance.

---

[14] It is a truism of statistical experiments that "approximately right is better than precisely wrong" (credited to J. W. Tukey).

[15] The analogy between mechanical/electrical descriptions in data sheets and software requirements is stronger for non-functional software properties, which can be expressed by a few parameter values. Chapter 20 to follow explores this situation in more detail.

Chapter 20
Functional vs. Non-functional Properties

T HE SYN tools used throughout this monograph measure (for components) and predict (for systems) two behaviors: output (usually called 'functional behavior') and run time (an example of a contrasting 'non-functional behavior'). As described in Chapter 14, the tools actually process as 'run time' an arbitrary secondary output from components and systems. The 'non-functional' behavior could be any property of interest, so long as there is a way to measure it at the component level and then to combine its component values into system values. For run time, measurement is straightforward using operating-system services and the series combination operator is addition, although concurrency introduces a bit of complication (Chapter 11). Throughout this chapter, run time continues to stand in for an arbitrary non-functional property. Reliability, which can be treated in much the same way as run time, is not at all straightforward and has its own Chapter 12.

Non-functional behaviors are the poor step-children of software requirements and development—they seldom receive proper attention. Capturing the functional requirements (and then implementing them faithfully!) are such demanding tasks for software that non-functional aspects are often relegated to afterthoughts. For run time, about the best that can be expected is a required upper bound on response, or in the case of large expected data sets, a requirement that for input of length n, the run time should increase no more quickly than by (say) $n \log n$. Requirements that prescribe the dependence of run time on state are rare indeed. If functional testing is seldom thoroughly done, non-functional testing may hardly be attempted, perhaps using only a few test points. Yet in principle, run time can be carefully subdomain tested along with functional behavior, as the SYN tools do.

20.1 Non-functional Depends on Functional

Composition in series is the fundamental operation by which components are combined. In series composition, test points fed to the first component reach the second component as outputs from the first. Thus the basic rule for composing run times

D. Hamlet, *Composing Software Components,* DOI 10.1007/978-1-4419-7148-7_20,
© Springer Science+Business Media, LLC 2010

is addition, but the value added from a second component in series arises from the first's output. Thus synthesis of non-functional behavior depends on synthesis of functional behavior. If a first-component's output is inaccurately approximated, a second-component's run time (as well as its output) in a series system will be wrong not only because it is itself an approximation, but also because it stems from the wrong input. The presence of component states literally adds an extra dimension to the dependence of run time on functional behavior. When a sequence of inputs is given to a first component in a series, its sequence of outputs depends on the resulting state sequence. The run time in a second component depends on those outputs, but also on a state sequence that results in the second component. Thus part of the run time predicted for a series system depends on four parameters and three of them are approximations. It is all too easy for one of the predicted states to drift away from its actual value, creating large errors in the predicted run time.

Yet in examples the SYN tools seem to do better at predicting run time than at predicting functional behavior. The explanation is simple: in the examples, run-time functions were not chosen to vary so widely as output functions, nor to align badly with subdomain boundaries. There is some justification for this choice, because variation in run times can only occur when code takes different branches. If the component tester has enough patience and time, subdomains can be chosen to correspond to execution paths; for each path subdomain the run time is a constant and the approximation is perfect[1]. In the examples chosen to stress the tools and subdomain-composition theory, it is the output functions that were made to behave badly. The chosen run-time functions may even compensate for inaccurate functional approximation because they change slowly from subdomain to subdomain. The tutorial in Chapter 9 provides one of several examples.

20.2 Non-functional 'Compositional' Properties

Intuitively, a non-functional property of software is 'compositional' if there is a simple rule for combining its component values into system values. This definition is somewhat vague because 'simple' is imprecise. It is simple to add run times in series, for example, but not so simple to adjust the input value for the second component in the series. Nevertheless, for some non-functional properties (and run time is the best example) it is intuitively clear that composite values come quantitatively from component values.

There are, however, clear cases of 'non-compositional' properties, usually called 'emergent' properties. For example, a property with a fixed, finite number of possible values cannot be compositional unless there are enough combinations to capture

---

[1] This insight about path behavior is due to Dave Mason [77]. Run times in a path subdomain are truly 'all the same', But only, of course, if all factors such as caching that affect performance in a modern computer are ignored. A more subtle point is that if paths are idealized, it would be fair to also idealize arithmetic instructions as of arbitrary precision, which would take more time for larger operands.

what happens in composition. In particular, a binary property V is often emergent. If there are two components each with V *false* that combine to make V *false*, yet another pair with V *false* that combine to make V *true*, there can be no rule for combination, simple or otherwise. 'Memory-leak-free' is an example of such an emergent binary property[2].

20.2.1 Run Time

For an executable program P, the run time is a function

$$T_P : D \times H \to \mathbb{R}$$

where D and H are the input and state domains of $\boxed{P}$. Unless P contains an indeterminate loop, it has a finite number of path subdomains and T_P is a step function, because for a given path the same set of P instructions is executed and the run time is the same no matter what value in $D \times H$ began that path. Thus for any set of subdomains that do not cross path boundaries, the approximation is perfect:

$$\ddddot{T_P} = T_P.$$

However, perfect run-time approximations do not necessarily combine into perfect run-time predictions for a system, since in a series construction the functional behavior of the first component is also involved in synthesizing the system run-time prediction.

In practice, a tester can use the SYN tools at the component level to obtain an apparently perfect run-time approximation function for component P, by examining the graphs and error analysis provided by Xcute and adjusting subdomains accordingly. The perfection may be false, only a consequence of lucky coincidence rather than isolating path subdomains, but in principle $\ddddot{T_P}$ is a better approximation to actual behavior than $\boxed{P}$. Furthermore, because the run-time range $\mathbb{R}$ *is* numeric, the most stringent assumption of the theory is always satisfied.

When a component tester adjusts a subdomain to reduce the measured error in functional value, it is improving the component's description of what values it supplies to other components. When a subdomain adjustment reduces the measured run-time error, the description of that component itself is better; other components are not involved.

20.2.2 Reliability

The SYN tools can substitute reliability measurements at the component level and reliability predictions at the system level for the similar run-time operations. Synthe-

---

[2] Paradoxically, Section 20.3.1 to follow demonstrates how the leak-free property can be synthesized algorithmically.

sis is accomplished by multiplying failure/success probabilities in place of adding run times. However, where run time is a straightforward software parameter, reliability most certainly is not, and Chapter 12 considers its many practical and theoretical difficulties. Where component measurements are concerned, the worst difficulty is that unless real failures are found, there is no way for component-level testing to provide feedback on the adequacy of the reliability-subdomain decomposition. If component C does not fail under test, there is no way to know if this means excellent reliability subdomains were used, or completely inadequate ones[3].

20.2.3 Safety Factors and Prediction Accuracy

It is characteristic of non-functional requirements that exact values may not be given. For run time, for example, the detailed behavior is seldom of interest. A set of requirements that prescribed the exact run-time function would be silly, because it would tie the hands of the developer to no purpose, perhaps forcing the insertion of busy-loops to waste time if the code was too efficient. A run-time requirement is more likely to be given as a bound. Thus non-functional software requirements look more like their mechanical analogs, e.g., "the beam shall not deflect more than 0.1 cm at its free end". The predictions of CAD tools like the SYN package are correspondingly more valuable. The maximum value predicted for run-time behavior can tell the designer whether or not a performance bound will be achieved. However, SYN predictions are only approximations, so their possible errors must be taken into account. To achieve a required system response time of under 100 ms, for example, a designer might insist on a prediction of better than 30 ms, a 'safety factor' of about 3. When an engineering discipline is young, safety factors are only guesses backed by (painful) experience. If the power supply fails when it was chosen to have twice the capacity of the predicted load, the next time it may be given five times the capacity prediction. A designer with wide experience acquires 'rules of thumb,' safety factors that have worked in the past. Bill Addis has investigated ancient building practices to identify the rules used in the construction of Greek temples, which were based on religious ideas of perfect ratios, adjusted to make the temples stand [2] (and some still do today).

As a discipline matures, however, it becomes possible to bring even safety factors within the realm of calculation. For the SYN tools, each component has an error analysis. Experiments such as the ones in Chapter 17 indicate that system prediction errors are roughly proportional to the average component error and the number of components. Hence in a system of seven components where their average measured run-time error is 3%, the predicted system run time might be off by a multiple of 21%[4]. Like almost all rules of engineering design, this one for estimating a safety

---

[3] The accuracy of the functional approximation $\lceil C \rceil$ is available as a quality metric, but the non-functional property is no help.

[4] If the proportionality constant is 1.5, the safety factor would be about 1.32. The engineer has not been born who will not use at least 2!

factor in meeting a run-time requirement is more precise than it is correct, as described in Section 20.3.3 to follow.

20.3 Predicting Emergent Properties

An intriguing paradox of mathematical proofs is that sometimes a result cannot be obtained by induction, yet induction can establish a generalization of the same result. By generalizing, the inductive hypothesis is strengthened enough for the proof to go through. Something similar occurs with some emergent properties R. R may be clearly non-compositional, yet another, more general property Q *is* compositional, and R can be obtained from Q. The definition of Section 20.2 is saved by noting that the composition rule for R is certainly not simple: it involves inventing Q and finding Q's composition rule, measuring not R but Q, and finally deducing R for a system from Q.

20.3.1 Memory Leaks

A component or system is *memory leak-free* iff the memory it holds at the end of any possible execution is the same as it held at the beginning of that execution[5]. It is obvious that if two leak-free components are combined, the resulting system is leak-free. But the property is emergent, because components that are not leak free can combine to be leak-free, but they also (usually) can combine into a leaky system. The former appears unlikely, yet for systems correctly comprised of a 'get-memory' component and a 'release-memory' component, neither of which is leak-free, the whole point of the design is to create a leak-free system.

Let R be the emergent leak-free property:

$$R(x) = \begin{cases} 1 \text{ if no leaks on input } x \\ 0 \text{ otherwise} \end{cases} .$$

A generalization Q of the leak-free property can be an address list of memory blocks changed. For simplicity, let components be stateless[6] and let $Q(x)$ be the list of address blocks obtained/released on input x. In this list a negative address means

---

[5] The intuitive sense of a 'leak' is that memory is obtained and never returned; the given definition prohibits this case, but also the case of returning memory that was not first obtained.

[6] When there is state, a component may very well use it remember memory addresses, permitting leaks in one execution to be corrected in another and vastly complicating R and Q. One paradigm that could be used for leak-free systems would then be to have each component keep track of its memory gain (releasing no memory) and at system termination invoke a clean-up component to release just the memory acquired. The complications in Q are no problem in principle, but for understanding it seems better to discuss the stateless case. Mixing state with leak detection places a very large premium on perfect detection of infeasible states because they may have 'leaks' that never actually occur.

memory released; a positive address is gained. Suppose that cancellations in the list have been removed[7]. Q is compositional. Intuitively, the Q composition rule for A and B in a series system U on system input x is to combine the lists $Q_A(x)$ and $Q_B(\boxed{A}(x))$ by removing element pairs of the same value but opposite sign. Then for a system U, $R_U(x) \equiv (Q_U(x) = \varnothing)$.

It would not be difficult to modify the SYN tools to measure and synthesize predictions of memory-address lists Q in place of run time, although this has not been attempted. Were this done, SYN synthesis could predict the leak-free non-functional property.

20.3.2 Security

Software 'security' is a catch-all term for any property that programs are required to protect, with the implication that there is reason for a malicious person to actively try to circumvent this protection. A typical example occurs in an on-line bank-teller program, which should protect accounts from access by anyone other than their owners, yet allow easy owner access. It has been rightly pointed out that in fact 'security' is not an isolated property like run time, because *any* aspect of software behavior might be exploited to compromise protection. Indeed, most successful security intrusions go around rather than through the intended security mechanism, exploiting an unrelated functional bug of some kind[8].

A memory leak as described in the previous section is one kind of security property—a leak could be used to deny service by crashing a system. Some other security mechanisms operate like memory allocation: for example, access permission is granted and withdrawn, and a violation can be like a leak—access is not withdrawn when it should have been. By defining generalization properties like user-keyed access tokens, the generalized property can be synthesized, and from it a security determination can be made. But the more interesting security situation is different. In it, the system obeys a correct security combination rule, and the components themselves may even be secure. Yet their synthesized combination is insecure. The composition theory behind the SYN tools provides a simple explanation for this behavior, and the tools can accurately approximate it. The security of a second component in series depends on the *functional* behavior of the first component as well as on the second's security behavior. Hence a mistake unrelated to

---

[7] It is assumed that the operating system does not permit list duplicates that signify obtaining or releasing the same block twice in a row.

[8] Here is a simple example: Suppose a bank-teller system has a 'verify-permission' component whose input is a user identification and a password, and which returns zero for failure, non-zero for success. Suppose the password is copied to a buffer for processing, and should that buffer overflow the run-time system returns an error code. Then a malicious user can identify herself with any account to be attacked and supply a super-long password that will overflow the buffer. The returned error code will look like a success return from the verify-permission component, giving the attacker access to an arbitrary account. (The exploited bug is the verify-permission programmer's failure to reject overlong passwords before using the buffer.)

security can have security consequences. In a SYN-like synthesis the mistake will be accurately represented in the predicted approximation, because it is present in the component approximations[9].

20.3.3 'Emergent' Prediction Error

It is plausible that the average prediction error in a system synthesis using the SYN tools will be roughly the sum of average testing-measurement error from each component involved, since each synthesis step passes on and could compound approximation errors in the previous step. The experiments of Chapter 17 bear out this predicted-error behavior. Average predicted error makes a good rule of thumb for calculating a safety factor, but unfortunately it's not really 'safe.' When a structural engineer uses a safety factor, he has continuity of the physical world on his side; the software engineer does not. Continuity validates averages, because when test points are near to each other, untested points between them must take values not too far from the average[10]. Discontinuous functions may behave arbitrarily badly between any two tested points, taking values wildly different from their average. Choosing test points closer and closer together almost always works for the structural engineer, soon bringing any variation within a reasonable safety factor; not so for software, where a discontinuity can occur when only the least-significant bit of some quantity changes. This too was demonstrated in Chapter 17, where shrinking a subdomain containing a discontinuity error only created a smaller subdomain with the same (or a larger) relative error. The last discontinuity straw on the camel's (software's) back is that discontinuities are an emergent property of the system—their locations cannot be predicted from independent component measurements.

To summarize the difference between safety factors for physical designs and safety factors for software: Both may be insufficient, but as component test points are brought closer together, a physical safety factor becomes accurate enough to really guarantee safety. For software, this may never happen, and no matter how many component tests are done and no matter how large a safety factor is chosen[11], actual behavior can deviate from prediction by too much. In the case of non-functional bound requirements like worst-case response time, this means that an engineer's best work can never be sufficient to guarantee performance. That software cannot

---

[9] In the buffer-overflow example of the previous footnote, instead of the functional measurement for the verify-permission component showing only isolated non-zero spikes at matching user-ID/password pairs, it will show a broad non-zero plateau across all user IDs for all long passwords. Of course, the component tester will not see this suspicious behavior unless passwords beyond the legal length are included in the component tests.

[10] Actually, continuity is not enough to guarantee this desirable behavior, although engineers often speak as if it were. What's really needed is that the functions involved be 'smooth,' in the sense of differentiable and the derivative bounded. Real-world properties are not always described by smooth functions, but it's the most common situation.

[11] Always excepting exhaustive testing, or a safety factor large enough to cover any possible result, neither of which is of any practical use.

be 'engineered' with trustable safety is a fact of life. Safety factors are valuable and calculating them imperfectly is better than ignoring prediction errors, but software development cannot in principle attain to the ideal of mechanical or structural engineering as they now exist. Instead, software will forever remain in the realm of immature engineering where inaccurate safety factors often save the day, but when there is an unanticipated failure, there may be no way to find the real root cause and do better next time[12].

---

[12] Perhaps it is little consolation to its owners that a building which collapsed in an earthquake was designed within its safety factors to withstand only smaller earthquakes. But it gives engineers some satisfaction to know that they did their job and the blame lies with the owners cutting corners on Mother Nature.

Chapter 21
Conclusion: Lessons Learned from I-CBSD

S IMPLIFYING the description of components and systems has enabled a detailed investigation of testing these software entities. A complete fundamental testing theory has been developed. Powerful tools have been implemented to support the theory. Working with the theory and experimenting with the tools has provided many insights about testing components and systems, which are summarized in this chapter.

21.1 Software Components are Unlike Mechanical Components

The natural mental picture of a 'component' is mechanical. Many physical parts are standardized and widely available, fasteners for one example, plumbing fittings for another. These parts can be completely described by simple diagrams and a few numerical values. In a large hardware store, parts will be laid out in bins and drawers, a kind of concrete catalog. Standardized parameters and tolerances are so well understood that they are usually not displayed: if the part looks right and has the right dimensions, it will usually do. A more-or-less complete range of fasteners requires on the order of 100,000 bins, a remarkably small number considering how comprehensive is the display. Non-standard mechanical parts are more varied and more difficult to describe, but an engineering drawing and a short table of parameter values usually suffices. The adequacy of descriptions is attested to by construction: a machinist could routinely make the part from its description. Most important, the manufacturing process for parts is well controlled, and their descriptions are trusted to be accurate.

Combining mechanical components is equally straightforward, and can be supported by CAD tools. Often a system is adequately described by its exploded view along with a parts list. Furthermore, the parameters of system description can be calculated from information about the parts and their connections. In all aspects of mechanics, it is continuity that allows a few descriptive measurements to suffice, and makes possible adequate safety factors in system calculations.

D. Hamlet, *Composing Software Components*, DOI 10.1007/978-1-4419-7148-7_21,
© Springer Science+Business Media, LLC 2010

Software components, like mechanical ones, are parts created to be assembled into systems, but the similarity does not go much farther than that. Software's discontinuous behavior may be the root of the difference (see the section to follow), but what is obviously different is software's complexity. A program's behavior is *not* described by a few numerical values. For comparison with 100,000 kinds of mechanical fasteners, take the PSTricks graphics package [96]. Its routines to place simple line drawings within TeX documents take floating-point parameters, but in most documents it would do as well to have about 1/8" gradations in a range of about 10". That is, it would be enough to draw (say) circles whose radii are 1/8", 1/4", ..., 9-7/8", 10", a total of 80 possibilities. There are roughly 75 different named routines[1]; they average more than three arguments each. In addition to explicit arguments, PSTricks behavior is altered by about 20 'graphics parameters' like color or line thickness; on average there are more than three independent values for each. Thus the number of PSTricks possibilities is greater than about $75 \times 80^3 \times 3^{20} > 10^{16}$, one hundred billion times more than the number of fasteners. Another way to put this is that simple graphics objects are a hundred billion times more complex than common fasteners.

One school of thought lauds this complexity, which allows software to attempt things never imagined with mechanical devices[2]. Another school eschews software complexity, but eliminating it is not easy: when a program is *supposed* to behave simply it may not. Certifying simplicity is at least as difficult as certifying baroque functionality, because it means demonstrating what the program does *not* do. No matter what software developers intend, their components behave in ways that require elaborate description, and there are no accepted standards for expressing or certifying a description.

Software systems also have complex behavior, even when their components are combined in less varied ways than in mechanical systems. To calculate how a system will behave, its complex parts require complex combinatorial rules. The SYN tools simplify things enormously in order to make these calculations; in practical CBSD development, there are no comparable tools.

21.2 Software Functions Are Inherently Discontinuous

Only about 40 years ago, digital encoding was the rich uncle of the signal-processing family. Quantizing signals and transforming the discrete samples was understood and worked perfectly in principle, but in practice the electronics was too slow, noisy, and expensive to compete with traditional analog methods. For example, a Fourier

---

[1] Omitting those like `pspicture` and `pscustom` which combine arbitrary other routines.

[2] For example, when mechanical/electronic devices to monitor nuclear reactor safety are replaced by software controls, it is possible for the new controllers to adjust the neutron flux so that the reactor runs closer to criticality and hence more efficiently. With the old mechanical controls, it was not safe to include more than a go/no-go functionality; critics say it is even less safe with software.

transform that required an hour to compute digitally[3] could be done in less than a minute by an analog harmonic analyzer; the digital computation required a million-dollar computer, while the analyzer cost about $20K. Today, semiconductors fabricated in the small have solved the problem of noise and made digital electronics fast and cheap. Although analog circuits can also be better built today than 40 years ago, the market for computer chips has made it convenient to use them for almost every purpose.

Digital circuits are discontinuous as a consequence of their quantized numerical storage. Ultimately, there is nothing between the 0 and 1 states of a flip-flop. In software implementing numerical algorithms, the consequent round-off errors matter a great deal. However, for less sensitive applications, the underlying hardware discontinuity can be ignored. For example, in process-control applications sensors measure physical quantities like temperature, which are given a discrete representation by an analog-to-digital converter. The resulting values have limited precision and constitute a discontinuous space. But no one cares. The process-control software compares temperature values in its algorithms, and a C conditional statement like

```
if (T > 90.0) { #too high, close valve ...
```
is insensitive to the small quantization error in the floating-point values. Unfortunately, software introduces its own high-level discontinuities, and conditional statements are the culprits.

When a mathematician defines a function by cases, it is usual to be careful about the boundary values. A smooth transition can be arranged and this is often natural and desirable. If the cases agree at their boundary, it is immaterial which case actually includes the boundary value. Programmers are seldom so careful. Definition by cases is their bread and butter, but boundary agreement is not. In the temperature example above, the program's behavior on one side of the boundary T == 90.0 is probably completely different from on the other side. To give just a trivial example, later writing

```
if (T < 90.0) { #still cool, continue ...
```
by mistake (T <= 90.0 is the right complementary test) could lead to a catastrophic failure. The fault does not lie with the slightly inaccurate floating-point values, but with the way they are examined.

The component Chopper used in the Introduction (Fig. 1.1) introduces discontinuities in a typical way: Chopper's code tests the input value, and periodically inserts a zero-output value. Not only is there no concern for agreement at the boundaries; disagreement there is the whole point. It is possible to replace a component that has internal conditional-created discontinuities with a system using a conditional component[4], but this merely displaces the discontinuous boundary into the conditional component.

---

[3] The fastest digital algorithm known used convolution; the FFT might have leveled the playing field.

[4] For Chopper, the conditional component would make the test and select either an identity component or a zero component.

21.2.1 Simple Component Behaviors Lead to Complicated System Behaviors

At a glance, every synthesis experiment conducted with the SYN tools displays system behaviors that are surprisingly complicated. Quite simple variations in component behavior replicate into convoluted system properties, for which component discontinuities are often to blame.

The tester must pay attention to component discontinuities. Indeed, case boundaries are the foundation of general test-coverage methods called 'boundary-value analysis,' in particular 'domain testing' [100]. Some of the most revealing mutations replace a relational operator with other relational possibilities [26, $\prec A \succ$][65]. In every example using the SYN tools, it was seen that subdomain boundaries must match points of discontinuity in order to get good component approximations. Thus it was an unpleasant surprise to observe in synthesis experiments that accurate component approximation does not always lead to accurate system-synthesis predictions. Once again, discontinuities are to blame.

When component C_1 is placed in series with C_2, how do their discontinuities contribute to the composed behavior[5]? For C_1 things are straightforward. If it has a discontinuity at input x_d, the system will also have one at input x_d[6]. C_1 maps inputs on either side of x_d to different values, hence the system discontinuity may be larger or smaller depending on what C_2 does with these values. Let $\Delta x > 0$. The size of system discontinuity is:

$$\lim_{\Delta x \to 0} \left| \boxed{C_2}(\boxed{C_1}(x_d + \Delta x)) - \boxed{C_2}(\boxed{C_1}(x_d - \Delta x)) \right|.$$

Since subdomains for the SYN tools system prediction are exactly the C_1 subdomains, aligning them with the C_1 discontinuity will result in system alignment. That is, good measurements of C_1 in isolation break the domain into the right pieces for system approximation. It is C_2's discontinuities that go wrong.

Let C_2 have a discontinuity at input y_d and $x_d' = \boxed{C_1}^{-1}(y_d)$[7]. A system discontinuity thus appears at x_d'. It is almost certain that x_d' falls strictly inside a C_1 subdomain, because when C_1 was approximated x_d' was in no way special—only the y_d discontinuity of C_2 makes x_d' of interest. Hence on the system subdomain containing x_d' (the same as the C_1 subdomain) the prediction must be constant, and therefore cannot agree with the discontinuous actual behavior. The larger the size of the actual system discontinuity, the larger the r-m-s prediction error. If the components' approximations are improved by refining their subdomains, it will not reduce the relative r-m-s prediction error in the subdomain containing x_d' unless by chance it falls on the refined boundary.

---

[5] The analysis to follow assumes the step-function approximation to stateless components. Other, more complicated cases are mostly THTC.

[6] Except in one unlikely case; see following discussion.

[7] Nothing very interesting occurs if $\boxed{C_1}^{-1}$ is not defined at y_d because of a C_1 discontinuity. The interval around y_d just has to be carefully examined, avoiding the point itself.

A discontinuity is the limiting case of a rapid change in behavior, so it might be expected that large but continuous variations in C_2 functional values would cause similar difficulties[8], and so they do. In a C_2 subdomain where there is rapid change, the actual system behavior for points that reach this subdomain through C_1 is also rapidly varying, but is calculated to be constant. It does not help to refine the C_2 subdomains in the changing region; what is required is to refine the C_1 subdomains that map there. But when C_1 is being approximated, there is no clue that this is needed. As C_1 subdomains are refined the system r-m-s prediction errors do decrease, just more slowly near points that map into the C_2 region of rapid change.

21.3 Testing Theory is Unlike Other Formal Methods

As a name for descriptions and analysis of software based on mathematical logic, 'formal methods' leaves a lot to be desired. The name doesn't mention logic, and 'formal' is not a universally understood code word for 'mathematical proof.' A software engineer can be forgiven for thinking that a Fagan code inspection [24] is a 'formal method.' It would almost be better to return to an earlier name, 'program proving.' A case in point is that program testing is often put up as an opposite of proof techniques, so perforce testing is not a formal method[9]. But the mathematical testing theory and its application to component composition presented here is formal (i.e., mathematical), though it lacks the subtext of proof. To paraphrase Dijkstra, testing doesn't prove anything.

The name 'formal methods' won't be used in the remainder of this section; 'testing' will be contrasted with 'proving.'

21.3.1 Conservative Reductions

One powerful trick for proving properties of a program is to alter it, show that the alteration preserves properties of interest, then carry out the proof on the altered program. Because this works best when the alteration is a simplification, it is called "reduction," and when properties are preserved, "conservative reduction." Loop unwinding, which was used to analyze iteration in Section 8.3.3, is an example of conservative reduction[10].

---

[8] In the piecewise-linear approximation things go wrong only if the wide variation is itself not linear.

[9] Bill Howden, when checking if a microphone was on, used to tap it and say: "Formal-methods 1-2-3...Formal-methods 1-2-3...".

[10] It is usual to take blackbox (functional) behavior of the program as the implicit property to be preserved. The proof that a reduced program is 'equivalent' is a proof of functional equality. Of course, other properties might *not* be preserved. Loop unwinding, for example, preserves neither run time nor state behavior.

Reduction can be considered for testing in two senses: A program might be reduced so that the results of a given testset are not changed; or, a testset might be reduced yet preserve (say) test coverage for the same program. Both of these are used in program 'trouble reports.' A person who encounters failure is encouraged to find and report the simplest case (testset) that fails; it is also helpful to eliminate parts of the program as surely not involved—failure still occurs if they are removed[11]. Any conservative reduction in the sense of functional proof will also preserve all functional test results, but most test-result-preserving reductions are not conservative in the proof sense[12]. Since a test provides no functional information except its finite-support function, other points of the domain could go wrong.

21.3.2 Special Role of Persistent State

Functional-semantics proof theories like those of Floyd, Hoare, and Mills do not include an explicit treatment of program persistent state. In principle, they associate with each identifier of an imperative program a mathematical variable, and describe the relationship between these variables that execution of the program establishes. Program analysis consists of proofs that some particular relationship of interest holds. For example, it might be proved that two identifiers X and Y in a program always hold the same values x and y, by proving $x = y$ in the theory[13]. By singling out special variables for input, variables whose values a program does not change, the proof theories can express statements about program functionality. In the example, if x is an input value, then proving $y = x$ means that as a function of x, y is identity.

A similar device could be used to prove statements about persistent state. Let identifier S be taken as the state, treated as a global in the program so that its value s exists at the start of execution. At the end of execution, any valid relationship among s and other variables related to program identifiers (including s's own initial value) might be proved in the theory. Using this machinery, statements about sequences of inputs can be proved. For example, suppose a program has input variable x, and that in the theory $s' = 2x + s$ is proved[14] along with a proof about some other variable of

---

[11] Program slicing, another powerful transformational technique, is a way of cutting out unnecessary syntax. It was first presented as a debugging method [99].

[12] Mutation testing provides a strange exception: certain mutation-adequate testsets 'determine' a program that passes them. There is a canonical program whose statements can be deduced from the test values; any other program passing the test must agree with the canonical one not just on the determining testset, but over the whole input domain [38]. Hence a transformation to this canonical program, preserving the determining-testset results, is conservative in the proof sense. The canonical program may be completely different from the original; it is a property of the testset.

[13] Perhaps the semantics of an assignment statement like Y := X in the program figures prominently in the proof.

[14] Using the convention that s is an initial- and s' a final value for state identifier S.

interest (say) $z = sx$. Take a 'reset' value of s to be 0^{15}. Then for a sequence of input values x_1, x_2, x_3 starting from reset, it will be possible to prove[16] $z = (2x_1 + 2x_2)x_3$. The theory does not treat S and its values in any special way, but a person chooses to use it to describe state.

The proof theories can be used to establish general principles regarding state, which were previously treated informally.

Unwinding loops fails with state. The unwinding equivalence (Section 8.3.3) used for stateless components does not hold in the presence of state, as described in the last part of Section 10.1.1. The proof makes use of any conditional (like the example above) in which the state changes on each execution: the unwound loop will then have one state change too many and hence disagree with the iteration.

State values are not inputs. Treating state values as inputs is wrong in principle as described in Section 10.2.2. This proof uses a program P_0 that never sets its state variable, but whose results do depend on the state-variable value. (The 'dome' component used in Section 10.2.2 will do for P_0.) Use the proof theory to derive a formula $f_0(x, s)$ for the functional dependence of some property on (input $\times$ state) (Fig. 10.2 graphs this function of two variables for run time in the example). Choose a particular state value s_1 that is not the reset value s_0 ($s_0 = 0$ in the example). $f_0(x, s_1)$ is defined for all x. (In Fig. 10.2, its graph is a slice through the dome parallel to the $x - z$-plane.) Then derive a formula for the result state on input x starting at reset: $g_0(x, s_0)$. In the example, because P_0 never sets its state variable, $g_0(x, s_0) = s_0$ can be proved for all x. Hence g_0 is constant, the reset state never changes, and $f_0(x, s_1)$ is not defined for any x. (In the example of Section 10.2.2, Figure 10.3 shows where f_0 is really defined.)

Floyd-Hoare proof theory is essentially relational—the theorems that can be proved about a program relate the values of arbitrary variables corresponding to its identifiers. In contrast, testing theory is inherently functional, distinguishing particular program 'input' and 'output' identifiers and expressing values of the latter in terms of the former. To capture persistent-state behavior of a program P without falling into a general relational theory, the extension of Mills's formalism in Chapter 10 defines a state mapping $\left(P \right)$ to parallel the blackbox behavior $\boxed{P}$.

21.4 The Several Meanings of 'Compositional'

CBSD, and I-CBSD presented here, start with the idea that component properties can be combined algorithmically to predict system properties. Reliability was the initial property of interest[17]—this is expressed by saying that reliability is 'com-

---

[15] There are many ways to handle state conventions. The example uses the simplest imaginable without explanation.

[16] And for input sequence $x_1, x_2, ..., x_n$, $z = 2x_n \sum_{i=1}^{n-1} x_i$.

[17] Chapter 12 shows that its theory is difficult.

positional.' Run time is clearly a compositional property. Chapter 20 investigates 'emergent' properties with the opposite character, and shows that some can be predicted in a roundabout way but others in principle cannot be deduced from independently determined component properties.

21.4.1 Compositional Properties

In a functional semantics for programs (Chapter 6) the composition of properties is elegantly captured by mathematical functional composition. However, the semantic functions themselves cannot be obtained algorithmically—finding the meaning of a program from its syntax is an undecidable problem[18]. But there is an additional practical problem in expressing functional meanings. The closed forms of semantic functions become more and more convoluted as meaning is built up from the statement level, so that even if in principle they are algorithmically defined, they may not be tractable for a particular program. Similarly, to compose two functions expressed in an intractable form may not be useful. Program testing, while it does no better with termination[19], does not suffer from the practical intractability of functional semantics. Once termination is assured, any program can be tested blindly, and even termination can be investigated without mental gymnastics—one can always try a test and wait awhile to see if there is a result. But testing does not compose (Section 8.1); independent testsets run on two components will not match at their interface if put in series. It is almost the same thing to say that testing does not *de*compose: a test of a series system, when execution reaches the interface between the components, will not pass values that match independent tests conducted for the second component.

21.4.2 Testing Can Be Made Compositional

The subdomain-based testing theory presented in Chapter 8 and extended in Chapters 10 and 11 solves the problem of matching test points in the middle of a series system by factoring component domains into 'the same' subdomain classes[20]. Func-

---

[18] In the Floyd/Hoare and Mills formalisms, the non-algorithmic difficulties arise in assigning meaning to iterative (or recursive) program elements. For Hoare's logic the non-effective step is finding a loop assertion. Loop/recursion termination poses a slightly different difficulty: the semantic function for an infinite loop is just the undefined function, but it is an unsolvable problem (Turing's halting problem) to decide if the undefined function is in fact a program's meaning.

[19] The halting problem for a single input point is as unsolvable as the general problem.

[20] If the subdomains were equivalence classes, then this would be like factoring an algebraic structure over a partition relation. Properties could be defined on the space of classes, with any member of the class serving as a representative. That subdomains are not equivalence classes is shown by the factored relation's properties' failure to be well-defined: taking different points as representative gives different results.

tional composition, the fundamental rule for series connection of components, can thus be approximated as subdomain-test composition. Any other (non-functional) compositional property of components defined by their inputs can also be approximated. Its compositional rule is applied subdomain-by-subdomain, but the correct input values for the second component in a series must be obtained from the functional (approximate) output from the first component. The non-functional testing calculation thus includes a triple approximation: the first-component functional value is averaged across an input subdomain, then this average value selects (perhaps incorrectly) another average (of the non-functional property) for the second component to combine with the average from the first component.

Whether or not the approximate test-based compositions are accurate depends on the subdomains used to test the components. Intuitively, as those subdomains are refined and matched to discontinuities and parts of the domain where rapid change occurs, the measured component approximations can be made arbitrarily accurate. The prediction accuracy for any system assembled from those components also then improves overall, but as an emergent property of the system it cannot always be completely controlled (Chapter 17).

21.5 Simple Tools are Remarkably Powerful

As they were originally conceived, the algorithms for synthesizing system properties from the measurement of components were applicable to just two stateless components in a series composition. The SYN tool package supporting a complete I-CBSD method evolved from this seed, each additional feature something of a surprise. The larger surprise is that tool development almost never ran into the barriers that usually arise in restricted cases. Usually, elaboration of a simple model quickly closes on itself. Nothing more can be implemented without relaxing the model's assumptions. Not so for the SYN tools: the only limitation seemed to be conceptual. When a feature could be imagined, it could be added without much difficulty.

The best example of serendipity in SYN tool development is the way in which approximation tables produced by COMP were converted to executable code, as described in Section 14.3. The germ of this idea arose naturally: the obvious way to check the tables was to compare them to actual executions. Turning a table into code is trivial—place the table in a wrapper that reads an input and returns an output looked up in the table. To then apply every feature of the tools to this table-lookup code was also trivial—the name of the wrapped code was substituted for the code-file name. In particular, whole systems could be synthesized from table-lookup code, and these were crucial in validating the synthesis algorithms, as explained in Section 14.3.1.

Other examples of serendipitous tool features:

Incremental algorithms. Regression testing—applying existing testsets to code that has been changed—is an area of research that seems promising, but results have been disappointing. The caliber of what has been learned is: A structural test of a path on which no code has changed need not be repeated. The reverse—applying a changed testset to unchanged code—has been studied only as an efficiency issue[21]. For the SYN tools, there is a common situation in which the testset changes but the code does not: In component testing, the error analysis supplied by Xcute shows that subdomain(s) are badly placed or sized, so the subdomain breakdown in a .ccf file is altered. It is obvious that only changed subdomains need be retested; the approximating values in the others are unchanged. This is an ideal incremental-algorithm situation, and apart from bookkeeping to keep track of what has and has not changed, it was trivial to add incremental processing to the tools (Section 9.6).

Concurrent components. The simple form of concurrency described in Chapter 11 was devised only to have a functional description, not to necessarily fit easily into tools. Yet its two-dimensional character so closely matches the data structures used to capture the two dimensions of persistent state that the implementation was easy.

Piecewise-linear approximations. At first it appeared that a piecewise-linear option for approximating component behavior was an easy addition to the existing step-function measurements. And indeed making the measurement and calculating from component fitted lines a predicted system line, was completely straightforward. However, the piecewise-linear component subdomains compose to form altered system subdomains (Section 9.4.2) and discovering the new floating-point end points turned out to be a touchy numerical problem that is only partially resolved. A better implementation should probably use an extended precision package, but this has not been attempted.

In another sense, the simple SYN model has strongly resisted extension. The tools' power and ease of implementation seems to stem from simplicity, which opens no path to applying their algorithms to more realistic components and systems. Adding state to components (Chapter 10) was by far the most difficult change to the SYN tools, and it appeared to be not so much an addition as a complete redesign. Worse, the addition of state cross-cut other features of the tools, which had to be painfully modified or implemented from scratch. For example, the measurement of internal interface profiles (Section 9.5) is quite different with state; profiles for systems with state are measured by conventional run-time instrumentation, not calculated.

It is sometimes frustrating to work within limitations of the SYN tools, but only in devising examples to try. Once started, each experiment reinforces the original premise: Unit testing works, and works better with proper tool support. When all difficulties at the component level are resolved, system testing can focus on problems of the overall design only, and much of it can be carried out with approximate

---

[21] The usual methodology is to assume the validity of some structural coverage method, and to eliminate as unnecessary test points that provide only redundant coverage. Since structural coverage is itself hard to justify (See Section 7.2.2), this is not a promising research plan. It may very well be that structural coverage works for accidental, hidden reasons, and that 'redundant' points are the very ones that made it work.

predictions, not actual executions. Never is the software developer put in the position of testing from scratch a system whose code is an incomprehensible monolith. There are substantial research problems raised in extending these benefits to more practical cases, but those problems are worth working on because they are at the heart of software testing.

Chapter 22
Open Problems

D EVELOPMENT of the SYN tools took place sporadically over about ten years. It was decided at the outset that the tools would be used as an existence proof for carrying out explicit measurements and calculations in full detail. In turn this goal dictated that some fundamental questions were not allowed to interfere with realizing working tools. Instead of wandering off into theory-land, the research made restrictive assumptions so that implementation could proceed. The result is tools that realize their full potential in the restricted case, but dodge important issues. The research decisions were good ones in the sense of making narrow progress; it is a truism of experimental, tool-based research that if one first solves difficult theoretical problems, there will probably be no tools or experiments. The problems that have not been tackled are long-standing ones in the general theory of testing.

22.1 Subdomain Testing in Non-numeric Domains

Testing theoreticians[1] have not been quick to extend their understanding to programs with state and concurrence[2], but have also been content to make the more basic assumption that program input domains are numerical, and hence ordered and dense. Subdomains can be defined easily enough for non-numeric domains, but their structure and sampling are hard to understand. Random sampling makes no practical non-numeric sense, and neither does equi-spaced systematic sampling. The space of strings over a finite alphabet is a concrete example that exhibits the difficulties. A program that processes strings usually treats most of them as illegal—a compiler is a good example that first checks the syntax of its input-program string. A

---

[1] All five of them? Or is it three?

[2] In this monograph, Chapters 10 and 11 extend the functional testing theory of Goodenough and Gerhart [34, $\prec A \succ$] and Howden [64, $\prec A \succ$]. However, extended functional testing theory may not be a small step in the right direction, as hoped for in Chapter 6, but a dead end that intrinsically cannot explain realistic program input spaces.

D. Hamlet, *Composing Software Components,* DOI 10.1007/978-1-4419-7148-7_22,
© Springer Science+Business Media, LLC 2010

substantial part of an algorithm may be devoted to illegal-string checking, which requires testing. But by definition illegal strings have no structure to capture with subdomains. Which of them are 'the same'? And even after attention is confined to 'legal' strings, subdomains are not helpful in testing. For a compiler, for example, 'assignment statements' might be a good subdomain, but how can it be sampled, how subdivided, and then subdivided again?

A good fundamental question to raise is a practical definition of random testing for a non-numeric domain like strings. It's not that the concept of 'random string' cannot be defined, but that the space is so large that no definition can be used in practical testing. A test composed of 'random strings' by any definition would not achieve functional coverage by anyone's standards—think of the compiler example. Falling back on structural coverage is a bit better—maybe a test point that falls in 'assignment statement' could be found by looking at a compiler's code. But what are the other points of such a subdomain, and how would testing coverage be judged? What is a 'random assignment statement'?

There is a starting point for investigation in the component-approximation theory: However subdomains are defined, on whatever domain, taking a single test point in each subdomain defines a step function on which the SYN synthesis algorithms can be used. In the limit as subdomains approach singleton sets a synthesis would be perfect. But there is no reason to believe it would be accurate away from the limit, and no way to reasonably refine the huge subdomains that are natural to a data type like 'string'.

22.2 Completing a Testing Theory including State

Among the welter of programming details needed to add local-state capability to tools that were originally for a stateless model, little consideration was given to the fundamental question of whether two-dimensional (input × state) subdomains are really the right way to capture the testing of component state values. A deeper investigation might produce a theory with fewer warts, but this is certainly THTC now.

22.2.1 Reliability in the Presence of State

Reliability is one idea that doesn't fit well with state subdomains chosen *a priori*, because the tester does not control the distribution of values that fall into them. If there is a notion of state-dependent reliability, it would not seem to be sampled as the SYN tools do. See Section 12.2.3 for more speculation on this topic.

22.2.2 Better SYN *Tools for State*

In retrospect, it was a mistake to model component local state as a single floating-point value. The precision was not needed in most examples, and for capturing discrete modes was counterproductive. It would have been better to have integer, or even discrete-character state values. The one case where continuous numerical values are needed—investigating a loop whose termination test is for convergence—foundered for other reasons (Section 18.4).

In several examples two parts of a mode were needed, which could be modeled by using the value and its sign, but not very naturally (for example, in Section 18.3.3). The difficulty of using the sign as a flag showed itself in a proliferation of subdomains to span the space $[-M, +M)$ instead of just near one end. Most subdomains in the middle were not meaningful, and added to the explosion in multiple dimensions. Things would have been better with states that were (say) a pair of integers. The original thought that when multiple values were needed they could be coded into one value, did not consider the gaps this would create in the state space and the subdomains to span them. However, the two-dimensional profusion of (input × state) subdomains is a real phenomenon that can be mitigated but not eliminated.

22.3 Limited Input Domain

Although in the examples throughout this monograph there was little difficulty in choosing finite domains on which to approximate each component[3], in general it will not be possible to synthesize a system when its components' sample domains have been chosen independently. The individual domains may do a good job of capturing the behaviors, but for synthesis one component cannot follow another unless the range of the first is a subset of the domain of the second. It is usually possible to achieve a system match with glue code that restricts the domain or range of the first component. What is not allowed under I-CBSD is to expand the arbitrarily chosen input domain of a second component. That would require retesting for a wider approximation, which would violate the immutable-components restriction. It does not seem a serious violation, however. It's not as if the component were being modified to make the system work; the adjustment is just in the scope of its finite description. To allow a system developer to add or modify subdomains or their sampling (that is, to supply .ccf files) would not require access to component code sources, or even unrestricted access to real executable code. In the SYN tools, the system developer would merely need the ability to run COMP, which could be arranged safely.

The strict separation of component- and system development that defines I-CBSD could be relaxed to allow domain/range adjustments, but it's a slippery slope. Once a system designer gets into the component-testing business, the idea of quality unit testing by component experts could be lost. Tools could help by (for example)

---

[3] The exception is the loop experiment in Section 18.4.

insisting that the approximation errors in any new subdomains be no worse than the originals that came from the component developer. System-driven retesting would solve other I-CBSD difficulties, too. It could be used to force profile matches at system interfaces as described in Section 19.3.2, or to improve system reliability by increasing sampling in critical component subdomains (Section 18.5). These transgressions against I-CBSD could be made unexceptionable if the tools require any retesting to be at least as extensive as the original.

References

Many of these citations are just that: giving credit where it is due, justifying by authority, or pointing to a source of information about a topic that is not fully explored in this monograph.

Annotations are provided for papers that have some special claim, sometimes to explain or excuse them, but most often because they deserve to be read in the original—the annotation is a kind of advertisement and testimonial. Citations for annotated items are marked with the symbol "$\prec A \succ$".

1. Adams, E.N.: Optimizing preventive service of software products. IBM J. Research and Development **28**, 2–14 (1984)
2. Addis, W.: Structural Engineering: The Nature of Theory and Design. Ellis Horwood (1991)
   Although Addis's book is out of print, it is well worth seeking in the library. He holds joint degrees in civil engineering and philosophy and is one of only a handful of writers on 'philosophy of engineering.' His historical studies of structural engineering are rich and detailed. This book is the only one I know that tries to explain what 'engineering theory' is and how it relates to practice. He makes a strong case that for an engineer, 'theory' is the same as 'design rules,' the codified ways that design is to be carried out. The fascinating insight Addis proposes is that good design rules are not necessarily in agreement with reality. If they can be followed easily and include adequate safety factors from past experience, they can be quite at odds with physical laws yet remain in successful use for years, or even centuries. Lorenzo Strigini first put me onto the book.
3. Addis, W.: Creativity and Innovation: The Structural Engineer's Contribution to Design. Architectural Press (2001)
4. Allen, R., Garlan, D.: A formal basis for architectural connection. ACM Trans. on Softw. Eng. Methodology **6**, 213–249 (1997)
5. Allen, S.F., Constable, R.L., Eaton, R., Kreitz, C., Lorigo, L.: The NUPRL open logical environment. In: Proceedings 17th International Conference on Automated Deduction, LNAI 1831, pp. 170–176. Springer Verlag (2000)
6. Antoy, S., Hamlet, R.G.: Automatically checking an implementation against its formal specification. IEEE Trans. on Softw. Eng. **26**, 55–69 (2000)
   The implementations of this paper are abstract data types written in C++ and the formalism is that of algebraic equations suitably restricted to eliminate difficulties like non-confluence. Its major contribution is Antoy's idea that the abstraction/representation mapping relating the concrete implementation of a data type to its abstract mathematical structure should be explicitly made part of the implementation. This allows random testing to be completely automated, thus extending the ideas of DAISTS [30] and Mills [29]. The example used for

illustratation exposes the weakness of random testing in the presence of state that it may fail to use enough long sequences.

7. Basili, V., Turner, A.: Iterative enhancement: A practical technique for software development. IEEE Trans. on Softw. Eng. 1(4), 390–396 (1975)
8. Boehm, B.W.: Software engineering. IEEE Trans. on Computers pp. 1226–1241 (1976)
9. Boehm, B.W.: A spiral model of software development and enhancement. IEEE Computer pp. 61–72 (1988)
10. Boehm, C., Jacopini, G.: Flow diagrams, Turing machines, and languages with only two formation rules. Comm. of the ACM 9, 366–371 (1966)
11. Boland, P., Singh, H., Cukik, B.: Comparing partition and random testing via majorization and schur functions. IEEE Trans. on Softw. Eng. 29, 88–94 (2003)
12. Bolton, F.: Pure Corba. Sams (2001)
13. Butler, R.W., Finelli, G.B.: The infeasibility of experimental quantification of life-critical software reliability. IEEE Trans. on Softw. Eng. 19(1), 3–12 (1993)

   The clear conclusion of this well-thought-out paper is that 'ultrareliability,' that is, failure rates below about 10^{-8}/run, cannot be investigated using testing. The number of test points required to obtain confidence in ultrareliabilty is too large to be practical, even under the best possible circumstances. The roughly 10^7 seconds in a work-year are not enough to conduct the roughly 10^9 necessary test runs. The paper considers a number of ingenious ways to try to get around this stubborn fact, and shows that each must fail. The technical device used to obtain results is hypothesis testing, which makes the derivations more forbidding than need be. Most of the results could be obtained with less statistical machinery using failure-rate bounds and upper confidence bounds as in Chapter 12.

14. Chen, T.Y., Leung, H., Mak, I.K.: Adaptive random testing. In: Proceedings of the 9th Asian Computing Science Conference, Lecture Notes in Computer Science, vol. 3321, pp. 320–329. Springer-Verlag (2004)
15. Chen, T.Y., Merkel, R.: An upper bound on software testing effectiveness. IEEE Trans. on Softw. Eng. (2008). (to appear)
16. Chen, T.Y., Tse, T.H., Zhou, Z.: Semi-proving: an integrated method based on global symbolic evaluation and metamorphic testing. SIGSOFT Softw. Eng. Notes 27(4), 191–195 (2002)
17. Cobb, R.H., Mills, H.D.: Engineering software under statistical quality control. IEEE Software pp. 44–54 (1990)

   Although some of the mathematics is garbled in the printed version, this paper makes a good case for prioritizing software failures for attention by frequency of occurrence. The paper popularizes very original work by Adams [1] in which he suggests that many failures are simply not worth fixing—they will probably never occur again. My own experience with operating-system crashes agrees: Bug after bug is fixed, often with great difficulty, but the failure rate of the system hardly improves because there is a large supply of very low-frequency failures.

18. Cohen, D.M., Dalal, S.R., Fredman, M.L., Patton, G.C.: The aetg system: An approach to testing based on combinatorial design. IEEE Trans. on Softw. Eng. 23(7), 437–444 (1997)
19. Cook, S.A., Reckhow, R.A.: Time-bounded random access machines. Journal of Computer Systems Science 7, 354–375 (1973)
20. Davis, M.: The Undecidable. Raven Press (1965)

   Davis has collected the papers of Gödel, Church, Turing, and Post written in the 1930s, which define the idea of mechanical or 'rote' computation, and explore its limits. Certainly these papers are among the most important and difficult in the history of mathematical logic. It is impossible to be sure of the effect this work had on the development of electronic computers in the following decade. It certainly did not suggest how real machines should be built— von Neumann's design is nothing like a Turing machine or a Post system, closer in fact to Babbage's mechanical engine—but the idea that from the simplest operations all possible computations can be built may have been important.

21. DeMillo, R.A., Lipton, R.J., Sayward, F.G.: Hints on test data selection: Help for the practicing programmer. Computer **11**, 34–41 (1978)
22. Duran, J., Ntafos, S.: An evaluation of random testing. IEEE Trans. on Softw. Eng. **10**, 438–444 (1984)

   Joe Duran was an early and tireless advocate of random testing, whose insights are well expressed in this paper. Its contribution was a way of analyzing subdomain testing (called "partition testing" in this and other papers) by simulating its distributions. It is not an exaggeration to say that this paper opened up a new area, generating many similar publications (some say too many), e.g., [55, 11]. The most recent development comes from T-Y. Chen and his co-workers, who are beginning to find fundamental explanations for the limitations of systematic testing [15], and perhaps will be able to unravel the way in which so-called 'faults' are expressed in a program's input space.
23. Ernst, M., Cockrell, J., Griswold, W.G., Notkin, D.: Dynamically discovering likely program invariants to support program evolution. IEEE Trans. on Softw. Eng. **27**, 99–123 (2001)
24. Fagan, M.E.: Design and code inspections to reduce errors in program development. IBM Systems Journal **15**(3), 182–211 (1976)
25. Floyd, R.W.: Assigning meanings to programs. In: Proceedings Symposium Applied Mathematics, vol. 19, pp. 19–32. Amer. Math. Soc (1967)

   Floyd's paper is generally credited with originating program proving, although Turing [95, $\prec A \succ$] and others had provided earlier examples. I first read the paper as a grad student, and I remember telling my thesis advisor that I was sure Floyd was onto something truly wonderful. I had previously written a paper for a class in which I attempted to describe Algol programs in first-order logic, a paper that received a B+ with the comment that the professor (Buzz Hunt) didn't think it was practical, so I was in a position to appreciate just how well Floyd had done. So far, Hunt appears to have been right.
26. Foster, K.A.: Error sensitive test cases analysis (estca). IEEE Trans. on Softw. Eng. **6**(3), 258–264 (1980)

   Foster's background was in hardware testing, and he was seeking to find for software an analogy to hardware tests for so-called 'stuck-at' faults (in fabrication technology that has now changed). It is a lack of fault models—details of how things might go wrong—that makes software testing very different from hardware testing. For hardware the engineer knows what might fail and tests for it; when it's not found all is well. For software the catalog of possible problems seems unlimited, so when all tests succeed it means almost nothing. The difference is that in hardware manufacture the whole point is to control and confine the possibilities for mistakes, but in software the point is to allow a human programmer as much power as possible.
27. Frankl, P.G., Weiss, S.N.: An experimental comparison of the effectiveness of branch testing and data flow testing. IEEE Trans. on Softw. Eng. **19**(8), 774–787 (1993)
28. Frankl, P.G., Weyuker, E.J.: An applicable family of data flow testing criteria. IEEE Trans. on Softw. Eng. **14**, 1483–1498 (1988)
29. Gannon, J., Hamlet, D., Mills, H.: Theory of modules. IEEE Trans. on Softw. Eng. **13**, 820–829 (1987)
30. Gannon, J., Hamlet, R., McMullin, P.: Data abstraction implementation, specification, and testing. ACM Trans. Prog. Lang. and Systems **3**, 211–223 (1981)
31. Geller, M.M.: Test data as an aid in proving program correctness. Comm. of the ACM pp. 368–375 (1978)

   For many years this paper stood alone as a serious attempt to aid program proofs using test data. (Other 'testing/proving' papers were mostly the obverse.) Geller recognized that in special cases a few test points constitute a proof in conjunction with knowledge of the program code. For example, if some part of the code can be seen to be implementing a linear function, it is sufficient to test two points to show that it is the correct line. This kind of analysis is exactly what takes place in the best unit tests. But Geller was able to come up with only a few examples, mostly for the integer data type. The current work in metamorphic testing [16] may be the long-sought generalization of this promising start.

32. Gelprin, D., Hetzel, B.: The growth of software testing. Comm. of the ACM **31**(6), 687–695 (1988)
33. Gerhart, S.L., Yelowitz, L.: Observations of fallibility in applications of modern programming methodologies. IEEE Trans. on Softw. Eng. **2**(3), 195–207 (1976)
34. Goodenough, J.B., Gerhart, S.L.: Toward a theory of test data selection. IEEE Trans. on Softw. Eng. **1**, 156–173 (1975)

    The tentative title correctly indicates that the authors present only the beginnings of a theory, long on definitions but short on theorems. They assume that programs have neither persistent state nor concurrency. Nevertheless, this paper set the standard for practially all subsequent theoretical work in software testing. It was a revelation because testing was treated using a functional mathematical model, in contrast to other treatments that were merely exposition of practical methods. The exciting prospect that opened up was the possibility of proving results rather than supporting them only with empirical studies. The workshop on Testing And Verification (TAV) first organized by Susan Gerhart and Bill Howden in Ft. Lauderdale, FL in 1979, which eventually evolved into the International Symposium on Software Testing and Analysis (ISSTA), had this paper and Howden's on subdomain testing [64] as prime motivation.

35. Gorton, I., Heineman, G.T., Crnkovic, I., Schmidt, H.W., Stafford, J.A., Szyperski, C., Wallnau, K. (eds.): Component-based software engineering, 9th Int. Symposium, CBSE9, LNCS 4063. Springer (2006)
36. Guy Steele, J., Woods, D., Finkel, R., Crispin, M., Stallman, R., Goodfellow, G.: The Hacker's Dictionary, A guide to the World of Computer Wizards. Harper & Row (1983)

    This original version, like Algol 60 in Hoare's aphorism, is a great improvement on its successor *The New Hacker's Dictionary*. It is out of print, but the text is mostly preserved at http://www.dourish.com/goodies/jargon.html. It is fun to read, particularly for former DEC PDP-10 assembly language programmers (if you did not have the good fortune to be at Stanford or MIT in the glory days). Many entries supply the obscure etymology for jargon in common use today. Some personal favorites are HACK, LOGICAL, MAGIC, RANDOM.

37. Halstead, M.H.: Machine-Independent Computer Programming. Spartan Books, Washington, DC (1962)
38. Hamlet, D.: "determining" tests. In: Proceedings Workshop on Effectiveness of Testing and Proving Methods, pp. 87–93. Avalon, CA (1982)
39. Hamlet, D.: Software component dependability, a subdomain-based theory. Tech. Rep. RSTR-96-999-01, Reliable Software Technologies, Sterling, VA (1996)
40. Hamlet, D.: What can we learn by testing a program? In: Proc. ISSTA, pp. 50–52 (1998)
41. Hamlet, D.: On subdomains: testing, profiles, and components. In: Proceedings ISSTA '00, pp. 71–76. Portland, OR (2000)
42. Hamlet, D.: Continuity in software systems. In: Proceedings ISSTA '02, pp. 196–200. Rome (2002)
43. Hamlet, D.: Invariants and state in testing and formal methods. In: Proceedings Workshop on Program Analysis for Software Tools and Engineering (PASTE), pp. 48–51. Lisbon, Portugal (2005)
44. Hamlet, D.: Subdomain testing of units and systems with state. In: Proceedings ISSTA 2006, pp. 85–96. Portland, ME (2006)
45. Hamlet, D.: When only random testing will do. In: Proceedings First International Workshop on Random Testing. Portland, ME (2006)
46. Hamlet, D.: Software component composition: subdomain-based testing-theory foundation. J. Software Testing, Verification and Reliability **17**, 243–269 (2007)

    A detailed presentation of the subdomain-based composition theory, but only for the stateless, non-concurrent case. The SYN tools are mentioned only in passing. The paper includes a brief review of related work.

47. Hamlet, D.: Collaboration among software components. In: Proceedings 27th Annual Pacific Northwest Software Quality Conference. Portland, OR (2008)

48. Hamlet, D.: Tools and experiments supporting a testing-based theory of component composition. ACM Trans. on Softw. Eng. Methodology **18** (2009)

   This publication was originally intended as the experimental companion to the stateless theory [46]. Its primary purpose was to investigate the behavior of measurement and prediction errors as subdomains shrink. But long delays in publication and referee demands allowed it to include cases with state (including a minimal theoretical treatment of state), and other case studies, for example on substituting one component for another. The SYN tools are heavily used, but without any attention to them in their own right.

49. Hamlet, D., Andric, M., Tu, Z.: Experiments with composing component properties. In: K. Wallnau (ed.) Proc. 6th ICSE Workshop on Component-based Software Engineering. Portland, OR (2003). http://www.sei.cmu.edu/pacc

50. Hamlet, D., Mason, D., Woit, D.: Foundational theory of software component reliability. In: Proc. 10th International Symposium on Software Reliability Engineering (ISSRE'99) - Fast Abstracts. Boca Raton, FL (1999)

51. Hamlet, D., Mason, D., Woit, D.: Theory of software reliability based on components. In: Proc. 3rd ICSE Workshop on Component-based Software Engineering [98]

52. Hamlet, D., Mason, D., Woit, D.: Theory of software reliability based on components. In: Proceedings ICSE '01, pp. 361–370. Toronto, Canada (2001)

   Although papers in the CBSE workshop [51] and ISSTA [41] first presented information on the subdomain theory of component composition that is the subject of the present monograph, its first detailed presentation was at ICSE 2001. (An identical paper was submitted to ICSE 2000 but rejected—the authors like to think this meant it was ahead of its time, but it probably only illustrates the wildly inconsistent reviewing of software engineering papers.) A slightly modified version appears in Lau's collection [53].

   There are three serious mistakes in this initial paper: (1) The non-functional property described is reliability rather than run time, which lets in all the issues described in Chapter 12, detracting from the theory; (2) It was not realized that the synthesis of loop approximations is algorithmic, so the paper is weaker than it might have been; (3) The use of a 'transfer matrix' from one component's subdomains to another following in series does not generalize to further compositions, compromising the paper's claim that an arbitrary system can be synthesized. It was the implementation of the SYN tools that exposed these mistakes.

53. Hamlet, D., Mason, D., Woit, D.: Properties of software systems synthesized from components, chap. 6. In: Lau [70] (2004). An updated version of [52].

54. Hamlet, D., Maybee, J.: The Engineering of Software. Addison-Wesley (2001)

55. Hamlet, D., Taylor, R.: Partition testing does not inspire confidence. IEEE Trans. on Softw. Eng. **16**, 1402–1411 (1990)

56. Hamlet, R.G.: Introduction to Computation Theory. Intext Educational Publishers (1974)

57. Hamlet, R.G.: Testing programs with the aid of a compiler. IEEE Trans. on Softw. Eng. pp. 279–289 (1977)

58. Hamlet, R.G., Haralick, R.M.: Transportable package software. Software – Practice & Experience pp. 1009–1027 (1980)

59. Harel, D.: Statecharts: A visual formalism for complex systems. Science of Computer Programming **8**, 231–274 (1987)

60. Heninger, K.L.: Specifying software requirements for complex systems: new techniques and their applications. IEEE Trans. on Softw. Eng. **6**, 2–13 (1980)

61. Hoare, C.A.R.: An axiomatic basis for computer programming. Comm. of the ACM **12**, 576–583 (1969)

62. Hoare, C.A.R.: Communicating sequential processes. Comm. of the ACM **21**(8), 666–677 (1978)

63. Howden, W.: Methodology for the generation of program test data. IEEE Trans. Computers **24**, 554–559 (1975)

64. Howden, W.E.: Reliability of the path analysis testing strategy. IEEE Trans. on Softw. Eng. **2**, 208–215 (1976)

In the title, "Reliability" does not refer to the engineering measure of probable success, but to the social-science notion that various attempts to judge something will agree with each other, often applied to diagnosis of mental illness. The various attempts are test-point choices from subdomains, and they agree if they all fail or all succeed; then in Howden's terminology such subdomains are "reliable." Despite the unfortunate choice of a technical word (in hindsight), this notion is just what a tester wants from a subdomain breakdown: not to be misled by success; to miss no failures. Using a functional model to define test success, Howden formally defines subdomain testing, then experimentally investigates the path-coverage subdomains for a set of programs containing common beginners' mistakes. His mathematics is sound and precise and the examples give an excellent insight into why subdomains sometimes work for testing and sometimes don't. The workshop on Testing And Verification (TAV) first organized by Susan Gerhart and Bill Howden in Ft. Lauderdale, FL in 1979, which eventually evolved into the International Symposium on Software Testing and Analysis (ISSTA), had this paper and Goodenough and Gerhart's [34] as prime motivation. A short summary and appreciation of Howden's paper appears in a retrospective session of ISSTA 98 [40].

65. Howden, W.E.: Weak mutation testing and completeness of test sets. IEEE Trans. on Softw. Eng. **8**, 371–379 (1982)
66. Kleene, S.C.: Introduction to Metamathematics. Elsevier (1980)
67. Knight, J., Cass, A., Fernandez, A., Wika, K.: Testing a safety-critical application. In: Proceedings ISSTA '94, p. 199. Seattle, WA (1994)
68. Knuth, D.E.: Literate programming. The Computer Journal **27**(2), 97–111 (1984)
69. Lamport, L.: How to tell a program from an automobile. http://research.microsoft.com /en-us/um/people/lamport/pubs/automobile.pdf (1997)
70. Lau, K.K. (ed.): Case Studies in Computer-based Software Engineering. World Scientific (2004)
71. Leveson, N.G., Cha, S.S., Knight, J.C., Shimeall, T.J.: The use of self checks and voting in software detection: An empirical study. IEEE Trans. on Softw. Eng. **16**, 432–443 (1990)
72. Linger, R.C., Mills, H.D., Witt, B.I.: Structured programming, theory and practice. Addison-Wesley (1979)
73. Lions, J.L.: ARIANE 5 – Flight 501 Failure – Report by the Inquiry Board. European Space Agency (ESA), Paris (1996)
74. Lyu, M. (ed.): Handbook of Software Reliability Engineering. McGraw-Hill, New York (1996)
75. Manna, Z., McCarthy, J.: Properties of programs and partial function logic. In: B. Meltzer, D. Michie (eds.) Machine Intelligence 5, pp. 27–39. Edinburgh University Press (1969)
76. Marick, B.: Experience with the cost of different coverage goals for testing. In: Pacific Northwest Software Quality Conference, pp. 147–164. Portland, OR (1991)
77. Mason, D.: Probabilistic program analysis for software component reliability. Ph.D. thesis, University of Waterloo (2002)
78. Mason, D., Woit, D.: Software system reliability from component reliability. In: Proc. of 1998 Workshop on Software Reliability Engineering (SRE'98). Ottawa, Ontario (1998)
79. Medvidovic, N., Mehta, N., Mikic-Rakic, M.: A family of software architecture implementation frameworks. In: Proc. 3rd IFIP working int. conf. on software architectures (WICSA), pp. 221–235. Montreal, Canada (2002)
80. Meinke, K.: Automated black-box testing of functional correctness using function approximation. In: Proceedings ISSTA '04, pp. 143–153. Boston (2004)
81. Meyer, B.: Object-oriented Software Construction. Prentice Hall (2000)
82. Mills, H., Basili, V., Gannon, J., Hamlet, D.: Principles of Computer Programming: A Mathematical Approach. Allyn and Bacon (1987)

Although intended as a textbook at the freshman (!) level, this is the best exposition of Harlan Mills's denotational-semantic calculus for the Pascal programming language. It first defines a minimal language subset ("CF Pascal" for "Character-File") that reduces the detail required in proof examples, then treats (most of) the full language. Two features of the formalism recommend it over (say) Hoare's axiomatic treatment: (1) The mathematical basis is functions rather than relations, and (2) The rules for proving loops are much easier to use than assertions. (The loop function must still be guessed, but checking it is more straightforward than the proof that Hoare logic requires.) The 'box' notation was introduced in this book; it is an adaptation of Kleene's [66] notational way of distinuishing a program (Gödel number) from the (partial recursive) function it computes. (Horrors! Most computer science papers confuse the two notationally.) As befits a textbook, there are numerous exercises.

Mills probably did not invent his calculus, but the extensive development in this text was new. At the same time the book was published, Mills and Hamlet wrote a summary for *Computing Reviews*. That paper was assigned to the database editor (!), who first "had difficulty finding referees," and never completed handling the paper. The junior author did not at that time grasp how unprofessional this treatment is (or even that such treatment was a possibility!) and was too diffident to complain effectively. The paper remains in limbo.

83. Musa, J., Iannino, A., Okumoto, K.: Software Reliability. McGraw-Hill, New York (1990)
84. Musa, J.D.: Operational profiles in software-reliability engineering. IEEE Software **10**, 14–32 (1993)
85. Myers, G.J.: The Art of Software Testing. Wiley-Interscience, New York, NY (1979)
86. Ntafos, S.: On required element testing. IEEE Trans. on Softw. Eng. **10**, 795–803 (1984)
87. Ostrand, T.J., Balcer, M.J.: The category-partition method for specifying and generating functional tests. Comm. of the ACM **16**, 676–686 (1988)
88. Parnas, D.: On a "Buzzword": Hierarchical structure. In: Proc. IFIP Congress, pp. 336–339. North-Holland Publishing Co. (1974)
89. Parnas, D.L.: On the criteria to be used in decomposing systems into modules. Comm. of the ACM (1972)

   Parnas is best known for his deep insights into software engineering and their expression in revealing concrete examples; there is no better illustration of these strengths than this famous paper. Its example is the design for a program for KWIC indexing, which now also serves the unexpected purpose of keeping this neglected variant of index-making alive. To the modern student, it seems that Parnas is just presenting object-oriented design in an unfamiliar way; this is chronologically reversed, since O-O was barely a glimmer in Alan Kay's and O-J Dahl's eyes when Parnas wrote. His ideas came from software engineering, not programming languages; he was mostly thinking of operating systems written in assembly language.

90. Petroski, H.: To Engineer is Human: The Role of Failure in Successful Design. St. Martin's Press, New York, NY (1985)
91. Sethi, R.: A case study in specifying the semantics of a programming language. In: Proc. POPL 1980, pp. 117–130 (1980)
92. Spivey, J.M.: The Z Notation: a reference manual, 2 edn. Prentice Hall (1992)
93. Szyperski, C.: Component Software, 2nd edn. Addison-Wesley (2002)

   Almost every citation to this much-cited monograph is pointing to its definition of *software component*, and justly so, for Szyperski was among the first to think deeply about this concept. Perhaps the close reasoning and careful abstraction that characterize the book were necessary to come to framing a suitable definition, but the general reader will find it hard going.

94. Turing, A.: On computable numbers, with an application to the entscheidungsproblem. London Mathematical Society pp. 230–265 (1936-37)

   Reprinted, including the correction (1937), in Davis's fine collection [20, $\prec A \succ$]. Davis's annotation of the paper is right on: "...read this paper for its general sweep, ignoring the petty technical details." But of course the sweep would not be there if the author had not been convinced that the details (hardly 'petty' unless all programming is, which Davis may very well believe) supported it. A modern proof of Turing's result is often component-based [56], in that a number of simple Turing machines are devised to solve various bookkeeping problems, then combined into a 'system' that is a universal machine. It is probably safe to say that none of the many 'implementations' of the universal machine is likely to be correct—there are too many details, and none has been tested! But carrying through the exercise is absolutely convincing. One sees clearly that it can be done, even as one makes mistakes trying to do it. The modern reader has difficultly keeping in mind just how little was established about computability in 1936, requiring Turing to feel his way cautiously to each application.

95. Turing, A.: Checking a large routine. In: Report of a conference on high speed automatic calculating machines (EDSAC inaugral conference), pp. 67–69 (1949)

This short paper is from Turing's second career as a programmer on the early machines. In it he anticipates some of what Floyd [25, $\prec A \succ$] would publish almost 20 years later. Mathematicians (his colleagues in his first career) lamented Turing's loss to the profession: What good work he might have done if he hadn't been seduced by those digital computers! Reprinted with corrections and annotations in "An early program proof by Alan Turing," L. Morris and C. B. Jones, *Ann. Hist. Computing* 6 (2) pp 129–143 (1984), and in *The early British computer conferences*, MIT Press, 1989, pp 70–72.

96. Van Zandt, T.: Pstricks: Postscript macros for generic tex, user's guide. ctan.org/tex-archive/graphics/pstricks/base/doc/pst-user.pdf (1993)

97. Vincenti, W.G.: What Engineers Know and How They Know It. Johns Hopkins University Press (1993)

This collection of chapter examples from aircraft engineering provides an invaluable insight into how engineers think about and solve problems. One particularly notable theme is the transition from pure guesswork in design to experimentation that determines the best combination of parameters. Before this is possible there must be enough theory to delineate the parameters to be monitored in experiments.

98. Wallnau, K.: http://www.sei.cmu.edu/pacc (links to CBSE proceedings)

99. Weiser, M.: Programmers use slices when debugging. Comm. of the ACM **25**(7), 446–452 (1982)

100. White, L.J., Cohen, E.I.: A domain strategy for computer program testing. IEEE Trans. on Softw. Eng. **6**(3), 247–257 (1980)

101. Woit, D., Mason, D.: Software component independence. In: Proc. 3rd IEEE High-Assurance Systems Engineering Symposium (HASE'98). Washington, DC (1998)

Appendix A
Tool Specifications

TIME was when program sources and the documentation describing them were an essential part of using computers. It was expected that software would require modification, both because it did not do what was wanted and/or it failed entirely. Every user was his/her own Mr./Ms. Fixit[1], which entailed long, hard study of code. Computing for the mass market took a quite different direction, first because software began to be sold rather than bundled free with the hardware[2] and second because customers were judged incapable of understanding code, or at least unwilling to spare the time for it. Software customers who buy executable copies of proprietary code *cannot* adapt or fix it, and must wait those months for the vendor to release fixed versions (for which they are expected to pay!). The current movement toward open-source software combines the best of both worlds: there is a legion of expert developers working on an open-source product; but the customer who is willing and able can fix problems too, and perhaps the work will be incorporated by the experts. The Internet is essential in helping a DIY user to find information and make changes in source code.

The availability of source code also means that documentation is public, and it makes a real difference in how code is written. Microsoft and its closed-source ilk try to make the executable code handle any and all contingencies; when the source and documentation is available, the requirements are less stringent. When

---

[1] Computing-service organizations provided their customers with fix-it service. In the late 1960s, Computer Center Corporation in Seattle sold timesharing access to DEC PDP-10 systems. C³ had on its staff a DEC hardware expert and three software experts, one for the PDP-10 operating system, one for compilers, and one for utility software. They also employed a self-titled 'Factotum,' part of whose job was to fly to Maynard, MA every few weeks and steal (if necessary) copies of the 'red DECtapes,' containing the latest unstable sources for PDP-10 software. The C³ staff compared these to their local sources and used or adapted bug-fixes they needed. Without the fix-it service, most C³ customers would have been forced to wait months for the repairs they needed to do their routine work.

[2] Selling software is a ridiculous idea on the face of it, but it is the foundation of a spectacularly successful business model at Microsoft and other corporations. It's ridiculous because software really costs very little (inflated claims about development costs notwithstanding); it's successful, because the traffic has been willing to bear wildly inflated prices, no one quite knows why.

D. Hamlet, *Composing Software Components*, DOI 10.1007/978-1-4419-7148-7,
© Springer Science+Business Media, LLC 2010

something goes wrong, a closed-source application must fabricate an error message that hides what is really happening (both to protect proprietary secrets, and to avoid acknowledging that the problem may be a software-development mistake), while an open-source error message can be more forthright, can even suggest what the user should change. Programs that hide everything are sometimes called 'intelligent.' The authors of wvdial, a self-confessed intelligent program for connecting to a dial-up Internet service provider (ISP), put it well in the BUGS section of their Linux man page:

> "Intelligent" programs are frustrating when they don't work right. This version of wvdial has only minimal support for disabling or overriding its "intelligence" ... So, in general if you have a nice ISP, it will probably work, and if you have a weird ISP, it might not.

(But wvdial is open source, so when it doesn't work, the motivated user can find out why and perhaps fix it.)

A.1 Documentation

The two schools of thought on documenting source code are the *narrative* and the *detailed*. Narrative documentation is to be read for high-level understanding, giving an overview of what programs do and roughly how they do it[3]. Narrative documentation for the SYN tools is presented in Chapter 14, backed up by the theory presented in Part III.

Detailed documentation is supposed to give full details necessary to understand (and modify!) the source code. Technically, it makes narrative documentation superfluous, but in reality that's not so. When software is complicated, no single person can grasp the sense of the whole from a plethora of detail. It is the trees, not the forest, that are described, and the old saying holds true[4].

---

[3] The best narrative documentation for a large program in the author's experience is *Introduction to the B5500 Master Control Program*, a booklet that gives the reader the low-down on a Burroughs machine with an unusual stack-based descriptor (capability) architecture and its way-ahead-of-its-time multiprogrammed operating system. This thin booklet sold at least one multi-million dollar system in the mid-1960s, to the University of Washington computer center in Seattle. The UW MCP was extensively modified over the first years of its operation to include very foreign features of less 'interactive' data-processing applications, which would not have been even contemplated without this narrative help. In compensation, the B5500 MCP (about 120,000 machine instructions written in a variant of Algol 60, this for core memory of only 32,768 words total) had no detailed documentation except the comments within its code, which were often plain lies. The most amazing thing about the UW MCP is that the source changes (amounting to perhaps 40% of the total code) were reported to Burroughs, and the systems programming group there released an official variant system. In these days of open-source, a comparable situation would be a single million-line 'patch' to Linux.

[4] To continue the example from the previous footnote, the description of the IBM 7090 IBSYS operating system of the 1960s is a set of manuals occupying about two feet of shelf space, a stack from which it is literally impossible to extract anything like a narrative description. Its very authors failed to do so, and the novice reader hasn't a chance. The IBM documentation fits, just

Detailed documentation is often combined with code by placing comments in the source. This is not at all satisfactory in a developing system, because even when comments are initially excellent, as the code is altered to create different functionality or to repair mistakes, programmers short of time do a poor job of changing or adding documentation. The only comments that are safe to trust after extensive code changes are the add one to X type on instructions like X += 1, universally acknowledged to be of no use whatsoever. The SYN tools have a modest amount of code commentary, and a modest effort was made to keep it up to date. Detailed documentation presented in a form separated from code is even more liable to be out of date, but it starts out better because it is not squeezed into code-comment format. Donald Knuth, surely one of the best minds in computing, has grappled with the problem of code documentation and implemented a system [68] that does a better job than any other to date. But it is complicated enough to keep it from wide use.

Finally, there is a form of detailed documentation called a 'change log,' which describes the chronological sequence of changes as they are made, including such information as date, reason for the change, size of the new/altered code, author, etc. The code lines may be tagged with a pointer to the log entry. A change log is invaluable for tracking what has happened to software, and for studying the maintenance process[5], but it isn't at all useful for understanding or modifying the code, except perhaps to identify the work of a programmer who is prone to blundering. A change log for the SYN tools would trace their evolution from integer domains for step-function approximation of stateless components, but such a log was never systematically kept. CVS version-control tools were used to backup the source files, but the 'commit' points and comments are haphazard.

A.2 SYN Documentation Tricks

The SYN tools provided with this monograph are from the old school that values source code and its documentation. To run them in any significant way will certainly expose their user to failures large and small, most of them easy to fix.. This Appendix contains detailed documentation for the SYN tools.

---

as the Burroughs documentation did: 7090 IBSYS is a bloated, unimaginative system (written in assembly language) for the most conventional of hardware. No one would have given a minute's serious consideration of modifying IBSYS to include MCP features; yet it was IBSYS features that the UW computer center staff added to the B5500. The 7090 outsold the B5500 hundreds to one.

[5] For example, the information that the UW changed 40% of the original MCP code comes from a change log.

A.2.1 Stand-alone Script Execution

Each script in the SYN tools can be executed by itself, independent of the others. Sometimes this coding style isn't helpful because a script relies on data files that are generated by other scripts. But since files can be made by hand with an editor like vi, it is often useful to create a simple case that isolates a script and may help in understanding its operation. For example, the utility script rms compares two files intended as data for 3-D plotting, perhaps files produced by Xcute. It is easy to fabricate two files each containing a single point to see how the comparison works. The header comments (Section A.2.5 to follow) or the message-discovery process described in Section A.2.3 to follow can be used to learn how the file names are given to rms. When the user sees that rms requires the files to have matched identical input values, he/she might want to modify its source to do better; the best test cases to use when developing a more sophisticated rms will be those of small hand-made files.

A.2.2 Error Messages

SYN scripts attempt to adhere to the error-message philosophy that a message must tell the script user how to correct the error situation. Often this is as simple as including in a message the name of a file the user must create (e.g., very little can be done without system.pscf), or a previous script that must be run (e.g., COMP before Xcute). But there is a much larger scope introduced by the assumption that the user will examine failing code and correct it. As an example, consider messages themselves. Suppose that in an imaginary script named poorscript, some particular file is required but missing, so the script terminates with the (lousy) message: "Can't find the file". But Perl routinely does better than that; it prints:

```
Can't find the file at poorscript line 23
```

unless poorscript as gone to extremes to prevent this[6]. Thus the user can look at poorscript line 23, find how the file name is stored (it will usually be in some easily identified Perl variable) and correct the message. However, there is usually yet a better correction. The user could be instructed in how to create the file. If that's by hand, perhaps it's enough to name the file and rely on documentation like that in Section A.3.1 to follow. For example, if told that a .ccf file is missing, even the SYN-novice user should know what to do. But in many cases the message might better name script(s) to be run before this one, e.g.:

```
The .ccfc files created by COMP are required
     --run COMP first
```

---

[6] And if it has, that itself is a mistake to correct. The offending line can be found by searching poorscript for the text of the message.

Section A.2.3 to follow suggests that messages provide a way to discover how a script works without reading any documentation.

Perl provides a number of mechanisms for printing messages, which SYN uses as follows:

Perl die *statement.* The script terminates with a message sent to STDERR, which should always identify the source-code location. Because one script may be executing another, this may set off a chain of termination messages, all but the first being of little interest except as a kind of call trace. (Or, by mistake, the upper-level script may ignore the death of its child.) In most scripts, the die construction is used within nested conditionals to avoid using else.

Perl warn *statement.* The message goes to STDERR, but the script continues. Sometimes it is appropriate to identify the source location, sometimes not. Most scripts have a 'verbose' option -V to enable extra informational messages; these most often are produced with warn. It is a mistake to make a message conditional on -V if a user action is needed.

Perl print *or* printf *statement.* The message goes to STDOUT and does not identify the source location. Except for a few peculiar cases (such as when a line is to be overprinted without a newline), print is not used for messages but for results calculated by a script, e.g., a table of r-m-s errors. Perhaps #debug statements (see below) should use warn, but they use print.

Perl exception messages. The Perl interpreter keeps track of values assigned to variables and does not permit certain 'impossible' situations, for which it sends a message to STDERR (but typically does not terminate the script). The source location is identified, and if reading from a file, its filehandle and record (line) number are also given. In the most common of these situations the variable must be dereferenced, but has not been assigned a value. For example, in an expression $X + $Y if neither variable has a value, the message is:

```
Use of uninitialized value in addition (+) at ...
```

and you'll get it twice. Somewhat less frequent is the message for

```
$X = "st"; if ($X > 2) ...
```

which is:

```
Argument "st" isn't numeric in numeric gt (>) at ...
```

It would be really helpful for debugging if Perl identified the offending variable, but it doesn't[7]. Receiving any such message is a clear indication of something badly wrong. The most frequent explanation is that a file in the wrong format was somehow supplied to a script. For example, if a document containing lines of character strings somehow finds its way into foo.ccf and that name is listed in system.pscf, a host of these messages will arise for almost any SYN com-

---

[7] Promises have been made for Perl versions 5.9.2 and beyond.

mand, one or more for each line of the file. The expected format for most lines of a `.ccf` file is three numerical values; the `...isn't numeric...` messages are printed when there are three or more text words on a line of the bad file; if fewer than three words, the `...unitialized...` message. If the first line in the bad file happens to contain `Now is the time`, the occurrence of 'Now', etc., in the messages will help to identify it.

In two exceptional cases, none of the Perl printing mechanisms are appropriate, so SYN uses logging. A script writes a file whose name ends in ".log" containing messages, and at the end of the run notifies the user that such a file has been created (using an unconditional `warn`). Log files are removed at the beginning of any SYN command. The first case requiring a log involves messages that are voluminous or repetitious that would obscure others more important. The best example occurs in `Calc` using the piecewise-linear approximation. The vagaries of floating-point approximation of interval endpoints creates strange situations that may occur hundreds of times in a synthesis calculation and so are shunted to a log. The second case is more interesting. The executable code for components and systems *cannot* write error messages, because both SYSOUT and SYSERR are in use for functional- and run-time values. So when SYN is controlling an execution, any exception message goes to a log. For the numerical domains SYN requires, exception messages can be recognized because they almost certainly contain non-numeric characters. During the execution of table-lookup code, there is a special, frequently-occurring error to log: an input may fall outside the domain of the table.

A.2.3 'Message-discovery' Documentation

A novel kind of self-documentation is employed in seldom-used scripts. If the script is run without parameters it will either perform its duties or terminate with a message stating why it can't. In the former case, if the user doesn't understand what has happened, there is naught for it but to consult the script header comments or other passive documentation. (But don't forget to try the verbose -V option that may elicit information.) But in case there is an error message, the user can supply the missing parameter, file, etc., and try again. A sequence of such attempts will quickly lead to understanding. This procedure is an extension of the (undocumented!) UNIX coding style that prints the man SYNOPSIS line in response to a command invocation that is wildly at variance with what's expected. Section A.3.4 to follow lists SYN command names and a very brief description of each. Taking a command name from the list, execute it without parameters and follow the messages to understand it. For example, the `profile` command displays an internal interface histogram for one component in a system. With no command-line argument, `profile` will demand the name of a `.ccf` file. When that's supplied, `profile` will require a file named `trace_report`, which is produced by the SYN command with options -G -P. Once a `trace_report` exists, examining it with an editor will clarify the whole `profile` algorithm, and suggest hand-edited simplifications as test cases, should `profile` fail.

A.2.4 '#debug' Statements

Almost every SYN script has failed badly at some stage of the research reported in this monograph. Mistakes were found and corrected by inserting 'debugging' Perl code in the script to gain information about the failures. This code (usually `print` statements) remains in the scripts, commented out with a leading '#' and including the tag '#debug'. Even without understanding very well, turning on these statements may be helpful. Again using `profile` as an example, it contains a subroutine `bar` with three parameters. Suppose that Perl complains about an undefined value within `bar`'s code. The subroutine contains a `#print` statement near the beginning of `sub bar` that prints its parameter values received, which will help begin the process of finding out why some value is missing.

A rough measure of how difficult each script was to bring to its present working (?) state is the fraction of its lines occupied by #debug. SYN and Calc top the list with about 4% debugging statements; COMP and its variants about 3%; Xcomp a bit less than 3%; Xcute about 1%. No script is much below 1% debugging statements.

A.2.5 The Script Header Comments

Each Perl script in the SYN tools begins with a comment that describes its parameters and describes its functionality in a line or two, then in more detail if this is not forbiddingly long. For example, the script `splitsub` begins with the relatively complete functional description shown in Fig. A.1.

For simple scripts like `splitsub` the Perl code is easy to read and provides the only detailed documentation on how the script works. When a functional description is too complex to compress into a header comment, its narrative documentation is given in the text of this monograph (e.g., in Section 9 for scripts like COMP), and for the most important scripts detailed documentation is provided in the next section.

A.3 Details of the Tool Scripts

It would be difficult to work on the script programs in SYN without the information provided in this section; that doesn't mean that enough information is provided. It is presumed that the reader can use the tools but is now interesting in modifying or repairing them.

```
#
# splitsub [N]
#
# Script to divide the subdomains of components in a system
#   in half repeatedly.
#
# Run in a base directory D, creates N new base directories
#   in the same parent named D2, D22, ..., D22222, ...
#   that are copies of D except that all subdomains in .ccf
#   files named in system.pscf are split in half (in D2),
#   then again in half in D22, etc.
#
# N may be absent (default is 5), and N must lie in [1,10].
#
# In each new directory, *.ccf[ct] approximation and theory*
#   prediction files are removed.
#
```

Fig. A.1 Header comments for the splitsub script

A.3.1 File Formats

SYN tools create and use a variety of files, but most of them are just a convenient
form of temporary internal storage. If the need ever arises to know what a transitory
file looks like, the best plan is to interrupt the program that creates it and take a
look[8]. Four files are ubiquitous and worth describing. The first two are created by
hand to define a component and a system; the last two are created by the tools in
response.

Component configuration file (.ccf*).* (Created by hand by a SYN user, one for
each component.)

All but one or two lines consist of three blank-separated numbers, the first two
numbers L R are floating-point and the third C a non-negative integer. The line
specifies a subdomain interval $[L, R)$ and a sampling count C for it. For a stateless component there is one block of these lines; for components with state or
concurrent components there are two blocks separated by a blank line. The intervals of a block must be ordered and contiguous. There must not be extraneous
blank lines. Line 1 is a header that begins with the file name of the executable-
component code. For a component with state, a blank and "state" follows; for
a concurrent component, a blank and "concurrent" follows. The first (or only,
for a stateless component) block below the header describes the input domain;
the second describes the state or parallel-input domain.

*System description file (*system.pscf*).* (Created by hand by a SYN user.)

---

[8] One useful #debug statement is to dump an internal file (say foo) with the Copy module's
copy("foo", *SYSOUT);.

Lines beginning with the second, name .ccf files for the components of the system. They are indexed by (line-number - 1), so component 1 is on line 2, component 2 on line 3, etc. These index values are used to refer to the components on line 1, the 'Polish' line. It describes the system structure in reverse Polish notation with operators S (sequence, two arguments); C (conditional, three arguments); L (loop, two arguments); and P (parallel, two arguments); and operands the component numbers. The table below defines these operators for numbered operands 1, 2, (and maybe) 3:

Polish	construction
1 2 S	1 followed by 2 in series
1 2 3 C	conditional with test 1, true-branch 2, false-branch 3
1 2 L	loop with test 1, body 2
1 2 P	concurrent execution of master 1 and slave 2

It is safe to have a different component .ccf name and also within the file a different executable-code name for every operand position in the Polish line, but in some situations the same operand and/or executable may be reused. State requires unique executable names; the SYN -P profile option requires unique .ccf names. When duplicates are not allowed, a repeated .ccf file and/or executable file must be copied and renamed to create distinct operands.

Stateless component approximation file (.ccft). (Created by COMP.)

Line 1 is a header containing "theory" followed by a code showing whether the measurements used the step-function (C) or piecewise-linear (L) approximation. Two-letter codes are mixed cases; for example, CL means that the functional approximation was step-function but the run time was piecewise-linear. The next fields are present only for reliability measurements: r followed by an integer in [1,99] that gives a confidence percentage.

Following lines have the form of blank-separated 6-tuples:

$L\ R\ m_f\ b_f\ m_r\ b_r$

$[L,R)$ is the subdomain interval; the lines appear in contiguous interval order. These subdomains are identical to those in the .ccf description file for the component. Two pairs of values follow, describing lines $y = mx + b$ for functional ($_f$) and run-time ($_r$) measurements on that subdomain.

Stateless system prediction file (.ccf). (Created by SYN.)

When two (or three) stateless components are synthesized to a prediction file, the latter's format is almost the same as an approximation file (.ccft) produced by COMP. It was early decided to name the prediction files "theoryN.ccf, where N is 1 for the first synthesis operation, 2 for the second, etc. It would have been a far better choice to use extension .ccft, since .ccf now names files with two completely different formats. The prediction file differs from a measured approximation file only in that its header code is always L (which does not imply anything about measurement), and following the calculated functional- and run-time slope/intercept values is a seventh field, TRUE, FALSE, SERIES, or CONC to indicate the type of synthesis. The first two refer to which branch a conditional took for this subdomain. The subtle difference between a predicted and measured file is that for a prediction of a conditional and for piecewise-linear predictions the subdomains are intersections of those in the constituents, so the file sizes may grow.

Component/system approximation/prediction for state/concurrency (.ccfc*).*
(Created by COMP for state/concurrent components; by SYN for systems with state.)

Line 1 is a header with five or more blank-separated fields:

TYPE n_S I_s S_{1s} $[S_{2s}...S_{n_S s}]$ $S0_1$ $[S0_2...S0_{n_S}]$ [r/u]

The initial 'TYPE' is state or concurrent for an approximation; theory for a synthesis prediction. The number of state dimensions is n_S (always 1 for a component approximation). The number of input subdomains is I_s. The n_S fields starting at the 4th field (S_{1s}) are the number of state (or parallel-input) subdomains in state (or parallel input) 1, state 2, ..., state n_S. The n_S values starting with $S0_1$ are initial values of these states. (Although it has no meaning for a concurrent component, $S0_1$ must be present.) In the last field, which is present only for measured files created by COMP, code r means the test measurements were random samples; code u means equi-spaced systematic sampling.

Following the header are $1 + n_S$ blocks of subdomain intervals $[L, R)$ with L followed by a blank and R, the count of intervals in each block being $I_s, S_{1s}, S_{2s}...S_{n_S s}$ in order.

Finally, there are $I_s \times S_{1s} \times S_{2s} \times ... \times S_{n_S s}$ lines of measured/predicted values, each line containing $3 + n_S$ blank-separated result values:

h Output Run State-1 State-2 ... State-n_S

for a component with state, or for a concurrent component just six values:

h Output1 Output2 Run1 Run3 Run4

The sequence position of the value line determines the subdomain. Indices vary in this order: Input, State-1, ..., State-n_S.

The first field *h* is a count of how often this subdomain was sampled (only 0 or non-zero are meaningful for a prediction). In the concurrent files, 'Output2' goes to the parallel slave while 'Output1' is the master's final output; the numbered run times are before, during, and after slave execution.

The confusing file names among .ccft, .ccfc, and .ccf can be blamed on that old villain 'historical accident.' As the tools changed and developed, new names were introduced but old ones were not retired because it seemed unsafe to change them. If it were not Too Horrible To Contemplate (THTC) the change, two formats would be enough: one for hand-made description files (say .ccf) and the other for measured/calculated approximations/predictions (say an amalgam of .ccft and .ccfc).

Two ideas have been implemented only for stateless components, using a complex of files that will not be described in detail:

Incremental processing. As described in Section 9.6, approximation measurements and synthesis need not be completely redone when there are only small changes to component or system descriptions. The incremental algorithms are implemented using files with a "b" appended to the name, e.g., "C.ccfb" for a component description file. These file are copied from their namesakes each time a processing step is begun, and later comparison exposes changes.

Conduction Matrices. The implementation of interface profiles[9] (see Section 9.5) uses binary matrices kept in files with names like theory1-C3.cm. There is a one at position (row *n*, column *m*) just in case subdomain *n* of theory1 can reach subdomain *m* of C3. These "conduction matrices" are recursively computed during synthesis starting with square base matrices like C3-C3.cm with ones on the diagonal.

A.3.2 Testing and Approximating Components: COMP and friends

COMP processes components one at a time, using the list in system.pscf. The work is done by COMPSt if there is state or concurrency; otherwise by COMPFt. All three of these scripts can do a collection of components, but inside the outer loop in COMPFt and COMPSt is the substance of the approximation algorithms for one component. In a word, the description of the .ccf file is turned into a subdomain-indexed table-lookup file .ccft or .ccfc, by sampling inputs, running the executable component code, and recording the result values by subdomain. The results always include a functional-output value and a run-time value; for state there is an additional result-state value; for concurrent there are additional output-to-slave and partial run-time values.

If the sampling is systematic or random in each subdomain, the work is done in nested loops, outer loop over subdomains then inner over test points (over two dimensions for state/concurrent). As each subdomain is completed in the inner-most loop, results go into the table-lookup file. In the step-function approximation, results are averaged over the subdomain; in the piecewise-linear approximation, a line is fitted to the subdomain results. In sequence sampling over the whole domain (when there is state), the nested loops are: outer loop over sequences, then inner over points within sequences. As each point is selected, it falls in some input subdomain; part of the execution outcome is a result-state value, which serves as input-state to the next input test point. Each of these states falls in a state subdomain. Thus each test point is associated with an (input × input-state) subdomain, and at the end of all sampling the results are collected by subdomain to go into the table-lookup file.

Xcute is the reporting script for component testing and approximation. Its outputs are graphs of a component's behavior, either as measured point-by-point in execution, or as approximated by subdomain. For stateless components this means

---

[9] The profiles for components with state are measured by instrumenting the SystemCode file in a conventional way.

four graphs over the input domain, two for functional output (measured and approximated) and two for run time (measured and approximated). These are displayed on a single plot. For state there are six graphs over the 2-D (input × state) domain, measured and approximated: functional output, run time, and result state. These are displayed as three measured/approximated pairs in projections of the 3-D graphs. Xcute always uses the approximation table-lookup files produced by COMP, and it tries to avoid rerunning the component code. However, it may happen that its options call for a new test-point granularity, which requires new execution. A new approximation could also be obtained in this way, but it would differ only slightly so it is not recorded or used by Xcute. To get a different approximation (in the .ccft or .ccfc file), one would have to go back to COMP with a changed .ccf file that specifies different sampling counts.

Because executable code is provided for each component, it can be executed without the use of Xcute; the approximation table-lookup can also be 'executed' with a wrapper that reads an input, looks it up in the table, and prints the table value. Sometimes this mechanism that avoids SYN tools is valuable in validating the tools. However, care is required when a component has state, which is modeled using a .state file. The component behavior depends on the contents of this file, and mixing SYN tool executions (say with Xcute) with direct executions via the platform operating system may lead to confusion. The confusion is worsened because the mechanism for accessing the .state file is different in the two cases: Xcute uses a named pipe mechanism[10] which if interrupted may cause subsequent file access to hang. The only safe way to mix execution modes is to remove the .state file each time.

A.3.3 Synthesizing and Predicting Systems: SYN and Calc

Even though the SYN tools take their name from this script, SYN is not the real engine of the synthesis algorithm, which is Calc. SYN has the pedestrian task of parsing the Polish system description in system.pscf and 'implementing' it as synthesis by repeatedly invoking Calc for each operator with its operands. At the leaves of the parse tree, operands are atomic component-table-lookup files created by COMP; however, the synthesized result of one operation enters another as an operand, so intermediate table-lookup files named in sequence theory1.ccfc, theory2.ccfc, ... are created[11]. The highest-numbered theory.ccfc file is the one for the complete synthesized system. Since these intermediate files are in the same format as those created by COMP, the algorithms for synthesis using them are unchanged; furthermore, Xcute can graph intermediate files.

---

[10] Not in Windows, although there is a non-standard Perl module that might be worth investigating if you must use Windows.

[11] An unfortunate early decision used the extension .ccf and a different format for stateless intermediary files. See Section A.3.1.

Calc begins by reading into internal data structures the table-lookup files (.ccfc, etc.) for the operands of one synthesis operator, and breaking out the fields in each line of these files into local variables. Then Calc switches on the operator to algorithms for series, conditional, loop[12], or concurrent synthesis. Within each section there is a block of code for stateless operands and a distinct block for other types, the latter including mixed cases of stateless/state and the former divided by whether the approximation is by steps or piecewise lines. These separations lead to duplication, but they isolate the simpler stateless algorithms so they are the least likely to be buggy. If Calc must be trusted, give it a step-function stateless case.

A.3.3.1 Series Synthesis Algorithms

Series synthesis is in essence a matter of finding where each subdomain of the first operand[13] leads in the second operand, and taking the synthesis results from the latter. The two table-look-up files for the operands are indexed by subdomain, so tracing from the first operand to the second is trivial for stateless components: to fill in a synthesis result subdomain, look it up in the first operand table, locate the subdomain in the second operand where the first output leads, and fill in the values from there. However, piecewise-linear synthesis is full of kludges to handle round-off errors at interval endpoints[14], and the portion of the linear-synthesis algorithm that creates new subdomains in the synthesized result is difficult to understand. Its mathematics is given in Section 8.3.1.

When the first operand has state(s) and the second is stateless, the synthesis result is a copy of the first's tables, but with each line's output and run time fields adjusted to include the second operand's modifications. The remaining cases, in which the second operand has state, are more difficult to describe. Taking a special case helps. In the rest of the series discussion, let the second operand have just one state domain S_2 with 3 state subdomains[15]. Let the second operand have 2 input-domain subdomains. Thus the special-case second operand has tables of size 6, in which its block of 2 input-domain subdomains is repeated 3 times corresponding to the 3 state values. Figure A.2 shows a schematic version of the second operand's table. In the figure, each horizontal dash represents an (input × state) subdomain line, and

---

[12] There is actually a fifth operator, 'compose,' used in loop synthesis, but it is almost the same as 'series.'

[13] Unfortunately, the operands to Calc are not always real components that have executable code and subdomains listed in a .ccf file. However, since the table-lookup files do not distinguish between real components and calculated intermediates, intuition won't go wrong in thinking of the operands as 'components' so long as these are not thought of as limited to a single state domain.

[14] It could be worse—most of the kludges that didn't work very well have been removed from Calc.

[15] In the discussion to follow, '3' is a kind of name for the subroutine count, much easier to talk about than a conventional variable like N_s. This idea is carried to an extreme by the formula (from a blackboard in an empty classroom at Cornell c. 1962): $\lim_{3 \to 4} \sqrt{3} = 2$. Using 1 (or 0!) as a variable instead of 3 makes discussion even easier, but a loss of generality is more likely.

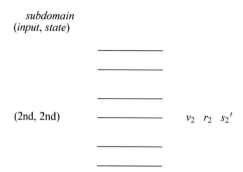

subdomain
(input, state)

(2nd, 2nd) v_2 r_2 s_2'

Fig. A.2 Schematic .ccfc file for an operand with 2 input subdomains and 3 state subdomains

these are artificially separated into groups of 2 (the input subdomains). The 4th line of Fig. A.2 displays some symbolic values for the table contents, an output v_2, a run time r_2, and a result state s_2'. The subdomain this 4th line describes is the last (2nd of 2) input subdomain and the middle (2nd of 3) state subdomain.

When the first operand is stateless with (say) 4 input-domain subdomains (hence 4 lines in its table) the synthesis result table with the second operand of Fig. A.2 has 3 times as many lines as the first component ($4 \times 3 = 12$), since it has a replication of the input block for each of its 3 states. Each group of 4 lines corresponds to the 4 input subdomains from the first operand; the group is repeated 3 times, once for each state subdomain of the second operand, with output- and run-time fields and a field for result values of S_2 in each line. Start constructing the result table by concatenating three copies of the first-operand table. Consider each line L of the 3 replications in turn. L contains some copied output value v_1 and run-time value r_1 from the first operand. Locate the second-operand input subdomain into which v_1 falls. L is in one of the 3 replication blocks; find the same block in the second operand description, and use its values on line L. Figure A.3 shows the case where L is the 7th line of the result table, the 3rd line in the 2nd input block. Suppose the output v_1 falls in the last input subdomain of the second operand. This L is in the middle of the state blocks of the result, so the line of the second-operand table to use is the 4th one in Fig. A.2. Thus the values placed on line L are v_2 (replacing v_1), $r_1 + r_2$ (replacing r_1) and the additional S_2 value s_2'. Had L been the 3rd line in Fig. A.3, the new values would have come from the 2nd line in Fig. A.2, and so on.

When both operands have state, the state of the synthesized result is their cross product. Creating these composite states is almost the same as in the previous case[16]. Again start to construct the synthesized result table by concatenating the first-operand .ccfc file three times, each line with an additional output-state field to hold result values for S_2. The new lines replicated from the first-operand table now themselves repeat input-domain subdomains more than 3 times, since there is a replication in the first-operand file for its state(s). The lines start out with as many result-state fields as the first operand has. Again consider each line L in the

---

[16] See Section 10.1.1 for a slightly more precise description using more mathematical symbols.

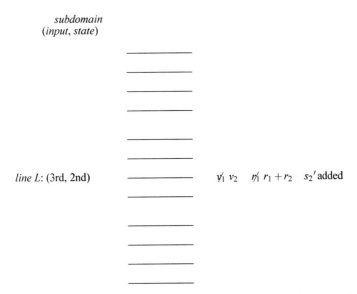

subdomain
(input, state)

line L: (3rd, 2nd) ———————— y_1 v_2 r_1' $r_1 + r_2$ s_2' added

Fig. A.3 Schematic synthesized .ccfc file for series of a stateless first operand with 4 input subdomains and a second operand as in Fig. A.2

synthesized result file. Once the proper line in the second operand file is identified, the output-, run-time-, and S_2-result-state values are changed in L, but the original result-state values from the first operand remain in place.

The reader will probably not want to draw the diagram like Fig. A.3 for a case in which the first operand has (say) 4 input subdomains and 2 states, the 1st state domain with 2 subdomains and the 2nd state domain with 3 subdomains. There would be $4 \times 2 \times 3 = 24$ lines in the first-operand table and these would be replicated 3 times in the result to make a synthesized table of 72 lines, each line with 3 result-state values.

A.3.3.2 Conditional Synthesis Algorithms

Except for complications introduced by state in the operands to be synthesized, conditional synthesis is the simplest of the operations performed by Calc. Given three subdomain-indexed tables (for the conditional and the two branches), the result table has lines copied from one branch table or the other. The input subdomains of the synthesized result table are all possible intersections among the input subdomains of the three operands. Thus in each result subdomain the conditional stays within one of its subdomains (and therefore takes a single truth value), and one of the branches also stays within one of its subdomains. Thus for each such result subdomain, the proper synthesized values can be read from one of the branch tables, where a subdomain must enclose the result subdomain. When the result subdomain comes from the IF branch, it is marked TRUE; it is marked FALSE if from the THEN branch. These marks are only used in loop synthesis, to be subsequently described.

State in the operands leads to a synthesized system with as many state dimensions as the sum of the number of state dimensions in the three components. For example, if a conditional construction is synthesized from a component with state as the test, another component with state in the ELSE branch, and a THEN branch that is a series of two components each with state, the result will be a system with four state dimensions.

The easiest way to describe construction of the table for the synthesized result is to form it as concatenated replications of a core table with its result lines adjusted, as in the series case just described. The core table is a copy of the table for the first operand to Calc (the test operand), but each input line is split to account for intersections with the input subdomains of the other operands. First, the original lines are marked TRUE if the test operand has output 1 there, FALSE if its output is 0. Because the test operand may have state, the input-subdomain lines of its table may be repeated many times; the core table has these repetitions. In the TRUE lines, the input subdomain is intersected with subdomains of the second operand (the IF branch); the FALSE line with subdomains of the third operand (the THEN branch). In the core table, each intersection is given a copy of the original test-operand line from which it was split. For example, if the test operand had a TRUE input subdomain $[10, 20)$, and the IF operand had input subdomains $[6, 14)$ and $[14, 30)$, the core table would have its line split in two for subdomains $[10, 14)$ and $[14, 20)$.

Next, adjust the lines of the core table to include the actions of the operands in the two branches. For each core line, find the corresponding input-subdomain line for the first state subdomain in the second operand (for a TRUE line) or the third operand (for a FALSE line). Adjust the values on the core line as follows: (1) Replace the output with that from the other operand; (2) Add the two run times; (3) Append the result-state values from the other operand. Now each line of the core table is close to correct for the conditional system: it contains an output from one of the two branches, a run time total from the test-operand and the proper branch, the result-state value(s) for the test operand, and the result-state value(s) for one or the other branch operand. But the pattern of result state values fails to include results for both branches. The 'branch not taken' states are missing, and result-state values for the two branches occupy the same positions on a line. The latter can be fixed by allocating result-state slot(s) following those of the test operand to the IF-branch state(s), then following with the ELSE-branch state(s), and moving those for a FALSE line to leave room for states from the IF branch. One group of result states is missing in each line. Because those missing states are the ones local to the branch that is not executed, the proper values to fill in are identity, since they do not change[17].

At last the core table is correct. But now it must be concatenated enough times to provide a line for every state of the synthesized system. Start with the second operand's first state dimension. That requires a concatenation of the core table as

---

[17] Unfortunately, a true identity is not available; the consequences of using a midpoint value for the state subdomain are described in Section 14.3.2.

many times as the first state has subdomains. In the repetitions, only the first is correct (the core table itself). For the others, the proper values come from lines in the second operand's table, changing the output, summing run times, and appending the result-state values. Similarly, replicate the larger table to handle the second state dimension of the second operand, and so on. When all the second-operand states have been added, continue with the third-operand states. As an example, suppose that a conditional synthesis is to be performed in which the number of intersected input subdomains is 7 and the number of state subdomains is given in the table:

Operand State	State	State subdomains
first (test)	1	3
second (IF branch)	1	4
	2	5
third (ELSE branch)	1	3

In this case the core table has $21 = 7 \times 3$ lines, 3 repetitions of the split input lines. Each line contains output, run time, and 4 result-state values. Adding the state replications successively yields tables of length $84 = 21 \times 4$ (first IF state), $420 = 84 \times 5$ (second IF state), and finally $1260 = 420 \times 3$ (ELSE state).

A.3.3.3 Loop Synthesis Algorithms

In Chapter 8 loops were treated as repeated composition of conditionals, in a series that must terminate for the subdomain approximations. For stateless functional behavior loop unwinding gives correct results, but unfortunately it is not correct for run-time synthesis, nor for components with state. The run-time error is minor, only repeating the conditional test once too often (in the last unwound loop and the residual loop, so the unwinding adds in the run time of the condition once too often). But when there is state, series composition gives quite the wrong loop result. Each composition would add new state dimension; but the correct semantics for a loop is that the state dimension remains as it is in just one unwinding—the state is subsequently updated 'in place.' Calc has a 'compose' operator to implement loop synthesis; Calc 'compose' is invoked recursively from its loop portion. The recursion mechanism is unusual: Calc makes a copy of the base directory in which it is working, changes to the copy directory, then invokes itself; on return, results are moved up to the original directory.

The loop operator has a first operand that is a conditional and a second operand for the loop body. Calc begins by synthesizing these as if they were a conditional with no ELSE. Let the result be a prediction table L_0. In L_0 the subdomain lines are marked by the conditional construction with TRUE or FALSE according to whether the conditional holds or does not hold on that subdomain. Should it happen that all lines are marked FALSE, that is, the vacuous ELSE was always taken, then L_0 is an identity table, which is the correct prediction for the loop, whose body is never executed. If any prediction lines are marked TRUE, then Calc invokes the 'compose' operator on L_0 with itself, producing a new prediction L_1. Calc 'compose' is careful to properly update the TRUE/FALSE marks on subdomains. Subdomains in L_0 that are FALSE have their prediction results copied identically to L_1. Subdomains in L_0 that are TRUE are traced through their outputs into new subdomains, and should they go to one marked FALSE, in L_1 the TRUE is changed to FALSE. This process is repeated, next composing L_0 with L_1 to form L_2, then L_0 with L_2 to form L_3, and so on. Termination is signaled at the first L_k where all the subdomains are marked FALSE.

If the pattern of FALSE marks does not change at some 'compose' step, then it can never change, since further applications of L_0 will be repetitions. But if the pattern does keep changing, then there will be at most K compositions, where K is the count of subdomains in the first operand[18]—one or more subdomains must switch each time. Hence Calc tests for a prediction that a loop will never terminate by comparing L_j and L_{j+1}, and it lists the TRUE subdomains as the domain of non-termination if they should be the same.

When there is state, Calc 'compose' is simpler than Calc 'series.' The number of state domains is the same in L_0 and all subsequent predictions. In the TRUE subdomains that actually compose, all the result values (output, run time, and result state(s)) are just moved from one place in the table to another.

A.3.3.4 Concurrent Synthesis

For a concurrent master-slave system synthesis, only the slave may have state. The first-operand (master) table looks like a table for a component with one state, the 'state' subdomains being those for the master's second input domain (from the slave). The synthesized result lines are replications of the master input-subdomain lines, repeated for each of the slave states in the way described for conditional synthesis above. In one such line for input subdomain I_1 that lies in the replicated block corresponding to a (in general, cross-product) state S of the slave, the values are obtained as follows. The master second output (to the slave) value lies in some slave input subdomain, say I_2. The $I_2 \times S$ line of the slave table has output v_2 and run time r_2 along with a sequence of slave result-state values. These result-state values are those of the synthesized result. To get the output and run-time values, look up v_2 in the second master input domain; say it falls in subdomain I_3. Then at master line for $I_3 \times I_1$ let the master first output be v_1 and the three run times be r_1, r_3, and r_4. The synthesis result line can now be completed with output v_1 and run time $r_1 + \max(r_2, r_3) + r_4$.

A.3.3.5 Summary of Synthesis Algorithms

The code in Calc that implements synthesis is complicated, but largely so because of the bookkeeping needed for multiple states. For understanding Calc it is rec-

---

[18] In the stateless piecewise-linear approximation, the bound is K^2, since the composition can create new subdomains, but at most K of them for each original.

ommended that the reader start with stateless step-function cases, and then examine cases in which one or more of the operands has a single state dimension. The most general case in the code will be used when each operand has a single state. It is more difficult to read the existing Calc code than it was to write it. The general pattern of implementation was to create a template of the synthesis result table, then consider one line. That line corresponds to a subdomain (input × state(s)) of the system, and to see what values should be in the line, it suffices to trace through what should happen for inputs and states that are described by that line. The information to collect correct values lies in the tables of Calc's operands.

The make-template-and-fix-lines descriptions here are complementary to the narrative descriptions of the underlying algorithms in Chapters 8, 10, and 11. The more abstract algorithms in those chapters may be helpful in seeing what Calc must do, but perhaps not in tracking how it does it. Believing that Calc is correct is no easier than believing in the abstract algorithms. As Section 14.3.1 says, the reason to trust the SYN tools (and trusting Calc is the major part of that) lies not in abstract description nor in studying code, but in the validation of comparing the tool predictions to direct execution of the table-lookup code. Should that validation fail in a particular case, the only remedy is tracing that case through the labyrinth of Calc, armed with dumps of the operand tables being synthesized.

A.3.4 Auxiliary Scripts

In most cases the header comments or the process of message-discovery execution adequately documents these utility programs. Not all of them are mentioned elsewhere in this monograph; some of them were written to support particular examples and are not well tested.

feedseq Executes a component's code with a sequence of inputs.

infeas Checks a component-approximation or system-prediction file for infeasible subdomains and creates a feasible version.

modes Searches a system prediction file (.ccfc) and a system measurements file (.datt) with two state dimensions for pairs that could be used as values for a single system state dimension.

profile Graphs the interface profile for a component within a system.

tracer Using only the table-lookup approximations, displays (down to component level) the input/output trace (with run time) through a system.

subddiff Compares two approximation files and lists subdomains in them where the approximate functional or run-time values differ.

rms Compares two plot files and computes the rms deviation of one from the other.

splitsub New base directory(s) are created in which all the .ccf files listed in system.pscf are modified by (repeatedly) splitting their subdomains in half.

smartsplit Similar to `splitsub`, but uses the error analysis of `Xcute` to choose the best subdomains to split.

sampcounts From the current directory xxx a new directory xxx-r is created in which the sample counts of all `.ccf` files are changed to random values.

XqtF, XqtS, XqtC Wrapper code for approximation table-lookup files (stateless, with state, concurrent respectively) that turn tables into executable code.

Xsys Executes the code file `SystemCode` that has the actual behavior of a synthesized system.

The following commands are used indirectly by the script(s) shown in brackets. The only reason to use them directly is to gain a finer control of options that are set by the parent script in a limited way, or to perform just part of the parent's sequence of operations. However, failures in the parent script are most likely those of these children.

Calc [SYN]. Don't use `Calc` directly. If it goes wrong, simplify the Polish line of `system.pscf` to restrict what `Calc` does to the offending case.

COMPFt *and* COMPSt [COMP]. These scripts do almost all the component processing, `COMPFt` for stateless, non-concurrent components, `COMPSt` for the others. With the `-S X.ccf` option, a single component described by `X.ccf` is approximated. However, it is often sufficient to use `COMP` to approximate all the components in a system, then remove a single (say) `S.ccft/S.ccfc` file and repeat `COMP`, which will process only `S.ccf`, the other components being up to date.

Smeast [SYN]. The historical name is a misnomer, since this script does not do system measurements. Rather, it 'compiles' the Polish in `system.pscf` into a Perl script `SystemCode` connecting the actual executable files (or the table-lookup code if `SYN -X`), so that when `SystemCode` is executed, it makes system measurements. But it is `Xcomp` (which may be used through `SYN -G`) and `Xsys` that actually do the execution. If `Smeast` is compiling bad code, it is sensible to run it stand-alone and examine `SystemCode` in a debugging cycle.

XS [COMPSt, Xcute]. Executing component code when it has state or is concurrent is complicated enough to make it worthwhile to have a script for that alone. However, `XS` exists more as a subscript to avoid duplication than as a useful stand-alone command.

Xcutel *and* Xcutet [Xcute]. These scripts do the work (for stateless-, and with-state or concurrent components respectively) of displaying actual code executions and comparing them to approximations.

Xcompl *and* Xcompt [Xcomp]. The real scripts behind stateless- and with-state comparisons between actual system execution and predictions.

Index

Page numbers in *italic* suggest the first place to look for information. Page numbers with a suffixed "n" indicate that the reference is in a footnote. When an index term is so frequently used that it would have a plethora of page numbers, those with less information content have been culled.

A

$\prec A \succ$ 8
-A (alternate plot) option 155
abstraction mapping   69
accumulating loop   284
adaptive random testing (ART)   94
Addis, Bill   55, 314
adequacy criterion   85
agile development model *58*, 143n
annotated citation   8
approximation   7, 98, 104
  checking quality   145, 159
  component measurement 99
  mixed cases   107
  piecewise-linear   *100*, 130, 234, 328
  run time   313
  step-function   100
architecture   39, 43
Ariane 5   193n, 225
artificial components   8, 118, 209
associative series composition 163, 262

B

bad code   228
bank-teller program   316
base directory   112, 113, 206
Bell component   4
bicycle   31
binary search   234
Bohr atom   9
bottom-up   46
boundary-value analysis 322
bounded variation   130n
box function   65
  approximation   100
  concurrent   73
box notation   69
buffer flushing   172
buffer overruns   26
bug   183, 219
busy work   78–80, 84

C

CAD   18
  tools   24, 27, *27*, 203, 306, 319
cascaded components   249
catalog   37, 38, 45, 305
  description   37

lies, fraud   307
category-partition testing 81
CBSD   2, 7, 34, 35, 46, *see also* I-CBSD
  ideal   46
certification   30
Chopper component   2
circle notation   69
clear drop   *2*, 2n, 6n
CMM level   37, 307
command-line editor   257
COMP command   113, 210
complex software   24, 302, 320
component   30
  approximation   5
  certification   25, 37
  commercial tools   41
  definition   33, 34
  description   37, 45
  immutable   45
  proving   109
  repository   4
  reuse   *see* reuse
  stateless   111
  substitution   36, 293
  SYN tools restrictions 38, 40, 207
  testing   38

D. Hamlet, *Composing Software Components,* DOI 10.1007/978-1-4419-7148-7,
© Springer Science+Business Media, LLC 2010

Breinigsville, PA USA
11 November 2010
249128BV00011B/110/P

9 781441 971470

Bib. # 581628

005.3
HAM

Ollscoil na hÉireann, Gaillimh

3 1111 40241 9996